The Road to Infamy
(1899-1900)

Colenso, Spioenkop, Vaalkrantz,
Pieters, Buller and Warren

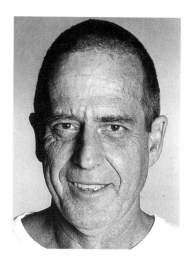

Owen Coetzer is a specialist senior journalist on *The Argus* in Cape Town. He was born in the Transvaal and educated at King Edward VII High School in Johannesburg.

He has worked on the South African Press Association, *The Daily News* as features editor in Durban, *The Diamond Fields Advertiser,* as chief sub-editor, both *Femina* and *Personality* magazines, as deputy editor, *The Argus* as feature writer, magazine chief sub-editor and chief sub-editor of *Weekend Argus.* Owen was also deputy editor of *Getaway* magazine, and one-time editor of the South African Navy's *Navy News.* He has worked for the *London Times* and several American publications. Owen travels extensively to Israel, the United States, Britain and Egypt, and has won awards for travel journalism. He has four children, a dog named Redvers, and lives in Cape Town.

THE
ANGLO-BOER
WAR

The Road to Infamy
1899 - 1900

by Owen Coetzer

**ARMS AND
ARMOUR**

Originally published in South Africa by
William Waterman Publications
A division of William Waterman Publications (Pty) Ltd
P O Box 5091, Rivonia 2128

This edition published by
Arms and Armour Press
A Cassell Imprint
Wellington House, 125/130 Strand, London WC2RR 0BB

Distributed in the USA by Sterling Publishing Co. Inc.,
387 Park Avenue South, New York, NY 10016-8810.

Distributed in Australia by Capricorn Link (Australia) Pty.
Ltd, 2/13 Carrington Road, Castle Hill, NSW 2154.

British Library Cataloguing-in-Publication Data:
a catalogue record for this book is available from
the British Library.

ISBN 1-85409-366 5

Dedication

To Geraldine,
*my constant war-graves companion,
friend and soulmate.
And to the spirit of*
Sir Charles Warren.

*"The evil that men do lives after them.
The good is oft interred with their bones."*
William Shakespeare – *Julius Caesar*

Contents

INTRODUCTION

I am not an academic, and this is not an academic work. Rather it is a catalogue of stirring, often emotional events – and many mishaps – that initially horrified the Empire upon which the sun, in 1900, never set.

The Natal Campaign of the Boer War.

Or the Anglo-Boer War, as it later became known. Or in Afrikaans, "Die Tweede Vryheidsoorlog", the second war of independence.

For four months – October 1899 to February 1900 – the might of the British Army was flung ignominiously from one side of the Tugela River to the other. From Colenso to Spearman's to Potgieter's, to Vaalkrantz, back to Colenso, to Pieters, and finally across the Klip River to Ladysmith.

In those bitter months – bitter for the British that is – reputations were made. And lost. Heroes of the Empire, on dusty pedestals for years, began a slow tumble to be shattered on the bloody rocks of ineptitude, jealousy and fear.

Accusations, ill-feelings, condemnation, criticism, censure – all figured in telegrams, signals, despatches and official reports.

Worse still, one top-secret despatch viciously and unfairly condemned the action of one General – even to Queen Victoria herself, who would not permit "the man who lost Spioenkop" to be given a mayoral welcome to Canterbury when invited to address the University there.

The General concerned knew nothing of the censure until the war was almost over. His reputation was irrevocably damaged, and in terms of an undertaking exacted by Field Marshal Lord Roberts, he was not permitted to speak out in his defence, nor to seek redress.

This work seeks in a small way to vindicate him.

For General Sir Charles Warren, whose "asperities of a peculiar temper", as *The Times* obituary quaintly calls it, was nevertheless the epitome of a Victorian Christian gentleman.

In 1865 as an engineering surveyor, he had "dug" Jerusalem as one of the pioneers of the then new discipline of archaeology and surveying.

His meticulous notes, plans and drawings were used – and are still being used – by Israeli archaeologists as they uncover the ancient City of David, clinging as it does to the ancient Temple Mount and the valley of the Ophel.

His conviction that rigid personal discipline made "men", (coupled with scrupulous adherence to Truth in all its forms, decency and, a strange, new, subject for Victorians, hygiene) also made him hard to get on with.

His deep involvement with the spiritual and physical education of young people led to him furthering and fostering the equally new world-wide movement founded by another hero of that War, Baden-Powell.

The Scouts, as Baden-Powell called them, were seen by Warren as the hope for mankind's future.

From the upstairs window of his house, The Oaks, in the tiny hamlet of Westbere, he could see across the land to the spires of ancient Canterbury cathedral three miles away.

Or he could look across the Sturry marshes, with its abundant bird life, or walk a hundred yards down the hill to the small church.

The scouts used his garden. In fact after the death of his wife, Fanny Margaretta, buried in the tiny cemetery at the bottom of The Oaks, his house became a sort of scout headquarters.

But in time, the house became too big for him and he moved to Weston-Super-Mare, where he died in 1927.

It was, however, in death a hero's return. His body lay in state in Canterbury cathedral, before being moved in solemn military procession, on a gun carriage draped in the flag of Goshen and Stelland, Boer republics whose future he had successfully secured for Britain in the heady days of Griqualand West diamond rushes.

Six hundred troops slow marched that day and crowded, as a guard of honour, into the tiny Westbere graveyard. Men who had fought with him openly wept.

The *Last Post* was sounded and the volley of farewell disturbed the birds. Then all was peace. The hero had come home.

Warren is buried next to his wife. Little has changed. The Oaks remains, as do the sweet-smelling country lanes. I know. I have been there.

Sir Redvers Buller wrote to Lord Roberts, after the battle of Spioenkop: "I cannot employ Warren in an independent command again."

Yet it was Warren who was given the task of masterminding the final, successful, push at Pieters that culminated in the Relief of Ladysmith.

You will find few battle descriptions here; few words on the political machinations of the Wolseley and Roberts "Rings" with which other authors have sought to begin their studies of the Boer War.

This work follows Buller through Natal to Ladysmith. By the time he had arrived, Talana and Elandslaagte, and Nicholson's Nek had been fought.

Copious works have articulated Ladysmith's grim fight for survival; few, if any, have used the evidence I do.

Further, the book is not about Ladysmith – but the attempts by the relieving force to get there.

Being a non-academic of course permits me a certain flexibility of style, with perhaps a cliché or two too many.

But, if I am able to take the reader into the heart, and the unemotional official mind, of this war which has often erroneously been dubbed "the last of the gentlemen's wars", I have accomplished what I set out to do.

And that is to bring out in bold gory detail how Tommy went to war – ill-equipped, ignorant of local conditions, scared stiff of South African lightning, but ready to fight the Boer.

Essentially it is a story around two Generals – Buller and Warren. The commander and his subordinate, both fiercesome, with tempered tempers. Antagonists of old . . .

No, you will not find many battle descriptions here.

The evidence of the Royal Commission into the War in South Africa, and the diverse telegrams, despatches and official reports I have used tell their own tale.

As do those of the official war correspondents attached to the Natal Field Force.

You will also find comment from pro-Boer Irishman Michael Davitt, who gave up his seat in the British House of Commons to join Kruger, calling the Boer War the most unjust of the nineteenth century.

Davitt is an expressive, compelling writer, and while some may question my use of him as a source, so must they then question my use of the British war correspondents as a source – they were fiercely pro-British (they would not be doing their jobs if they were otherwise). Davitt is just as fiercely anti-

British. But all weave wonderfully descriptive word patterns full of colour and life.

As a non-academic my comment has been kept to a minimum. But in places where events need connecting and comment, I have done so.

But, probably for the first time, the Natal Campaign – fought in the searing heat and melting humidity of summer, and in unprecedented rain storms and rivers of mud – has been minutely examined from official, and unofficial, sources.

"Thank God," Sir George White is reported to have said when Ladysmith was relieved, "we kept the flag flying."

But it took an awful long time for the Army in Natal to get there . . .

OWEN COETZER
Cape Town

General Sir Charles Warren, the man who masterminded the Relief of Ladysmith, the gentleman soldier, whom Buller blamed for "losing" the Battle of Spioenkop. But Warren was ordered not to speak out in his own defence, and has gone down in history as a failure. He was not . . .

St Stephen's House, on the London Embankment. In this building the Royal Commission into the War in South Africa was held. Heroes and villains in that war passed through the front door to give evidence. St Stephen's House no longer exists – it was pulled down in 1994, with a whole complex of buildings which backed on Cannon Row. The site will become a tube station. (Picture: Gorry Bowes-Taylor.)

PREFACE

What the Commission wanted to know

The Royal Commission on the War in South Africa sat in St Stephen's House, Victoria Embankment, London, in late 1902, and early 1903.

It sat on 55 days to hear 114 witnesses. What they had to say is recorded in two volumes of Minutes of Evidence, and contains answers to 22,200 questions.

Asking them were Victor Alexander, Earl of Elgin and Kincardine; Reginald Balliol, Viscount Esher; Sir George Dashwood Taubman-Goldie; Field Marshal Sir Henry Wylie Norman; Admiral (Rtd) Sir John Ommanney Hopkins; Sir John Edge, and Sir John Jackson.

It was their job, and an exacting one, to determine whether Britain had been prepared for the costly war (some £223 million) in terms of both money and men in South Africa. Worse, it was their job to inquire into the supply of men, ammunition, equipment and transport by sea and land. They wanted to know how effective it had been and what could be done to improve it.

Assisting them were Donald Alexander, Baron Strathcona and Mount Royal, British High Commissioner in London for the then Dominion of Canada; and Sir Frederick Matthew Darley, Lieutenant Governor of the State of New South Wales, Australia, and Chief Justice of the Supreme Court there.

The warrants for the Commission were issued by King Edward VII in September and October 1902, and were signed at Balmoral, under the words: By His Majesty's Command.

Specifically, under the King's orders, the Commission was to be given access to all books, documents, registers and records the members felt it necessary to call for.

Their task: To question the heroes of the British Empire on what they had, or had not, done during the war, and what could be done to improve the might of His Majesty's Army (Queen Victoria died in 1902) should there be any future wars.

Lord Roberts, Sir Redvers Buller, Sir George White, John Denton Pinkstone French, Lord Wolseley, Evelyn Wood, Sir Charles Warren, Lord Baden-Powell, Sir Arthur Conan Doyle, William Gatacre, Lord Methuen, Rear Admiral Hedworth Lambton, Lord Lansdowne and a host of other not so household names, faced the Commission.

The commissioners had full power to call before them such persons as they should "judge likely to afford . . . any information upon the subject of Our Commission; and also to call for, have access to, and examine, all such books, documents, registers, and records as may afford . . . the fullest information on the subject . . . by all lawful ways and means whatsoever".

There was some urgency about the whole matter too: Lord Kitchener, for instance, was about to sail for India, and it was important that he gave evidence. But the Commission had only been fully constituted on the day before he left. His evidence was understandably, and regrettably, hasty.

It also became obvious, while there were many other considerations, that the object of the Commission was to discover inefficiency or defects in administration of the army, shown up by the war, and to indicate their causes wherever possible.

And it became essential to examine the main features of the military system in Britain as well as in the field.

Also it was not the task of the commissioners, and they made it quite clear, to pronounce judgment on questions of strategy or tactics, or to review the decisions of superior authority on the conduct of individual officers.

The Preface to the Report states: "The general course pursued has been to obtain the evidence of the leading actors in the War, arranged, so far as possible in chronological sequence, and of other competent officers who could speak as representatives of the various arms of the service."

While they pointed out the Commission was not a history of the war, statements which could be termed historical were invited from three Generals only, all of whom had held the position of General Officer Commanding in Chief – General (in 1903 Field Marshal) Sir George White, General Sir Redvers Buller and Field Marshal Earl Roberts.

But in the end, many others were called.

Says the report: "Differences of opinion will be found here also, and still more in some statements from other officers," but this did not mean that they were necessarily accurate as the Commission did not possess facilities for minute and prolonged examination of eye-witnesses.

Which is a nice way of avoiding embarrassing (the British Government) by statements made when someone got into a corner and blamed someone, or something else, such as the mysterious workings of the War Office – and there is enough testimony on that fact!

The Commission, too, sat in private. The report says that it was necessary at the outset to determine the amount of publicity which could be given to the proceedings. "It was obvious that highly confidential documents must come under the notice of the Commission, and that great inconvenience would ensue if the examination of witnesses regarding them were postponed or hampered. It is also an honourable tradition of the British Army that the conduct of superior officers should not be publicly canvassed by their subordinates; and lastly, in cases of personal imputations or grievances it was impracticable, without dislocating the order of the Inquiry, to prevent intolerable hardship to individuals by statements published day by day remaining unanswered for weeks. The Commission therefore resolved to sit in private and are satisfied that this decision has been justified.

"We have been enabled not only to demand the production of papers, but to receive explanations and evidence given with an outspoken frankness which has been vital to the proper performance of our duties. We have throughout kept in our own hands the whole question of publication. We have found no desire to conceal anything which could properly be made public, and we have insisted on the publication of much information which under ordinary circumstances would be treated as confidential, and our wishes in this respect have been fairly met by the officials concerned.

"We claim, therefore, that our assurance should be accepted that our records contain everything which can be made public with due regard to the interests of the public service."

No-one escaped the Commission's eye: Lord Wolseley, who had been

Commander-in-Chief in London at the start of the war, appeared before it, as did Lord Lansdowne, who had been Secretary of State for War and The Right Honourable St John Broderick, who superseded Lansdowne.

Among the documents discussed were the Courts of Inquiry into the British Army's surrenders, most famous of which was Nicholson's Nek where some 939 British troops and officers surrendered to the Boer forces after a night of disaster.

There were 225 surrenders listed between October 1899 and the occupation of Pretoria. The facts of each are noted, the officer in command identified, the reasons why the surrenders took place, and how many men were affected are noted. The decisions of the Courts of Inquiry are also noted. In all but two cases, the men were exonerated.

What did the Commission achieve? It changed the way Britain made war in the future. It changed the structure of command. It changed the attitude to the common soldier, and it spelt the end of the cavalry charge that struck fear into the hearts of the simple Boers at Elandslaagte.

That was said to be history's last cavalry charge.

With the advent of a powerful rifle, which could fire long distances on a flat trajectory and smokeless powder, the cavalry were no longer needed. Future wars would use artillery and manpower. The tank had not yet been thought of.

Besides all of this, the war in South Africa had cost, in the years 1899–1902, a staggering total of £230 000 000.

The Road to Infamy, the title of this book, exists. It is some two kilometres on the Ladysmith side of the small town of Colenso, where a sign indicates a road to the right.

Today it is tarred, and connects the KwaZulu industrial site of Ezakheni, on the far outskirts of Ladysmith, with Colenso, and the N3 route to Durban.

It was a different scene 94 years ago. In 1899, it was the road to Ladysmith, meandering through the foothills of Grobbelaarskloof, along the Tugela River, and then up through Pieters, with the Platrand far on the one side and Bulwana close on the other and down into the small town.

It was a peaceful place. The silence was broken only by the whiplash of wagon drivers and now and again, the clip-clop of horses' hooves as mounted riders sped to Durban or Pietermaritzburg.

In 1899 the Natal Government Railways line had also reached Ladysmith, hugging the contours of that same road most of the way – to the distress of the wagon transport riders, who saw their business going up in puffs of smoke and huge steel driving wheels.

The train could do in one day the mileage they could do in a week or longer.

When Buller began the push to Pieters as the fourth and last-ditch attempt to relieve Ladysmith, troopers rushed along and over the road. And they fought, and many died, on it.

Perhaps the worst battles of that war were fought across it, and blood mingled with the dust.

Churchill called Hart's Hollow, the valley beneath Inniskilling (Hart's) Hill, the "hill of hideous whispering death" – such was the sound and fury of Mauser bullets as they swept away gallant soldiers.

It was unnecessary.

Had Buller the courage to persevere, initially by taking Hlangwane hill at Colenso, or left things to Sir Charles Warren (as he did in the final push),

Redvers Henry Buller, General of Downes, reads the plain inscription on his grave in Crediton, Devon. But he was more than that. A Victoria Cross holder for his heroic action at Hlobane, during the Zulu War, he was knighted for his South African War services. But he complained steadily that he had not sufficient men to fight the Boer, took four attempts to get through to Ladysmith, and ultimately was sacked out of hand for angrily disputing his "surrender" telegram to General Sir George White.

Ladysmith could have been relieved in December 1899 or certainly in January 1900.

It was an infamy that British soldiers should have been made to carry the burden of indecision, and land up in graves along the road to Pieters.

The road to infamy.

IT all began some seven years ago. They were lonely figures on a never-ending veld landscape. Silhouetted here and there against the skyline, they wandered, seemingly without direction or pace.

Or down valleys of brown Natal summer grass, lost for a time in dips, but emerging after a while on to the hills.

Most wore hats to fend off the brutal sun, and like sensible travellers in summer climes, had shorts, high socks and useful boots. Some had expensive cameras or gadget bags slung around the shoulder, or haversacks with army-issue water bottles.

When they drew close, it could be noticed that beneath the arm, or in the hand was The Book.

And, like the British Tommy of nearly 100 years ago as he gazed across those endless plains outside Ladysmith, a look of puzzlement would appear, and The Map (in The Book) would be consulted, and turned this way and that.

Was it here Buller turned? they would ask themselves aloud. Was it there Long's guns got into trouble?

And when you met them (and you still do) at an hotel or the motel on the outskirts of Ladysmith, the Truth would be revealed – they were following the measured tread of the Soldiers of the Queen as they trudged from weary, wary battle to battle.

Perhaps it had been their great-great-grandfather, or uncle who had fought the "Boo-er". Perhaps they had come across a bundle of faded, forgotten letters.

More likely they had been gripped – as thousands are every year – by The War.

I have met seekers from Britain, Canada and Australia tramping the battlefields between Colenso and Ladysmith, that had once ran with British and Boer blood.

And watched how the quest became a pilgrimage to the shrines of war.

But there is a question that no-one has bothered too much about. Black troops fought – officially or unofficially – on both sides. And they died. And they were buried without headstones, without memorials.

Perhaps visionaries in the New South Africa should address this – and if the sites can be identified, memorials should be erected to the unsung, often confused, labourers in a white man's war. Above all, they should ensure that all monuments and memorials, graveyards, cemeteries and single lonely graves to Briton and Boer should be well maintained for the future.

The consequences of the white man's war became the black man's future. Colonialism, which painted most of the map of the world, and Africa, red, is long dead. The ideology of Queen and Country and Empire lies exposed in graveyards throughout the world, heroes all. Manipulated, exploited, soldiers of the Queen.

They must be remembered.

There are a few people whose patience has been sorely tried by my enthusiasm. I would like to thank them, and in a way this is their book as much as mine. There is Helen Griffin who, as a young schoolgirl in Pietermaritzburg, was so incensed by what I had written in a series of newspaper articles about the lonely, uncared-for graves on the Back Route, that she offered to keep a watch for me on how things were progressing, if in fact they were.

Her enthusiasm for this book has been unbounded, even though she has long left school and is now a qualified veterinarian and living in Pretoria.

Fiona Barbour, at the Alexander McGregor Museum in Kimberley, is the most astute and enthusiastic military historian it has ever been my pleasure to meet.

It is not her field, as she keeps on telling me. But one cannot live in the shadow of the Magersfontein massif and not become embroiled in its history. So Fiona did, and is without doubt the Magersfontein expert, sought by historians throughout the world.

She has always gone out of her way to help me in any way she could. She is extremely busy – I know, I have seen her desk – but somehow she always found the time to sort out my problems.

Magersfontein may be a long way from Ladysmith, but it is indelibly intertwined in the Natal Campaign by the soldiers and sailors, comrades all, who fought – and died – on the brown veld.

Valerie Haddad and Kathy Drake of the South African Library found documents that I had given up hope of ever seeing, and identified as Commander the Hon. D'Arcy Lambton the anonymous writer "Defender" who, in 1902, wrote "Sir Charles Warren and Spioenkop a Vindication". My daughter, Diane Gavin, who was living in London at the time, turned up valuable copies of the London *Daily Mail* of 1900, and to her, thanks.

My other children, Catherine, Mathew and Nicholas, gave their unwavering support too.

Ryno Greenwall, enthusiastic expert and collector of Boer War art allowed me to use one of his pictures as the cover illustration.

Paul Mills, too, of Clarke's bookshop in Long Street, Cape Town, deserves mention for his unfailing interest and enthusiastic help. And thanks too to David Long for his time and patience in converting the computer text for this book.

Gilbert Torlage, who heads the Research Section of the KwaZulu-Natal Provincial Museum Service, checked the book for factual accuracy. It must be noted, however, that the final conclusions are entirely the author's.

Thanks go to the late George Tatham who hiked me around Ladysmith time and time again, and to the late Llewellyn Hyde, historian *extraordinaire*.

Richard Tubb, of the Whitehall Library in London, sought documentation as well. John Beresford, who owns Sir Charles Warren's house, The Oaks, in Westbere, near Canterbury, Kent, kindly allowed me to wander about, and I would like to thank Sheila Tait, of the All Saints Church at Westbere, for taking me to Sir Charles Warren's grave. To get there swift transportation was provided by Grahame and Lorraine Herbert. To them, thanks too, and to the Duty Officer at the Aldershot Provost Office who allowed me free access to the Caesar's Camp military training ground, behind the town, and detailed an officer to take me there. It is no wonder British troops called Ladysmith's Platrand "Caesar's Camp". It is an absolute replica of a hill near Aldershot.

Finally, this book would never have been written without the enthusiastic help of the late Dr Fred Clarke, who went out of his way to inform me of happenings along the "Back Route," and took a great interest in what I wrote.

OWEN COETZER
Cape Town, 1995

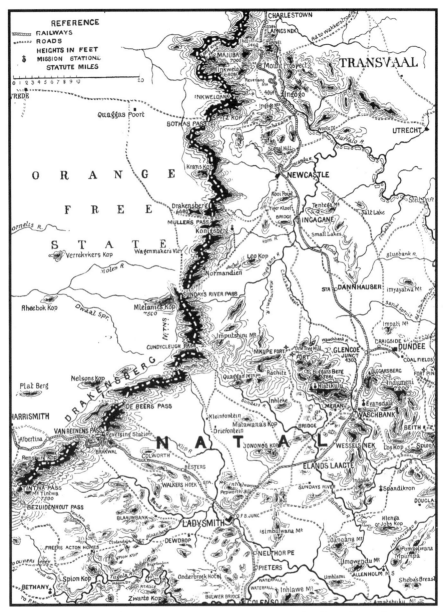

A contemporary map of the Natal Campaign, with roads and railway lines. Place names are those which appear in the official reports. One needs an explanation. Inhlawe Mountain, to the immediate right of Colenso, is to the right of the much-disputed Hlangwane, which is between it and Colenso. The map also does not show the Frere or Chieveley.

CHAPTER ONE

The Trappings of War

Deficiencies and Dum-Dums

They appear as a single column of minute type, do these simple trappings of war. For the most, they are cold statistics on page 188 of *Volume Four (Appendices)* of the Royal Commission into the War in South Africa, which sat at St Stephen's House on London's Victoria Embankment late in 1902.

For instance, there were issued 1,022,696 pairs of socks, to be thrust into 508,930 pairs of shoes or leather boots, to be tied with 690,318 pairs of laces. Keeping the socks up were 3,350 garters.

Around them would go 467,595 puttees.

Hitching up 644,797 pairs of trousers over 428,080 pairs of drawers, were 92,374 pairs of braces and 731,142 flannel or woollen belts.

Of course there were shirts, 449,346 of them, to be tucked into the trousers and covered by 621,747 khaki frocks, worn like working aprons.

The Scots and the Irish regiments were issued with 232,660 kilts.

And for the night-time cold, and no-one expected them to be used, 232,660 jerseys were given to Her Majesty's troops heading for the worst of Natal's summer months, November, December, January and February.

But by 1900, they were exceedingly grateful to the men of Her Majesty's Army Clothing Department for their foresight. Nights beneath Natal's starry skies can be bitter ones. And in the torrential rains, and terrifying thunderstorms that raked the veld that year, the jerseys kept Tommy Atkins reasonably dry and warm beneath his 303,254 Bell tents.

But he was also wrapped up in 138,837 greatcoats and cloaks with 203,287 helmets to keep away the scorching sun, and some of the rain.

Once they were off his head, he would use one of 22,726 hairbrushes, or 88,100 combs to neaten down his thatch.

For those who eschewed the helmets, Tommy could use one of 203,571 worsted caps, or, to go with the kilts, 88,019 Glengarrys.

There were lanyards, for whistles, revolvers and a hundred and one other uses – 249,866 were issued.

He 'ad to eat, dinn'ee? The inner man was issued with 170,616 forks, 139,282 table knives, and 160,418 spoons. These delved into 97,518 mess tins, and afterwards hands and faces were cleaned with 176,168 towels.

He would also lather his face with 44,946 shaving brushes, attack it with 467,595 razors, and sharpen these with 2,022 razor strops.

If he felt inclined, he could use one of 1,515 nail brushes to keep the nails clean.

Then there was the question of the soap.

There wasn't any.

Colonel Sir W.O. Richardson, KCB., Deputy Adjutant-General for Supplies in South Africa for the years 1899–1900, told the Commission in 1902: "Soap, that is an Army Ordnance supply, but as the Army Ordnance

Department have comparatively few depots, the troops are often unable to obtain it, and it would be preferable to make soap an Army Service Corps supply as whenever there are troops an ASC depot will be near at hand from which a supply could always be obtained.

"Owing to the absence of soap, or to the difficulty of getting soap in the field, half the force in South Africa became verminous, so that although it seems a petty thing, it is really most important.

"Sixteen years ago [that is in 1884] it was laid down that soap should be an ASC supply!

"Soap should be issued as a free ration in the field. It should be looked upon as a necessity, not a luxury."

Soap indeed, but not enough of it, made its appearance among the supplies shipped from Woolwich Arsenal – 384,062 bars of it, among the 298,019 water bottles, 466,055 blankets, 41,106 camp kettles and 101,831,000 rifle and machine gun rounds, with 1,800,228 pistol ammunition rounds thrown in.

To carry his equipment (including the soap), Tommy was given, if he was cavalry, 17,080 kit bags. If he was regular army, or a volunteer, 57,097 kit bags. Among them were 10,000 waterproof bags.

From Woolwich, too, came 303,254 waterproof sheets, 20,647 tents, 942 marquees, 27,404 felling axes, 39,435 pick-axes, 47,028 shovels and 14,645 spades, among other necessary implements.

Armaments, which Woolwich knew a great deal about, were supplied from British Ordnance factories. For instance there were 11,400 6-inch shells. For breech loading guns, 54,963 5-inch; 287,322 15-pounder; 91,224 12-pounder, and 16,308 4.7-inch shells.

For quick-firing guns, 33,400 12-pounder and 529,920 37-mm shells were sent.

One figure needs emphasising: 101,831,000 rifle and machine gun rounds. Tommy meant business . . .[1]

The "Boer" War, as it was known lasted, officially, from October 11, 1899, to June 5, 1900, the day of the official surrender of Pretoria.

The "Guerrilla campaign", as the British euphemistically called it, went on for another 18 months, culminating on May 31, 1902 when the document containing terms of surrender was signed at Melrose House in Pretoria at 10.15pm by the Boer representatives and Lord Milner, British High Commissioner in South Africa.

By that date, according to the Commission, 448,435 British troops had been sent to South Africa, swelled by a total of 52,414 locals. Opposing them were some 5,000 Boers.

In fact, at one time there were more than 900,000 British troops in the country.

The remarkable material figures quoted above are for the period September 1899 to June 1900 only.

During that time, the British Army had reeled, stunned, from actions at Colenso (where Sir Redvers Buller had lost his guns), to the horrifying (for the British) disaster at Spioenkop; the Methuen debacle at Magersfontein and the Gatacre surrender at Stormberg.

Mafeking, Kimberley and Ladysmith had been besieged.

And there had been early surrenders: one officer, a Lieutenant Nesbitt, and 16 men of the Protectorate Regiment in the first action of the war on October 13, 1899 near Kraaipan in the Northern Cape; 10 officers and 213 men, commanded by Colonel B.D. Moller of the 18th Hussars, at Adelaide's Farm, near

Dundee, and the one, once it was cleared from censorship, that sent waves of shock throughout Britain, Nicholson's Nek on October 30, 1899 when ten and a half companies, 954 officers and men, surrendered to the Boers.

A gentleman's war, it was not.

The bearded fellows, with bandoliers slung casually around their shoulders, who had first appeared on the crest of Talana Hill, outside Dundee, at dawn on October 20, 1899 to open the Natal Campaign, were about to exact a heavy toll on the Soldiers of the Queen.

Sir William Penn-Symons, commander at Dundee, was taken by surprise as Boer shells suddenly began bursting among his soldiers' tents in the valley between Talana and the small town.

"We'll have them by tea-time. They're only farmers!" one source has him shouting, as he buckled on his weapons and took the lead, followed by an orderly carrying a lance with a red burgee, so that his officers and men (and the enemy) knew where he was, guiding his troops up the small rise to a belt of trees and a stone wall on the way to the base of the Talana Hill.[2]

A small, pyramid-shaped cairn, in the grass to the left of the corrugated-iron-roofed farmhouse, near what is today Dundee's museum, marks the spot where he was mortally wounded in the stomach, bravely urging his troops on.

He is buried in the English Churchyard nearby.

The farmers had come to stay.

And, instead of victory, the British troops, leaving their tents up, many with lamps still burning, and their wounded behind, retreated overnight to the dubious, hilly safety of an about-to-be-besieged Ladysmith, and Sir George White.

That doyen of war artists, Melton Prior of the *Illustrated London News*, who was to be holed up in Ladysmith at the time, drew a superb picture of the citizens vying for a vantage point on the kopje outside the dusty town as the long column, under Brigadier General James Yule, was gathered in.

It was a victory, Yule insisted. The British, not the Boers, had drawn first blood, driving them from the hilltop.

But the Boers had only displayed a tactic that was to torment the British from that moment on. They, indeed, had struck the first, unexpected, blow. Then, they merely waited until Penn-Symon's troops were well and truly on their way up the hill, before they retired, getting on their horses and riding away.

Talana was a mess. The general was dead, and so were many troops, several killed by their own shells as they reached the crest of the hill and British gunners kept on pounding it. By the time they were stopped, it was too late.

Natal is the battleground of South Africa. The picturesque rolling hills and verdant valleys have witnessed the rise and fall of Shaka, the raids up and down the country by thousands of his superbly trained Zulu impis, conquering land for their leader.

It has seen the brutal murder of Voortrekker leader Piet Retief and his followers by Dingane, who, with his half-brother, Mhlangane, had earlier assassinated Shaka.

The moonlight has been party to the lightning Zulu raids on sleeping Voortrekker families in laagers at Blaauwkrantz, near Colenso, Saailager, near Estcourt and other sites nearby as women and children waited for Retief to return.

One survivor had 88 assegai wounds.

There was the Tugela massacre too, as Britons at the small settlement of D'Urban went to the Voortrekkers' aid, and were wiped out on the Zululand side of the swiftly flowing river. The cream of Natal's English pioneers fell to the impis' assegais, as gleaming hordes swept on to destroy the settlement. Pieter Retief had been known, and liked, by many of the English. He had fought for them in the Frontier Wars, and had lived among them in Grahamstown.

There was the "Zulu" War which culminated in the British army's greatest defeat in any colonial war on the plain of death in front of the Sphinx-like massif of Isandhlwana.

Here 1,300 British and black soldiers were massacred at lunchtime, under an eclipse of the sun, on January 22, 1879, enveloped by the famous "horn" formation of the Zulu army.

Those who could, fled down along the narrow tracks to the Buffalo River and Rorke's Drift. Few made it across the tumbling river as Zulu impis followed the trail of death.

Heroism was the name of the day, and 11 VCs were won in the small buildings that clung to a small plateau at Rorke's Drift.

The great-great-grandfather of Minister of Home Affairs in the South African Government of National Unity and leader of the Inkatha Freedom Party, Dr Mangosuthu Buthelezi, was commander-in-chief of the Zulu army on that day.

But thousands of British troops, stealthily brought up to three starting points on the banks of the Tugela, faced the impis. By sheer weight of numbers, as in the Boer War that was to come, they were finally able to "win" the war, and King Cetshwayo, who had fled deep into the Nkandla forest, was captured and interned in Cape Town's Castle.

Later, he was paraded before Queen Victoria in London, and sent back to serve out a prison term with another "dissident", Langalabelele, who had earlier rebelled against the British in the foothills of the Drakensberg, and was sent to Robben Island.

The two, one a monarch, the other a leader, were sent to while away the days at the Maitland Mill, opposite the Observatory in Cape Town.

When Cetshwayo was freed, his kingdom had been dissolved: the British had seen to that. Soon afterwards, he died, and some sources say he was poisoned, and lies buried in a secret grave in the heart of the Nkandla forest where he was captured.

But there was more. The conflict of 1881, known in South Africa as the First Boer War, involved the humiliating British defeat, again by a handful of farmers, at Amajuba mountain which borders the Transvaal and Natal, with Laing's Nek in a saddle.

"Avenge Majuba!" was a frequent British rallying cry during the early days of the Boer War.

Majuba was avenged on February 27, its 19th anniversary, when General Piet Cronje surrendered on the banks of the Modder River at Paardeberg, and the same day the British won the battle of Pieters in their final attempt to relieve the Ladysmith siege.

How well were the British equipped for the war? What would have happened if, say, Russia, a vast nation friendly to the Boers and with observers, aides and individual troops fighting in South Africa, had decided also to go to war with Britain?

Could the British cope, with an armada of ships pouring soldiers into South Africa?

The answer is, no.

The day of the battle of Colenso, December 15, 1899, General Sir Henry Brackenbury, GCB, KCSI, Director General of Ordnance, compiled a telling, damning report.

Some were small items; others, like guns, large and looming, In the end he wrote: "This is sufficient to prove that we are attempting to maintain the largest Empire the world has ever seen with armaments and reserves that would be insufficient for a third class military power."

This is what he found:

Horse artillery

"We had 10 batteries of Horse Artillery 12-pdrs on the Home and Colonial Establishment at the beginning of the war, and in reserve only the materiel of one battery; and that battery had been converted to an experimental QF (quick firing) system.

"In order to send out the materiel of one Service battery, as a reserve, to South Africa, we have to arm one of our Service batteries at home with this experimental equipment, and send its Service equipment to South Africa."

Field artillery

"We had 50 batteries of Field Artillery 15-pdrs on the Home and Colonial Establishment at the beginning of the war, and in reserve the materiel of 11 Service batteries, of which two had been converted to an experimental system, leaving only nine available.

"Fortunately eight more are under manufacture and approaching completion, but five of these are appropriated to batteries to be raised in 1900–01.

"At the beginning of the war we had three batteries of 5-inch howitzers, and, in reserve only one 5-inch howitzer, one carriage and two ammunition wagons. To send out three howitzers to South Africa to replace casualties, I have had to take two from those appropriated to [the category of] moveable armaments of fortresses."

Gun ammunition

"In addition to the 300 rounds per gun with batteries, ammunition columns, and parks, we had a reserve of 220 rounds per gun for each horse and field and mountain gun or howitzer.

"The whole of this reserve has long since been absorbed by the demands for South Africa.

"The whole powers of the Ordnance factories and the trade have been turned on to further supplies, and all the naval orders for ammunition have had to be held in abeyance since the beginning of October. [The war began in the second week of October.]

"We have borrowed from the Navy, and from the Government of India.

"Nevertheless, I was unable to meet Sir R. Buller's demands for 5-inch howitzer ammunition and 7-pdr ammunition till a fortnight after they should have been complied with . . .

"I have had to deplete the authorised quantities of ammunition for the siege train in order to supply the 5-inch howitzers in South Africa and to take guns from the moveable armament of Plymouth to meet Sir R. Buller's demand for long-ranging guns.

"I have received a request from General Officer Commanding, Malta, for 1,000 rounds a gun for the howitzers in his moveable armament, a reasonable demand with which it is impossible to comply, the authorised complement being 200 rounds a gun, and ammunition not existing."

Harnesses

"We had 500 single sets in reserve, less than sufficient for five batteries. I have already had to send 800 single sets to South Africa to replace casualties."

Machine guns

"The authorised number is 1,224. Of these we only had 898, leaving 326 deficient. We have had to draw on machine guns provided for moveable armaments of fortresses to meet South African requirements."

Cavalry saddlery

"We had only 500 sets in reserve at the beginning of the war to meet wear and tear of 16,000 sets in possession of the troops. I have already had to order 600 sets to be sent to South Africa to meet casualties."

Infantry accoutrements

"We had about 10,000 sets in reserve to meet wear and tear of 364,000 sets. I have had to send 6,000 sets to South Africa to equip rifle regiments and the balance to replace casualties. We have none left."

The list goes on. Many of the vehicles for the Army Service Corps were obsolete and fit only for good roads in peacetime – not the rutted, boulder-strewn roads and veld in South Africa.

Brackenbury says: "We have sent or are sending all our serviceable general service wagons, and have had to order no less than 600 vehicles from the trade in this country, besides great numbers ordered locally.

Mule harnesses

"We had 1,700 sets. We have had to buy the equivalent of 24,700 single sets from the trade."

Cavalry swords

"The authorised reserve was 6,000 but owing to a change of pattern having been under consideration for a long time, it had been allowed to fall to 80. We have sent 500 to South Africa."

Tents

"We had an authorised reserve of 5,000 single circular tents and 100 hospital marquees. I have had to send 17,000 circular tents and 900 hospital marquees to South Africa."

Camp equipment

"We had 2,000 camp kettles in reserve. One single demand from Cape Town is for 5,000. Our reserve of picketing pegs, ropes, mallets was not sufficient to supply one-fiftieth of the demands from South Africa."

Small arm ammunition

"Our authorised stocks on 31 March 1899 were 151 millions. I have sent out over 50 millions to South Africa and am supplying Sir R. Buller, at his demand, with about 3 millions weekly. The Ordnance factories and the trade can only supply two and a half millions weekly."

His dismal litany goes on, and on. "Our fortresses [here he is talking about Britain] are chiefly armed with an obsolete armament of muzzle-loading guns, defective in range and energy, and practically useless against ships armed with modern armour . . .

"The ammunition sanctioned is only 200 rounds a gun for fortresses abroad, and 100 rounds a gun for fortresses at home, and there is NO ordnance reserve, except an estimated supply for two years' practice, which is insignificant.

"The greater part, about 73 percent, of the moveable armaments consists of obsolete guns and obsolete ammunition.

"There are only 200 rounds of ammunition per gun abroad, and 100 rounds at home, and no ordnance reserve of either guns, carriages, or ammunition, and no provision has been made for new guns, or for reserves of ammunition."

He goes on:

General stores

"Our reserve of general stores was utterly inadequate to meet the demands. We have had to buy in the market wherever we could get. As an example, we had an authorised reserve of 52,000 sets of horse shoes and no mule shoes. I have to send 35,000 sets of horse shoes and 40,000 sets of mule shoes to South Africa monthly to keep the animals shod. I have to go to Germany and Sweden for horse shoes, and to the United States for mule shoes."

Clothing

"Our reserves of clothing were inadequate to meet even peace requirements; and before this war broke out I had asked for a reserve to be provided equal to six months' ordinary issues, which would cost £320,000. This demand has received no answer. The whole trade of the country is occupied for us, and the clothing factory has been working to its full power.

"We have borrowed from India all the helmets and boots they could give us. It has just been possible to clothe the troops sent out . . . but I am unable to send out the reserves to South Africa."[3]

Tommy in the field

Now, what of Tommy in the field. How did he cope with fighting in the blazing Natal heat and torrential downpours that made his life so different from manoeuvres on Salisbury Plain?

With the biggest Empire in the world backing him, how did he fare?

Poor chap, he had a hard time of it. For instance, he had to heft a one pound tin of preserved meat with him for lunch.

But, thundered Colonel Sir William Richardson, Deputy Adjutant General for Supplies and Transport in South Africa for the year 1899–1900: "Probably nothing tends more to foul camping grounds than the unconsumed portion of the biscuit and meat ration thrown aside by the soldier, to breed flies and spread disease during the process of decomposition."

The entire ration, he said, was seldom eaten, and three-quarters of a pound would be enough. The same for the one pound biscuit tin poor Tommy had to take with his meat tin.

It was, said Richardson, a waste! There was nothing wrong with three-quarters of a pound for biscuits either.

Of course, it depended, he said, on the action and the commanding officer.

But now, how about the lids to those tins?

Tinned supplies such as preserved meats, butter, milk and jam should be secured by a metal band, soldered down and easily torn off by means of either a key or ring.

It was also found, said Richardson, that wooden trade cases were too weak to withstand the rough usage they were subjected to over the rough roads, and those made at Woolwich were necessarily strong and hard to open.

The weight of all packages supplied for use on active service should be reduced to a minimum, he said. The less the weight, the larger number of rations carried.

Circular tins of meat and jam caused a great waste of space in packing cases. All tinned supplies should be packed in wedge-shaped tins, he argued.

Then there was the tea.

As no Boer could possibly fight without coffee, and in fact refused to do so on many occasions,[4] so poor Tommy could not do without his tea.

But he had a problem. The tea came in one big compressed cake. To make tea, he had to pour water over the whole lot, which then became a soggy powerful brew. There was nowhere he could keep the mess once the water had permeated it, so often enough he was forced to throw it away.

It was like seeing his life blood ebb away on the ground.

Richardson suggested that the tea be supplied in compressed cakes, yes, but of only one or two ounces in weight, so that Tommy could brew up in satisfaction, and then light up.

And that was another hot point: The tobacco came in huge, heavy wooden cases, hard to move around, so that poor Tommy was dependent on some wagon or other being able in the first place to load the tobacco, and secondly to find him.

It was hardly possible for the wagon, marked "Tobacco", to trundle into the field of battle.

And the temptation. Tommy, unloading stores in the blistering heat, was able after a time to decipher the cryptic lettering designating the contents of packing cases he was hefting.

If he saw the letter C, a short line, 24p, another short line and the letter H, he knew that inside was just the thing for a thirsty man – 24 pints of Heidseick champagne. Or if he saw the letter J, a short line, 48lbs, another short line, and the letter A, his stomach would probably begin to rumble. What he was looking at was J for jam, 48lbs and A for apricot.[5]

Richardson called for a new system of marking to obviate what he called "numerous robberies" from the packing cases.

Once Tommy had settled down to eat, he had another problem, apart from the tins of preserved meat and biscuits.

There were the vegetables, tinned. What he opened, often enough, was unfit for human consumption.

Says Richardson: "The manufacture of [tinned] meat and vegetable rations requires careful inspection as a large proportion of those sent to South Africa were found to be unfit for human consumption."

And in the morning, our hungry Tommy would look for a *loovrly poiec o' bacon.*

No go: Lean bacon only should be supplied, said Richardson. "In a warm climate the fat tinned bacon is uneatable, and is besides useless for cooking purposes."

So how about some milk, then? "Hold it," said Richardson, "preserved milk requires to be carefully selected as many brands will not keep good for any length of time in a warm climate."

Ravenous Tommy now breaks open his emergency rations. At last! food! But no – "None of the emergency rations can be said to be entirely successful," says Richardson.

At this point, Tommy looks hopefully for the "Boo-ers". Only one bullet from them would end his misery, but first nature calls.

But there is no latrine paper. It is only for use in field hospitals. And besides, like the soap mentioned elsewhere, it was not clear whether it was an Ordnance or an Army Services Corps supply.

As a result, it was always in short supply.

So, Tommy resolves to end it all by jumping over a cliff in the dark. Just in case he changes his mind, he searches for a candle and a lantern. But the candle won't fit the lantern because the lantern is too small. And there's no point in lighting it in the torrential rain – it leaks.

And then there are the matches. "Where the bloddy 'ell are them flamin' matches, 'ey Bert? Wotcha mean, you doan't 'av any?"

But there were other hardships Tommy Atkins faced. Problems from home.

Parcels for soldiers, Sir William said, were much abused by people at home.

Useless parcels of old school books, sermons, meteorological reports, papers and periodicals, many years old, were shipped in large quantities to South Africa.

And a firm of tobacconists sent hundreds of cases containing small packets of cigarettes and tobacco addressed to individual soldiers which had to be distributed at considerable trouble and expense by the military authorities, who were thereby used as agents to enable the firm to make a profit.

"Instances occurred in which bottles of spirits and beer, matches, cooked food – for instance a pig's head which arrived in a decomposing state – were sent by their relatives to soldiers serving at the front.

"By a single vessel as much as 400-tons of parcels would arrive. The ship's agents who conveyed them free of charge took no responsibility for them.

"The parcels were consequently pilfered before shipment, during the voyage and after they landed.

"In one instance, out of 30 cases of brandy sent to the Red Cross Society only eight cases reached their destination."

Taking these parcels to their destination were military transport vehicles. But Sir William had much to say about them, too: " . . . these vehicles are by no means well adapted for service in a country like South Africa where the roads consist of roughly defined tracks over the veld, and where the smallest stream is usually to be crossed at a drift with steep banks on either side.

"Many of the baggage wagons, ambulances and tongas brought out . . . were of little use, and were virtually money thrown away. In many instances the harness supplied with them was of faulty construction, and had to be altered before it could be used. It could hardly have been examined by experts before purchase.

"On a journey across the veld in an ox or mule wagon, the service pattern folding lantern in tin case seldom lasted for more than a fortnight, by which time the jolting of the wagon had broken every pane of glass in the lantern. A combination of glass and metal are not satisfactory."

And the traction engines that did such sterling service on Buller's march from Frere to Spearman's?

"The present type is unfitted for field service. Those sent to South Africa ruined the roads in the towns, and constant complaints of them were received from the municipal authorities.

"On the veld they could not travel more than a few miles away from water," he said.[6]

And so Tommy walked to war . . . loading his rifle with . . . DUM-DUM BULLETS – or did he?

Early in the war, both sides hurled damning accusations at each other. The Boers had used terrible expanding bullets which tore away flesh, mangled limbs and killed nauseatingly, claimed the British.

What's more, they had the evidence: a green substance had been found coating the slug. Undoubtedly poison.

Not only that, deadly poison. More effective than a straight bullet. That a bullet killed anyway didn't seem to enter their heads, and even had the recipient survived the initial impact, he would be likely to die later of intense shock.

It is likely, says Emanoel Lee, who (until his death a few years ago) was a consulting surgeon at Oxford, that the substance found on captured bullets was green fat, used to lubricate the chamber and barrel of the Mausers.[7]

Nothing else.

But what of poor Tommy Atkins? At Kraaipan, in the Northern Cape, one of the first battles of the war, General Piet Cronje wired the following to Pretoria: "Dum-Dum bullets were found with the enemy."

In December 1899, outside Mafeking, General Snyman told Pretoria: "Cartridges taken from the enemy during the morning's battle were Dum-Dum bullets."

And when General Erasmus took possession of Dundee after Talana, and the British had retreated leaving their stores behind, he reported that he had found "huge quantities of Mark IV ammunition".[8]

The Mark IV expanding bullet was to be Britain's main ammunition during the war.

Let General Sir Henry Brackenbury explain:

"There was," he told the Commission of Inquiry on October 21, 1902, "one great difficulty we had with regard to the supply of small-arm ammunition, which perhaps I had better mention here.

"Owing to the experience of the Chitral [India] campaign, it was considered desirable that we should have a more deadly bullet than the ordinary Mark II ammunition which was in use with the .303-inch calibre magazine rifle.

"The Mark II ammunition bullet is, as you know, a very small bullet, less than one-third of an inch in diameter, including the cupro-nickel envelope with which it is covered, and it was found from the experience of the Chitral campaign that it had not what was called sufficient stopping power against the rush of Ghazis, and accordingly in this country, as well as in India, an effort was made to find a satisfactory bullet which would have a more deadly effect.

"In India they produced Dum-Dum ammunition, in which the head of the bullet is not covered by the nickel envelope.

"In this country we produced a bullet in which there is a small cylindrical hole in the lead at the top, and this is left as an opening, and is not covered over with nickel.

"This bullet was an expanding bullet. We had every intention of using this bullet and making it, in fact, the bullet for the British Army all over the world, and, I think, about 66 000 000 of it up to March 31 1899 had been delivered, and formed part of our stock of 172 000 000.

"It was known as the Mark IV. We had an exceptionally hot summer in [July] 1899, and it was found that, especially in the hands of the volunteers, where the rifles had not been kept particularly clean, there were several instances in which this bullet stripped, to use the technical term; that is to say the lead of the bullet squirted out through this opening in the top of the nickel envelope, and left the envelope behind in the rifle.

"Then if there was a second load, you were apt to get an accident, a blowback in the breech. This happened at Bisley, and it happened in several other places with volunteers. There could be very little doubt of what was the cause of it; it was due to exceptional heat, and it required a rifle that was not clean.

"We carried out a great number of experiments to try and reproduce this, and we always found it most difficult to reproduce, and the only conditions in which we could reproduce it were the conditions of great heat and dirty rifles.

"Those two conditions, great heat and a dirty rifle, were exactly the conditions which were likely to occur in war, and, therefore advised the Secretary of State, that none of this ammunition should be considered serviceable for war, and consequently, 66 000 000, or thereabouts of our reserve was non-effective for the purposes of war."

There was more to come.

"It was about the same time, also in that summer that the Hague Convention sat, and passed a resolution against all expanding bullets, but our Government was not party to that Convention, and they declined to be bound by it; nevertheless it is impossible to avoid a feeling that it had a certain moral effect, and that it was not considered desirable to use an expanding bullet in time of war.

"The reason why we did not use an expanding bullet in South Africa was not the Hague Convention, however, but because the Mark IV ammunition, our expanding ammunition, had proved to be unfit to be used in war.

"Consequently, about two-fifths of our reserve of ammunition could not be used.

"We were driven to great straits at one time, because we had actually got reduced in this country to two or three boxes of Mark II ammunition, so that if we had had to go to war with an European power we should have had to fight them with expanding bullets . . ."

But how many cases of Mark IV expanding bullets were shipped out, for instance, to Ladysmith, a British army depot since 1896, before that long hot summer of 1899? And how many were actually withdrawn between, say July 1899, the start of the summer in Britain, when the defect was discovered, and October 1899, when the war began?

The chances are, very little, despite the evidence on October 17, 1902, of Sir Ralph Henry Knox, Permanent Under Secretary of State for War until January 1901.

Asked by Sir Henry Norman whether the Secretary of State or the Under Secretary of State at all times knew what articles were deficient, Knox replied:

"One of the difficulties that arose on the eve of war was with regard to the small arm ammunition. It was decided that the Mark IV ammunition should not be used, and the greater part of our reserve consisted of this Mark IV ammunition, which had been approved.

"Mark IV and Mark V were both under consideration, and it was decided that it was a bad form of ammunition, and in order that they should not be used, the stock, having been, as it were condemned or regarded as obsolete, was reduced to something very low indeed . . ."

QUESTION 1368: (Sir Frederick Darley): "Mark IV is an expanding bullet, is it not?"

KNOX: "It is a cup-nosed bullet."

DARLEY: "Mark V was also in the same category?"

KNOX: "Yes."

DARLEY: "They I suppose were withdrawn on account of the Hague Conference?"

KNOX: "The question was very much discussed, and although I think our representatives took the view that it was an admissable bullet, still the government came to the decision that it should not be used on this occasion."

DARLEY: "In South Africa?"

KNOX: "In South Africa."

DARLEY: And it was not?"

KNOX: "It was not."

What, then, did the Boers find? Or was it just propaganda?

And finally there were the rifles. Some years before the war it had been decided to change from the Lee Metford to the Lee Enfield.

When war began, there were some 200 000 new Lee Enfields available, and some 25 000 troops had gone out to South Africa with them.

That's when they discovered the mistake.

Sir Henry Brackenbury again: "The calibre is exactly the same, the mechanism is the same, and everything else, but there is a difference in the rifling; that is to say in the number, and depth and width of the grooves. . .

"When we began to hand these Lee Enfield rifles to the Imperial Yeomanry for trying the recruits, to see whether they could shoot before they were accepted, reports came in to use that this rifle was shooting 18 inches to the right at 500 yards, which seemed a most extraordinary thing.

"We made inquiries and had the matter tested, and found it was true. We then immediately went into the question of how the rifle was sighted, and we found it had been sighted on the experience of a certain number of rifles, on the recommendation of the chief superintendent of the ordnance factories, and that it had been sighted differently from the Lee Metford rifle, and although the twist (1 in 10) of the rifling was exactly the same in the two, so that you would think the sighting ought to have been exactly the same in the two, it was not; a considerable difference had been made in the sighting of the Lee Enfield as compared with the sighting of the Lee Metford."

SIR GEORGE TAUBMAN-GOLDIE: "When was that discovered?"

BRACKENBURY: "It was discovered in the winter of 1899. I think in December, when the Imperial Yeomany were first enlisted . . . we immediately proceeded to make a back sight with a differently placed notch on the leaf, and we sent these out to South Africa to be put on the Lee Enfields already there, so that they could alter their rifles at once.

"But it was an awful blow just at the moment when we were beginning to take this new weapon into use to find that this mistake had been made."[9]

And thus poor Tommy went to war . . .

SOURCES:

1. *The Commission on the War in South Africa.*
2. *Black and White Budget, 1899.*
3. *The Commission on the War in South Africa.*
4. *Kommandolewens Tydens die Anglo Boere Oorlog*, by Fransjohan Pretorius (1991).
5. *The Commission on the War in South Africa.*
6. Ibid.
7. *To the Bitter End*, by Emanoel Lee (1986).
8. *The Boer Fight for Freedom*, by Michael Davitt (1903).
9. *The Commission on the War in South Africa.*

Durban's landing place, at the Point. It was here, in 1899, that thousands of British troops landed during the early days of the war. This contemporary picture shows soldiers awaiting the arrival of their regiment, while civilians stand about. The boats with their lateen sail, conveyed passengers to and from the roadstead. Troops and equipment were often loaded into lighters which were then towed ashore. Smaller ships were allowed in to dock. (Picture: Author's collection.)

CHAPTER TWO

Setting the South African Scene

When Durban trembled with fear

Rear Admiral Sir Edward Chichester, Bart., CB, CMG, RN, was caught in a shaft of wintry sunlight as he sat before the Royal Commission that cold Tuesday morning, December 2, 1902.

Chichester had been principal transport officer in South Africa from October 1899 to November 1900, when thousands of British troops began to pour in, and he smiled wryly remembering the swaying palm trees that fringed the Durban embankment, the Bluff and heat and the humidity.

But the chairman wasn't really amused and Chichester only caught the last few words of his question . . . "was the method pursued?" It was enough to reply to.

Chichester sat up straight, thrusting the Durban summer of a long time ago out of his mind. This was now serious business. He said: "I commenced at Durban, where I was first, which is a capital port, the best of the lot. The ships came in there, and we got even as big a ship as the Majestic in at one time. They went in alongside the wharf, and we got men and horses wharved practically out of the ships alongside.

"The native labourers there are wonderfully good men – the Zulus; they would tear their fingers off for the English, and there was hardly ever a ship kept outside . . . there was very little delay there all the time . . ."

Chichester later volunteered the information that he had been transport officer in Durban before, during the war of 1881, and indeed, loved the place.[1]

In 1899 he was back, but he found a Durban trembling with fear.

As invasion followed ultimatum in October 1899, thousands of Natal volunteers, hundreds of whom had never heard a shot fired in anger, rose to resist the Boer and protect their homes.

Meanwhile, London *Daily Telegraph* correspondent Bennett Burleigh was in Pretoria the day war was declared. Hurriedly, he managed to get on a train heading for Natal – a train full of Boer commandos. Squeezed into the guard's van with him were some Middelburgers, and as he eased himself into the hard seat, they whooped with delight.

They were going to invade Natal, they told him, eat fish in Durban, and then, if the English did not submit to being thrashed, sail over to London to finish the job![2]

Not only Durban trembled.

Three months later, Vice Admiral Sir Robert Harris, who commanded the naval station at the Cape in 1899, took the stand. It was March 17, 1903, the 47th day of the Commission.

Asked by the chairman what it was like in Durban at the time, Harris replied: " . . . The position began to get critical. It was not so much at Durban at first; it was most critical at Pietermaritzburg."

HARRIS: "The Governor of Natal at the time, Sir Walter Hely-Hutchinson, was very apprehensive that the Boers might leave Ladysmith and approach by the Greyton road and come down and carry Pietermaritzburg very easily.

"It is a place I knew very well, and I thought it was quite indefensible, and so it was arranged that in the event of any difficulties to retire on Durban and pull all the archives and things on board a man-of-war stationed there . . . then as the Boers began to invest Ladysmith more closely, and we thought they might come down to Durban, the burden of protecting Durban was thrown upon my shoulders by the Admiralty by telegram which said I was to protect the towns, so I despatched the (HMS) *Terrible* there and asked that the Captain of the *Terrible* might assume complete control of the place as Military Governor.

"Both the governors [Natal and the Cape] concurred and they appointed Captain Percy Scott as Military Commandant at Durban, and he, about 48 hours after his arrival telegraphed to me that Durban was in a state of complete defence, which relieved all our anxiety on that score . . ."

No-one in Durban had met anything like the enterprising Captain Percy Scott before. On the one hand, the Admiralty – with whom he fought – were happy to see him so far away from Whitehall where he had caused untold anguish; on the other hand they were relieved he was in command in Durban.

By the time his appointment had been made official in November 1899, his ship, his enterprise, his guns and his name had become household words in South Africa and Britain.

When Sir George White, about to be besieged in Ladysmith, had cabled urgently to the Cape for guns, who was to give them to him? Why, Percy Scott, of course – and what was wrong with naval guns anyway?, he asked. They fired shells. Of course, they were fixed aboard his ship – but he would merely take them off.

Scott, the entrepreneur, did just that.

They were originally anti-torpedo boat guns. Situated aboard the one-year-old Cruiser, the 12-pounder, 12-cwt guns were menacing the formidable, put there to smash the darting, fast torpedo-boats that were the fashion of the European navies in 1899.

Captain Scott, with fine waxed Victorian moustache and beard, had caused several angry explosions in Whitehall when, after taking over the ship from her first commander, Captain Charles Grey Robinson, he wrote: "I made an inspection of HMS *Terrible* and found the gun sights of the 9.2-inch guns were wrongly constructed and unserviceable; that the gun sights of the six-inch guns were unserviceable, and that as for the bow guns" [the 12-pounder, 12-cwt guns already mentioned] "put in for firing when chasing the enemy, the object of the pursuit would be invisible through the sight as the port was not big enough, and the guns could not be loaded for want of room to open the breech . . ."

Whitehall, he could have added, were nincompoops. Yes, Whitehall was glad Captain Scott was in South Africa.

The *Terrible* left Plymouth on September 20 on a routine voyage to the China station to take over from her sister ship, HMS *Powerful*. The rumblings of war in South Africa certainly had reached Naval command, but *Powerful* needed to come home.

The warships were instructed, however, to sail for the Cape. *Terrible* arrived in Simon's Bay on October 14. *Powerful* arrived a day earlier, but had berthed in Cape Town harbour to put off some troops of the 2nd Battalion, King's Own Yorkshire Light Infantry which *Powerful* had picked up from

The caption to this contemporary picture states: "Making sure of results. Testing the bolts and mountings by actual firing at Durban." This is one of Percy's Scott's 4.7 in guns, taken off HMS Terrible *and mounted on timber. In the background is Durban's Bluff, and the picture was probably taken at the rocket station near the north pier. The gun is being fired by lanyard, its recoil throwing up sand. Interested spectators line the building at the one side. (Picture: McGregor, Museum, Kimberley.)*

their duties in Mauritius.

Powerful, too, had stopped at Durban on October 9, but after discussion and deliberations with the Natal government, sailed almost immediately for Cape Town where, it was thought, the troops she was carrying would be better needed, as the main push north was expected to be from there, through Bloemfontein to Pretoria.

War was declared on October 11.

The next day the invasion of Natal began. Three days later, *Terrible* reached Simon's Town, and Captain Percy Scott sprang into action . . .

"After being 24 hours at the Cape," he wrote ironically to the Admiralty, "I realised the seriousness of the situation. We had insufficient troops to resist the Boer invasion; our base was 6,000 miles from the scene of operations, and we had no artillery to cope with the enemy's, either in power or in range . . ."

Something had to be done. Captain Scott was the man to do it. But how?

His eyes lit upon the errant 12-pounders bolted solidly, but uselessly, to *Terrible*'s deck plating. There, he thought, was the answer. The guns were superior in range to any field artillery that, as far as he knew at the time, the British and Boer forces had on the ground.

"Get Carpenter Jones here immediately," he instructed, striding towards the guns in the bows. "We need wagon wheels and an axle-tree," he told his bemused First Lieutenant. "Go and see if you can buy some, there's a good chap."

The First Lieutenant departed, taking with him a young Midshipman, Edward Chichester, born in January 1883, son of the Rear Admiral who was so enamoured with Natal. Young Chichester was soon, however, to transfer to HMS *Powerful* – and landed up for the duration besieged in

28

Ladysmith, here we come! One of Captain Percy Scott's 4.7 in guns, on its prefabricated wooden body, is pulled down past Medwood Gardens in West Street, Durban, by sailors from HMS Terrible. Bemused spectators line the streets, some leaning nonchalantly up against the garden wall. The war had come . . . (Picture: Middlebrook Collection, McGregor Museum, Kimberley. MMKP 3490.)

Ladysmith.

It took 24 hours, with the carpenter, some shipwrights and blacksmiths, to convert one of the 12-pounder, 12-cwt guns into a highly manoeuvrable land artillery piece.

What had Scott done? He said: "We made a mounting, consisting of a log of wood to form a trail, mounted an axletree with a pair of ordinary Cape wagon wheels. On to this was placed the ship carriage, bolted down and secured in such a manner as not to interfere with its being put back on board, should circumstances have required it."

Later, he said: "I could see no difficulty in mounting these guns on wheels for service ashore. It seemed natural . . .

"To make sure everything was right, we fired a few rounds and the mounting behaved well . . ."

Now work began on transforming the other 12-pounders, and Captain Percy Scott was about to leave his indelible mark on the Royal Navy and the South African War.

The Battle of Elandslaagte, which closely followed the disaster at Dundee, where the British troops retreated leaving their tents up, marked a milestone for Captain Scott, and the world of gunnery in far off Simon's Town.

The Boers were nearing Ladysmith, and the British needed guns, big guns, urgently. Could anybody help?, asked Sir George White.

HMS *Terrible* had massive 4.7-inch turret guns. If, thought Scott, he could make the 12-pounders manoeuvrable, why not the two 4.7s? Heavy baulks of timber were brought hurriedly aboard, and again Scott's shipwrights and blacksmiths went to work.

The mounting consisted of four pieces of timber, 14 feet long by 12 inches, placed in the form of a cross. On to the centre of this was placed the ordinary ship mounting, bolted through to a plate underneath. The pedestal and timbers were thus all securely bolted together. Next, the gun carriage was dropped over the spindle and secured down to its clip plate.

Scott's urgent work was watched with anticipation and curiosity.

"The admiral," wrote Scott, "asked me if I could . . . get them finished by the following afternoon. It was rather a rush; but they were ready by 5pm, put aboard the *Powerful* and she started with them, and four 12-pounders, for Durban."[3]

There, the guns and their straw-hatted gunners were entrained immediately for Ladysmith. Theirs was the last train in to the town. Forty-eight hours after their arrival the door was closed and the garrison remained beleaguered for 118 days.

But Scott's guns were a godsend. Without them Ladysmith would have fallen. And, in fact, after the war, General Louis Botha told Scott: "If it wasn't for your guns, the Vierkleur would have flown over Durban."[4]

Scott's legacy to the Royal Navy is enacted at every naval base throughout the world and at every military tattoo – The Gun Run, where two teams compete against each other, unlimbering and limbering 12-pounder 8-cwt guns and taking them across imaginary rivers and dongas.

It was first performed with a single 12-pound 8-cwt gun, not the 12-pounder 12-cwt bow guns that Scott's men used at Ladysmith. The smaller version that unlimbered quickly was used. The Gunnery School in Portsmouth was the first venue for this exciting event it was performed before the Lords of the Admiralty in 1900 and then at the Royal Tournament in front of the Prince of Wales.

By the way, there was no question (as some military tattoo programmes will have it) that these guns were manhandled between Durban and Ladysmith by enthusiastic sailors of the Naval Brigade. It would have taken them a full year to get through the Valley of a Thousand Hills on the way, if at all!

No, they went by train.

Scott left Simon's Town on November 3 for Durban. On her speed trials, HMS *Terrible* had notched up more than 22 knots in the English Channel, until a fog descended and it became impossible to see her bows, and speed had to be reduced.

Nevertheless, there was no way *Terrible* could do 22 knots in the Indian Ocean and against the Mozambique Current. But early in the morning of November 6, she arrived off the Back Beach, or the Point as it has become known today.

Because of her draught, she could enter harbour, but, just to be on the safe side, guns, ammunition and supplies were loaded into lighters to be pulled by tugs to the Point wharf, while *Terrible* wallowed in the heavy swell.

The next day the men were landed and when the last lighter tied up, 30 guns – two 4.7-inch, 16 ship's 12-pounder 12-cwts (on Scott's carriages), two 12-pounder 8-cwts, one nine-pounder and one seven-pounder light field guns; two three-pound Hotchkiss, two Nordenfeldt machine guns and four Maxims – manned by 450 officers and men were safely ashore.

By 10am the force was in motion and to their assigned positions in and around Durban – a march that took several hours.

The whole party was given a tremendous ovation as passed the Town Hall (today the main Durban Post Office) where much later a hero called Winston Spencer Churchill would address an admiring crowd on how he had managed to escape from Boer captivity.

On the outskirts of the town, the brigade divided into three separate commands, going in three separate ways. One battery of 4.7s, six 12-pounders and two Maxims went up the Berea Road past the Toll Gate and took up position facing Pietermaritzburg, on either side of the road. The batteries were connected by something new in technology – a telephone.

A second battery of six 12-pounders went westward to Cleremont. They were to guard the western approaches and the railway upcountry.

On the eastern side six more 12-pounders headed out towards the Umgeni River. A detachment from HMS *Thetis* manned the Bluff fort guns which overlooked the harbour entrance and western routes, and a crew from HMS *Tartar* supplied the men for an armoured train.

There were other sites too, private houses taken over by the military – Fort Denison was a home belonging to a citizen near what is today the Windermere shopping centre, and Fort Hartley, a house belonging to a citizen of that name, on the way to the Umgeni.

Scott moved in. Within 48 hours he telegraphed to the Cape that Durban's defences were in place and the town was secure.

J.E. Middlebrook was a British photographer who had set up a business in Durban. As the British troops began landing, he took his camera (with Scott's permission), and catalogued, on pristine, clear glass negatives, the arrival of Her Majesty's troops. He took a photograph of Scott and his staff too, in what was obviously the Middlebrook studio.

Scott cuts a dashing figure in his white navy uniform, pith hat and knee-high black boots. He looks, unsmiling, directly at the camera. With him are three other Royal navy men – R.A. Laycock, who was his clerk, as was E.C. Blanchflower, while Assistant Paymaster W.F. Cullinan sits, holding a swagger stick.

Others on Scott's staff were Sergeant E.H. Brooke, Natal Police; R. Alexander, who was the Superintendent of the Durban Borough Police (both his sons became newspapermen in Durban), T.O. Fraser, who was the then much-hated press censor, and Major H.R. Bousfield, of the Durban Light Infantry, who was Scott's Staff Officer.

Writes George Crowe, of HMS *Terrible:* "Telegrams arriving in quick succession both day and night, and the mass of naval, military and civil correspondence that flowed interminably through the Commander's office for the next five months, imposed a continuous duty upon the staff of an onerous and important nature.'"[6]

Or, in other words, they were kept very, very busy.

Natal, the British liked to think, was a hotbed of spies, criminals and suspiciously friendly Boers who had crossed the borders to get away from the advancing Commandos as they avalanched down through Volksrust and Newcastle.

Scott took his job seriously. For one, he refused to allow an ambulance and its staff, sent from England by humanitarian Sir James Sievewright for the Boers, to leave Durban. Later, the same ambulance, which had by then been sent to Delagoa Bay (today Maputo, in Mozambique) was refused by President Kruger, who said he did not want an ambulance from an Englishman!

Life in Durban was tough. Under Martial Law, all bars closed at 9pm, and a system of night passes was instituted. No one was allowed out in the streets between 11pm and 5am without a pass. Whoever flouted this law faced arrest and detention until sufficient proof was forthcoming as to the person's identity.

Scott himself was twice arrested for being unable to produce his permit

– once when out to test the vigilance of the police, and the second time when he was late leaving the *Terrible* and his permit lay safely on his office table. He was stopped by a Borough policeman who refused to believe what he called Scott's "fantastic" tale about being the Commandant of Durban. Scott was locked up until he was identified some hours later by his secretary, who had been telephoned from Scott's office.

The constable, trembling now in his boots, was warmly praised by Scott for doing his job properly.

However, the stringent controls were soon to be relaxed. Once the first contingent had left for the front on November 27, the Cleremont battery was withdrawn to the town camp, or Town Hall camp as it became known (it was alongside the Town Hall, where the Medwood Gardens are today).

On November 28, Buller wired from Pietermaritzburg: "I think you can now make yourself as snug as possible, parking your guns where most convenient for your men, and where giving them the least duty. I cannot say for another week or 10 days that Durban is absolutely safe, but it looks as if, at present, it is not in immediate danger."

Scott withdrew the Fort Denison battery and other outlying batteries towards the Umgeni, and regrouped them in the town, giving him time to perfect yet another invention.

Because Ladysmith had now been cut off, there could be no communication with the garrison, or Sir George. So, thought Scott, how about a "Flasher" – which is what his men called it. Scott drew up plans and submitted them to Buller. "Agreed", came the answer.

Scott's "Flasher" was born. Lieutenant Ogilvy and Engineer Murray, with their respective electrical and artificer staffs, came ashore from the *Terrible* and began. First a seachlight was borrowed from *Terrible*'s bridge, a dynamo was commandeered from a dredger, a locomotive boiler requisitioned from the Natal Government Railways, and connections were made, some in the onshore engineering foundry of the NGR, now the exquisite shopping mall known as The Workshop in central Durban.

Three railway trucks, too, were borrowed on which the apparatus was to be fixed. Says Crowe: "About noon on November 30, within 48 hours or receiving the general's telegram [Buller's telegram] the searchlight train – for that is what it was – steamed out of Durban . . . for Frere."

The "Flasher" was used every night to communicate with Ladysmith by means of code, and also its light was used to show up the destroyed Frere bridge while engineers were constructing a by-pass at night. Until then Scott's "Flasher" pigeons had been used with great success to carry messages to and from Ladysmith, including a plan of the situation in the town which Sir George wanted to send to Scott.

Sir George had the plan photographed down, but even then it was found to be too heavy for one bird to carry, so it was cut into four sections, each of which was entrusted to one pigeon. They all arrived safely with an interval of about 25 minutes between the first and the last – flying time, some six hours.

Another pigeon brought this message: "From general Sir George White to H.R.H. The Prince of Wales: The General Officer Commanding and the garrison of Ladysmith beg to congratulate Your Royal Highness on the anniversary of your birthday. A royal salute of 21 shells will be fired at the enemy at noon in honour of the occasion – Ladysmith, November 9, 1899."

For the record: The *Terrible*'s men left Ladysmith after its relief on March 11, 1900 and arrived in Durban the next day to a tumultuous welcome.[5]

32

HMS *Terrible* sailed from Durban at noon on March 27 for the China Station (and the Boxer Rebellion in which she once again upheld the might of the Royal Navy.)

Natal volunteers, after an unparalleled spell of a year in the field, returned home on October 8, 1900.

SOURCES

1. *Commission on the war in South Africa.*
2. *The Natal Campaign*, by Bennet Burleigh.
3. *The Commission of HMS Terrible*, by George Crowe.
4. *The Siege of Ladysmith*, by Gerald Sharp.
5. *The Commission of HMS Terrible*, by George Crowe.

General Sir George White, VC (he won it in India), the man who, averred Buller, "allowed himself to be shut up" in Ladysmith. White, however, called his action the salvation of Natal – because he had kept more than 12,000 Boers from fighting in other areas. At one stage – after the battle of Colenso – Buller telegraphed him to "fire away all your ammunition" and make the best deal possible with the Boers. White and his staff were shocked by the telegram, and thought it had been sent or intercepted by the Boers. Sir George's heroic stand is unique (with Mafeking) in the annals of warfare.

CHAPTER THREE

Ladysmith

What it was all about

Major Hubert Gough sharply pulled up his wet horse in the swirling dust of the main street. The cheers rang around his ears as he tried to face Sir George White and, at the same time, keep his horse steady as the troopers who had ridden hard with him milled about.

Sir George looked at him, smiled and said, "Hallo, Hubert, how are you?"

It was all very quiet and unemotional, wrote Gough later.

"I had known Sir George very well when he was Commander-in-Chief in India and had often dined at his house, Snowden, in Simla."

Hubert Gough, one of the youngest commanders of troops in the war, was the first man of the relieving force to enter Ladysmith. Fittingly, he commanded men made up of Colonial irregulars – Natal Carbineers, Natal Mounted Rifles, Border Mounted Rifles, Natal Police and the Imperial Light Horse.

An hour earlier, he had been stopped and handed an order from Major-General Lord Douglas Mackinnon Bailie Hamilton Cochrane Dundonald, scouting between the Tugela and the Ladysmith approaches, ordering him to "retire at once" after some Boers had been seen on the nearby hills and some shells had been fired at the British troopers.

Writes Gough: "From where I was, I could look across the plain to Ladysmith and see the tin roofs of its houses three miles away. I had not the slightest intention of obeying the order to retire. I just crumpled up the note and threw it to the ground, telling the orderly who had given it to me to return to Dundonald and report that he had delivered the message."

But he first asked the messenger to wait a minute.

" . . . I now made up my mind to proceed straight on into Ladysmith, but two things had to be done first. I wrote a message back to Dundonald and said that I was already within the Ladysmith perimeter and was going on to the town at once."

Only then did he dismiss the orderly.

"The second matter to arrange was our entry into the town. It had to be conducted with dignity and in order . . . who was going to be the first to enter the beleaguered town?

"I think I came to a solution worthy of a Solomon. All scouts were recalled and the squadrons were told to ride in side by side, each in double file, so we still presented a front of fours.

"I rode at the head of the whole column."

The time was 4pm on February 28, 1900. The slouch-hatted mounted troopers of No 5 Estcourt–Weenen squadron of the Natal Carbineers were led by Major Duncan Mackenzie, and the slouch-hatted troopers of the Imperial Light Horse by Captain Herbert Bottomley.

These two outstanding soldiers commanded the only companies of the Natal Carbineers and the ILH that were not besieged in Ladysmith.

There was a sequel for Gough.

The next morning as he was parading his men, his brother, John, who had spent his whole time in Ladysmith, rode up. As he recognised him, Hubert ran forward to greet him affectionately.

John, having suffered the pangs of starvation for several months, was evidently struck by the hearty well-fed appearance of his brother, and instead of indulging in any heroics about the Siege or referring in any way to fights or battles which they had been through, looked down from the superior height of his pony and said, "Well, Hubert, how fat you have got!"

The garrison was on one and a quarter biscuits a day each when they were relieved, and had only four days' supply of these!

Officially, Dundonald was peeved. When his orderly returned in a rush with Gough's message, Dundonald, on his way back to the Tugela–Colenso line, wheeled about, selected some officers (including Winston Churchill) and some troopers, left his brigade, and thundered off for Ladysmith. As he neared the town, he sent back a message for Buller – "Am in Ladysmith: Dundonald."

Says Gough: "He did not mention me, nor his strict orders to prevent me pushing on . . . If I had carried out his orders, he would not have been in until the next day!

"I was washing my hands for dinner with Sir George when Dundonald (and Winston Churchill) arrived, I suppose nearly two hours after I had crossed the Ladysmith lines . . ."

Well, was Gough really the first person to enter the besieged town?

Churchill writes: " . . . up and down hill, over boulders and through the scrub, Hubert Gough with his two squadrons . . . were clear of the ridges already. We turned the shoulder of the hill, and there before us lay the tin houses and dark trees we had come so far to see and save."

But according to Gough, Dundonald and Churchill were at least two hours behind.

Dundonald writes: " . . . we reached Ladysmith some few minutes after the Natal Carbineers and the Imperial Light Horse had passed across the river into the town."

But a resident, Mr Herbert Watkins-Pitchford, writing to his wife from Ladysmith, says, in capital letters: "DUNDONALD HAD NO MORE HAND IN THE RELIEF OF LADYSMITH THAN I HAD.

"And all the reports as to his brilliant action in being the first into the place, are false!"[1]

Some precious, hoarded prizes were laid out for dinner that night, while a few short miles away, 75 wagons of medical supplies and food for the Ladysmith hungry and sick lay immobile near the Tugela.

Buller seemed unmoved, and ordered only that the wagons begin to "move in the direction of Ladysmith".

And while his men made haste slowly, the Boers loaded their notorious Long Tom gun into a train at the foot of Bulwana and headed off up the line for Modder Spruit.

If Buller had attacked the Boers during this somewhat chaotic with-drawal, could the war have been shortened?

This is what Deneys Reitz says in his book *Commando*: "In all directions the plain was covered with a multitude of men, wagons and guns ploughing across the sodden veld in the greatest disorder. Whenever a spruit or nullah barred the way there rose fierce quarrels between the frightened teamsters, each wanting to cross first with the result that whole parks of vehicles got their wheels so interlocked that at times it seemed as if the bulk of the transport and artillery would have to be abandoned, for the mounted men pressed steadily on without concerning themselves with the convoys. Had the British fired one single gun at this surging mob everything on wheels would have fallen into their hands, but by great good luck there was no pursuit and towards afternoon the tangle gradually sorted itself out."

Buller had given emphatic orders that the British forces were not to pursue.

Lieutenant-Colonel R.H. Sim, Royal Engineers, on Sir Charles Warren's staff, wrote: "Sir Charles had implored Buller to send up a battery as soon as the road to Green Hill [or Railway Hill as it became known] was practicable for artillery yesterday, but he would not, and so the enemy were able to get away unharmed." [2]

Later, Buller said: "All that I know worth knowing about rearguards I learned from the Boers whom I commanded in 1879; and I was, and am still, deeply impressed with the belief that unless there is some paramount object to be gained, an attempt to force a Boer rearguard is merely a waste of men . . . Moreover the reprovisioning of Ladysmith became a matter of supreme importance." [3]

But the Boer was on the run. Had Buller once again tied up their forces outside Ladysmith, by moving even one-quarter of the troops (some 25 000) into action, many of those who had ridden to support General Piet Cronje far down in the Free State at Paardeberg would have been forced to return, thus weakening further their ability to hit the British forces under Roberts then on their way through the Free State to Pretoria.

Also it is ironic that the man on the last train out of Ladysmith, as Boer guns began opening up on the town and commandos sealed it off, was the man who indirectly succeeded in its salvation.

Cavalry Commander John Denton Pinkstone French was one of hundreds who were crammed aboard that train. His work was now elsewhere.

It was French, later, whose cavalry attacks in the Orange Free State forced the Boers to hasten from Ladysmith to defend Cronje before his surrender at Paardeberg, symbolically on Majuba Day, which marked the Boer defeat of General Colley in the "First" Boer War of 1881.

But Buller lived up to his name – "Blunder". While the food wagons laboured at ox-pace towards the town, his unofficial entrance into Ladysmith was from the opposite side, the people all having congregated at the iron railway bridge entrance.

It was soon sorted out, as were the wagons with the supplies.

On March 3, 1900, Buller's army made its formal entry into Ladysmith, prompting Lieutenant-Colonel Grant, who was among those who had been in the town for four months, to write: "Like all the really pregnant things of the earth, it is beyond the art of the word painters, who have tried their skill upon it and often spoilt it painting cheering, dancing figures, tears and antics of joy, embracings. There was none of this; the garrison were but just able to stand, much less dance; hundreds could not stand, but crouched or sat in the ranks, a piteous guard of honour." [4]

Sim called the triumphal march into the town "one of the most mournful pageants that could be devised by idiotic generals". [5]

And Warren wrote: " . . . I cannot even now bear to think of it: the march of 20,000 healthy men triumphant and victorious, through the ranks of the weary and emaciated garrison, who were expected to cheer us and who actually tried to do so – it was an ordeal for me and many another."

Trooper H.M. Stainbank, of the Colonial Scouts, a member of Warren's personal escort, wrote home to his parents on March 3: "Today was appointed for the great triumphal entry into the town. The Ladysmith garrison lined the street as far as the road leading to Tin Town, the permanent military camp.

"They looked very white and thin beside the Relief of bronzed and dirty-looking fellows, all stout and in splendid condition.

"The garrison had smiling faces, but some of the men could hardly stand up they were so weak. They cheered as hard as they could, but what a miserable sound it was from so many men.

"They had hardly the strength to cheer. One poor Lieutenant of the Gordons could only lean on his sword.

"General Buller led the way with his escort and General Warren with his. Warren was soon recognised and spoken of as the 'fighting' general, and it seemed to me that the cheers for him were more hearty . . ."

Indeed, Warren was the "fighting" General. How is explained in the closing chapters of this work.

Warren later wrote: "All the incoming soldiers handed their day's rations and everything out of their kitbags to the garrison. Tommy is awfully generous. He knew he would have to go without food for the day, but he did not care.

"I was sent back to conduct the wagon to the camping ground, and as we passed through the streets, children, women and soldiers came up asking for biscuits. We had four days' reserve rations, biscuit and bully, on the wagon, but the sergeant and I managed to get rid of the lot. I am afraid there will be a row about it, as we shall have to apply for more . . ." [6]

George Steevens, of *The Guardian*, who together with Bennet Burleigh, of the London *Daily Telegraph*, were the two foremost war correspondents of their day, wrote from Ladysmith: "Beyond is the world – love and war. Clery marching on Colenso, and all that man holds dear in a little island under the north star. But you sit here to be idly shot at. You are of it but not in it – clean out of the world. To your world and to yourself you are every bit as good as dead, except that dead men have no time to fill in.

"I know now how a monk without a vocation feels. I know how a fly in a beer bottle feels.

"I know how it tastes, too . . . ." [7]

The anonymous chronicler of exploits of the Natal Mounted Rifles tries some levity: "We formed a band called the Ladysmith Siege Band, the instruments being tubs with sheepskins and tin whistles. The band played daily for our physical drill, and also at our concerts."

But the flies: "Flies thrive in a siege. In our mess we had a punkah, and even then it was a race from plate to mouth lest the flies should swoop down and scoop the meal!" [8]

To Louis Creswicke, who wrote *The Transvaal War* from the seclusion of his London office, working from despatches and newspaper reports, all the British were good and all the Boers unwashed and bad.

But even Creswicke had to write before the Relief: "Still the garrison was resolved to hold on to the last, preferring death by starvation or disease rather than surrender. The malodorous surroundings were borne with patience, the diminution of the supply of medicines watched with pathetic resignation . . .

"How they longed, how they prayed for the great hour! They believed in Buller; they knew he would come, they said to themselves. But when, O when? An echo answered – When?" [9]

Was Buller well received?

There are conflicting reports. Some say Sir George White was aloof and distant. Others say the same of Buller, the conquering hero who had taken too long to travel the 19 kilometres between Colenso and Ladysmith.

Ian Hamilton, Chief of White's Staff, wrote the following to Roberts: "Buller was very rude to Sir George and spoke to him in the vilest way of you and Kitchener, whom he appears to dislike, and to attribute dishonest motives to, almost as much as he does you. I never gave him the chance to be nasty to me, but contented myself with a very distant salute."

Sir Frederick Treves, eminent London surgeon who headed the Natal medical operation, arrived in Ladysmith on March 2, days after Gough's arrival and Buller's certain knowledge of conditions in the town.

He wrote: "I had no food at my disposal . . . on walking into Starvation City one's first impression was that of the utter emptiness of the place . . . the people we met were pallid and hollow-eyed, and many were wasted. All were silent, listless and depressed. There were no evidences of rejoicing, no signs of interest or animation, and indeed (as far as they were concerned) Ladysmith was still unrelieved."

On his way there, Treves found, at the top of the ridge across the Tugela pontoon bridge (the British had used the iron bridge for target practice for the Navy 4.7 in guns after the battle of Colenso and blown it up), "the mighty convoy of ox-wagons with food for Ladysmith. The wagons could be counted by hundreds and the cattle by thousands. The hubbub could not be surpassed. The lowing of the oxen, the shrieking of the Kaffir boys, the bellowed orders of the convoy conductors, the groaning of colliding wagons, made a compound of sound worthy of the occasion.

"Among the rabble would be seen ambulance wagons, water carts, isolated gun carriages and ammunition wagons, bread carts, mounted officers hurrying through, weary pickets returning to camp and a few Tommies tramping along with cheery indifference to the restless, struggling crowd." [10]

By the time Buller came in, some of the food had been distributed. But there were others, like Gough and Dundonald, who knew supplies could have been got up sooner.

It is interesting to record that in the Commission on the War, Buller blamed White for getting "holed up", as he put it, in Ladysmith in the first place.

Buller faced searching questions from the members of the Commission and got himself tied up in knots over a series of telegrams – and was reprimanded too.

He had never, he said, approved of White staying in Ladysmith.

When it was pointed out to him that the Commission was in possession of a telegram he had sent to White telling him to stay in Ladysmith, he said: "I merely want to call the attention of the Commission to the fact that the telegram of mine was sent in reply to a telegram from him in which he said he could not leave it.

"It is in my statement as follows: 'A few hours later I received a further telegram from Sir George White saying he could not withdraw from Ladysmith, and that he had sent a single battalion to guard the bridge at Colenso as the best step that he could take for the protection of Natal'.

"When he sent me that telegram, I replied that he had better stay in Ladysmith. There was nothing else I could reply."

SIR HENRY MORGAN: "Did he not send that battalion there to guard the bridge at Colenso in consequence of representations to him that he should send some force there?"

BULLER: "Not from me! I made no representation to him at all except that I wanted to get his cavalry out."

MORGAN: "If there was a telegram from the Commander-in-Chief drawing his attention to the necessity of guarding Colenso, that would account for his action in that matter, would it not?"

BULLER: "I do not think it would at all! The Commander-in-Chief was 7,000 miles away and could not possibly know what he [White] ought to do . . ."

Later, SIR GEORGE TAUBMAN-GOLDIE asked: "Is it not the case that he represented that sending the one battalion to Colenso was all he was doing for the safety of the Colony because that by staying at Ladysmith, he hoped to contain the Boers and prevent them going further south?"

BULLER: "I was reading what he said; 'I wired Natal government yesterday that I would send the Royal Dublin Fusiliers to guard the bridge at Colenso as the best step I could take for the protection of the Colony'; those were his own words."

GOLDIE: "Yes, but that has to be read with the rest of the telegram . . ."

BULLER: "Well, I knew, not at that time on the 31st [October 1899] but three days later that he had been driven into Ladysmith . . ."

GOLDIE: "Without going in to that now, I only say you must not pick out one sentence from a telegram and present it as the whole of what he was doing for the protection of the Colony."

BULLER: "When he says that he would contain as many Boers as he could and that they would not go south without attacking him?"

GOLDIE: "Yes."

BULLER: "I merely took the telegram as I read it, and I read it that he could not leave Ladysmith.

"He did not send out the cavalry that I wanted, but he sent out one regiment. He should have sent out more. After all, a stationary force can contain no more of the enemy than those who choose to stay round it, and at that time, contrary to his belief, the Boers were actually moving south and invading south Natal."

GOLDIE: "You said you hoped you would have had all the cavalry out of Ladysmith?"

BULLER: "Yes."

GOLDIE: "Do you think that the force in Ladysmith would have been capable of defending the place without the cavalry?"

BULLER: "Yes, I think they would have defended it more easily. The cavalry really did nothing, except on January 6 when they were brought into action."

GOLDIE: "Do you think they were only brought into action on January 6?

BULLER: "I learned that was the only day they had anything to do! They were used on November 1 and 2nd, but they went back again. Beyond that I don't think they did anything." [11]

All it implied was that he, Buller, had had to fight long and wearisome battles, while White had been inactive in Ladysmith.

The fact that White had serious problems, the most important of which was Buller (known in the town as "Sir Reverse") himself, did not enter Buller's mind.

And the Boers: What did they think?

Michael Davitt, the British Member of Parliament, resigned when war was imminent and sailed for South Africa to join the Boers, because he felt it was "the most dishonourable and unchristian war which has ever disgraced a civilised age" and the "greatest infamy of the nineteenth century".

His masterful work *The Boer Fight for Freedom* was banned in Britain, but was published in America and available in Holland, Germany, Scandinavia and Russia.

Davitt travelled a lot, gleaning what he could from Boer leaders and commandos who had been involved in the fighting on all fronts.

As far as Ladysmith was concerned, Davitt gave the breakdown as follows: The laagers were roughly divided into four, situated more or less to the points of the compass.

Joubert was to the north, Schalk Burger to the east, Lukas Meyer south, and Prinsloo, with the Free State contingent, to the west.

Their mobility deceived White into believing he was opposed by 25,000 men – an over-generous estimate of his opponents' strength which, if true (and it wasn't), left Buller, Gatacre, Roberts, French and Methuen almost without Boers to fight.

During November, writes Davitt, the Boer laagers around Ladysmith attracted visitors of both sexes from the Transvaal – non-combatants who travelled down to witness the siege.

The prowess of Long Tom, which was legendary, made the two guns on Lombard's kop and Bulwana objects of almost religious regard for the thrill-seekers.

Says Davitt: "Ladies by the hundred came from Johannesburg and Pretoria to enjoy the sensation of besieging an English army, and to experience the satisfaction of touching a big Cruesot gun."

But Davitt, wise in the ways of politics, if not defence, grudgingly writes: "This siege has been one of the few real British triumphs of the war; but a triumph by virtue of endurance rather than by striking military performance, and chiefly owing to the lamentable blunder . . . by which General Joubert played into the hands of his adversary's purpose.

"General White has clearly explained what his governing object was in consenting to so large a force of British troops submitting to so long a siege: 'I was confident of holding out at Ladysmith as long as might be necessary, and I saw clearly that so long as I maintained myself there, I could occupy the great mass of the Boer armies and prevent them sending more than small flying columns south of the Tugela, with which the British and Colonial forces in my rear, aided by such re-inforcements as might shortly be expected, could deal without much difficulty'" (White to Roberts, *SA Despatches*, Vol. XI, p. 15.)

Joubert, says Davitt, deluded himself with the notion that the successful keeping of some 12,000 soldiers inside Ladysmith would result in a second post-Majuba peace pact. He died broken-hearted with the knowledge that his policy had been the means of tying up the great mass of Boer armies in the task, watching one English general, while Botha, Cronje and De la Rey had to fight three armies, one of them four times as large as General White's, with the small flying columns which were spared from the field of siege operations in Natal. [12]

Finally, the actual situation in Natal in those early days was far more serious than was realised anywhere outside of Ladysmith.

Whatever consoling descriptions correspondents may have been allowed to apply to the main battles, they nevertheless had a hard time of it. For instance, Bennet Burleigh complains that no correspondents were allowed to mention Buller's arrival in Natal, despite the fact his operations could be observed from near and far with a good pair of binoculars or spy-glass.

The ruling applied to Colenso, Spioenkop, Vaalkrantz and Pieters, despite the fact that civilians working for the army were allowed close to the battleground.

Leo Amery, who edited *The Times History of the War*, blames White, too, for holding on to his cavalry, and did so despite strong objections by French and Sir Archibald Hunter.

It seems, says Amery, that White did not realise that there was no longer any object in retaining any part of the Natal Field Force (as the composite army was known) that was not essential for garrison purposes.

Based at Colenso and Chieveley, the cavalry could have done invaluable work in preventing Boer raids across the river and could have helped the relieving force.

Amery had no love for Buller, yet vindicated his later Commission stand by stating that the cavalry were far less use inside Ladysmith than out.

"They added to the number of mouths to feed, and the presence of so many horses in a confined space was largely responsible for the insanitary condition of the town and the consequent sickness which so greatly reduced the garrison." [13]

By the time the Natal Field Force was disbanded on October 19, 1900 – just over a year after the war began – some 75,000 troops, 30,000 horses, 120 guns, 90,000 livestock and 300,000 tons of supplies were received and forwarded, and 25,000 men, Natalian and Uitlander, Zulu and Hindu had been raised to defend its majestic borders. [14]

And on the brown, hot plains, they died.

Perhaps the final comment should go to General Neville Lyttleton, who, in a letter, was with Buller.

"Few commanders," he wrote "have so wantonly thrown away so great an opportunity."

He was referring to the flood of Boers in retreat, jammed up just outside Ladysmith. "They were at our mercy," wrote Lyttleton. And Buller did nothing about it.

The Siege of Ladysmith had lasted from November 2, 1899 to February 28, 1900, a total of 118 days.

Regiments in Ladysmith during the siege

Naval Brigade; Natal Naval Volunteers; Royal Artillery, with 13th, 21st, 42nd, 53rd, 67th and 69th Batteries; No 10 Mountain Battery; Natal Hotchkiss Detachment; 5th Dragoon Guards; 5th Lancers; 18th and 19th Hussars; Natal Carbineers; Natal Mounted Rifles; Border Mounted Rifles; Natal Mounted Police; Imperial Light Horse; 1st Liverpools; 1st Devons; 1st Gloucesters; 1st Manchesters; 1st Leicesters; 1st and 2nd King's Royal Rifles; Royal Irish Fusiliers; 2nd Gordon Highlanders; 2nd Rifle Brigade; 2nd Dublin Fusiliers; 23rd Field Engineers; Balloon section; Telegraph section; Army Service Corps; Army Ordnance Corps; Town Guard.

SOURCES

1. *Thank God we kept the Flag Flying*, by Kenneth Griffith.
2. *Life of Sir Charles Warren*, by Watkin Williams.
3. *Commission on the War in South Africa*.
4. *From Cape Town to Ladysmith*, by G.W. Steevens.
5. *Life of Sir Charles Warren*, by Watkin Williams.
6. Ibid.
7. *From Cape Town to Ladysmith*, by G.W. Steevens.
8. *Natal Volunteer Record*, Robinson and Sons, Durban (1900).

9. *Transvaal War*, by Louis Creswicke.
10. *The Tale of a Field Hospital*, by Frederick Treves.
11. *Commission on the War in South Africa*.
12. *The Boer Fight for Freedom*, by Michael Davitt.
13. *The Times History of the War*, edited by Leo Amery.
14. *Natal Volunteer Record*, Robinson and Sons, Durban (1900).

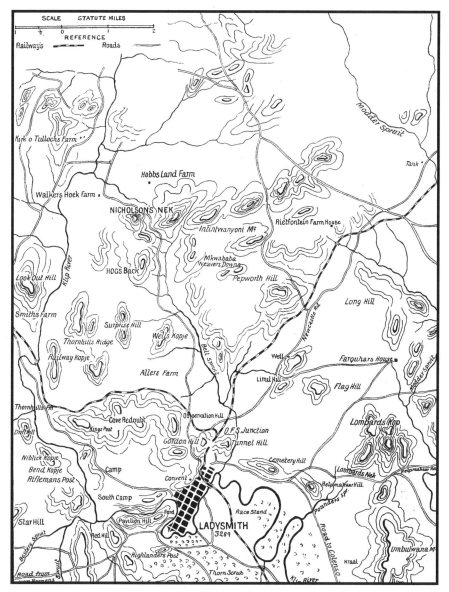

Contemporary map of the area north of Ladysmith, showing the railway line junction to the Orange Free State and Northern Natal. Nicholson's Nek, north of Ladysmith, was the scene of Britain's biggest wartime surrender – some 900 men – an event that hit Whitehall like a Creusot shell. It was kept from the public for weeks while the situation was evaluated.

CHAPTER FOUR

Sir George Explains

Why I stayed in Ladysmith

When Tommy reached for his well-worn pipe and tobacco, or, if he was enlightened and aspiring to keep up with the gentry, searched for his cigarettes, his fingers probably found a tin of Three Castles, with its eight-pointed star emblem and gold lettering. The tobacco kept him comfortable over long, bitterly cold nights, or helped him spend an hour or two over a veld dinner.

Three Castles was manufactured by Messers W.D. and H.O. Wills, of Bristol and London. And, in the patriotic fervour of the time, they also put out a 22-page hard-cover booklet – *British Commanders in the Transvaal War 1899–1900*.

The right-hand side pages contained portraits of the fighting heroes – Roberts, Kitchener, Buller VC, Forestier-Walker, Methuen, Warren, Rundle, Gatacre, Kelly-Kenny, French, Hunter, Fitz-Roy Hart, Hildyard, Lyttleton, Colville, Carrington, Brabazon, Macdonald, Dundonald, Baden-Powell, Kekewich, Plumer – and of course, Sir George White, VC.

The left-hand pages contained the words, a potted, truly British biography. This is what they had to say about the man Buller accused of letting himself be "locked up in Ladysmith".

"Lieutenant-General Sir George White, VC: The subject of our portrait, born in 1835 is, as are Lord Wolseley and Lord Roberts and many other gallant and distinguished soldiers, an Irishman.

"He entered the army in 1853 and first saw active service in the Indian Mutiny, where he gained great distinction. In 1879, General White fought with the Gordon Highlanders during the war in Afghanistan. At the actions of Charasiah, Kandahar and others our (then) Major behaved with such conspicuous gallantry that he was awarded the Victoria Cross. For distinguished service in Burmah he was promoted to the rank of Major-General, and soon after, in 1893, was appointed successor to Lord Roberts as Commander-in-Chief of India.

"The existencies of the situation in Natal during the Autumn of 1899 necessitated the sending out of this distinguished General to command the troops there. His splendid military abilities were immediately evidenced in his methods of dealing with the strategies of the Boer Commanders, but on November 3, he found his communications cut off and the Siege of Ladysmith commenced. For 117 days [it was actually 118], "General White heroically defended the town against the attacks of the Boers, the most daring and prominent of which occurred on January 6, 1900 when the enemy were repelled with a loss of over 800 men. Eventually on February 28, the glad news of the approach of the British relief column and the retreat of the Boers was announced, and so ended one of the most memorable of modern sieges." [1]

Stirring stuff of which heroes are made!

Sir George White had embarked at Southampton for South Africa on September 16, 1899, like Buller, without orders. This is what he told the chairman when he was called to the Commission on Monday, February 16, 1903. "I may here mention, as the point has been referred to in the evidence I have been allowed to see, that, previous to starting, I had received no orders, except that I was to assume command of the forces in Natal; and that the General Officer Commanding at Cape Town was to exercise his command independently of me.

"I was not informed of any plan of campaign against the Boers, or asked to operate on any given lines. I therefore considered myself unfettered in meeting the emergencies which I had to face immediately on landing, as I thought best for the preservation of Natal."

Sir George had a brief interview when he arrived in Cape Town on October 3, 1899 with then Sir Alfred Milner.

"From what he told me I was convinced that Natal would be the main objective of the Boers, and that war was imminent. I accordingly changed my plan of going by sea to Durban from Cape Town and proceeded that same evening overland to East London where the Durban mail steamer had been detained for me."

Sir George arrived at Durban on October 7, 1899, where he was met at the docks by Major General Sir William Penn-Symons.

WHITE: "I may perhaps here say that at Durban I met Captain Holland of the Indian Marine, who was helping in the transport service, and who had served with me when I was commanding the field force during the war in Upper Burma.

"I asked him about the coal supply, and urged him to get as much as possible from outside sources, as even then I had grave doubts as to my ability to cover the Dundee coalfields in the North of Natal."

White found most of the troops in Natal had been moved by Penn-Symons between the coalfields at Glencoe (some 3,000 to 4,000) near Dundee, and Ladysmith (some 8,000 to 10,000).

Penn-Symons had been sent in May 1899 to Natal to take precautionary measures in the north should there be a war with the Boers, and spent much time reconnoitring the countryside – much of which he was familiar with, as he had fought, with distinction, in the Zulu War of 1879.

But he was not, however, at Isandhlwana – as chance would have it, he was away from his regiment on special duty.

Penn-Symons came of a Cornish family, the founder of which was a Norman Knight who arrived in Britain with William the Conqueror.

Penn-Symons was born in 1843 and in 1863 joined the South Wales Borderers – the famous 24th Regiment of Foot.

He became a Lieutenant in 1866, Major in 1881, Lieutenant Colonel in 1886 and Colonel in 1887. The first action he saw was in 1877 against the Calekas in the Frontier Wars. In 1885 he served as Deputy Assistant Adjutant and Quartermaster General organising and commanding the Mounted Infantry in the Burmese expedition, and was honourably mentioned in Despatches for his services with the Chin Field Force.

In 1889–90 he was given a brigade in the Chin-Lusha Expedition, was again mentioned in Despatches, made a Commander of the Bath (CB) and received the thanks of the Government of India.

He commanded a brigade of the Waziristan Field Force in 1894–85 and then moved to the notorious North-West Frontier of India in 1897–88, after which he was made a KCB. In 1898 he gave up his appointment in India and took command of the British troops in Natal.

Creswicke, in *The Transvaal War*, says Penn-Symons was one of the best shots in the army, his military hobby being musketry, and was an authority on mounted infantry.

When White arrived in Durban he immediately took the train to Pietermaritzburg, and on October 10th – the day the Boer ultimatum was handed to the British government – discussed the military and political situation with the Governor of Natal, Sir Walter Hely-Hutchison.

WHITE: "The Governor of Natal . . . informed me on the 10th October that the outbreak of war on the 11th October [the next day] was certain.

"On learning the disposition of the troops I had been much impressed by the exposed position of the force at Glencoe, and had discussed it with Sir William Penn-Symons. He had given the subject great thought, had consulted the Colonial Office and local civil authorities, and was most confident that he had sufficient troops there to hold his own against the Boers.

"He also dwelt to me on the advantages that the ground round Glencoe offered for the tactics of his trained troops against burgher levies.

"Notwithstanding his opinion, I considered the Glencoe force should be withdrawn.

"Ladysmith appeared to me the most advanced post that could practically be held against the two main divisions of the Boer Army. We knew that both Transvaalers and Free Staters were making every preparation to take the initiative and to assume at once an active offensive . . .

". . . The facility with which the enemy could cut communications behind me if I had given them a long line to strike at, would have involved me in probable disaster.

"Feeling that Ladysmith was the most advanced post that I could hold on in force to use as a shield to cover the vitals of Natal, I sought an interview with Hely-Hutchison."

Hely-Hutchinson baulked. He had a most decided opinion that a withdrawal from Glencoe would be disastrous, involving the probability that the Dutch, not only in Natal but also in the Cape would throw their lot in with the Boer armies.

WHITE: "He further said that the effect on the natives, of whom there are some 750,000 in Natal and Zululand, might be disastrous, and that loyalists would be discouraged and disgusted.

"He also informed me that the opinions that he had expressed were not his only but were shared by the Prime Minister [of Natal] and by every member of the Natal Government.

"The dangers described have since been referred to as mere political considerations, which should not have been allowed to over-ride military principles; but I submit that to dismiss them thus, after the danger is past, is to deprive them of the weight that was due to them when I had to decide. The issue that appealed to me with greatest force was the rising of 750,000 of perhaps the most warlike and bloodthirsty natives in our Empire." (No doubt Sir George had in mind the Zulu War 20 years before.)

"Had it taken place, it would have been as great a disaster in a military sense as in a political. With reference to the probability of these results I was bound to give the greatest possible weight to the opinions of the Governor and the Ministers. They had all the threads of information, both as regards Dutch and native feeling, coming direct to them, and they had experience of these races for years.

"If I had ordered withdrawal, and their anticipations had turned out to be true, it would have been said, with reason, that after a few hours' experience of a country in which I had never been before, I had acted in direct opposition to the opinions of all by responsible advisers on such a point, who for years had had their fingers on the pulse of native opinion, and that I had thus brought about a most terrible disaster.

"On the other hand, there was a chance of success . . . and (our troops) turned an over-weening confidence with which the Transvaalers crossed the frontier into a hesitancy . . ." [2]

More to the point, however, Hely-Hutchinson was terrified the Boers would reach, and destroy, Maritzburg, and then Durban. As it was Durban was heavily fortified; Maritzburg was not. And Hely-Hutchinson was in Maritzburg.

So White decided to let matters be – without changing his opinion on what he called a military error – and the following day took the train to Ladysmith, with Symons going on to Dundee. [3]

That evening the Boers crossed the frontier from Volksrust – the war had begun.

In March 1900, an already ill Sir George White, on his way back to Britain, and the Governorship of Chelsea Hospital, wrote his despatches from Cape Town.

In them he tells why he stayed in Ladysmith to be besieged, an action that was severely criticised by Roberts and Buller, and later by Lord Wolseley, Commander-in-Chief in Britain.

In fact, White the VC hero, was never given another military command, most likely on the recommendation of Roberts. Being in Ladysmith ended his career.

In the *South African Despatches*, White writes: "It will be remembered that during October 1899, the forces of the Orange Free State and the South African Republic had been gradually converging on Ladysmith from west and north, and that, although my troops had successfully encountered portions of the enemy's armies at Talana, Elandslaagte and Rietfontein, the battle of Lombard's Kop on 30th October had proved that the numbers and mobility of the Boer forces, when once concentrated, were too great to admit of any prospect of victory should I continue with inferior numbers to oppose them in the open field.

"The task before me was the protection from invasion by the Boers of as large a portion as possible of the Colony of Natal, and especially Pieter-maritzburg, the capital of that Colony and the seat of its government; and I now had to consider how this could be best insured.

"On 31st October, General Sir Redvers Buller telegraphed to me as follows: 'Can you not entrench and await events, if not at Ladysmith then behind the Tugela at Colenso?'

"On the same date I replied stating my intention to hold on to Ladysmith and on the 1st November I received Sir Redvers Buller's approval of this course in a telegram which commenced as follows: 'I agree that you do best to remain at Ladysmith, though Colenso and line of Tugela river look tempting.'"

(Buller's explosive testimony on this has been reflected in the previous chapter.)

Wrote White: "It may be well to state here shortly the reasons which governed my choice of this position. Ladysmith is the most important town in Northern Natal, and there was reason to believe that the enemy attached very great and perhaps even undue importance to obtaining possession of it.

"It was suspected then, and the suspicion has since been confirmed, that the occupation of that town by the Boers had been decided on by the disloyal

Dutch in both colonies as the signal for a general rising; as, in fact, a material guarantee that the power of the combined republics was really capable of dealing with any force the British Empire was able to place in the field against them.

"Our withdrawal would therefore have brought about an insurrection so widespread as to have very materially increased our difficulties.

"Strategically, the town was important as being the junction of the railways which enter Natal from the Transvaal and the Orange Free State, and until the Republics could gain possession of that junction their necessarily divergent lines of supply and communication prevented their enjoying to the full the advantages of combined action.

"Tactically the place was already partially prepared for defence and offered a natural position of some strength; and although the perimeter that must be occupied was very great for the number of troops available, yet it afforded a possibility of maintaining a protracted defence against superior numbers.

"On the other hand, the mere fact of a retirement behind the Tugela would have had a moral effect at least equal to a serious defeat, and would have involved the abandonment to the enemy of a large town full of an English population, men, women and children; and of a mass of stores and munitions of war which had already been collected there before my arrival in South Africa, and has since been increased.

"The line of the Tugela from the Drakensberg to the Buffalo River is some 80 miles long, and in a dry season, such as last November, can be crossed on foot anywhere. Against an enemy with more than double my numbers, and three times my mobility, I could not hope to maintain such a line with my small force, and any attempt to prevent them turning my flanks could only have resulted in such a weakening of my centre as would have let to it being pierced.

"Once my flank was turned on the line of the river the enemy would have been nearer Maritzburg than I should have been, and a rapid withdrawl by rail for the defence of the capital would have been inevitable. Even there it would have been impossible to make a prolonged defence without leaving it open to the enemy to occupy the important port of Durban, through which alone supplies and reinforcements could arrive, and for the defence of which another retreat would have become eventually essential; thus abandoning to the enemy the whole Colony of Natal from Lang's [Laing's] Nek to the sea.

"On the other hand I was confident of holding out at Ladysmith as long as might be necessary, and I saw clearly that so long as I maintained myself there I could occupy the great mass of Boer armies, and prevent them sending more than flying columns south of the Tugela, which British and Colonial forces in my rear, aided by such reinforcements as might be shortly expected, could deal with without much difficulty.

"Accordingly, I turned my whole attention to preparing Ladysmith to stand a prolonged siege." [4]

And indeed he did. He told the Commission: "I may here state definitely that my ultimate hopes of saving Natal from being over run by the Boers were centred in holding Ladysmith. Personally I never underrated the enemy's fighting power. I knew they were fighting for what they knew was national existence, and according to their national instincts.

"I had had letters from officers and men of my own regiment who were engaged at Majuba, and who had fought under me all through the Afghan war 1879–80, and I knew that the Boers who had forced Ian

Hamilton, Hector MacDonald and others to surrender were no despicable enemies. . ."[4]

So what did Wolseley, who had appointed White in the first place, have to say?

Field Marshal the Right Honourable the Viscount Wolseley was Commander in Chief of the British Army between 1895 and 1901.

As Sir Garnet Wolseley, he was almost as familiar with the Natal and Zulu countryside as a Boer. He had replaced Lord Chelmsford after the disastrous Battle of Isandhlwana in the Zulu War – but had not been at the final battle of Ulundi where the Zulu army had been defeated.

Later, it was Wolseley who declared that the Transvaal would forever remain British – a statement that endeared no Boer to him, and was the direct cause of the war of 1881, culminating in the British disaster at Majuba.

Wolseley was called to give evidence before the Commission on November 27, 1902, saying: "The Generals commanding in the field were in no way, so far as I know, interfered with by any order from home as regards their plans or their operations. One of the very few instances where even a caution that I can remember was conveyed to officers in the field was sent at the end of September [1899] by myself with reference to the proposed forward movement upon Glencoe.

"I always thought those forward movements were dangerous, and I pointed that out; but at the same time, a man sitting at home in his office in England is very chary naturally of trying to prescribe to anybody in the field as to what operations he should do.

"But at last I thought it was so serious, pushing this force on, that I did send the General Commanding [Penn-Symons] a warning telegram. I warned him against such a position until reinforcements in sufficient numbers had arrived. He was desired to keep a month's provisions always with him at his advanced posts and subsequently he was told that he should keep two months."

VISCOUNT ESHER: (who was asking the questions): "To whom was that telegram sent?"

WOLSELEY: "To the General Officer Commanding in Natal. Sir Coleridge Grove [an assessor] tells me it was sent to Sir George White, but it was intended, of course for General Symons. He was the man it was intended for, and I think it went to General Symons."

ESHER: "What Sir Coleridge Grove is thinking of is perhaps the telegram of the 31st October. That is the telegram in which you say: 'White's telegrams lead me to fancy he means to hold on and let himself be besieged in Ladysmith . . .' "

CHAIRMAN [of this session was the Earl of Elgin and Kincardine]: "Of course the holding of Glencoe or that district, at any rate, was part of the local scheme of defence?"

WOLSELEY: "Yes, but it was never intended, if I may say so, and I cannot fancy any scheme of defence for Natal in which it could be contemplated for a moment to hold on at Glencoe with a small advanced post when 30,000 Boers were coming in to attack it. Advance posts must fall back or be cut off when seriously attacked."

CHAIRMAN: . . ."I understood that in the case of Natal there have been demands sent from home to the General Officer Commanding, General Goodenough [who died in Cape Town just before the war started] in the first place, and General Butler [who took General Goodenough's place and in fact took over as High Commissioner while Sir Alfred Milner was in Britain] afterwards, for schemes of what the operations would be in the case of an outbreak of war, and that those schemes in both cases involved the holding of Ladysmith and an advance post, either at Glencoe, Dundee or Newcastle?"

WOLSELEY: "Yes, I have no doubt of that; but it was not intended, I presume, that a man should allow himself to be cut off at Glencoe. He was of course to fall back on his main support which would be in the neighbourhood of Ladysmith. No one ever thought that the troops would occupy Ladysmith. The district in front of Ladysmith is called Biggarsberg, a very strong position. Ladysmith is in a hollow. It is no position at all."

CHAIRMAN: "But it was surely the distinct intention that the force in Natal should hold Ladysmith?"

WOLSELEY: "I do not know . . ."

CHAIRMAN: "But I am going back to the schemes of defence. Surely those schemes of defence, which went on the supposition that two months' supplies should be accumulated in Ladysmith, involve the holding of Ladysmith on an outbreak of war?"

WOLSELEY: "I should not think so."

CHAIRMAN: "You did not interpret it so?"

WOLSELEY: "No. I should think if ever the enemy forced their way down into the neighbourhood of Ladysmith, and he was unable to hold the Biggarsberg, I am only expressing an opinion, he would fall back behind the next position, which was not Ladysmith, but Colenso."

CHAIRMAN: "Did you see the correspondence with the General Officers Commanding, who sent home those local schemes of defence?"

WOLSELEY: "I may have, but I cannot remember."

CHAIRMAN: "Because my impression from reading them is that they were all on the intention of holding these advanced posts in the event of a war as being the only means of protecting the Colony until reinforcements came from home or elsewhere?"

WOLSELEY: "I do not know that. I have never heard of anyone proposing to hold Ladysmith that I am aware of."

CHAIRMAN: . . . "General Goodenough's letter . . . says: 'It appears to me that the aim of a force such as that now in Natal, while waiting for reinforcements, should be: – To place itself in a secure position as to its communications while keeping the enemy in uncertainty as to the ultimately intended line of advance; – To reserve to itself the power of making, at will, offensive raids or sallies under favourable conditions, profiting by any mistakes the enemy may commit; and – To cover and protect as much of the railway towards the frontier as can be reasonable effected.'

"And in order to do that he provides for holding Ladysmith and Glencoe by an entrenched position. That would mean holding them, surely?"

WOLSELEY: "Yes, but I think that a man who had that scheme in his head never would have contemplated that he was going to be attacked by 25,000 men. It would be absurd for a man to think he was going to hold Glencoe . . ."

CHAIRMAN: . . . "Would it have been a practical operation on October 31 1899 to have withdrawn from Ladysmith to the line of the Tugela without at any rate great loss of supplies and munitions of war which were concentrated there?"

WOLSELEY: "I can only answer from what I would do myself . . . If I was in command of such a force as was then in Natal, and hearing at that time – because they did – that there was a large force of the enemy coming for me, nothing in the world would have induced me to stay in Ladysmith. I would have burnt my supplies sooner than have stayed there. I would have fallen back to the next line which was at Colenso, and behind the river . . . I can only say what I would have done myself . . ."

CHAIRMAN: "Was there any information or report in the War Office showing that Ladysmith, while it might have been tenable by a small force against a comparatively small force, was not tenable against a large force?"

WOLSELEY: "I think all who had ever been at Ladysmith knew that, and I think that anyone who was on the spot must have realised that it was a very bad position, whereas the position in front of it, the Biggarsberg position, is a very strong position indeed, and was always, so far as I remember, for a long time before the war took place, looked upon as the best defensible position for an army in the North of Natal."

CHAIRMAN: "But it was never recommended as a position to be held?"

WOLSELEY: "I do not think, as far as I am aware, that any instructions emanating from this country [Britain] were sent to any General Officer Commanding in the field as to the positions he was to hold, and where he was to defend himself. That must always be left to a Commander's own discretion . . ."

CHAIRMAN: . . . "No preference was expressed as to the best scheme of operations?"

WOLSELEY: "None . . . and if I may say so, when Sir Redvers Buller went to Natal himself, he went there on his own hook entirely [Not even Milner knew he had gone. Buller made secret arrangements to leave the Cape for Natal.] and at his own instigation, and I do not know that I even knew, until he had started, or was about to start, that he was going there."

Now an extremely interested Viscount Esher took over the questioning.

ESHER: "Did you have any . . . discussions with Sir George White before he went out?"

WOLSELEY: "I have no doubt I had. I cannot remember personally having any."

ESHER: "Did you ever discuss with him the question as to whether he should or should not adopt the position of Ladysmith?"

WOLSELEY: "Never. I fancy he felt himself forced at the last moment to remain at Ladysmith. He found this enormous accumulation of stores there and he probably thought he should not leave them.

"You will find a telegram . . . which I have no doubt you will have from Sir Redvers Buller, in which he says something to this effect, 'As I expected, General White is shut up in Ladysmith, because he finds it impossible to get away.'"[5]

But back to Sir George's evidence at the Commission. He had read what Lord Wolseley had to say, and was understandably upset. After all, he had been there. Wolseley had not.

WHITE: . . . "Lord Wolseley says: 'No one ever thought that the troops would occupy Ladysmith. The district in front of Ladysmith is called Biggarsberg, a very strong position. Ladysmith is in a hollow. It is no position at all.' "To this I can only reply that when I arrived in Natal, and I believed before, there was a general opinion that Ladysmith was a point to be held. Its selection as the principal station for troops in Natal received the very high sanction of Lord Wolseley himself . . .

"The Biggarsberg was not provisioned, and the main routes and the railway from the Orange Free State entered Natal in rear of it. Had I therefore posted my force on the Biggarsberg, Ladysmith, their [the Boers'] most coveted possession, would have lain open in my rear. The position Natal would then have been in needs no explanation . . . .

"With regard to Ladysmith being in a hollow, I held the heights around, and took advantage of the hollows, which were screened by the heights from

51

the enemy's observation, for hospitals, ammunition parks and others.

"With reference to its being no position at all, I can only urge that I defended it for 118 days against the headquarters and united armies of the South African Republics.

". . . On the 31st October, General Sir Redvers Buller telegraphed me as follows: 'Can you not entrench and await events, if not at Ladysmith, then behind the Tugela at Colenso?' On the same date I replied, stating my intention to hold on to Ladysmith, and on 1st November I received Sir Redvers Buller's approval of this course which commenced as follows: 'I agree that you do best to remain at Ladysmith, though Colenso and line of the Tugela River look tempting.'

"It will have been observed that Field Marshal Lord Wolseley considers that the proper strategy to resort to before the superior forces of the Boers was to retire behind the Tugela.

"Field Marshal Earl Roberts, on the contrary, attributes the subsequent difficulty to the neglect in the opening campaign of the great principle of advancing against the enemy's armies with massed forces while they were still separated.

"When two such very high authorities take views so exactly opposite of what the right course was, it may, at all events, be allowed that strategy is not a very positive or exact science, the study of which leads to uncontentious conclusions . . ."

So that their eminences didn't miss the point, Sir George stated:

WHITE: . . . "I would like to submit to His Majesty's Commissioners that my resolve to hold Ladysmith and its successful accomplishment resulted in the complete overthrow of the Boer plan of campaign. That plan was to overwhelm the British in Natal before their reinforcements could arrive, and by a rapid coup, conquer that province to the sea.

"The overthrow of that plan had been accomplished even before the reinforcements landed. During the time the Boers could have carried out their plan, they were held at Ladysmith. The holding of Ladysmith therefore saved Natal. My task was thus fulfilled.

"If I could keep the Boers around Ladysmith, and thus preserve the integrity of Natal as a province, its capital city of Maritzburg and its seaport of Durban, during the interval, when the Boers' power of early mobilisation and concentration on Natal enabled them to attack with greatly superior numbers, I had every confidence that after that interval the greater resources of the British Empire would be put forth to help my force.

"I cannot justly be held responsible for the losses incurred in the relief . . ."

CHAIRMAN: ". . . Another consideration which I understand weighed very much with you in acceding to the views of the Governor [Sir Walter Hely-Hutchinson] was the presence of the natives on the frontier?"

WHITE: "Yes."

CHAIRMAN: "That you considered a serious danger which you were obliged to take into account?"

WHITE: "I thought it a most serious danger. I was probably the only one in South Africa at the time who had been all through the Indian Mutiny, and I felt a very heavy responsibility in acting against the advice of my responsible, I might say, my constitutional, advisers on what the effect of a given order of mine might be upon 750,000 natives.

"I pressed the Governor with regard to it. I said, You have put before me terrible risks with regard to the result of my proposed action that I think I would not be justified in facing.

"He adhered to his view most firmly, and also he told me that it was not only his opinion, but that it was the strongly-held opinion of every member of his local government. I think it is only fair that people judging on that decision of mine should put themselves absolutely in the position that I was in at the time when I had to decide.

". . . If it is not wasting time, I would like to say exactly how it was put to me by a men who knew both the Boers and the Zulus. I was told that the Boers had come over the passes, declaring that one Hollander was worth four Englishmen; that the fool Englishmen would be in a red coat and white hat, and stand at the top of the hill and the wily Boer would shoot him, not over a rock, but from round the side of a rock. That over confidence was knocked out of them at Talana . . ." [6]

And Roberts? He was called to the Commission on December 4, 1902. "Bobs" the hero, the dapper little General, Lord of Kandahar.

With him was General Ian Hamilton, who had been Sir George White's Chief of Staff.

The Commission gives Roberts his full title: "(V.C.) Field Marshal The Right Honourable Earl Roberts, K.G.; K.P.; G.C.B.; O.M.; G.C.S.I.; G.C.I.E.," the man whose son lay buried in a grove of trees, almost three years dead, alongside the railway line between Estcourt and Colenso. At Chieveley, where there had been a massive field hospital, they buried the Honourable Frederick Sherston Roberts.

CHAIRMAN: " . . . I understood you to say that Sir George White had no general instructions when he went to Natal?"

ROBERTS: "No instructions."

CHAIRMAN: "Nor any plan of defence . . . ?"

ROBERTS: " . . . I made sure of that . . ."

CHAIRMAN: "Of course there was what was called a local scheme of defence for Natal, was there not?"

ROBERTS: "Not that I am aware of. Sir George White confirmed to me that: 'When I arrived in Natal, I had no instructions in regard to the wishes of the Government as to any particular plan of campaign, nor was I aware of any general plan of operations in South Africa.' This is what he telegraphed to me."

CHAIRMAN: " . . . The schemes of defence were certainly formulated by the two officers I have mentioned [Goodenough and Butler] and the reason I allude to them is this, that according to them, Ladysmith and some point about Glencoe were two of the points which were to be held in case of a defence of the colony?"

ROBERTS: "Well, Ladysmith was not in any way defended for that purpose; there was no protection around Ladysmith, not a sod turned, when Sir George White arrived there, and I have been to Glencoe myself, it is a basin surrounded by hills, and I cannot conceive a worse place for anything like a depot or frontier station."

CHAIRMAN: "The point I want to get to is this, who was responsible for the selection of these two places which, certainly, were mentioned in the local schemes of defence which we have seen, and which were submitted by the two Generals in command?"

VISCOUNT ESHER: "These [handing some papers to Sir Ian Hamilton] are the papers relating to the scheme of defence, and perhaps, Sir Ian Hamilton will look at them, and see if he ever saw them before?"

HAMILTON: "Having examined them, I do not think that these papers would ever have been considered applicable to Sir George White to the situation he went out to face."

CHAIRMAN: " . . . I have before me a paper presented to Parliament in 1899, a despatch from the Governor of Natal, who sent on a scheme of defence from the Colony and sums in up in this way: 'General outline of defence – The general outline of defence takes the following form, viz: (a) a base at Maritzburg with auxiliary sea base at Durban; (b) a line of communications from Durban and Maritzburg to Ladysmith and Glencoe Junction; (c) concentration of regular troops in two bodies at (1) Ladysmith, guarding the railways from Colenso to Sunday's River Bridge (inclusive), and from Ladysmith to Van Reenens; and observing the roads leading into Orange Free State to the north-west. (2) Glencoe, holding Biggarsberg passes and Dundee coalfields, observing roads into Orange Free State and South African Republic . . . guarding the railway from the Sunday's River to Newcastle, and as far north as possible.

'From Ladysmith and Glencoe, columns could move and concentrate in any direction to oppose the advance of the enemy's forces from the passes of the Drakensberg, or the drifts over the Buffalo River . . .'"

ROBERTS: "That seems to me to be a very ambitious scheme with the very small force at their disposal . . ."

CHAIRMAN: "But the point I wanted to bring out was that the existence of that scheme of defence would influence the action of the local authorities, and possibly of Sir George White, if it was before him, in holding Glencoe in the first instance and Ladysmith in the second?"

ROBERTS: " . . . Ladysmith he was forced to hold. I do not see that he could have avoided it . . ."

CHAIRMAN: " . . . Ladysmith, you think was a bad selection of a base?"

ROBERTS: "I think Ladysmith was a bad selection in this way: That it had a practically impassable river a few miles behind it, and was not in any way fortified for protection."

Then the chairman called attention to a telegram from the Colonial Office in 1897: "Ladysmith approved by War Office" which, he said confirmed the selection of Ladysmith as a post. And, said the chairman, Ladysmith was fast accumulating stores.

CHAIRMAN: "Those stores, it was explained to us, were on the sea or were being landed at the time Sir George White arrived in Natal, and were hurried up; and a question has been put whether it would have been a possible operation either not to put those supplies into Ladysmith or to have carried them back again?"

ROBERTS: [Capitulating] " . . . Ladysmith was in existence, with everything there, and had been approved of as place to hold on to, and I do not see how he could have attempted to leave it. His one object would be to get every supply he could into the place, so as to be able to defend it." [7]

And there, m'lud, the defence rests . . .

SOURCES:
1. *British Commanders in the Transvaal War 1899–1900.*
2. *Commission on the War in South Africa.*
3. *The Boer Fight for Freedom*, by Michael Davitt.
4. *South African Despatches*, Volume II, Natal Field Army.
5. *Commission on the War in South Africa.*
6. Ibid.
7. Ibid.

CHAPTER FIVE

Ladysmith

Sir Archibald to the rescue

To Sir George White's support came an influential, good looking General with a profound knowledge of oriental languages. It was no fault of Sir Archibald Hunter's that he became Sir George's Chief of Staff instead of Chief of Staff to Sir Redvers Buller as was originally intended. When Hunter had arrived in Ladysmith, Buller had not – and White's need was therefore greater.

And it was Hunter who gave Sir George unqualified support – support for the man who, in the words of other generals, had "allowed himself to be shut up in Ladysmith."

Sir Archibald Hunter, K.C.B.; D.S.O., at one time, the youngest Major General in the British Army, and the man who led the highly successful attack on Lombard's Kop in the early days of the siege, was called before the Commission on the 13th February 1903.

Throughout the evidence on Ladysmith, (as expounded in the previous chapter) the Commissioners were intrigued by the defence plans sent to Britain before the war by Generals Goodenough and Butler, which no-one seemed to know anything of. What they referred to was the alleged vulnerability of Ladysmith.

Time and time again, these questions came to light. Sometimes subtly thrown in, other times deliberatley phrased. The answers all, however, pointed to one vital thing – Ladysmith had to be held at all costs.

Sir George White had done the right thing, Sir Archibald explained.

CHAIRMAN [for this session was the Earl of Elgin and Kincardine]: " . . . Ladysmith, being full of stores, it was necessary to hold it?

HUNTER: "Yes.

CHAIRMAN: "The withdrawal of any large strengths from Ladysmith would have left it open, would it not, on the Orange Free State side?.

HUNTER: "Yes it would.

CHAIRMAN: "There might have been that risk in those operations.

HUNTER: "Yes. You know (I suppose it is generally well known) that there was a scheme to concentrate the whole of the forces in Natal at a place called Sunday's River Camp. I can tell you the reason why that concentration did not take place.

"I was present at Pietermaritzburg when Sir George White arrived there on the 6th October 1899. He stayed there the night of the 6th and, I think, the night of the 7th. Then he went to live with General Penn-Symons, and I think it would be the 8th or the 9th October that he came after dinner to Government House, to Sir Walter Hely-Hutchinson's house, where I was living.

"He asked to see the Governor, and he asked that I might be present. He came then to advocate the withdrawal" (from Glencoe) "and then concentration under his own command, of all the troops in Natal, and, undoubtably, from a military point of view, he was indisputably correct; there is no question about it.

"But at the time, he asked Sir Walter Hely-Hutchinson what political effect it would have, and he said: 'I have nothing to do with the military disposition of your force, but there are 70,000 Zulus" (Sir George in his evidence, said there were 750,000 Zulus – more than likely the correct figure) "sitting waiting on the border waiting exactly to see which side of the fence to take, which side to jump, and how the cat is going to jump.' I think those were his words or words to that effect.

"He further said: 'If you withdraw now, without a blow having been struck, the Zulus will interpret it and accept it as a sign of your being afraid to meet the Boers, and they will acknowledge the Boers as your masters, and the future effect I shudder to contemplate.'

"For that reason the divided distribution in Natal was maintained".

CHAIRMAN: "And you were present at that interview?"

HUNTER: "I was present at that interview and perhaps it is somewhat presumptious to say so, but I was practically asked to give a casting vote!"

CHAIRMAN: "I know you had been asked for your opinion."

HUNTER: "I knew that what had happened that night was a very serious thing. I know Sir Walter Hely-Hutchinson intimately well. I was his best man, and I have known him all my life.

"At that time, he slept in his own dressing-room, and had given me his wife's bedroom. So much was I impressed with the seriousness of what had happened that night that before I went to bed (and we did not separate until quite 1 o'clock, perhaps later) I sat down and wrote to Sir Evelyn Wood" (Adjutant-General from October 1, 1897 to October 1, 1901. Afterwards General Officer Commanding 2nd Army Corps, and Buller's Zulu War commanding officer) "so far as I could remember word for word everything that happened that night – a letter of several sheets of foolscap.

"In the morning, just after Sir Walter Hely- Hutchinson had had his bath, he came into my room, and he saw the papers lying on my table and said: 'Hulloa, whom have you been writing to?' I said: 'I wish you would run your eye over this and see whether it is a correct description of what took place last night.'

"He sat down and read it, and said: 'I sat down and wrote home also' (I presume he wrote to the Colonial Office), 'and my version of it practically tallies with what you have said.'

"That really is the inner history of why the forces in Natal remained divided. That has nothing to do with whatever reasons they were divided on, but that is why they continued to be divided.

"Sir George White, as Military Commander, wanted to have the whole of the troops concentrated at some point in Natal, under his own command, where all could combat any advance either from the Transvaal border on Natal, or from the Orange Free State border."

CHAIRMAN: "And in that decision you concurred?"

HUNTER: "I concurred in the decision that he was right from a military point of view, but I remember in summing up I said, 'Taking the long and short, thick and thin, you are far wiser to leave things as they are, and abide by the result.'

"He was very much concerned with what would be said in the future as to his military arrangements, and I told him that at any rate the truth would be told, and it would be known in the future (we could not all die), and it must be known eventually that he wanted to have the troops concentrated under himself, but for the political considerations; and that the political considerations were two-fold: on the one side was this big force of savages waiting to see what we were going to do, and of course the Boers would have sent their agents among them, and have pointed out that we had run before we had been hit, which would have had a very disastrous effect – it might even have led to the massacre of every white man, woman and child they could get at, and the whole of the eastern part of the colony, in Natal, at the foot of their mountains, would have been absolutely at their mercy, and also it would have had a very exhilarating effect, to say the least, upon the Boers themselves."

CHAIRMAN: "Which was the point, did you say, at which Sir George White had insisted to concentrate?"

HUNTER: "I remember him consulting Sir Penn-Symons. There was a camp, called Sunday's River Camp, Sunday's River bridge, a point north of Elandslaagte, about 20 miles north, if my recollection serves me right, of Ladysmith. There was a big bridge there across the Sunday's River, a big iron bridge and beautiful water, and it was reported to be a very defensible camp. I never was beyond Ladysmith myself until after the siege; I never was as far north anyhow."

CHAIRMAN: "You never saw that position?"

HUNTER: "I never saw that position."

CHAIRMAN: "But it was north of Ladysmith. Was that with the object of covering Ladysmith?"

HUNTER: "It would have covered Ladysmith, and you would then have been ready to advance over the Biggarsberg, and to have met, and, I think, successfully contended with any force coming down from the Dundee Junction, and also you were, as it were, straddled across the junction in the part of the country where the two forces must join coming from the Transvaal and from the Orange Free State, as it was then."

CHAIRMAN: "It has been said that a position on the Tugela was the proper one; what is your opinion as to that?"

HUNTER: "With regard to any position south of the Tugela, if you look at the map, the Tugela would strike most people as being the best place, but the south bank of the Tugela is dominated altogether by the northern bank; therefore for a defensive position I think I would have gone north of Ladysmith myself."

CHAIRMAN: "It does not follow, when you say south of the Tugela that it need be on the banks; it might have been a defensible position, but south of the river?"

HUNTER: "But for a big military force like that you would have been confined to the banks on account of the water."

CHAIRMAN: "Estcourt has been suggested."

HUNTER: "I do not know the country well, except from maps. I only passed up once from Pietermaritzburg, and down again in the dark."

VISCOUNT ESHER: "Such a concentration as that would have been still more open to the political objection than the one that was contemplated, would it not?"

HUNTER: "Do you mean a withdrawal further south?"

ESHER: "Yes."

HUNTER: "Still more; that would have said they had got you into the sea; that is how the Boers would have translated it – that you were making back to your ships."

CHAIRMAN: "But the decision having been taken, is it your opinion that it was necessary to hold Ladysmith?"

HUNTER: "Yes, absolutely indispensible. I do not see what else you could have done."

CHAIRMAN: "You could in the time withdrawn the stores which had been accumulated there?"

HUNTER: "No. I do not mean to say that we could not have marched out. We could have marched away, and left the women and children, and burnt all our stores.

"Ladysmith is a great locomotive centre. There were large stores of coal for the railways, and everything that is required to feed and maintain an army in the shape of ammunition, food, medical stores and engineer appliances, and a large amount of railway stuff as well. There was a large Natal Government Railway accumulation of stuff there, sleepers and coal and rails."

CHAIRMAN: "Ladysmith itself was not a place easy to defend?"

HUNTER: "No, it was not. It was the bottom of a teacup. Ladysmith became Ladysmith merely because it was where, in the old days, the roads from three or four different places came down, one from Newcastle in the north, another from Harrismith and another from the Zulu border, where they all met, and a place where the Klip River was easily forded, which was the reason why the roads all directed themselves to that particular place, to those drifts across the river."

CHAIRMAN: "And there had been no preparations for defence in Ladysmith?"

HUNTER: "None whatever; and the conditions of the life of the garrison there were such with the local farmers, and so on, that you dare not go off the roads. The cavalry officers were supposed to do reconnaissances every year, and to send in sketch maps to show what work in this respect they had been doing. But there were simply sketches of the line of the track; they dare not go off it.

"Every farmer was a Boer or a Dutchman with Boer sympathies; and there was not a single man (Briton) who had been on the top of Bulwana, except one and he is dead now – Captain Valentin of the Somersetshire Light Infantry. He had been asked by one of these young farmers to go out for a day's shooting, and in the course of the day, he crossed over the top of Bulwana Hill and down the other side, and he was the only man who had ever been on the top. Nobody knew whether there was water on the other side or whether there was not."

CHAIRMAN (Incredulously) "Do you mean that before the war, in our own colony, a British officer could not sketch the country? I mean that in our own colony in the neighbourhood of Ladysmith, that is to say within a girdle of ground that would be naturally occupied in any system of defence for the town, covering stores and so on, there was not a single officer except this Captain Valentin who had been on the main feature or any of the features that dominated a position that had to be held?"

HUNTER: "Not one."

CHAIRMAN: "Because the farmers would have offered violence?"

HUNTER: "No, they would have summoned them before the magistrate for tresspass, and the magistrate would have given a decision against them, and they would have been bound by the magistrate's order."

CHAIRMAN: "Did it ever happen?"

HUNTER: "It was threatened . . ."

SIR GEORGE TAUBMAN-GOLDIE: "Just going back to the argument that was used about the 70 000 Zulus (sic) sitting on the fence in case we withdrew from the northern apex of Natal; as a matter of fact nothing did happen when we were driven out the northern apex by the Boers?"

HUNTER: "No. But then of course we were driven out as a result of a fight. It was not as if we had turned tail before we were hit, and the result of the fight was an acknowledged British success."

TAUBMAN-GOLDIE: "And the 70 000 Zulus were aware of that fact?"

HUNTER: "Yes they were, and they saw us always holding out. And I think it is an acknowledged thing throughout the whole of South Africa that the fall of Ladysmith was to be accepted as the promised sign. They are very biblical in their ways of thinking, and so on, and the Cape Colony, and the Zulus and everyone else, who were watching to see who was going to be master, were practically asked whether they would accept the fall of Ladysmith as the sign, and it was generally conceded, I think, by them all that they would accept it as the sign. Therefore if Ladysmith had fallen, I believe all the Dutch in the Cape Colony would have risen, the Zulus and everyone else. They would have plumped then for the Boers as their future masters."

Of all the witnesses Sir Archbibald Hunter came across as dynamically the best. He raised points that others had not.

One (in later evidence) was that popular instrument without which the world of the 1990s would never exist.

The telephone.

It was used for the first time to direct a battle on January 6, 1900, during the bloody fight for Wagon Hill when Boer forces almost succeeded in driving the British off Platrand.

HUNTER: "On that day I was practically directing the operations, because I think on that day, Sir George White was in bed – at any rate he was not at the office, and I went to him at various times during the day and told him how things were going.

"It was, I suppose, the first time on record of a fight over a considerable area ever being directed by the telephone. In the house that we had as Headquarter Staff House a telephone exchange was arranged on the verandah, where a British officer sat day and night, all the seven officers in that house taking it in turns to relieve one another so that there was always someone there.

"In that way they got word from all parts; not only was the telephone connected up with the headquarters of each defence, but the headquarters of each defence were in telephonic communication with their outlying places, and they could be put straight through with one of these; they were just connected with one of them, and they could hear the firing quite well on the telephone . . ."

Then, near the end of his evidence, the motor car came in for discussion. The exchange went like this:

TAUBMAN-GOLDIE: "Have you ever studied the question of how far motor carriages might be utilised for moving heavy guns about?"

HUNTER: "I have seen that traction engines were used."

TAUBMAN-GOLDIE: "Steam?"

HUNTER: "Yes. These present day Twentieth Century motor cars I know nothing about. But there is one example, where if you had surplus officers you could sensibly employ them, in staff rides, for example, on motor cars. Take my case for example. If Scotland is invaded, I would be held, I presume, responsible to deal with the invader" (Hunter was, from 1901 to 1903 commander of the Scottish District) "If I had motor cars and a surplus of officers, I should be employing them in every Volunteer, every Militia regiment and every Yeomanry regiment in going about the country in intimately learning, so as to do it in the dark almost, the various parts of the country that would be most liable to be attacked."

CHAIRMAN: "You are speaking now of course of a country with good roads as Scotland has?"

HUNTER: "Yes, but then in Austria, I know they have been used on awful roads, and I have seen them in France going over the ordinary harvest stubble fields."

CHAIRMAN: "There does not appear to be any reason why something in the shape of a motor carriage should not be able to move guns about."

HUNTER: "I think it is one of the developments that this century will see brought to a high state of perfection."

Prophetic words. He did not fight in World War 1, but as General Sir Archibald Hunter, he was at Aldershot training men for the war with Germany. With motor trucks and vehicles.

And Hunter stirred controversy. Asked if he had any remarks to make on the (artillery) guns, he said:

"I think our guns were, up to the limit of their range, very good.

"Our gun-laying in the Army, judging by comparison, and so on, is infinitely better than the gun-laying in the Navy. I know I am treading on very delicate ground when I criticise Naval gunnery, but I say, and I know that it will not be contradicted by a lot of men who were in Ladysmith, that the naval gunnery . . . left everything to be desired.

"The naval guns were fired from fixed, permanent platforms; there was no motion in the platform to disconcert the gunners, but the practice made with the naval 4.7s was – I do not want to use too harsh a term – well it was such that I offered to take the girls out of the school to come and serve the guns, and make as good practice . . ."

SIR FREDERICK DARLEY: "May the light have had anything to do with that – the clearness of the atmosphere?

HUNTER: "But this did not extend over one day, it extended over the whole siege. They never profited today by the experience of yesterday. And they were firing off a fixed platform at a fixed target, not a moving target as the Boer guns did."

DARLEY: "At a known range?"

HUNTER: "Yes, at a known fixed range. It was the same, probably, for more than a month – the Boer gun was in position in the same place. It never changed . . ."

The Navy's answer came from Rear Admiral the Honourable Headworth Lambton, C.V.O., C.B., who was in charge of the naval guns during the siege, and gave evidence some weeks after Hunter.

Hunter's statements were read to him, and Sir John Hopkins asked: "Is there any truth in that statement?"

LAMBTON: "None whatever . . . Of course he shows himself to be an extremely ignorant man. He is a very gallant man, but it is bravery and stupidity combined in his case.

"He talks about a fixed range when the range was always varying.

"There were several numbskulls there" (in Ladysmith) "and apparently he is one of them, who had not sufficient intelligence to understand that though the distance was always the same the range was always altering.

"General Hunter is a very young General and a great friend of mine, at least I thought he was, and a very brilliant man; but I do not suppose he has ever seen a big gun before, and he certainly knew nothing whatever about the shooting – the firing.

"You cannot make any comparison whatever between military and navy shooting.

"The military shooting you may say is like a man going out in a duck punt and firing at a flock of duck. They only have time shrapnel; you all know what time sharpnel is; they burst it; they do not try to hit any one object.

"Our shooting is shooting as a rifle is shot. You cannot compare the two things at all; it is ludicrous; there is no possible comparison. The military never fired at a mark at all; they fire in the air . . ."

But anyway, as far as Ladysmith was concerned, Sir Archibald Hunter had made his point: It had to be held at all costs . . .

SOURCES
Commission on the War in South Africa, Evidence of Sir Archibald Hunter, and Admiral Lambton.

CHAPTER SIX

Frere Interlude

Of flies, Frere camp, and the weather

John Black Atkins said it all. He was the *Manchester Guardian*'s Man at the Front and wrote from Frere camp: "Take it for all in all, this is a great country for campaigning. It would be ideal if there were fewer flies . . . justice has not been done to the dangerous qualities of the South African domestic fly.

"Its persistence is beyond belief. It calls you in the morning early, and it spends the day with you in close attendance upon your head; finally it goes to bed in your tent near your head, in order that it may be ready to call you again the next morning.

"It is sometimes a little late in getting up on a cold morning, but then it is always too early for you.

"Its faithfulness would only require to be less distressing to be admirable.

"I can ride, for instance from here to Chieveley camp, seven miles, and take the same fly with me all the way there and back. After a long journey he may go to bed a little earlier, I don't know, but I am sure he does not get up any later the next morning." [1]

Frere today is a mere collection of small houses on the main railway line to Johannesburg. They are mostly railway staff houses, although many of them are now disused, and the small shell of a church.

Today, too, the railway bridge that carries the long container and passenger trains to and from the City of Gold passes swiftly beneath the rolling wheels.

The main N3 highway passes nearby too.

It is a peaceful place, perched on a ridge between Estcourt and Colenso. There are bluegum trees alongside the railway line; there are dirt roads and nothing very much goes on.

But in 1899 it did.

Boer forces blew the bridge up as they headed back towards Ladysmith after the battle of Brynbylla at Willow Grange.

The Boers were heading forcefully towards Pietermaritzburg and Durban, and probably could have made it there, too, had General Piet Joubert not curtailed the activities of a dynamic, young commander named Louis Botha. It is of course a matter of history that this commando got no futher than Willow Grange – but speculation, and terror, ran rife all the way down the line to the sea. The Boers reached at least as far as Mooi River.

"We'll eat fish in Durban," some Middelburg burghers told another war correspondent, Bennet Burleigh, as he travelled down from Pretoria to the Natal border with them. [2]

They could have, but were stopped.

In Frere, J.B. Atkins studied the blown-up railway bridge.

"It is a beautiful job," he wrote. "The bridge has been lifted bodily from its masonry piers and lies in the river bed, the iron framework and girders contorted like a tangle of forest creepers.

"The countryside for a few hundred yards around was bombarded with shell like pieces of iron. Only one omission makes the job short of perfection; the masonry piers are uninjured. They were loaded with explosives, but as an expert explained to me, it was put in horizontally instead of diagonally and so had not the necessary lifting power . . . electric wires lay about the wreckage, from which we gathered that the explosion was caused by electricity . . ."

And electricity, as any good Victorian lady knew, was bad for the complexion.

When Atkins arrived, a trestle bridge had been constructed by a team of Royal Engineers, and the first train had tentatively steamed across it.

Atkins writes: "Ten days ago Frere was a little dark green plantation hiding a few iron-roofed houses, and set in the midst of a heaving sea of downs. Then a camp came, and today there is a patch, nearly two miles square of brown, trodden and dusted grass with brown tracks radiating from it into the grassy distance."

Burleigh, who was there a little earlier, has this to say: " . . . the spruit is a poor thing, where we draw khaki water for drinking and cooking . . . [it] holds only but a succession of muddy pools, and the water only flows when there are heavy rains.

"Frere is in the scrubless region. It is the name of a railway station . . . around is the veld. To the west, piercing the clouds, stands the lofty pinacled Drakensberg chain, colloquially known as 'the berg'. Cathkin Peak, Giant's Castle, and all the great kops or kopjes stretching away to the north are clearly visible.

"On the arrival of Lieutenant-General Clery at Frere, he established his headquarters at the windowless, doorless, looted house of the stationmaster.

"It is, despite the interior wreckage wrought by the Boers, a pretty pavillion-roofed East African homestead, begirt by verandahs and trellis work, the whole set in a little orchard of peaches, hedged by stately eucalyptus . . .

"Day by day the camp increases in size; the heavily-freighted frequent railway trains from Durban and Maritzburg bring soldiers, horses, mules, guns and abundance of munitions of war.

"In the order named, from left to right, the Border Regiment, Queen's, and West Yorks hold the low ridges to the North of Frere, about one and three-quarter miles to the front. Their tents lie in the hollow behind the hill. The picquets' outposts have protected the position by digging shallow trenches, and raising low stone walls impregnable to musketry fire.

"Lieutenant Jones RN, with his bluejackets, has also got his 12-pounders in excellent positions." [3]

Camp life was becoming somewhat hectic.

The locals had never seen anything like it, and visitors, when they were allowed through by officious Army personnel, trekked from Estcourt to take a look.

The best description comes from Frederick Treves, one of Queen Victoria's surgeons, who headed medical operations in the field.

He writes: "The water is the colour of pea-soup, and when in a glass is semi-opaque and of a faint brownish colour. The facetious soldier when he drinks it, calls it 'khaki and water.'

"In the lowest pool, immediately above the iron railway bridge which has been blown up by the Boers, Tommy Atkins bathes with gusto in what seemingly is a light-coloured mud. Here also he washes his socks and his shirts.

"The centre of the camp is the railway station, and that of Frere is the smallest and most unpretending that any hamlet could pretend to. It is however crowded out of all reason, and its platform of hard earth is covered with boxes and baggage and sacks and saddles in as much disorder as if they had been thrown in panic from a burning train.

"Between the little goods shed and the little booking office are several stands of rifles. A sentry, proud apparently in his covering of dust, is parading one end of the platform, while at the other end a motley crowd of perspiring soldiers are filling water bottles at the tank which supplies the engine. In the waiting room a tumbled mass of men are asleep on the floor, while on a bench in front of it two men-of-war's men are discussing an English paper six weeks old.

"Outside the station are ramparts of provision boxes and cases of ammunition, and iron water cisterns and mealie bags, and to the fragments of a railing which surrounds the station, horses of all kinds and in all stages of weariness, are tied.

"A ragged time-table on the wall dealing with the train service to Pretoria, and with the precise hour of the arrival of the trains there, seems but a sorry jest.

". . . When we reached the camp, it was stated that 30,000 men were under canvas. A camp this size must of necessity present an endless scene of bustle and movement. Nothing seems at rest but the interminable array of white tents and the rows of baggage wagons. Cavalry would be moving in one direction and infantry in another. Here a mounted patrol would be riding out or a couple of scouts coming in. There would be a long line of kaffirs carrying bales and boxes to a temporary depot, and here a troop of eager horses hurrying to the river to drink . . .

"There was no shade of any kind, and the camp during the day lay dry, dusty, parched and restless under a blazing sun, but at night there was a cool wind and cheery camp fires, and a darkness that blotted out the dusty roads, the dried-up river, the dismal pile of stores and the general picture of a camp in a desert of baked earth.

"The British soldier looked very smart in his khaki suit when embarking at Southampton, but at Frere he showed the effects of wear, and his tunic, his belt, his pouches, his boots and his face, had all been toned down to one uniform tint of dirt colour. He was of the earth earthy. He was unshaven. His clothes had that abject look of want of 'fit' that is common to clothes which have been slept in, which have been more than once soaked through, and which have more than once dried on the body of the owner . . ." [4]

It is near Frere that the victims of the Armoured Train Incident lie buried beneath the curiously shaped gravestone with its legends picked out in spent bullet casings.

When John Atkins arrived at Frere in December 1899, the wreckage of the train was still there.

He says: " . . . a melancholy heap with one truck on its side (a military cobbler was using its shelter as his shop), another upside down with its wheels sticking up into the air, two others standing on the line.

"There at the curve, at the bottom of the decline down which the train tilted at full steam after the enemy had been seen, is the broken rail successfully designed to send the train to destruction. And there on either side of the line are the ridges, profitably close, from which the Boers poured their fire.

"The trucks are ripped through and through with shells, the holes around them as clean as a whistle where the shells came in, and jagged and gaping where they passed out, and spattered over with the marks of lead." [5]

But there was more . . .

SOURCES
1. *The Relief of Ladysmith*, by J.B. Atkins.
2. *The Natal Campaign*, by Bennet Burleigh.
3. Ibid.
4. *The Tale of a Field Hospital*, by Frederick Treves.
5. *The Relief of Ladysmith*, by J.B. Atkins.

CHAPTER SEVEN

The Armoured Train Incident

And the reluctant hero

Winston Churchill, with red hair, an irritating lisp and an obnoxious, enthusiastic manner, was in Estcourt by November 6. He had arrived in Cape Town aboard the *Dunottar Castle*, the same ship carrying the man whom they knew wouldn't let them down: Sir Redvers Buller.

Also aboard was John Black Atkins.

Both Atkins and Churchill had one mission – to get to Ladysmith before it was cut off from the world.

From Cape Town Churchill wrote: " . . . the fact is now abundantly plain to those who are acquainted with the local conditions and with the Boer character, that a fierce, certainly bloody, possibly prolonged struggle lies before the army in South Africa".

On November 5, he telegraphed to London: "Last night I started by rail for East London, whence a small ship carries the weekly English mail to Natal and so by this circuitous route I hope to reach Ladysmith . . . We have thus gained three days on our friends who proceed by the Dunottar Castle and who were mightily concerned when they heard, too late to follow, of our intentions . . ." [1]

He says no more. It is left to Atkins to fill in the exciting details. And he does . . .

"At the offices of the Castle Line some of us found that it was possible to reach Natal sooner – and Natal meant the fighting – by leaving the Dunottar Castle . . . It was worth trying, and [we] decided to make the attempt.

"How much there was to be done before nine o' clock that night! For one thing my luggage was all stored in the hold of the ship, all labelled for Natal. The manner in which I cajoled the baggage officer into turning over some hundreds of tons of luggage and extracting mine from the bottom, and all this when he had been turning the same luggage over and over again all day long and had just packed it away, as he thought for the last time, would appear less persuasive in the description than it was in fact . . .

"The passengers got wind of our plan when it was too late for anyone else to join in it . . ." [2]

With Churchill and Atkins was Captain the Hon. Arthur Campbell who was the correspondent for Laffan's agency, and theirs was the last train allowed to leave.

Says Atkins: "The first law of the correspondent's life is to get there, and the second is to get there, and the third is to get there . . ."

At Beaufort West, on that Mournful Monday they learned of the Nicholson's Nek disaster and surrender of some 923 British troops. Racial feeling, wrote Churchill, ran high with Dutch farmers talking loudly and confidently of "our victories", meaning those of the Boers.

At De Aar they found armoured trains – little did Churchill dream then how one was to become a major part of his life – patrolling the line and small parties of armed police guarding the bridges, and infantry and artillery detachments occupying the towns.

The train reached Stormberg early the next day. "No more traffic north of this", they were told by the station master. "Yours is the last train through from De Aar, too. I shall send away all my men by the special tonight. And that's the end as far as Stormberg goes."

He was right. In December, the Stormberg battle went down as part of Black Week with the battles of Magersfontein and Colenso.

At East London, only Atkins and Churchill boarded the small steamer, *Umzimvubu*, for Durban – still with the English mail.

Atkins says the ship was awash the whole trip. In fact, he wrote, he had never seen anything like the waves off the Transkei (Eastern Cape) and Natal coast.

Churchill wrote: "The little steamer reached Durban safely at midnight on November 4, and we passed an impatient six hours in a sleeping town waiting for daylight and news. Both came in their turn. The sun rose, and we learned that Ladysmith was cut off."

Churchill, finding that the hospital ship *Sumatra* lay close by, went in search of people he might know. One officer, severely wounded at Elandslaagte, told him ominously: "All these colonials tell you that the Boers only want one good thrashing to satisfy them. Don't you believe it. They mean to go through with this thing to the end!"

An hour or so later, Churchill and Atkins were on their way to "the front", the sleepy town of Estcourt. It was November 6.

But it was not until November 15, 1899, in the pouring rain, that the real drama was to begin.

Churchill, with that in-built Sagittarian inquisitiveness and, in the face of danger, an attitude of immortality, had been aboard the armoured train a few days before, as it had crept closer and closer to now-abandoned Colenso, while the soldiers aboard became increasingly apprehensive of a Boer attack from the silent streets.

Churchill was fascinated by the empty town, the damaged houses, and the eeriness of it all. But the Boers merely watched, and in fact did not even show themselves.

Churchill had no illusions of what concentrated Boer fire would do, should the burghers decide to suddenly open up. Worse, if the enemy tore up the track.

On November 14, the train had gone out again, past Frere and Chieveley stations to where the line had, in fact, been damaged by an explosion. [3]

While platelayers were repairing the track that day, an African appeared and warned the officer that there were Boers close by.

Within minutes they had opened fire. A party of the Border Regiment aboard the train fired back, and the train, huffing and chuffing, began its long trip back to Estcourt.

Significantly, the Boers were said to have had a mobile gun with them. The action was reported – as was the possibility of the enemy suddenly springing a trap. But for two weeks, the train had run between Estcourt, Frere and beyond Chieveley towards Colenso without mishap. [4]

No precautions had even been taken – like a few mounted men, scouting on either side of the line, to accompany it. Why should it all change now?

When Churchill had the chance to ride with the train again on November 15, he eagerly took it. The irony is that he ought never have been allowed to go along. Trips for correspondents were normally rotated. But that rainy, misty morning, others whose turn it was, were either too sleepy or indifferent, and did not show up.

The officer in charge of the train that day, however, was grateful to the enthusiastic reporter.

Captain Aylward Haldane, DSO, Gordon Highlanders, had been wounded at Elandslaagte, but not sufficiently badly enough for him to head down to the hospital in Pietermartizburg or Pinetown Bridge.

He had not been out in the train before, and did not relish the idea at all. He did not know the terrain, and in fact could be said to have been coerced into the job.

The man who did that was to feature in a battle not yet planned, and have heaped upon him the ignomity of the gunner who lost his guns – no less than Colonel Charles Long.

Haldane wrote later: " . . . he told me, as if he was lavishing a favour, that besides my company of the Dublin Fusiliers, he was giving me another of the Durban Light Infantry, a volunteer unit, and a 7-pounder gun, with its detachment from HMS *Tartar*." [5]

Haldane, said an enthusiastic Colonel Long, sitting in for Colonel Wolfe-Murray who was in Pietermaritzburg, would reconnoitre with caution towards Colenso. There was nothing strange about that – it's what the train had been doing for weeks.

But still Haldane wasn't happy, and when he spied Churchill standing nearby with a group of other correspondents, suggested he might like to accompany the train the next day, as he had travelled the route before.

Churchill, says Haldane, was not all that keen but arranged to be at the station on the morrow, regardless. And early the next morning, with a "presentiment of coming evil", Haldane ordered his servant to pack up his things and take care of them. [6]

The train, hissing quietly in the bleak, wet early dawn, was made up of an ordinary truck which carried an antiquated 7-pounder muzzle-loading gun, served by four sailors from HMS *Tartar*. Then came an "armoured" truck, open to the air, and fitted with loopholes, carrying three sections of one company of the Dublin Fusiliers, followed by the engine and tender, two more armoured trucks carrying the fourth section of the Fusilier company, one company of the Durban Light Infantry and a small civilian breakdown gang.

At the tail end was an ordinary truck with the tools and materials for repairing the railway line – in all, five wagons, the locomotive, one small gun and 120 men. [7]

Haldane and Churchill were in the leading truck with the 7-pounder.

At Frere station, a contingent of Natal Police told them they had observed no Boers and Haldane telegraphed this back to Estcourt. Then without waiting for a reply, he ordered the train to puff as slowly as they could towards Chieveley.

And into history.

That morning, 100 Wakkerstroom commandos were posted on the side of a high cutting a few kilometres beyond Frere, near Chieveley station.

Another force was concealed closer to Frere, with instructions to allow the train they knew would soon be coming to pass them unmolested towards the ridge where the first body of commandos lay hidden. This group were then ordered to attack the train.

And, suddenly, there it was.

The commandos opened fire with Mausers and pom-poms, taking the train and its crew by total surprise.

It shuddered to a stop, and began backing off at full steam, the driving wheels spinning on the wet track, as the British began firing back at an enemy they could now see at the top of the rise.

The train gathered speed – and within minutes was out of range – as it rocketed down the slope back towards Frere, which those on board could now see through the rain.

Only a sharp curve to the left remained, and Frere – and safety – was only a matter of a few hundred yards further on.

It was not to be.

The rails had been damaged, and with a fearful crash and jolt, the leading truck, carrying stores and railwaymen, left the track and landed upside down.

The armoured truck next to it was derailed and thrown on its side, spilling out its occupants, pinning some of them underneath it, and crushing one. The next armoured truck came to a stop halfway on and off the track, leaning over on one side but obstructing the line – trapping the locomotive and other trucks. [8]

The real cause of the derailment isn't really known.

Michael Davitt says a rail "had been displaced". [9]

Official Boer accounts say that "stones" were put on the line; the *Times History of the War* says that stones were "placed between a guide rail and the outer rail", but correspondent Bennet Burleigh states the Boers had removed the fishplates and propped up one of the rails with stones. [10]

Mr R.A. Curry, driver of another light engine which had piloted the train as far as Frere, is emphatic that bolts were removed, and had to be replaced by plate-layers. As he was in close touch with the railwaymen, his testimony seems to have had weight. [11]

When the Commandos opened fire on the wreck, it was returned with alacrity by the sailors from HMS *Tartar* with their small 7-pounder – until a direct hit smacked into the barrel and smashed the trunnions, knocking it right off the truck, spilling sailors to the ground.

Churchill dropped over the side of the armoured truck – it kept bullets away, but shells would tear into the plating like paper – and ran towards Frere.

Haldane writes: "For a few seconds I was so dazed by the suddenness of the crash that the power of collecting my thoughts to decide what had best be done deserted me, but Churchill, quick witted and cool, was speedily on his feet . . . [and] volunteered to see what the situation was . . . " [12]

Men were lying wounded in the maelstrom and Churchill decided the only way out was to use the locomotive as a battering ram, to shift the truck that was half across the line. Haldane agreed.

Churchill ran off seeking the engine driver as the British troops and Natal volunteers began a hail of return fire.

Churchill found the driver in the shelter of one of the overturned trucks, blood streaming down his face cut open by a shell splinter.

Initially refusing, the driver finally succumbed to Churchill's fast-talking enthusiasm, and ran the gauntlet of bullets to get back into the cab. First job was to unhitch the engine from the rest of the trucks, and then to drag, or batter, the partly derailed truck backwards until it was clear, and the train could hitch up and go.

Kenneth Griffith writes in *Thank God We Kept the Flag Flying*, and here is the crux of the matter: "of course Churchill underrates his own contribution. Not only did the young man inspire the driver, but he inspired soldiers to come out into the open with him to assist in the work." [13]

But another problem was suddenly obvious. The couplings of the engine were some 15 cm from those of the truck. Immediately a search was begun to find a spare link, and says Churchill: "By a solitary gleam of good luck one was found."

For over an hour they hammered away, using the engine, backwards and forwards, but the dead weight of the truck was too much, and the engine wheels slipped time and time again. Finally, with the help of nine volunteers, exposed to terrible danger, the truck was drawn back far enough for the engine to give it one final shove to pass.

In the sound and fury, the men cheered.

But there was one more obstacle – the engine was about 16cm wider than the tender, and the corner of its footplate could not pass the corner of the freed truck.

The sounds have been catalogued: clanging, rending of iron, repeated explosions of shells and artillery, the noise of the projectiles striking the trucks, the hiss as they passed in the air and the grunting and puffing of the engine. Fearful of damaging the locomotive, the obstruction was at first gently bashed, but then a shell struck the front of the engine setting fire to the woodwork. The terrified driver turned on the steam and struck the truck with a grinding crash, the engine staggered, checked and then surged forward and broke past.

But it signalled yet another calamity. The trucks lay, still, on the Chieveley side of the obstruction – and there was no way back for the engine. Now in the hail of fire, an attempt was made to push the trucks to the engine, but the Boers poured down so much fire that it was impossible.

Haldane decided to get as many people to safety as possible – if only to a group of houses on the outskirts of Frere station, 800 metres away.

Piling the wounded on the locomotive, the train set off for Frere, with some soldiers running alongside protected by its bulk.

"Meanwhile the engine was struck in several places by shells. The feed-injector was broken. A shell passed through a corner of the tender, killing one of the wounded men and maiming others as they lay prone upon the coal sacks, whilst another missile struck the smokebox and missed penetrating the boiler by the merest shave, but it started a leak or two," writes Bennet Burleigh. [14]

Some soldiers, running alongside, could not keep up as the engine went faster and faster.

The main body of those left behind, enfiladed, surrendered, a mis-interpreted signal, an unfortunate wave of a white handkerchief perhaps. But nevertheless, a surrender. Haldane could only stand and watch, and be taken prisoner with the rest.

Churchill, leaving his handgun in the engine cab, jumped off after a short while and began running back in an endeavour to help bring the trapped soldiers into Frere. He had no idea the others had surrendered, and ran right into the muzzles of a couple of Boers.

Later, Louis Botha claimed that he himself had captured Churchill. Churchill corroborated it. But this was many years after the war.

Three of a series of Boer telegrams tell the story: "General Joubert: TD ZAR 21.11.1899

"From Commandant General, H.Q. Ladysmith

"To Government, Pretoria, begins —

"19.11.99. I understand that the son of Lord Randolph Churchill claims to be nothing more than a press correspondent and as such entitled to release. From a newspaper dated the . . . (Memo Telegraph dept.: No date filled in here) his status appears to be something totally different. Thus I deem it advisable that he be guarded and regarded as one potentially dangerous to our war effort.

"In short, he must be imprisoned for the duration of hostilities. It was through his active participation that a part of the armoured train escaped. – ends."

It was followed by another:

"TD ZAR 28.11.1899

"From Commandant-General, Colenso

"To Secretary of State, begins —

"I see a rumour that Lord Churchill's son, Lieutenant Churchill, the *Morning Post* correspondent will soon be released by the Government. I strongly object to this procedure. If this person is released, so can any other P.O.W. be released. He was most active in directing the soldiers in their efforts to extricate the armoured train and while thus engaged in stultifying our operations, made a prisoner of war. He must therefore be treated as any other P.O.W. and if needs be, guarded with even great vigilance. – ends."

Danie Theron, later to become known as the Boer's greatest intelligence agent, wrote;

"TD ZAR 28.11.1899

"From Captain Theron i/c Dispatch riders, Colenso

"To Secretary of State, Pretoria, begins —

"I beg to inform you that on the 17th inst. full reports have appeared in the *Natal Witness* and *Natal Mercury* of the active and prominent part played by the press correspondent Winston Churchill in the fight with the armoured train at Frere station. When the officers were in difficulties, Churchill called for volunteers and was their leader.

"According to the *Volkstem* and the *Standard* and *Diggers News* he now declares he took no part in the fight. This is a pack of lies; nor would he stand still when warned by Field-Cornet Oosthuizen to surrender or do so till covered by the latter's rifle. In my opinion he is one of the most dangerous prisoners in our hands. The Natal papers make a great hero of him – ends." [15]

The Churchill saga does not end there. Winston, the adventurous, incarcerated in the Boys' Model School, went over the wall, hid beneath a railway bridge on the outskirts of Pretoria and jumped a train to Lourenco Marques. From there he took ship to Durban.

But, of course, there is controversy. Michael Davitt ever watchful, publishes this correspondence:

"From Churchill, to Editor, *Standard* and *Diggers' News*. Am now writing How I escaped from the Boers; but regret cannot, for obvious reasons, disclose many interesting details.

"Shall be happy to give you any you may require when next I visit Pretoria, probably third week in March."

The Editor of the *Standard* and *Diggers' News* replied thus, says Davitt, in print: "The *Standard* and *Diggers' News* has been honoured by Mr Winston Churchill's evident desire to become a contributor to its columns, where, in about the third week of March, he would relate his experiences under the title *How I Escaped from the Boers*. We are sorry indeed to have to disappoint so promising a youth; but unless Mr Churchill can offer something much more interesting to the general public, we must decline the promised contribution.

"Mr Churchill is a very young man who has his way to make in the world, and we would, from our maturer experience, venture to suggest that it would be advisable to bear in mind the old adages, *A still tongue makes a wise head, Least said, soonest mended.* And to demonstrate to our journalistic fledgeling the true appreciation of his particular desire we would recommend that he alter the title of his lucubration to *How I Was Allowed to Escape from the Boers,* a precis of which would read: *A moonlight night, easy-going guards, Netherlands Railway Station. A coal truck.*

'*Ressano Garcia station. Begrimed and miserable object. Arrived at Lourenzo Marquez.*

'*Admittance to British Consulate. Departure by French steamer. Typeritten telegrams. And the key to the whole:* 'Scene: Pretoria War Office: 9am, Mr Churchill reported missing; orders of arrest issued to police authorities. 11am: Receipt of official letter by morning's mail from Commandant-General Joubert, ordering release of Mr Churchill as non-combatant. Orders to police authorities not to execute the warrant of arrest.'" [16]

How true that scenario was is of course a matter of conjecture. Point is, Churchill did escape and returned to the front, as a hero.

SOURCES

1. *From London to Ladysmith:* by Winston Churchill.
2. *The Relief of Ladysmith:* by J.B. Atkins.
3. *The Durban Light Infantry,* Vol. I, regimental history.
4. Ibid.
5. *A Soldier's Saga,* by General Sir Aylward Haldane.
6. *Thank God We Kept the Flag Flying,* by Kenneth Griffiths.
7. *From London to Ladysmith,* by Winston Churchill.
8. *The Durban Light Infantry,* Vol. I, regimental history.
9. *The Boer Fight for Freedom,* by Michael Davitt.
10. *The Natal Campaign,* by Bennet Burleigh.
11. *The Durban Light Infantry,* Vol. I, regimental history.
12. *A Soldier's Saga,* by General Sir Aylward Haldane.
13. *Thank God We Kept the Flag Flying,* by Kenneth Griffiths.
14. *The Natal Campaign,* by Bennett Burleigh.
15. *No Charge for Delivery,* by C.W.L. de Souza.
16. *The Boer Fight for Freedom,* by Michael Davitt.

By The Dawn's Early Light

The battle of Colenso – Part 1
December 15, 1899

"I never attacked on the 15th at all. I have been accused of doing so, and it has been said that every military man condemned the execution of that attack. But I made no attack . . ."
Sir Redvers Buller, Commission on the War in South Africa

"This is the day of the long expected battle, and we are to push on to the front. The real fighting is to begin, and there is not a man who is not possessed by the conviction that the Boers will today be swept from the Tugela – if they have not already fled – and that General Buller will have a 'walk over'.

"One cannot but be reminded, many times since, that the advance to Ladysmith was always spoken as a walk over . . .

"On this particular morning the sun rose gloriously. Out of the gloom there emerged rapidly the grey heights of the far-off Drachenbergs [sic], and as the light of dawn fell full upon them, their ashen precipices and pinnacles became rose coloured and luminous; and the terraces of green which marked the foot of each line of barren cliff seemed so near and strangely lit, that many a man, busy in the work of striking camp, stopped to gaze on these enchanted mountains . . ." [1]

The words are by Surgeon General Frederick Treves.

He continued: "The day was blazing hot, and thirst proportionate. The heat oppressed one with the sense of something that had weight. Any breeze that moved was heavy with heat . . ."

Treves did not say it, but foreboding too was in the oppressive air. The morning of the battle . . . And he and his meagre staff were soon to make their first acquaintance with the bloody circumstances of war.

Treves, standing on the long ridge of what is today the Clouston Military Cemetery, in among more of Captain Percy Scott's massive 4.7 in guns, looked down across the sloping plain to the small village of a few houses that was soon to ring disastrous bells in England.

Under the shelter of the ridge, and close to the great guns, four little field hospitals were pitched.

And the Boers watched. In total silence.

In their sangars and trenches, built in to the hills on the Ladysmith side of the sluggish Tugela River, they had been told by General Louis Botha that no response of any kind should be made to the enemy's artillery until the actual assault by his infantry was delivered.

Not a shot was to be fired by gun or Mauser, no light was to be shown at night, nor movement of men by day that could reveal to English ears or eyes at what place in the seven miles of defensive Boer positions – from Hlangwane to the bridle drift – guns or men would be ready for the challenge to the possession of the way to Ladysmith.

December 15 was scarcely one hour old when scouts brought word to General Botha's tent that the enemy were about to move . . .

Michael Davitt wrote: "The morning was beautifully clear, with a cloudless South African sky as the men from Botha's laager, with bandoliers well filled and Mausers charged, took up their allotted positions behind the Tugela.

"Away south at Chieveley the countless lights of the enemy's camp could be seen . . .

"Gradually those lights began to fade as the brightening dawn stole across . . . and eager eyes scanned the far-stretching veld in anxious watchfulness for the active foe.

"The hours moved slowly, as it seemed, until the fuller light of the awakened day revealed the forward lines of Buller's army maching steadily over the intervening plain.

"The whole of the enemy's forces could be clearly seen when, at about 5 o'clock, they began to take the form of well defined columns of huge proportions . . . .

"The scene . . . was one of unparalleled attraction, as the sun peeped over the eastern hills and sent its rays down upon the embattled British legions proudly marching on their way to combat. There would be death to many, possible defeat to all, in that huge disproportionate array of England's might and military pride, now sweeping on in majestic motion, like a resistless flood, over the resounding veld.

"It was war in all its spectacular glory, as seen from where the little force of warrior farmers and beardless boys gazed with fascinated but fearless eyes upon the wondrous living picture of 20,000 marching men; and war with all its horrors to the fathers and sons of families who looked upon these thousands of their country's foes whom they must in a few moments meet in the shock of deadly strife." [2]

Michael Davitt had touched on the truth – it was to be a defeat.

At Chieveley, J.B. Atkins also touched on the truth.

"The Boers", he wrote, "had contrived a conspiracy of invisibility . . .

"Before daylight on Friday December 15th I woke to the sound of men and horses tramping and the cries of the native drivers to their mules. There was not a spark of light in the sky till half the mounted brigade had wound past my tent in a walking column; here and there a pipe or cigarette glowed in the column; the men were silent, or if they spoke rallied one another on the expectations of the day; the horses, in the grasp of the prevalent sickness, threw their heads down from time to time and coughed.

"But take it for all in all, the camp was filled with a steady, continuous, sweeping noise which resembled silence.

"This was the morning of a battle. Look where you would, you were conscious darkly that the field moved before your eyes; troops in masses, still too vague for recognition, coiled and uncoiled till the light fell on an army that had resolved itself into its disposition.

"The dust from the arid downs floated up in an ethereal powder, and the column at my tent door passed through it like men wading through a white level tide which reached the middle of men and the bellies of horses.

"I cannot but remember an incident which happened as the column wound past my tent, perhaps because it was one of those incidents which are trifling enough to seize the mind peremptorily on grand occasions.

"A Zulu driver lashed out with his long whip at his mules, and instantly let drop from his left hand, with a curious native cry of despair, that

Correspondent Bennett Burleigh in acrimonious conversation with General Redvers Buller, on horse. Rigid censorship was imposed on all newspapermen at Frere. No-one was even allowed to mention the fact that Buller had arrived. However, as the correspondents pointed out, servants, traders and anyone with a good pair of eyes could see him. (Author's collection.).

cherished Kaffir instrument, a concertina. The moving column moved on, not all the piety nor wit of the Zulu could lure it back to recover the concertina. But the leader of the mounted company coming behind noticed the instrument lying on the ground. 'Mind that concertina!' he shouted. 'Pass the word!' He pulled his horse aside, the word was passed, a line of horses in the middle of the company swerved, the forest of legs passed, and, behold, the concertina lay untouched . . .

"And thus all the rest of the brigade passed, hurrying to use all the latest and most civilised means for killing men and destroying property, and minding the concertina tenderly as they went; so that when all the dancing sea of legs had passed over it the concertina still lay unscathed on the ground, and I picked it up and took it into my tent . . ." [3]

Well? Did Atkins seek and find and give it back to the driver? He doesn't say – but let's assume he did. It is not mentioned again.

Bennet Burleigh, the *Daily Telegraph*'s man, had other things on his mind that morning. Like deadlines.

Three days earlier, he had formally addressed a letter to General Sir Francis Clery, commanding officer of the Natal Field Force, signed by most correspondents, protesting the rigid censorship that had been in force since Buller's arrival.

None of the war correspondents were allowed to write anything about Buller – not even that he was in Frere.

And, on two occasions, said Burleigh, "we correspondents have been prevented from going forward with the cavalry.

"The first was when a reconnaissance was made towards Colenso, General Buller himself moving out with the force. Instance number two was yesterday when Major-General Barton's column advanced and occupied Chieveley.

"In each case Press correspondents were By Order stopped at the Frere Camp picquet lines."

Burleigh's letter read in part: "The hardship is the greater in that while we were stopped at the picquet, civilian visitors in camp, correspondents' cyclist servants, and others, have been permitted to accompany the troops afield

"We ask that, as licensed correspondents who are subject to an active censorship, and as gentlemen honestly seeking to do our duty, we be permitted to discharge those functions for which we have been Commissioned."

Burleigh, and the others, were later given the permission they sought, but only after being visited by Buller himself, who hinted darkly that press telegrams sometimes gave the enemy more than just food for thought.

But Burleigh still wasn't happy – until the very early morning of December 15, when the correspondents were allowed almost free reign.[4]

And here, with the dawn, the question has to be posed: Was Buller ready?

His original intention was to advance through the Free State to Bloemfontein and then, perchance, to Pretoria.

Natal had not come into the operation. No plans for its defence had been organised, and those that had been made by Generals Butler and Goodenough, also reported elsewhere, no-one was prepared to put into action.

Natal would, he knew, be the battleground of South Africa. Particularly since, as he had put it, White had allowed himself to be "shut up" in Ladysmith.

On November 3, soon after he arrived in South Africa, Buller telegraphed from Cape Town to London: " . . . I shall despatch the first reinforcements I receive to Durban, but I cannot conceal from myself that if the enemy previously occupy even with small force the countryside south of Mooi River the relief of White by troops just landed will, unless he can hold out six weeks at least from now, be an almost impossible operation. (*Telegram No 9, cypher*). [5]

On November 11, he telegraphed, also from Cape Town, optimistically: ". . . The advance of the enemy seems to have been so thoroughly checked by the defence of Ladysmith that I have now some ground for hoping that the successful relief of Ladysmith and Kimberley may terminate opposition . . . (*Telegram No 27, cypher*).

But Buller was still in Cape Town.

As reports of fighting around Ladysmith came in day after day, Buller decided. On November 20, he telegraphed London: "On the evening of 22nd November I propose to leave for Natal" (*Telegram No 37. cypher*).

Milner obviously did not see it as he reported he had no idea Buller had even left.

Thus it was that the Zulu War VC hero of Hlobane, a hundred miles or so to the north-east, arrived at Frere, on December 6, one day before his 60th birthday. Then as Burleigh reported, he swept the Colenso hills with his telescope and made one or two sorties, without the presence of the war correspondents.

He did not like what he saw.

There was an air of forboding. Like Treves, and Botha and Atkins, Buller too felt it.

On December 12 (one day after the Magersfontein disaster and Gatacre's defeat at Stormberg – the first of the Black Week reverses) he telegraphed to London: "After a careful reconnaissance by telescope I came to this conclusion, that a direct assault upon the enemy's position at Colenso, and result of it, would be too costly. The approach to the drift this side is a dead flat without any cover, and the enemy have a very strong position which they have systematically fortified just the other side of this drift.

"When that is passed, there is a steep defile commanded on both sides by high rocky hills to be ascended, and at the top is a very favourable position for the enemy . . .

"I have determined therefore to leave the 6th Brigade [Barton's] in position in front of Colenso, and to march on the night of the 13th with the whole force available to Springfield [Winterton today], force the passage of Potgieter's Drift, and then advance to Ladysmith by the Acton Homes–Ladysmith road.

"It is open country to Springfield, and open country again about 2 miles the other side of the Tugela to Ladysmith; but I shall have a train of about 400 ox wagons, and shall have 4 miles of difficult country about the drift. The operation therefore is not a very pleasant one, but has this great advantage, I am sure to get water; on the other road, the 9 miles of fighting from Colenso to Onderbrook would have been in waterless country . . . .

"I should mention that, having no cavalry bearer company here, and no divisional field hospital, and expecting a severe fight at Potgieter's Drift, which is 25 miles from the railway, I have organised a local bearer company of half whites, half natives, who will carry out any wounded."

(The Springfield–Acton Homes route was to come up again a month later after the battle of Colenso. Buller hadn't forgotten it, and when Charles Warren was faced by the brooding mass of Spioenkop, Buller suggested this route.)

Poor Buller. His soldiers were slavering for a fight, champing at the bit to get to close quarters with the Boers.

They had even revived the old story that after the Zulu War, Buller had admitted that a Boer commandant, Pieter Uys [the same Piet Lafras Uys a legend in South African history] had taught him more about the art of war than he ever knew before.

Now they were wondering.

Instead of fighting, he passively sent reconnaissance troops out towards Springfield and Potgieters, ordering them to report back to him as soon as possible. They were not keen to go in the first place – they were almost within spitting distance of the Boers, and here Buller wanted them to go somewhere else miles away.

But, as Burleigh reports: "For a score of miles to east and west of Colenso the Boers have established posts and raised defences of various kinds – stone walls, trenches and little emplacements for cannon. They watched us from valley and hilltop . . ." [6]

It was a dilemma for Buller – solved, finally, by the Magersfontein loss.

On December 13, Buller wrote to London: "I posted a letter to you yesterday, which, I believed contained my last word before my advance on Ladysmith.

"At the time of writing, I was fully impressed with the idea that the force under Lord Methuen was strong enough to overcome any opposition he might encounter. That hope has proved fallacious, and I heard last night that Lord Methuen's attack upon a position occupied by the enemy near Spytfontein [Spytfontein was the nearest railway station to Magersfontein. It does not exist today] had failed. I may observe that in Natal we heard this through Reuter, via Pretoria and Delagoa Bay, some hours before I heard it from the Cape.

"This has altered the general situation for the worse, and in my opinion, so much so, that I do not think I am any longer justified in proceeding with my plans for the relief of Ladysmith by a flank march through Springfield and Potgieter's Drift.

"This operation involved, as was evident from the first, the complete abandonment of my communications, and, in the event of want of success, the risk that I might share the fate of Sir G. White and be cut off from Natal.

"I had considered that . . . this risk was justifiable, but I cannot think that I ought now to take such a risk.

"From my point of view it will be better to lose Ladysmith altogether than to throw open Natal to the enemy.

"I have arrived at this decision with considerable doubt. The real fact is the enemy have the whip hand of us ever since the war began, and we have had to attack with inferior force their superior forces in selected positions.

"I certainly hoped to have found the relief both of Ladysmith and Kimberley less difficult than it has proved to be. I appear to have failed in Kimberley, and the undertaking in front of me is a very grave one . . . .

" . . . Lord Methuen has, it seems, failed at Kimberley; I hope I shall not do the same at Ladysmith, but even if I do, I shall, I think have enough troops in hand to secure South Natal . . ." (*Written despatch*). [7]

Well, there's the answer, and not the one his troops wanted to hear.

Buller seemed to have no will to fight, with phrases like "The whip hand of the enemy. Our inferior force; their superior force". And the hint – barely a hint, but nevertheless there – of failure.

Buller sought to back up his written despatch with a telegram to London: " . . . Gatacre's misfortune and Methuen's failure sensibly affected my position. I was this day starting to march via Springfield and Potgieter's Drift on Ladysmith. From the first it has been clear that as soon as I crossed the drift my communications would be quite uncovered, and the undertaking meant in fact burning my boats, but I considered this action justifiable, as I hoped the news of the relief of Ladysmith would dishearten the enemy.

"The reverse unfortunately has occurred, and I thought it too great a risk to make a flank march of 45 miles with an enormous wagon train across the front of a successful and active enemy [the same reasoning applied a month later when he decided in fact to move to Springfield after Colenso] when the communications of our only effective force in the field would be thereby uncovered.

"Therefore I am today advancing to attack and try to force the direct road.

"I fully expect to be successful, but probably at heavy cost. From the first I have foreseen that the advantage gained by the enemy at the outset might only be recovered by our greater staying powers . . ." (*Telegram No 79, cypher, December 13*).

That same day, he telegraphed to White: "I have been forced to change my plans. Am coming through via Colenso and Onderbrook Spruit" (*No 78, cypher, December 13*).

To which White replied: "Your No 78 of today received and understood. Shall be very glad if you will let me know your probable dates" (*No 30, December 13*).

Now, does Buller say: "Tomorrow!" or "the next day"?

No, instead he sends: "Three brigades concentrate at Chieveley today. Fourth brigade go there tomorrow. Actual date of attack depends on difficulties met with, probably 17th December" (*No 83, December 13*).

Poor White. How was he to know Buller would suddenly take it upon himself to attack on December 15th?

(A bemused Sir Frederick Darley asked White at the Commission: "Have you any idea why he changed his plan?"

(WHITE: "I have not an idea. I do not know whether the first was a ruse or not, and I have never known. I might here state that I published a Special Natal Field Force Order on the 14th December in anticipation of having the opportunity of helping Sir Redvers Buller's force . . . "

(The order detailed an offensive strike force led by White himself comprising 5th Dragoon Guards, 5th Lancers, 18th Hussars, Imperial Light Horse and a supply column; 1st Battalion Devonshires, 2nd Battalion Gordons, two companies 1st Battalion Royal Irish Fusiliers and a supply column; five companies 1st Battalion Liverpool Regiment, six companies 1st Battalion Leicestershire Regiment, 2nd Battalion Rifle Brigade, and a supply column; 13th Battery Royal Field Artillery, 21st Battery RFA, 53rd Battery RFA, 67th Battery RFA, 69th Battery RFA, two guns No 10 mountain battery Royal Garrison Artillery; 1st Brigade Division Ammunition column, 2nd brigade DAC, 23rd company Royal Engineers and telegraph section, Natal Carabineers and Border Mounted Rifles.)

No, White was ready.

On the wrong day.

"I dwell on this," said White, "to show that I had before me intelligence which led me to believe that an attack would take place on the 17th December, that I got that information on the 13th December, and that I immediately issued that order with a view of having everything in readiness, when I got the opportunity of moving out, to assist as far as my means would admit of the advance of Sir Redvers Buller's force.

"These are directed towards the attacks which have been made upon me for not co-operating!"

(When no attack was forthcoming from General Buller, White stood his troops down.)

Buller, meanwhile, had requested more troops.

The fact that he had, already, the biggest army ever assembled in Africa didn't deter him.

And so the scene was set. History was on the march that dawn morning of December 15, 1899.

The world waited . . .

Until the 16th of December.

"From General Sir R. Buller to General Sir G. White. Clear line. No 88, 16th December . . .

"I tried Colenso yesterday but failed; the enemy is too strong for my force, except with siege operations, and those would take one full month to prepare.

"Can you last so long? If not how many days can you give me in which to take up a defensive position.

"After which I suggest you firing away as much ammunition as you can and making the best terms [with the Boers] you can . . . "

Buller had failed.

With some 23,000 men, Buller had failed.

And sent the 20 words that, ultimately, sealed his fate – the Surrender Telegram: "*After which I suggest you firing away as much ammunition as you can and making the best terms you can.*" The furore over that, however, was still to come.

To London, at 6.20pm on December 15, Buller telegraphed: "I regret to report a serious reverse. I moved in full strength from camp near Chieveley this morning at 4am. There are two fordable places in the Tugela and it was my intention to force a passage through one of them; they are about 2 miles apart and my intention was to force one or the other with one brigade supported by a central brigade.

"General Hart was to attack the left drift, General Hildyard the right, the main road, and General Lyttelton, in the centre to support either.

"Early in the day I saw that General Hart would not be able to force a passage and directed him to withdraw. He had however attacked with great gallantry and his leading Battalion, the Connaught Rangers I fear, suffered a great deal.

"Colonel Brooke was severely wounded. I then ordered General Hildyard to advance, which he did, and his leading regiment, the East Surrey, occupied Colenso station and the houses near the bridge.

"At that moment I heard that the whole of the artillery I had sent back to that attack, namely the 14th and 66th Field Batteries and 6 Naval 12-pr QF guns, the whole under Colonel Long, RA, were out of action, as it appears Colonel Long in his desire to be within effective range, advanced without any scouts or effective infantry supports close to the river.

"It proved to be full of the enemy who suddenly opened a galling fire at close range, killing all their horses, and the gunners were compelled to stand to their guns. Some of the wagon teams got shelter for troops in a donga, and desperate efforts were made to bring out the field guns, but the fire was too severe and only 2 were saved by Captain Schofield and some drivers whose names I will furnish.

"Another most gallant attempt with 3 teams was made by an officer whose name I will obtain. Of the 18 horses, 13 were killed, and as several of the drivers were wounded I would not allow another attempt. It seemed they would be quite useless sacrificing loss of life in gallant attempt to force passage unsupported by artillery.

"I directed the troops to withdraw, which they did in good order. Throughout the day a considerable force of the enemy was pressing on my right flank, but was kept back by mounted men under Lord Dundonald and part of General Barton's Brigade.

"The day was intensely hot and most trying to the troops whose conduct was excellent. We have abandoned 10 guns and lost by shell fire 1. The losses in General Hart's brigade are, I fear, heavy though the proportion of severely wounded is I hope not large. The 14th and 66th Field Batteries also suffered severe lossses. We have retired to our camp at Chieveley" (*Telegram No 0215, December 15*).[7]

Poor Buller. At 11.15pm, aching and sore in the ribs where a fragment of shell had hit him earlier in the day, and with the reports of the Colenso catastrophe still coming in and being collated, again telegraphed to London: "A serious question is raised by my failure today; I do not now consider myself strong enough to relieve Ladysmith. Colenso is a fortress, which, if not captured by a rush, could I think only be taken by a siege.

"Within the eight miles from the point of attack there is no water and it exhausts the infantry. The place is fully entrenched. I do not think we saw either a gun or a Boer all day, but the fire brought to bear on us was very heavy. The Infantry were willing enough to fight, but the intense heat absolutely exhausted them.

"I consider I ought to let Ladysmith go and to occupy good position for the defence of South Natal and so let time help us. But I feel I ought to consult you on such a step.

"20,000 men, I consider, faced us today; both in arms and in position they had the advantage. They admit indeed that they suffered severely, but my men are dispirited because they have not seen a dead Boer. My losses have not been very heavy; much heavier indeed I could have made them, but the moment I failed to get on the run the result would have been the same. I was beaten. I now feel I cannot say that with my available force I can relieve Ladysmith, and I suggest that for me to occupy a defensive position and fight it out in country better suited to our tactics is the best thing that I can do" (*Telegram No 87, cypher, 15 December*).

But the Boers opposing Buller numbered not 20,000. There were just 4,500.

Buller's losses were 1,139, of whom 74 were officers. 143 men, of whom seven were officers, were killed; 756 men, of whom 47 were officers, wounded. Five died the following day.

Botha's casualties were 38 men, of whom seven were killed, one drowned in the Tugela and 30 injured. One later died of his wounds.

Buller's telegrams wreaked havoc in the Cabinet in London. There was only one conclusion – Buller must go. However not yet. And not completely.

But, a new, and even, for Buller, more worrying phase was about to begin.

A gentleman officer had reached Cape Town and was on his way with his 5th Army Division to the Modder River with instructions to take over command from General Lord Methuen after the Magersfontein debacle.

However, the officer and his men were stopped at De Aar station and immediately ordered back to Cape Town, and a new destination – Natal. His name was General Sir Charles Warren, and he was not amused.

Buller had wanted more troops – now he was about to get them, on orders from London.

Although no-one knew it at the time, Warren was to be Buller's Nemesis.

When he had arrived at Cape Town, Warren found he had been given the Dormant Commission, a decision taken by the Cabinet before he left the War Office. A letter of appointment had been waiting for him.

If anything happened to Buller, Warren had the authority to take over as Commander-in-Chief in South Africa.

Not only that, should the War Office terminate Buller's appointment, for any reason other than death, Warren would step in and take over.

While Buller had approved Warren's appointment, he was not happy with it. It meant, simply, he would have to be careful – extrememly careful, and not ruffle Whitehall feathers. Or make mistakes.

The fact that Warren had been given the Dormant Commission meant also that London considered him as competent as Buller. But was he?

They were not strangers to each other, and Buller no doubt thought of the acrimonious exchanges the two had had over the years. Warren was no yes-man, but scrupulously fair and honest.

At Colenso, Buller had failed.

He had better not fail a second time – if there was to be a second time.

How could he fail, with Warren now on his staff, and the War Office watching every move?

So Warren, Buller decided, could take charge of the next operation, wherever it was going to be.

On that same day, Lansdowne telegraphed from the cold of a London winter: "The abandonment of White's force and its consequent surrender is regarded by the government as a national disaster of the greatest magnitude.

"We would urge you to devise another attempt to carry out its relief, not necessarily via Colenso, making use of the additional men now arriving if you think fit" (*Telegram No 53, from the War Office*).

In other words, don't fail again!

Other historians have probed the political machinations of the next move, and written on the power struggles that, unknown to the British public, were going on behind the crenellated walls of Westminster, and down Pall Mall and the Victoria Embankment.

Suffice it to say that while telegrams were burning the wires to London and back, Buller was expecting some sort of censure.

It was not long in coming.

And it was with trepidation Buller received and read this telegram from London: "In Natal and Cape Colony distinct operations of very great importance are now in progress.

"The prosecution of the campaign in Natal is being carried on under quite unexpected difficulties, and in the opinion of Her Majesty's Government it will require your presence and whole attention.

"It has been decided by Her Majesty's Government under these circumstances, to appoint Field-Marshal Lord Roberts as Commanding-in-Chief, South Africa, his Chief of Staff being Lord Kitchener" (*Telegram No 57, cypher, War Office, December 18*).

Buller had not expected Roberts. He had expected his champion of many years, the aged Lord Wolseley, to be appointed to the command in South Africa.

Now it would be Roberts.

And Warren.

And Kitchener.

Later Wolseley wrote: " . . . Were I in his [Buller's] place I should resign at once, and [he told Lansdowne] I think you will have his resignation as the answer to your telegram . . ."

Buller did not resign. How could he? It would mean admitting defeat and returning home, not the hero, but the villain (the man who had "lost Colenso").

Wolseley also told Lansdowne: "Buller is much the abler soldier of the two," meaning Roberts.

Later, too, Buller wrote to Landsdowne: "I received two telegrams on the 18th December, 1899, one from the Government I thought brusque, the other from the Secretary of State for War I thought brutal. I confess I deeply resented the cruel and, as I thought, quite uncalled for sneer contained in the latter."[8]

The sneer? A personal telegram from Landsowne saying: "Private and personal. Decision communicated to you in my telegram No 57 may, I fear, be distasteful to you, but we have arrived at it from a strong sense that the step is inevitable. I have seen Lord Roberts, and I am quite sure you need have no misgivings as to your relations with him" (*Telegram No 58. cypher, December 18*).

But Buller did. Roberts had taken his job . . .

Not only that, Buller felt remorse – numbing remorse – that indirectly he was responsible for the death of Roberts's only son, the Honourable Frederick Sherston Roberts, who had gone to rescue Colonel Charles Long's guns on the outskirts of Colenso when they had overrun their position, and were lost to the Boers.

For that gallant act, Freddie Roberts had been awarded a VC

No, Buller was not looking forward to "Bobs".

And on December 20 he wrote to Lansdowne: "If I may be allowed to say so, I entirely agree with the reasons that guided the action of Her Majesty's Government. I have for some time been convinced that it is impossible for any one man to direct active military in two places distant 1500 miles from each other. I was aware when I left the Cape for Natal that I was, so to speak, leaving the front door open, but the conditions here were so critical, and the General Officers coming here were all so anxious that I should be present myself, that I felt I had no other course open to me. Lord Lansdowne is kind enough to suggest that the decision may be distasteful to me, but I trust that any decision intended for the interests of the Empire will always be acceptable to me." [9]

SOURCES

1. *The Tale of a Field Hospital*, By Frederick Treves.
2. *The Boer Fight for Freedom*, by Michael Davitt.
3. *The Relief of Ladysmith*, by J.B. Atkins.
4. *The Natal Campaign*, by Bennet Burleigh.
5. *Commission on the War in South Africa.*
6. *The Natal Campaign.* by Bennet Burleigh.
7. *Commission on the War in South Africa.*
8. *Buller's Campaign*, by Julian Symons; also: *The War to Date*, by an Absent Minded Beggar (1900).
9. *Thank God We Kept the Flag Flying*, by Kenneth Griffith.

CHAPTER NINE

The Battle of Colenso

Part 2
The evidence, the guns, the surrender

Tuesday, February 17, 1903. London had been washed by early morning rain. More was expected, said the *Daily Mail* weather forecaster. The Thames was murky brown – the repository of road and garden sand washed down in rivulets and streams.

It was Sir Redvers Buller's turn at the Commission today. He wasn't looking forward to it.

Not at all.

It was three years since he had last been in Natal. But Natal was very much in his mind. He had had a lot of time to prepare for this moment. Even while on the train from Exeter, the nearest main line station to Downes, the vast Buller estate at Crediton, in Devon, he had been making notes.

The Exeter station waiting room held tragic memories for him – it was where his mother had taken ill, too sick to be moved, and three days later died. He was a lad of 16. It is said he never left her side. Nor forgot it.

It had been a long journey to London. He didn't know how long he would be staying there either, but was not expecting to go home for some days, if not weeks.

He had been asked to prepare a summary of his operations in Natal, which he had done and sent in to the Commission months earlier.

Now he was to face the tribunal and if that's what it was going to turn out to be, well he was ready.

Let Sir Redvers tell of his December 15, 1899 battle of Colenso. And in a hushed St Stephen's House hall he reads –

" . . . On that evening [December 14th] I assembled my commanders, and in the presence of them all explained to each his part in the dispositions for the morrow.

"Each commander with his troops was to occupy a specified place, and to await the result of a general bombardment before leaving it.

"On the morning of the 15th December, the troops moved into their appointed positions.

"My intention was that they should remain there, out of fire and at ease, while from Gun Hill [present-day Clouston], I ascertained by practice the accurate range of all the points from which opposition could be offered to our advance.

"As the guns were getting into position I noticed that the 5th Brigade [General FitzRoy Hart, heading for the loop in the Tugela River to the left] were advancing beyond the position that I had allotted to them, and sent at once to stop them. My messenger was delayed by bad ground, and the brigade, continuing to advance, came under fire.

"Very shortly afterwards they received from me an order by a second messenger to withdraw at once out of range. This they complied with; but as they were doing so I saw a considerable body of Boers moving to a position

One of the huge 4.7 in. Naval guns about to belch fire and shot. The guns were located to the right of the railway line. Others were at Clouston, where Buller first had his headquarters. (Picture: Author's collection.)

from whence I thought they intended to make a flank attack upon the now retreating 5th Brigade.

"I therefore directed General Lyttleton, who was in reserve, to move to his left, and cover the withdrawal of the 5th Brigade, supporting him by Colonel Parson's brigade division.

"While this was passing I had observed that Colonel Long, with Hunt's brigade division, and the Naval 12 pounder guns, had also advanced beyond their allotted position. He had come into action, and was firing so rapidly as to satisfy me at once that he was too close to the enemy.

"I immediately despatched an officer, whom I directed to ascertain if the batteries were suffering from the enemy's fire, and if so, to order them to withdraw immediately.

"He went, returned and told me that the batteries were all right. Very shortly afterwards they ceased firing. Surmising that something must be wrong, I at once galloped off to my right, meeting as I went, two officers who had been with Colonel Long.

"Each of them informed me that the guns had been abandoned, having fired away all their ammunition – one of them said, 'Very nearly all – and lost every officer and man of the detachments killed or wounded.' Colonel Long himself was described as dangerously wounded.

"I at once went to General Hildyard and told him that the guns had got into trouble and that I was going to try and extricate them, that I thought it would be impossible for me to attack at all that day, and that for the present I certainly could not.

"I directed him to advance two of his battalions, and open as much fire as he could from a position I pointed out on the left of the guns, but charged him on no account to commit his men. Proceeding to a point behind the guns, I made an endeavour to withdraw them, sending out four limbers for that purpose.

"Of these two were successful, and withdrew two guns. The horses and men of the other two limbers were shot down. I then moved to my right, and saw Colonel Lord Dundonald and General Barton. Dundonald's men were engaged with the Boers, who were attacking from Hlangwane. General

Barton had only two battalions left in hand, having at Colonel Long's request supported him with one battalion and a half, while the remaining half battalion was in charge of the parked transport and baggage.

"Returning to my former place behind the guns, I withdrew the wagons, and made another but unsuccessful attempt to withdraw some guns. I consulted on the spot with General Clery as to the possibility of devising some means to save the guns without sacrifice of lives absolutely disproportionate to their value. As we, neither of us could conceive of any means by which they could be extricated, I, with his concurrence, decided they must be abandoned. I have only to add that, in my own belief, their withdrawal on that day or night was a physical impossibility, and that it was equally impossible to prevent their withdrawal by the enemy . . . I then ordered the retirement of the whole force to their bivouac, which was effected without the least trouble." [1]

But it was not impossible for the enemy to take away the guns – during the late afternoon, Boers crossed the Tugela and took them away.

Buller sat back, his mind reeling from the vision of veld and dust and explosions. And death. He felt his own wound too, remembering how a piece of shell had flown into his side from somewhere, badly bruising his ribs.

But his summary was a masterpiece of understatement. There is no mention of the Boers' invisibility, nor their absolute silence – until Hart drew close to the banks of the Tugela and one Boer soldier could take it no longer.

Bang! His Mauser crashed – as did the whole Tugela line after that. At close range.

The stupendous volleys gave the lie to the British assumption that the Boers held the high ground. In some places they did, but in the majority they were just on the other side of the river.

Hart, said Buller, "came under fire".

It was a devastating fire. And from it, the British reeled. Perhaps in panic.

But, in 1903, it was another time; another place. Far from the present pleasant comfort of the huge hall, and His Majesty's Commissioners who led Buller through the day with questions on Ladysmith and troop movements.

Buller brought a wry smile to the court when he said: "I knew the Boers were afraid of me – I will not pause to discuss whether I deserved the compliment – but I knew it."

The first day had not been too bad, Buller must have reflected. However, it was not over yet. In fact, it was only beginning . . .

On Wednesday, February 18, the screws turned, and were tightened.

The Chairman shuffled some papers and said: "We now come to the point of your summary which is headed *Events of the 15th December* and I take it this is the account that you wish us to accept from you of those events . . . do you wish to amplfy them?

BULLER: "There are only two matters which I want to be sure that I have made clear.

"I hope I have practically made it clear that I never attacked on the 15th at all.

"I have been accused of having done so, and it has been said that every military man condemned the execution of that attack. But I made no attack. I stopped at the very earliest moment in the morning every General from moving, and no attack was made on Colenso at all on the 15th of December. I have tried to make that clear here."

CHAIRMAN: "You stopped the movements as soon as you discovered the position?"

BULLER: "My left brigade [Hart] moved too soon, contrary to my orders, I did not succeed in stopping it, but withdrew it at once.

"But no other troops, except some artillery that got into the wrong place, moved forward at all for any purpose of any attack.

"And if I have not made that clear I should like to read General Hildyard's view, who commanded the 2nd Brigade, the attacking column; three or four words from his own account of what happened . . .

CHAIRMAN: "Very well."

BULLER: "I have here the autograph report of General Hildyard, of the action of his Brigade on the 15th December and these are the very few lines that I want to read: 'The orders received were to seize the kopjes north of Colenso when the bombardment had made itself sufficiently felt. Before this moment arrived the Commander-in-Chief [Buller] informed me that owing to the loss of the guns the attack could not be carried out today and that the retirement of the artillery was to be covered by the 2nd Brigade.

" 'The 2nd Queens and 2nd Devons were informed accordingly, and directed to cover its retirement, the former west of the railway, the latter east of it, taking care not to be involved more than could be helped in an engagement with the enemy.'

"I only wanted just to read that to show that there was no attack at all – The word Retirement in General Hildyard's letter should have been Withdrawal – and that the only military action that I directed that day was a series of attempts to recover some guns which had been taken into a position into which, in my opinion, they ought never to have been taken." [2]

Let us diverge a bit here. Michael Davitt was sitting on the Boer side of the Tugela, watching and waiting as the more than 20,000 troops marched towards him in that spectacular dawn that he described so well . . .

The British opened fire, he says, from the rising ground between Chieveley and Colenso. A cloud of smoke from 10 guns. Fort Wylie (on the Ladysmith side of the Tugela, constructed by the British before they retreated from Colenso, but since occupied by the Boers) was the target, and lyddite shells and shrapnel pounded the river bank and the surrounding ground.

"The guns," writes Davitt, "continued to roar their thunderous challenge to the sunlit kopjies 7,000 yards away, but there was no response.

"The echoes of the naval battery reverberated over the plain and up among the hills beyond the Tugela, but no sound came back . . . to indicate the presence there of a single gun." [3]

And the British marched on, and on. Closer and closer to death.

Buller was indeed attacking, and had been doing so since the pre-dawn. Later on, Buller admitted it.

VISCOUNT ESHER: "Had you intended to attack?"

BULLER: "Fully. I had given all my orders the day before."

But Sir George Taubman-Goldie wanted to hear more. About the guns. He said: "I think you ought to have an opportunity of giving your reasons with regard to those guns, why you say it was equally impossible to prevent their withdrawal by the enemy, and which you say you would be glad to give."

BULLER: "I offer myself rather more to be cross-examined."

Big-hearted Buller. The man with all the answers.

He went on: "It is difficult to fight against a man of straw; that is my position really. I state it as a fact, and I have seen a certain amount of fighting.

"The guns went down into a place where they were within 300 yards of cover, which was in occupation of the enemy, and within 1,200 yards of a fortified hill, which was held by the enemy.

"The fire from that hill, principally from the hill, as I was given to understand at the time, but also from the bushes, the cover, disabled the guns by either killing or wounding the whole of their men, and I was not informed of it by the officer in charge until he had abandoned his guns . . ."

"I got down to the nearest place I could, with anything like safety, approached behind the guns, which was a large donga, and from there I directed certain endeavours to retrieve the guns.

"But they were absolutely in the open. The first two we got away; I don't think the Boers realised what we were doing; the men while under fire managed to hook two on to the limbers I sent out, and brought them back; but the horses and men of the other two limbers I sent forward were shot down and either killed or wounded.

"At any rate they did not come back, and when a further attempt was made later in the day the limbers only got half way; there was nobody with the guns to hook on; they were entirely abandoned . . .

" I could have pushed forward and got to the river, and having got to the river I might possibly have managed to get live horses or men up to the guns to draw them back, yet the whole of the time the guns would be under fire from the entrenchments on top of Fort Wylie, which commanded the plateau we were on by about 150 feet, and looked down on everything. I believe myself that it was absolutely impossible." [4]

But Sir George Taubman-Goldie had not finished. "I wished rather," he said, "to direct your attention to the last few lines of the last paragraph in your statement. You are aware that it has been said that if it was impossible for us to get the guns away, it might have been made equally impossible for the Boers to take them away?"

BULLER: "Yes, but I do not think it has been said by anybody who has seen the place. Of course, anybody here may say it. I do not think that anybody who had seen the place could have said it . . .

" My men were very much exhausted that day by want of water; there was no water at all on the ground they were fighting on, and I was very much impressed, I admit, afterwards by their exhaustion.

"They were very ready to fight, but they went to sleep, and anyone who witnessed the trouble I had to get men out of the donga to make the efforts which they did make to get the guns back, would have, I think, entirely agreed with me, as did all the officers who were present . . .

" What would they have done in the night? There were more Boers there than I had men, and they would have come across the river – there was nothing to prevent them – and we should have had a rough and tumble on the banks of the Tugela in which I fully believe we would have been worsted. I do not think it was possible. I do not believe any living man could have got those guns away. I do not think so. Of course I could have kept the guns under our fire, but there was no use in that if I could not withdraw them and I could not." [5]

The questioning was now taken over by Lord Strathcona and Mount Royal. "You say here in your statement that shortly after the return of the officer you had sent to Long's Brigade Division the guns ceased firing?"

BULLER: "Yes."

STRATHCONA: "Was the account he gave you on his return of the actual position of the batteries at that time correct?"

BULLER: "It was not correct. He told me that the guns were comfortable. I went to the only place whence I could see the whole of the ground from which I had intended to have directed the attack, and the guns went beyond the position that I had allotted to them; they were out of my sight, so that I merely saw them go down, and when I saw them go down I sent after them, thinking that they had gone much too close, and the officer came back and said the guns were all right; but they were not all right."

STRATHCONA: "Then you do not consider that he carried out your orders correctly?"

BULLER: "As I told him the following day, he failed to carry out my orders. But I do not wish to discuss this. He was a good man and served me well; anyone may make mistakes." [6]

While Buller censured that officer, what of the officer who had "abandoned" his guns?

Colonel Charles Long had this to say in a letter to the Commission from his home at Radburne Hall, Derby.

"The idea of abandoning the guns never entered my head, nor did it occur to any of the battery officers. Had I done so, it would have been an easy matter to disable the guns, and this would, of course, have been done.

"I consider the guns were deserted of support . . .

" I must beg to be allowed to refer to a paragraph in Sir Redvers Buller's Despatch" [after the battle] which, if allowed to stand, would seriously affect my reputation. It says: '. . .I had personally explained to him to come in to action and with the naval guns only as the position was not within effective range for his field guns.'

"I beg most respectfully to state that I knew nothing whatever of such an order until when in hospital I read it in the *Natal Witness* [the Pietermaritz-burg daily newspaper] of 20 February. I see it quoted now in every paper.

"It is a duty I owe to myself to state the absolute truth as far as I am concerned, that Sir Redvers Buller never gave me that order . . . Had I received such an order I would have come into action at 5,000 yards or even more, and I am quite certain that such was not the intention of the General officer Commanding.

"CJ Long, Colonel RHA, Late Colonel on Staff Commanding RA, Natal Field Force." [7]

Later on, another General was to read amazing facts about himself in the local newspaper. But that comes under the heading of Spioenkop.

Buller's own notes, as reflected in C.H. Melville's *Life of General the Right Hon. Sir Redvers Buller*, are worth looking at here.

On the Colenso operation he wrote: " (1) With regard to my left flank I should have had but few losses had not my messenger got bogged. Let all English commanders recollect that the keenness and elan of the advance into action of the British soldier who has received no training except that of peace manoeuvres, must in the first few fights of a campaign be moderated by careful and effective staff work.

"(2) The range of artillery is twice as far as that of infantry. If, at the commencement of an action, the artillery force themselves into a position which they are unable to hold without crying out for the support of the infantry, it is evident that they sacrifice the whole of the value to their General of the extra range of their arms.

"(3) To be efficient the three component parts of an army – the Cavalry, the Infantry and Artillery – should co-operate to the same end, but should each have regard to the limitation and peculiarities of their own particular arm. An officer in difficulty must of course do the best he can for his command, but he must never forget in that emergency the plan of his chief Commander, and whatever he does should be subject to the consideration that it is his duty to assist that plan to the utmost.

"On the 15th of December Colonel Long's advance converted his General's intention of seizing a position into an attempt to save some guns that had been placed where they never ought to have been placed. To my mind any officer may make the mistake of selecting an unfortunate position.

"If he lives through it he will know better next time, and, I think, if he realises the mistake he has made, will probably be so much the better officer.

"But no officer commanding a unit is justified in being selfish and in thinking only of himself. The moment Colonel Long realised that he was in an untenable position – and he must have realised that the moment he opened fire – he ought to have sent at once to his General, reported the circumstances, and in the interim devoted himself to the consideration of how, in case he had to retire, he could best arrange to do so.

"Colonel Long did nothing of the sort, but he sent continual messages demanding support. What was the use of support? He was perfectly safe from capture, as he had the river between him and the enemy and was in the open.

"He sent no one to direct the supports, and he did not attempt to utilise the supports sent for the only purpose for which they could have been profitably used – for an attempt to withdraw the ill-placed batteries.

"On the other hand supports sent to him were wasted for the purposes of his General, as he was not at the point where the Infantry were intended to cross, and the supports he called for were withdrawn from troops who were intended for totally different purposes.

"So far as the fight on the 15th of December goes, my intentions for the day were frustrated by the action of my subordinates. Of that fact I do not in the least complain.

"A General one day may find himself in difficulty because a subordinate has not done right, and another day he may reap immense and unexpected advantage because a subordinate does right, though contrary to his orders, at the critical moment. But these are the chances of war. To gain the balance of those chances on one side the co-operation of all Commanders towards the success of the principal idea is necessary, and it is because Colonel Long forgot to realise the necessity for this co-operation that he is, in my opinion, to blame . . ."

Long was not the only one who came in for scathing criticism. General Geoffrey Barton, too, felt it necessary to explain his actions at Colenso.

In an appendix to his evidence before the Commission, he writes: "While I was serving in Pretoria, in May, 1902, and when peace was daily expected, my attention was called to the second volume of *The Times History of the War* in which I am most severely criticised in regard to my action on first arrival in Natal and at the battle of Colenso."

But he was to feel, like others, the indifferent hand of Roberts – Our Bobs – who, after the war, seemed disinterested in the plight of the officers who had served under his command.

After all, the war was won.

Barton writes: "I was unable to procure this volume, and only saw extracts therefrom; but on arrival home I personally referred the matter to the Commander-in-Chief, Lord Roberts, and claimed his protection.

"I also asked that the matter might be referred to a Court of Inquiry, which his lordship said was not possible."

What had Barton done?

Asked by Dundonald to support his attack on Hlangwane, the hill to the right of Colenso overlooking the river and later referred to as the "key" to Ladysmith, Barton refused.

Buller, while ordering Dundonald to "endeavour to take up a position on Hlangwane", had told Barton to protect Hildyard and later move up to Hlangwane.

When Dundonald found Hlangwane occupied by the Boers, and saw he was getting nowhere, he says he called for Barton's help, and Barton refused.

The Times History of the War claimed that it was because he "feared to take responsibility".

Barton disagreed.

"I have reason to believe that Buller thought Hlangwane was not held by the Boers, or I think he would have made other dispositions for its capture.

"I had no report or message from Dundonald, and did not know he was being seriously repulsed . . .

" Nothing had been ascertained of the strength or positions of the Boers south of the Tugela, nor of their means of reinforcing or withdrawing their men.

"It was a question whether Buller wished to hold the hill Hlangwane permanently; and under every rule and principle of war it was my duty to refer to him before committing any part of my infantry brigade to offensive action at such a distance, namely five miles, from the place assigned to it by Buller himself . . .

" At this time I saw Buller crossing the plain towards us; he observed the situation for himself, and then, far from wishing me to move towards Hlanwange, he blamed me for having brought one of my battalions so far to the right, and he ordered me to retire it nearer to the place he had appointed for my brigade . . .

"The following evening at 6pm Buller sent for me and had a long conversation with me about the battle. He again said I had taken one of my battalions too far to the right, but added that I was quite right not to support Dundonald further in a venture that could then gain no result : . .

"I am most anxious and desirous that the fullest publicity may be given to the part actually played by myself and my brigade at Colenso, and am ready to give full information and proof of every act and incident that came under my observation.

"I never made any secret of Dundonald's request and my refusal . . ." [8]

Colenso was beginning to become a messy place. And the question of the guns would not now go away. Hildyard was called.

ESHER: "Was the river fordable at that point. [Opposite the donga where the guns lay]?"

HILDYARD: "It was fordable with difficulty."

ESHER: "They [The Boers] would have to swim?"

HILDYARD: "They could have got across a drift there."

SIR JOHN EDGE: "Do you know where the Boers came from to that donga where our men took refuge?"

HILDYARD:"They came from the other side of the river. They had a bridge; it was broken down, but they had a footpath there where the men got across, and they came by that footpath down to the donga where our men were."

DARLEY: "How did they get the guns away; in what direction did they take them away?"

HILDYARD: "Nearly due north."

DARLEY: "Was there any drift that they could get the guns across there?"

HILDYARD: "Yes, there is a drift there, not very far from the bridge. I do not know whether they went over that drift or not, but there is a drift there . . ."

TAUBMAN-GOLDIE: "Could they [the British] have got the guns away that night?"

HILDYARD: "They could have got the guns away that night by remaining there till night in the positions they were in. The reason that was not done was that the commander on the spot [Buller] saw that the men were exhausted and saw what they would have had to undergo from want of water, the sun and so on, if they had lain out there all day, and ordered their withdrawal."

LORD STRATHCONA: "Would there have been much danger in remaining in that position?"

HILDYARD: "Oh, we should have lost men. If we had not tried to move, I do not suppose the losses need necessarily have been very great, but the physical suffering, no doubt, would have been great because it was a very exceptionally oppressive day, and lying in the sand there was very trying work . . ." [9]

The point to be made is that there were no Boers on the south [or British] side of the Tugela, even though the British might have thought so, hence their saying the onslaught came from 300-400 yards away. Therefore, had the men stayed where they were, the guns could have been saved.

The river. The guns.

Before the battle, British war correspondents were treating the Tugela like a stream, easy to cross. Almost in one hop. But after the battle, as they sat at Frere camp, and looked across the gently sloping plain towards Colenso, things changed.

For instance, Bennet Burleigh writes: "They [the Irish Brigade] found that the enemy had planted the ground with barbed wire entanglements.

"Even in the bed of the river barbed wire had been laid." [10]

A gleeful Michael Davitt writes: "The Tugela near Colenso is a steep-banked river 150 yards wide, and was about four feet in water at the time of the battle . . .

"The northern bank of the Tugela at Colenso offered no formidable obstacle to General Buller as his own and the British war correspondents' descriptions would indicate. There is a consistent exaggeration of the natural strengths of the positions held by Botha's small army in the English reports of the battle; the obvious purpose being to magnify the difficulties which General Buller had to face in a fight that proved so disastrous to his own generalship and to the prestige of the British army."

For instance, he quotes Lord Roberts (in *South African Despatches,* Vol. II, p. 13) who wrote: "As Sir George White explains in his Despatch, the Tugela at that time of the year was not a formidable defensive obstacle."

"Yet," says Davitt, "when General Botha held this same river at Colenso with 5,000 Boers against General Buller and 23,000 British, it became, in the military view of all the British Generals and all the war correspondents, one of the most formidable positions which English troops could possibly face." [11]

And it was Botha who ordered Long's abandoned guns be taken across the river.

Says Davitt: " . . . he ordered a couple of hundred burghers to cross the river and bring in the guns. These men were led by Field Cornet Cherrie Emmet, brother in law of General Botha, and Lieutenant Pohlman of the Johannesburg Police . . .

"Most of the men swam the river with their horses, while others who were unmounted waded across the stream, holding their rifles above their heads; a crossing which showed that, had the British an equal determination to reach the north side of the Tugela in the fight of the morning, there was no insuperable difficulty in the depth of the river to prevent them.

"Pohlman and his police advanced on the first donga, occupied by 50 British officers and men, and called on them to surrender, which they did without firing a shot. They were sent across the river to the Boer lines. Emmet waited for the return of Pohlman and his men before advancing on the second donga, nearest the abandoned batteries . . . " [12]

There lay Colonel G.M. Bullock, officer commanding the Devons. With him, says Burleigh, were about 100 of the Devons with Major MacWalter and Captains Goodwin and Vigors. There were also 14 gunners and a badly wounded Captain Congreve.

They had not been given the order – or had not heard it – to retire, and were stuck out in no-man's land between the abandoned guns and the Boers.

What happened next was the subject of a Court of Inquiry on Colonel Bullock held at Rhenoster, in the Transvaal, on August 6, 1900.

It makes dry, but heroic reading in the Commission of Inquiry's reports: "Colonel Bullock gave evidence and stated that his battalion, which formed part of the 2nd Brigade [Hildyard's] was ordered to capture the wagon bridge over the Tugela and a drift 50 yards to the east of it.

"As he was moving he recieved an order to move towards the railway bridge [the bridge on the far side of Colenso, not the wagon bridge] and subsequently a further order to cross the railway line to the east side and support some guns which were in difficulty.

"Witness then pressed on in the direction in which he believed the guns to be, and after passing through a heavy fire he arrived with the remains of his leading company at a little donga, where he found Colonel Long and a number of other wounded officers and men of the Royal Artillery . . .

"While witness was making a short reconnoitre one man of his battalion reached him from the rear and reported that all the troops had retired, and witness then knew that his little party was quite cut off.

"The position was desperate; the donga was untenable against a strong assault as it was quite exposed on two flanks, and a messenger whom witness had sent back for aid was shot dead.

"At 3pm a stretcher party joined witness. Half an hour later the Boers came up in front and on the flanks and his men fixed bayonets and opened fire.

"Witness heard the Boer commander shout something about Wounded and went out of the donga to speak to him. The Boer commander asked him to surrender, but he refused and told the Boer to get back as he was about to open fire again.

"A wounded gunner who had been captured was then sent in from the Boers with a message stating that if witness did not surrender the Boers would shoot the wounded and the men they had already captured.

"Major Babtie, Royal Army Medical Corps, volunteered to go out and speak to the Boers, but this availed nothing.

"Meanwhile a white flag appeared on the left flank and a Boer advanced into the donga. Witness ordered him back as he had no proposition to make, and meantime more Boers continued to come up covered by this flag of truce.

"He then himself went to the Boer Commander, who had already got into the trenches, and told him to take his men back as he did not intend to surrender and that these men had got into the donga under a flag of truce.

"While speaking to the commander (the flag of truce being still in the donga) two Boers rushed at him from behind and another hit him in the eye with the butt of his rifle. He became dazed, but not insensible. A melee among the wounded ensued.

"As the British ambulances were in the open in front and the Boers had already been firing upon them, and as three of the enemy's guns and a pom-pom commanded the donga, and 500 Boers were in position to command the donga with rifle fire, he suffered himself to be disarmed and surrendered.

"The finding of the Court was that Colonel Bullock was taken prisoner by reason of the chances of war."

On 15 June, 1900 a Court of Inquiry on six officers and 46 men of the Royal Field Artillery was held in Pretoria.

"Lieutenant Colonel Hunt, R.A., narrated briefly how the guns were attacked; Colonel Long and himself were both wounded at an early stage of the engagement and carried to the donga.

"Major Bailward R.A. stated that on Colonel Hunt being disabled the command fell on him. The batteries continued in action for another half an hour, when witness decided, after consultation with Major Foster, to withdraw the detachment under cover – the ammunition being exhausted – and to await the arrival of infantry support. It was impossible to bring up fresh supplies of ammunition on account of the heavy fire. Soon after they had taken cover they were joined by Colonel Bullock with his officers and men.

" . . . The court exonerated all concerned."[13]

As they did two officers and 24 men of the Devons who appeared at yet another Court of Inquiry at Irene, near Pretoria, on August 8, 1900. [14]

I have dwelt long on the battle of Colenso. Certainly because it was the biggest battle of the end of the nineteenth century, and should have foretold the future.

It was a turning point in warfare for several reasons, among which was the use of smokeless powder by the Boers, and the long, accurate distances over which the new Mauser rifle bullet could travel.

But Buller missed its significance. As he had missed the significance of on-the-spot reconnaissance. Not through a telescope as he had done from Frere, but by sending in spies, for want of a better word, to check the ground.

Buller had held "the key" to Ladysmith – a word he was later to use – in his hands, but could not turn it.

Nowhere in Buller's battle orders, issued by General Sir Francis Clery the night before, was there ordered an attack on a small hill that overlooked Colenso.

Hlangwane was occupied, the orders stated, "by a large (Boer) camp".

Dundonald commanding the mounted brigade was told to "endeavour to take up a position on Hlangwane" where he was to enfilade the kopjes north of the Colenso iron bridge.

Despite all odds, had Buller flung everything he had at Hlangwane in the dawn hours of December 15, he would have turned "the key" and opened the door to the relief of Ladysmith, as was done months later.

From Hlangwane, Botha's commandos would have come under British big gun bombardment, and it is doubtful if they would have been able to withstand it. He would have been caught between two British armies. No doubt White, with Buller advancing, would have sent what remained of his calvalry to sandwich Botha, and force his withdrawal up through Grobbelaarskloof.

It was to be months before Hlangwane was taken in Buller's final push through Pieters to relieve Ladysmith.

So important was Hlangwane that Botha blamed a French war correspondent for giving away its secret.

Says Davitt: "With Colonel Villebois-Mareuil [a dapper Frenchman who had joined the Boers, was killed in a later campaign outside Boshof in the Free State and is buried at Magersfontein] as a spectator of the battle was another French officer, Lieutenant Galapaud of the 9th Chasseurs who acted as military correspondent for *Le Matin* of Paris.

He wrote a brief account of "this great Boer victory", and embodied in his report Villebois-Mareuil's view of the vital value of Hlangwane to any attempt on the part of Buller to cross the Tugela at or near Colenso.

This view appeared in *Le Matin* early in February, and the next – that is the fourth – attempt by Buller to reach Ladysmith was made with Hlangwane hill as the pivotal point in his plan of operations, and was successful.

So convinced was Botha that Buller had been advised by cable of the opinion thus expressed within Boer lines that he caused the following letter to be published in the Boer press:

"Sir – In the issue of 29th March last there appears a translation of an extract from a description of the battle of Colenso, which took place on the 15th December, 1899, and which was published in February last in the French paper, *Le Matin* . . . The extract reads: An important point, and where the main attack was expected, was the Langwani Hill, on the southern bank of the Tugela, which was occupied by only some 800 Boers, who were, however, selected from the best shots.

"Had the British made themselves masters of this position, they would have commanded all the Boer positions on the flank. A couple of British cannon there would mean a flight to us, and a victory to the British. As they were unacquainted with the weakness of this position, we watched it with the greatest anxiety.

"In February this report was published in the Paris newspaper by some one who knew of the weak points of our position in this hill, and it was not until the 11th of that month that Buller made his attack upon the position, which he had formerly and for some time afterwards carefully avoided . . .

"I wish therefore through the medium of your paper to impress most seriously upon correspondents the great need of caution in the furnishing of reports, so that the possibility of advantage being thereby afforded to the enemy may be entirely excluded . . . "

The letter was signed by C. Sandberg, Botha's adjutant.[15]

There is a postscript. One of Long's guns, back in British possession, of course, was later used as a gun carriage for Lord Roberts's funeral.

SOURCES

1. *Commission on the War in South Africa.*
2. Ibid.
3. *The Boer Fight for Freedom*, by Michael Davitt.
4. *Commission on the War in South Africa.*
5. Ibid.
6. Ibid.
7. " " (Long's letter: Vol. VI, p. 341).
8. Ibid.
9. Ibid.
10. *The Natal Campaign*, by Bennet Burleigh.
11. *The Boer Fight for Freedom*, by Michael Davitt.
12. Ibid.
13. *Commission on the War in South Africa.*
14. Ibid.
15. *The Boer Fight for Freedom*, by Michael Davitt.

The Heroes

The VCs

"Off the three went for the guns – I saw them go – Schofield, Sir Redvers Buller's ADC; Congreve, of the Rifle Brigade, who had been quietly giving me notes out of his pocket book for an hour before up near the naval battery; and young Roberts, of Sir Francis Clery's staff.

"Roberts was looking over his shoulder at Schofield, laughing and working his stick with a circular motion, like a jockey, to encourage his horse."

In the dust and swirling bullets Congreve got hold of some loose horses and hooked them into the gun limbers, while Roberts stopped to hold Congreve's horse.

Then tragedy.

"He was in the full exhilaration, that is to say, of a man riding to hounds, when the first bullet found its billet.

"Poor Freddy Roberts! he was shot three times, and fell mortally wounded . . ." [1]

One of them took him in the groin.

Congreve saw Freddy Roberts disappear, but could not stop.

When the others reached the guns, through what Congreve describes as a "Tornado" of bullets and shell fire, one gun had the spade clamping gear jammed.

He ran to another, with Captain Schofield's help limbered it up, and then ran back to the first gun, found a pin and managed to limber it up as well.

Helping him, also seemingly unscathed, was Corporal George Edward Nurse, limbering up as though it was just a summer day's outing.

Another team, commanded by Captain Hamilton Lyster Reed, was on its way too – but they were "bowled over".

Reed was wounded, as were five of the 13 men who rode with him. Most of the horses were killed before they carried the men halfway to the guns, and were forced to retire.

During the mad drive, Congreve felt bullets strike him twice, but they only hit his clothes. Then his riding cane was shot in half as he held it in his hand, and finally he was shot in the leg, and tumbled from his horse.

As the bullets spurted sand around he crawled for the dubious cover of the donga, where others were – including a delirious and injured Colonel Long, calling for his guns, and praising his gunners.

Congreve could see Fred Roberts writhing in agony close by – but there was nothing then he could do about it. Every time someone stuck their head above the donga, the bullets threw up sand.

Even then, writes Congreve: "I had not been [in the donga a minute] before another bullet hit the toe of my boot, went into the welt, travelled up, and came out at the toe cap, two inches from the end of the toe. It did not even scratch me, but I shifted my quarters pretty sharply to a better place, where I found Colonels Hunt (wounded) and Long . . . " [2]

Also in the donga was Major William Babtie – a surgeon who had ridden through the maelstrom to help, on a horse that had been hit three times.

Earlier he had gone from person to person, a magical figure seemingly untouchable by Boer bullet, standing up and bending down.

Now he slithered across to Congreve, pulling him to safety.

"We've got to get Fred Roberts in," called Congreve. But no man could move, and live.

Finally, Congreve and Babtie inched out of the donga through the sand towards Roberts who was lying absolutely still in the blazing sun.

Gently, through the dust, they pulled him back to the shelter, under another storm of bullets.

"There we lay from 11 [in the morning] to 4.30 [in the afternoon]; no water, not a breath of air, no particle of shade, and a sun which I have never felt hotter even in India.

"My jacket was taken to shade Roberts' head . . ." [3]

Poor Freddy. He had a lot to live up to, particularly at his father's old school, Eton, where he won the regard of all by his open-hearted and chivalrous nature.

Thomas Packenham says he was slow-witted and had failed the Staff College entrance exam – by a record margin.

Roberts had pleaded with Wolseley to admit his son on his special recommendation as Commander in Chief. Wolseley refused – it was up to Lieutenant Roberts to show by some feat of gallantry that he deserved to be admitted. [4]

Young Roberts did go to the Royal Military College at Sandhurst and at the age of 19 was gazetted on June 10, 1891 to the King's Royal Rifles as 2nd Lieutenant.

He was immediately sent to India, where he joined the 1st Battalion of his regiment at Rawalpindi. Here he put in the first few months of his service.

A brother officer wrote, a few weeks after his arrival: "Sir Frederick Roberts' son has just taken up duty. Officers and men are delighted with him, for he is full of enthusiasm and ever ready to enter with spirit into any sports.

"Modest and unassuming, he has made friends on all sides, and is an undoubted acquisition, but is burning to receive his Baptism of fire."

He had not long to wait, for his wish was gratified in 1892 when a small expedition, including the 1st Battalion KRR was sent to Isazai in an action against dissident tribesmen.

Freddy was made a full Lieutenant on June 22, 1894 and was chosen by Sir William Lockhart to act as his aide de camp in the Waziristan expedition of 1894-5.

He acquitted himself so well that the general made a flattering mention of him in his Despatches, and the young Roberts received the Frontier War Medal with clasp.

In the Chitral expedition he was aide de camp to General Sir Robert Low, when he was again mentioned in Despatches and obtained a second war medal.

He went back home in December 1895 to join his father's staff in Ireland as aide de camp. But anxious for more excitement, he went to Egypt in 1898 for the expedition to Khartoum and became one of Horatio Kitchener's aides de camp.

Here he was, for the third time, mentioned in Despatches and received both the Queen's and Khedive's War Medals.

And now, he lay mortally wounded in the dust of Colenso . . . [5]

Late in the afternoon the Boers came for the guns and the prisoners. And the British ambulances came for the wounded, in terms of a truce.

Fred Roberts, in excruciating pain, was taken to the hospital tent at Clouston.

Surgeon Frederick Treves, who begun the first of the Colenso chapters, takes up the story.

"After a busy afternoon, among the field hospitals under the naval ridge [Clouston], I returned in the evening to Chieveley, in the hope, now that the bulk of the work was over, of getting something to eat.

"I had not been at Chieveley long when an orderly arrived with a letter to tell me that Lieutenant Roberts had been brought in wounded, and to ask me to go back to the naval hill at once.

"It was now dark, and I had at that time no horse. However the hospital train was standing in the station, and to the fertile brain of Major Brazier-Creagh, who was in charge of the train, it occurred that we might detach the engine and go down on it to the ridge, since the field hospitals were close to the railway.

"There was the difficulty, however, that the line was a single line, and a water train had already steamed down to the ridge, and was expected back at any moment. It was the simple problem of an engine on the one hand and of a train on the other, proceeding in different directions at night on a single line of rail.

"The case being urgent, the engine was detached and we started. Major Brazier-Creagh and Captain Symonds came with me.

"It also happened that we went tender first. The railway line appeared to us to go up and down with many undulations, and at the top of every rise we expected to meet the water train. Fortunately the moon was coming up, and the blackness which oppressed us was fading a little.

"We proceeded slowly, with much whistling and considerable waving of a red lamp. At last there was made out the dim outline of the water train coming towards us at fair speed.

"We stopped and there were redoubled efforts in the direction of whistling, lamp waving and shouting. These exhibitions had an immediate effect upon the water train, which, after some hysterical whistling, stopped, and backed promptly out of sight.

"The driver told us afterwards that he thought a whole train was coming down on top of him at full speed and that he might well have backed down into Colenso.

"We got out some way above the ridge and walked on to the field hospital I had so lately left. The gallant officer I came to see was comfortably bestowed in a tent, was quite free from pain and anxiety, and was disposed to sleep.

"From a surgical point of view the case was hopeless, and had been hopeless from the first, and no idea of an operation could be entertained . . . "

The doctors had given Roberts morphine.

That night Treves slept in Clouston.

The following day: " . . . Lieutenant Roberts, whom I had visited at intervals, went up by train [to Chieveley] and was placed in No 4 field hospital.

"Here a bedstead, with a comfortable mattress and white sheets, was waiting for him . . . " [6]

Buller was weary. And melancholy. We would today probably call it depressed. He had watched, from horseback close to the donga, the three eager heroes ride out with the limbers into the rain of bullets.

He had watched Freddy Roberts struck, and fall from his horse, the cane that he had waved so jauntily a few minutes before flying from his hand into the veld.

And he knew, with sinking heart, that he would probably never rise again.

He had watched, outwardly impassive, as Captain M.L. Hughes, his personal doctor, who had been next to him, was cut almost in two by an exploding shell.

It had all gone wrong.

Atkins writes: "Sir Redvers Buller and his staff came by me on their return. The General climbed down limply and wearily from his horse like an old, old man. I thought he was wounded with vexation; I did not know then that he was wounded – badly bruised about the ribs by a fragment of shell.

"The horse of General Gerard, one of his A.D.C.s had been shot in the neck; Captain Hughes, the doctor on his staff, had been killed – half blown to pieces – by a shell . . . " [7]

It was Buller who had suggested Freddy Roberts be appointed to a safe staff billet as ADC on his own personal staff when it was being formed for South Africa. [8]

Freddy Roberts, says Julian Symons, in *Buller's Campaign,* wanted to join Dundonald's Mounted Brigade, but Dundonald's request for him was refused – because he was an only son, and mounted men were so constantly in action.

It was thought safer for him to be aide de camp to Buller. But when he arrived, he was made ADC to General Sir Francis Clery, who then commanded the Natal Field Force.

Frank Stewart's representation of saving the guns at Colenso. Gunners lie already dead as orders are shouted and terrified mules begin to pull. Two guns were saved at Colenso and this is how one of them got away.

Now Buller had the task of flashing the tragic message to London.

Lord Roberts was in Dublin when the telegram from Buller came. Freddy, it stated, had been dangerously wounded at Colenso in an attempt to save the guns and had been recommended for a VC!

At the same time, Lord Roberts received another telegram from London asking him to be prepared to sail at once to take over the Command in South Africa.

But before leaving he and Lady Roberts sent a telegram to Freddy, at Frere, telling him of their pride in him and that they were praying for his recovery.

He did not live long enough to receive it.

He died on Sunday, to everyone's grief.

"He just faded gently away."[9]

Burleigh writes: "I regret to say Lieutenant Roberts succumbed to his painful injuries this [Sunday] morning.

"He was buried with five soldiers, each in separate graves close to Chieveley Railway-station.

"The pall-bearers . . . were Major Prince Christian Victor, Colonels Buchanan, Riddell, Versicke, Copley and Major Stuart Wortley, all of them riflemen . . ." [10]

However, Ladysmith historian R.E. Stevenson corrects Burleigh, naming Prince Christian, Colonel Buchanan Riddell, Captain the Honourable Reginald Cathcart, Versicke, Copley and Major Stuart Wortley as pall bearers.

Three of them did not survive the war – Prince Christian, a grandson of Queen Victoria, born at Windsor Castle, died of enteric in Pretoria; Colonel Buchanan Riddell was killed on Twin Peaks at Spioenkop after "recklessly" standing up in the open (in disgust, says Stevenson, at being ordered by Buller to retire) and Captain Cathcart, a descendant of a Governor of the Cape Colony, was killed at Tugela Heights in the final relief push on Ladysmith. [11]

On December 15, six Victoria Crosses were awarded – Babtie, Congreve, Roberts, Reed and Nurse. Schofield – Captain Henry Norton Schofield, Buller's ADC – was, said Buller merely doing his job, and that did not warrant an award.

But it did, and in 1901, Schofield's VC was gazetted.

J.B. Atkins writes of Schofield's action: "I can't believe it even now," Schofield told me afterwards, "that we got on so well." And then he went on: "I'll show you how cool those drivers were. When I was hooking on one of the guns, one of the drivers said, 'Elevate the muzzle, sir'. That's a precaution for galloping in rough country. But I shouldn't have thought of it – not just then. Pretty cool, wasn't it?' " [12]

Could Freddy Roberts's life have been saved had he been got to the hospital tent sooner?

While Treves says it was a hopeless case from the very beginning, was it?

No mention in the sources I have indicate what other wounds Roberts had received, apart from the one in the groin.

Emanoel Lee writes: "Lord Roberts' son, Fred, was wounded in the abdomen . . . It was not until the First World War that abdominal operations on war casualties were undertaken routinely." [13]

Septicaemia set in almost immediately, one local doctor told me, and in the primitive medical conditions of a field hospital, it was hopeless.

And from Ladysmith, Lord Rawlinson wrote in his journal: "Today I had news which affected me more than any since the beginning of the war. Little

Freddy Roberts was killed at Colenso. The Helio message says: He was shot in the groin . . .

"He was such a charming and fine lad, and I fear to think of the effect his death will have on his family." [14]

There was a popular story at the time that while in London Roberts went to his club where he was given a list of casualties. He is said to have read it

Freddy Roberts lies buried in the small war cemetry just beyond Chieveley station. His grave stands out from the others who died from injury or enteric fever in the Chieveley hospital tents, attended to by Surgeon Frederick Treves and his staff, The Chievely cemetery is an oasis of peace, beneath huge trees, where today few go. (Author's picture)

aloud to several fellow members without a falter in his voice when he came across the name of his son among those who had died of wounds.

In fact, it was Lord Lansdowne's lot to find Roberts and break the news to him. More than 20 years later he wrote to Lady Aileen Roberts: " . . . The blow was almost more than he [Lord Roberts] could bear and for a moment I thought he would break down, but he pulled himself together . . . Two hours later he was in the boat-train bound for Dublin to pack his bags and collect a war staff . . . " [15]

Dawn at Chieveley is an emotional time. Every morning, the sun catches the grave. It tinges the white cross with red, picking out the capital lettering *Thy Will Be Done* on its background of stylised flowers.

The inscription is on a three-stepped base: "In Loving Memory of Frederick Hugh Sherston Roberts, V.C. Lieutenant King's Royal Rifles. Only surviving son of Field-Marshal Lord Roberts, and Nora his wife.

"Who fell mortally wounded in an attempt to save the British guns at the Battle of Colenso on the 15th December, 1899, and died two days afterwards. Aged 27 years and 11 months.

"Blessed are the pure in heart for they shall see God."

The grave is set forward of the wall of other crosses that mark the final resting place of British heroes – the willing men who went to the battle of Colenso and returned mortally wounded, to die in the British tented hospital nearby.

Nothing disturbs the silence of Chieveley military cemetery, other than the passing trains on their way, 96 years later, between Durban and Johannesburg.

There are cows in green meadows, huge trees that cast their shade over the graves, and, nearby, a line of old railway houses.

A contemporary picture shows no trees, just a barbed wire enclosure with some graves on the bare veld. Chieveley is almost uninhabited today. There is nothing much to keep people there anymore, particularly on a main line that is electrified.

The cemetery is well kept. And seems to be away from mischievous hands which have, over the years, wreaked destruction of monuments in the Ladysmith and Colenso area.

SOURCES

1. *The Relief of Ladysmith*, by J.B. Atkins.
2. *The Transvaal War*, by Louis Creswicke.
3. Ibid.
4. *The Boer War*, by Thomas Packenham.
5. *Army Celebrities* (undated), circa 1900.
6. *The Tale of a Field Hospital*, by Frederick Treves.
7. *The Relief of Ladysmith*, by J.B. Atkins.
8. *The Life of Lord Roberts*, by David James.
9. *The Natal Campaign*, by Bennet Burleigh.
10. Ibid.
11. *Pamphlet: British Soldiers' Graves* (Ladysmith Historical Society).
12. *The Relief of Ladysmith*, by J.B. Atkins.
13. *To the Bitter End*, by Emanoel Lee.
14. *The Great Anglo-Boer War*, by Byron Farewell.
15. *Life of Lord Roberts*, by David James.

CHAPTER ELEVEN

Interlude
From the Commission's Report

Buller, the man with no orders

BULLER, like White, was a man with no orders. And it became apparent when he was called to give evidence on Tuesday, February 17, 1903 that the war, for him, had been a time of confusion.

CHAIRMAN: "You have been good enough to prepare for us a summary of evidence as to your operations, and if you have no objection, we will take that as the answer to the first question in your evidence, and then proceed to ask any questions which we may have, or to hear any comments you may desire to submit with regard to any part of it as we go through it. Will that suit you?

BULLER: "Quite so."

(Chairman then read the following from Buller's statement): "In June 1899, I was summoned from Aldershot by Lord Lansdowne, who told me, in the event of a war in South Africa, I had been selected to hold the command-in-chief.

"After submitting to him what seemed to me a preferable arrangement, I accepted the command, and we proceeded to discuss the question of military policy to be pursued.

"I maintained that the only practicable route was that through the Free State. He declined even to discuss this. Ultimately we agreed that one Army Corps, a Cavalry Division, and seven battalions for the lines of communication would be a sufficient force, if the object of the government were merely to attack the Transvaal. But I added that to leave the Free State out of the account, was to my mind, impossible.

"After leaving Lord Lansdowne, I saw the commander-in-chief [Wolseley] at the War Office, gave him a summary of my remarks, and received from him a promise of every assistance that he could afford. I begged both Lord Lansdowne and Lord Wolseley to recollect that I was not in the same position as Lord Wolseley when he organised the Egyptian Expedition of 1882, for he was then adjutant-general and had the whole of the War Office at his back, whereas I was fully employed with my work at Aldershot.

"INTERVIEW WITH LORD LANSDOWNE: "I heard no more of warlike preparations until the 3rd of July when I was summoned by telegram from Devonshire to London. There Lord Lansdowne informed me that he had under consideration a proposal to send out to South Africa one division of infantry and one brigade of cavalry.

"I asked wither these troops were to be sent, and with what object? I found there was no definite object, but that it was considered desirable to send some troops to some part of South Africa.

"I went to the War Office to see Lord Wolseley, but he had gone. I sent him a memo (July 6, 1899) summarising the views which I had expressed to Lord Lansdowne:

"1: Strengthen the Cape Colony and Natal garrisons to the extent that local authority not think sufficient to protect these colonies;

"2: Make up your mind as to the route and definitely to the attitude to be adopted towards the Orange Free State;

"3: Commence the formation of magazines on the intended line of route, and the mobilisation of the active force;

"4: Send out this fighing force.

"The proposal to send out these 10,000 men came to nothing. I pressed hard at this time . . . that our colonies might be garrisoned in accordance with a proper scheme of defence. I urged this again and again without success."

Poor Buller, indeed. He had been appointed, but to what? From that date until August 15th, matters moved but slowly at the War Office. Buller continues: "No council of war was held; no campaign was adopted; no regular military preparations were undertaken. In the middle of August, I heard that all preparations for war in South Africa entailing expenditure had been stopped, and that the Secretary of State of War had gone to Ireland. Mr Balfour, during his absence, came to the War Office . . . I heard that it was believed an Ultimatum was to be sent to the Transvaal on 11th September.

"The condition of affairs seemed to me to be alarming, for the intelligence given in the newspapers made it impossible to believe that war could be avoided. Not knowing what else to do, I approached the private secretary to Lord Salisbury, Prime Minister and Foreign Secretary, at the time, until 1900, I presented my views to him, and he thought it his duty to lay them before Lord Salisbury the following morning. On the 5th I heard that Lord Salisbury desired my views on the military situation . . . "

And that was a few weeks before war was declared!

But to return to the Commission.

VISCOUNT ESHER: "One of the points you mentioned in your statement is that no council of war was held.

"Do you wish to suggest that one should have been held?"

BULLER: "Well, I do suggest to the Commission that I was placed in an uncomfortable position. I made no complaint myself . . . I think there should have been a consideration of the intended expedition at which the commander-in-chief designate should have expressed his views before the Army Board or the Defence Committee of the Cabinet, or before some board who would have heard what he had to say, and he would have had the opportunity of raising a large number of questions . . . but I never had any opportunity."

ESHER: (*Incredulously*): "You were never called before a Defence Committee of the Cabinet at all?"

BULLER: "No, I was never called before anything."

ESHER: "And you were not present at any meeting of the Army Board at the War Office?"

BULLER: "Not one . . . I was never consulted on anything, nor was I ever given any questions to consider and answer by anybody."

ESHER: (*More incredulously*): "But you did not see the Prime Minister or the Colonial Secretary, or any other member of the government?"

BULLER: "No, nor did I see any of the correspondence that was passing at the time between the Cape and the Colonial Office."

ESHER: " . . . There is a heading in your statement which begins, 'general considerations affecting the plan of campaign'. Did you ever lay these considerations before Lord Lansdowne, or any other member of the government?"

BULLER: "No, I was never asked for my opinion on anything of the sort . . ."

ESHER: "And these general considerations were not laid before the government because you were never asked to state your opinions to any Minister of the Crown?"

BULLER: "Never. I was asked for nothing."

The questioning was taken over by Sir Henry Norman, who was anxious to find out more: "Do I understand, Sir Redvers, that before your departure for South Africa, you received no letter of general instructions as to what the government wished to be done?"

BULLER: "None."

NORMAN: "Nor on your arrival there?"

BULLER: "None."

NORMAN: "Or after your arrival?"

BULLER: "None. The usual letter of service."

NORMAN: "But that is a mere letter of appointment.

BULLER: "Yes."

Then Sir Frederick Darley took up the questioning: "Speaking broadly, your opinion is that the commander of a force such as you had under you at the time should be taken into the confidence of the government?"

BULLER: "I think so. I think I suffered myself a tremendous disadvantage by not having the smallest idea when I arrived at Cape Town of the course which negotiators had been taking, and the attitude of mind in which I should find Lord Milner [then Sir Alfred Milne] . . . I was told to treat my appointment as confidential and I was not able to discuss matters and it would have been an advantage for me to be able to go before a body of gentlemen and say, 'I think so and so.' "[1]

But what did Lord Lansdowne have to say about all this? He was called to the Commission on Thursday, 26 March, 1903 and asked by the Chairman what all this was about.

LANSDOWNE: "My attention has been called to a statement contained in the summary of Sir Redvers Buller's evidence to that effect.

"I think Sir Redvers Buller is under a complete misapprehension. I should like in the first place to dwell upon the extreme unlikeliness of the Government having deliberately withheld from Sir Redvers Buller anything that it was desirable that he should know; after all he was selected by the Government; he carried our fortunes and it was not very likely that we should keep him in the dark systematically, which is what I understand he alleges.

"We warned him in good time that he was to be asked to take command of the force, with the object that he might have ample opportunity of considering on what lines he should conduct these operations.

"I also wish to say that upon the occasion when I intimated to Sir Redvers Buller that he had been designated for the chief command I went out of my way to tell him that from that date anything that the War Office could supply him with in the way of information was his to ask for. If he wanted information and did not come for it, I submit that he had only himself to blame . . .

"It seems to be assumed that there was a great deal of secret political intelligence which was within our knowledge and which was not within his, and which ought to have been imparted to him.

"That was not the case; everything that happened during the course of these negotiations appeared from day to day in the columns of the newspapers.

"There was really nothing that we could have imparted to him which he could not derive from the ordinary sources of information.

"He certainly had access to me, and as a matter of fact, he did on several occasions come to me at the War Office, although not often.

"He certainly had access to the Commander-in-Chief, and to the Intelligence Branch, and it is also to be remembered that Colonel Stopford, who was designated as his Military Secretary, was at the time in charge of the Mobilisation Department in the War Office. Sir Redvers Buller could certainly have found out through him what was happening in the War Office; but I am bound also to say this, that Sir Redvers Buller's position in the War Office, although he had ceased to be a member of the Headquarters Staff, was such that he really could have obtained from anybody anything he wanted in the way of assistance or information.

"He had been, as the Commission knows, for years in a quite exceptional position of authority in the War Office; he was Adjutant-General when the Duke of Cambridge was Commander-in-Chief, and at that time a great part of the work of the War Office was really conducted by Sir Redvers Buller, and by him alone.

"I say, having served in the War Office with Sir Redvers Buller, and knowing his relations with the War Office staff, that there was not a room in the War Office that Sir Redvers Buller could not have walked into whenever he pleased with the certaintly that whatever assistance he could get in that room would be given to him without demur.

"I have known Sir Redvers Buller for some time and it never occurred to me that he was a particularly difficult person, or very easily intimidated, particularly by civilians. Therefore, if I may say so, coming back to a point you mentioned just now, the suggestion that Sir Redvers Buller was, so to speak, boycotted at the War Office, and that it was because of that that he had to find out the Prime Minister's Private Secretary and appeal through him to the Prime Minister, seems to me to be a rather preposterous representation of the facts. I cannot put it more gently than that."

CHAIRMAN: "At any rate there was no intention of yours to deny him any amount of your confidence?"

LANSDOWNE: "I cannot put it too strongly that it was, not only far from my intentions, but I think it would have been a monstrous thing if, having invited Sir Redvers Buller to undertake this extremely important command, I, or anybody under me, had stopped short of giving him all the assistance that could possibly be afforded him."

Cecil Headlam, who edited the *Milner Papers*, writes that when Buller arrived at Cape Town, he brought with him a "Spirit of depression", which increased upon his arrival.

Although he had formerly fought in South Africa, and was now past his prime, he had never held any independent command in the field.

His inability to handle large bodies of troops had been alarmingly displayed at manoeuvres in 1898. Yet the force with which he was now entrusted was twice as large as any Marlborough ever commanded in Flanders or Wellington in the Peninsula or at Waterloo, writes Headlam.

The weight of responsibility and the magnitude of the task appeared to have overwhelmed him.

"The spirit in which he had accepted the command had been ominous.

He seems to have been aware that he was not fit for it, and expressed the intention of returning home as soon as possible.

"It was hoped that Buller would achieve a brilliant success upon the Tugela. What happened was the deplorable defeat at Colenso . . . " [2]

Meanwhile, at Frere, the British army waited. Any hopes the troops may have had of moving elsewhere to take on the Boers were dashed.

Says Burleigh: "We correspondents all moved a few days ago to this place, Frere, in order to be near the headquarters of General Buller and neighbourly with the new Press censor, Major Jones.

"Press censorship soldiers, as a rule, find it a thankless and uncongenial task; there have been six changes in the office within two months.

"It is no easy function for the sagest to discharge, and experience has taught me that the Press censor, like the poet, is born not made. The hard official rules and the zeal to prevent even minor matters being made known through official channels – though the enemy and our public may be in possession of the information from other sources – are the stumbling blocks to journalistic enterprise with our troops in the field.

"Nay there is another deterrent repressive feature, of which you may or may not be aware, connected with war news.

"On great days – battle days – no message of any kind can be forwarded until the General's official despatch has been transmitted. You millions at home may be panting for the news which we, your representatives, are burning to send. But no; for hours you and we must wait, and therefore the censor's Clear the Line – the imperative signals which precede the General's message – put aside all other telegrams, however glutted the cables are . . . " [3]

J.B. Atkins goes for another topic: "The latest diversion in our preparations here is the arrival of the traction engines and a balloon. The traction engines go faster than any I ever saw.

"The balloon has not yet risen. The fact is there has been a miscalculation. The balloon is designed to ascend 4,000 feet, which is excellent at Aldershot; but here we are up 3,500 feet already, so the balloon has a margin in hand of only 500 feet.

"I hope the aeronauts will manage to get it up by relieving it of the cradle and sending up some light, acrobatic observer in the ropes. Otherwise I fear that when we get to a still higher place in the hills the balloon will try to go through the ground!" [4]

Burleigh writes: "Two other important adjuncts to Buller's army's fighting power and mobility have also arrived in this holiday season. The first of the accessions alluded to is a war balloon, which is now with all its equipment at Frere.

"Why an Aldershot balloon, or half a dozen of them, have not been sent here two months ago, or since Sir George White has been pent up in Ladysmith, is a problem for which I offer no solution . . .

"Weather permitting, the half-score or so of strong Aldershot tractionengines, which have at last been detrained here and at Chieveley will do much to making General Buller's army compact and mobile. Without them the troops would require an astounding length of ox and mule wagons . . .

"Yesterday and today these wheeling puffing Billees have been running to-and-fro transporting stores from the railway siding . . . they leisurely descend into spruits, roll across, and wheel up stiff, long climbs, like flies walking up a wall . . . On the flat, dry veld the steamers strip along at a brisk eight miles an hour." [5]

Later, he writes: " . . . I had omitted to refer to the new and big camp re-created at Estcourt. I am not alluding to troops required for guarding our line of communication . . . but to Sir Charles Warren's division, or to the major portion of it.

"Some six battalions or more of that command have arrived at Estcourt to reinforce the relief column. There all are encamped waiting for the order to go forward to Ladysmith. The losses at Colenso on December 15 last have all been made more than good . . . " [6]

SOURCES.

1. *Commission on the War in South Africa.*
2. *The Milner Papers* (Vol.II), edited by Cecil Headlam.
3. *The Natal Campaign,* by Bennet Burleigh.
4. *The Relief of Ladysmith,* by J.B. Atkins.
5. *The Natal Campaign,* by Bennet Burleigh.
6. Ibid.

CHAPTER TWELVE

Prelude to Spioenkop

"Jerusalem" Warren

He sits on a campstool beneath the meagre shade of a gnarled, ancient olive tree. His hair is closely cropped, almost a crewcut, and he wears a trimmed beard and moustache.

With him, three companions are posed in the classic Victorian manner of the time.

Captain Charles Warren's trousers have ragged ends, and incongruously, he wears cufflinks. He looks a resourceful, powerful man. And indeed he was.

The picture was taken after he had begun what still ranks as the biggest underground archaeological exploration of Jerusalem, and his pioneering work remains a model of precise archaeology.

His neat notes have been used over the last few years by Jerusalem specialist, the late Benjamin Mazar, and are still being used by Mazar's granddaughter, Eilat – and others – carrying on his work.

Much of the excavations at the southern, south-eastern and south-western ends of the Temple Mount beneath the walls of what was once Herod's magnificent temple (and upon which now rests the golden mosque of the Dome of the Rock) were done using Warren's observations. And in the mid-1990s Eilat re-excavated two of his tunnels, dug more than 100 years before.

For Warren was an engineer, and his speciality was tunnelling.

His brief, in the years 1867-70, was to explore and report on the underground area beneath the walls, one of which remains today as Judaism's holiest site, the Western Wall.

He was told: "The priority in Jerusalem is to answer the main questions still troubling biblical scholars: Where on the Temple Mount was the exact location of Solomon's Temple? where were the three city walls described by Josephus? where had the pre-Solomonic city of David been situated? and finally, what was the true site of the Crucifixion?"

Warren was a bright, enterprising officer. Some would have called him an obnoxious rebel. He was educated at Cheltenham and Brignorth, regularily obtaining top marks for whatever he did.

He was sent to Sandhurst to "get the stuffing knocked out of him" as his headmaster wrote, and emerged as the youngest and most brilliant of the officers of his year. He went on to Woolwich to study a new discipline – surveying – again graduating with top honours.

But nobody knew exactly what to do with him. However, he was the War Office's problem, and, after lengthy deliberations, they sent him as far away as possible – Gibraltar.

"Have a look," they said, "at our impregnable defences. See if you can improve on them," they smiled. No-one, they knew, could better the existing defences.

But Warren did. He built scale models of the Rock, one three metres high, detecting as he did so where there were flaws in many of its existing defensive measures.

He proposed a solution to a startled War Office – and was told to go ahead and remedy the faults. At the same time, he invented a fitment to gun carriages to supersede the truck levers – an invention objected to at the time because it was made of iron, but subsequently it was adopted.

In the end Warren was the man who, indeed, made the Rock impregnable.

But it was to Jerusalem he went in that summer of 1867. For some time the British press had been full of stories of the "scandal" of the Holy City which had an inefficient and almost non-existent sanitary system and absolutely no running water.

The accumulated rubbish of millennia lay heavily on the consciences of Victorian gentry to such an extent that a fund was raised towards making a plan of the underground portion of the city so that its water supplies could be better organised.

The stink was too much for delicate Victorian noses. So it was that the Palestine Exploration Fund (PEF) approached the British Army for help.

First, Captain Charles Wilson, an engineer who had a penchant for archaeology, was sent out. He was followed by Charles Warren.

While Wilson looked towards above-ground archaeology, Warren went underground. And so began a methodical and thorough exploration beneath Jerusalem to lay bare the tantalising secrets of passageways and caverns alongside the Temple Mount, long hidden from the eyes of infidels – Jerusalem was under Turkish rule at the time. Warren was strictly forbidden from entering the Temple Mount and digging right up against it. All his "digs" had to be made at least 10 metres from the walls.

Those who know Jerusalem today, with its Ottoman crenellated walls rising up out the Tyropoean and Kidron Valleys, will no doubt be puzzled by what follows.

But when Warren dug Jerusalem, only the top section of the walls – about three metres – were above ground. The rubble of ages had not been cleared, filling the Tyropoean valley and much of the southern face.

There is a contemporary picture of the top of one of Warren's shafts a few feet from what is today Robinson's Arch in the south-west corner of the Temple Mount. Trees and bushes grow out of the archway.

The rubble has, in the intervening years, been cleared away, and today Robinson's Arch stands some 20 metres from the ground level.

In the early 1990s, for the first time since the destruction of the Temple in 70CE (Common Era), the tunnel running the entire Western Wall, all 400 metres of it – was revealed by archaeologist Dan Bahat. Dan Bahat told me, during a recent visit to Cape Town, that he would undertake absolutely no archaeology in Jerusalem without "consulting Warren's two magnificent books" on his work over 100 years ago.

The last person to use the tunnel before Charles Warren was Herod The Great. At its northern end, Herod had ordered it blocked up – that was 1200 years ago.

Warren's greatest contribution, however, was the discovery of Hezekiah's tunnel built in 701BCE (Before Common Era) to ensure Jerusalem's continuous water supply as the Assyrian Senaccherib tried unsuccessfully to take the city.

The shaft Warren found is today known as Warren's Shaft, and bisects the underground passageway known as the Gihon spring.

In all, Warren dug 14 sites around the old city in appalling conditions. He correctly identified the site of Herod's Antonia fortress (north-eastern end of the Temple Mount, where Pontius Pilate is said to have condemned Christ to death). He investigated the Herodian substructures to the south-east, known as Solomon's Stables, access to which was forbidden in his time, and still is by the Muslim *Waqf* authority which handles religious sites.

He was the first explorer to try and follow the line of Jerusalem's pre-Ottoman ancient walls, and dug at the Golden Gate – where he discovered what he identified as the wall of the Ophel (south-east corner of the Temple Mount), the ancient City of David. He also examined the ancient Israel Pool (Birket Y'israel) at the Lion Gate.

But as to the true site of Solomon's Temple, like the archaeologists of today, he was unsuccessful, although theories abound.

Warren's was a survey of "lucky escapes". Huge stones were day after day ready to fall, and sometimes did, on their heads. One of Warren's men was injured so severely that he could barely crawl out into the open air; another extricated himself with difficulty, torn and bleeding, while another was actually buried under the ruins. It took an hour before he was pulled out alive.

Sometimes they were almost suffocated by the stifling heat; at other times they were plunged for hours up to their necks in the freezing waters of some subterranean torrent; and sometimes their way was blocked by a falling mass without light or escape. Of course they did . . .

Sir Walter Besant, the secretary of the PEF, wrote in 1870: " . . . It is certain that nothing will ever be done in the future to compare with what was done by Warren.

"It was Warren who restored the ancient city to the world; it was he who stripped the rubbish from the rocks and showed the glorious temple standing within its walls 1,000 feet long, and 200 feet high, of mighty masonry; he it was who laid open the valleys now covered up and hidden; he who opened the secret passages, the ancient aqueducts, the bridge connecting the temple with the town. Whatever else may be done in the future, his name will always be associated with the Holy City which he first recovered."

In the end, they called him "Jerusalem" Warren.

In 1870, he went home to put together his report, and in 1871, returned to military duty and was posted to Dover. For the next year he was employed on the fortifications of Dover Castle and Castle Hill and Fort (Fort Burgoyne), moving later to take charge of the Gunpowder and Small-arm factories at Waltham Abbey and Enfield.

In October 1876 he was asked by the Colonial Office to lay down the boundary line between Griqualand West and the Orange Free State following rival claims by Chief Waterboer of the Griquas and President Brand of the Free State.

The British Government had acquired the rights of Chief Waterboer, and later the Free State abandoned its claim after being paid out some £90,000.

It was Warren who placed under British control the fabulously rich diamond town of Kimberley in the then Northern Cape. When the survey had been completed, it was inspected by officials from both the Cape and the Free State; Warren was entertained by President Brand at Bloemfontein, met the Volksraad at dinner and was publicly thanked.

His work over, Warren headed for Zanzibar by way of Kimberley, Pretoria, and Delagoa Bay – but there he was ordered back to Cape Town to see Sir Bartle Frere who appointed him Special Commissioner in Griqualand West for six months to investigate various land cases that were due to come up in the Supreme Court.

Warren was made a CMG for this.

And then Warren went to war – first in the Transkei in 1878, in command of the Diamond Field's Horse (it was here, at Perie Bush, that he first met a young, bearded officer by the name of Redvers Henry Buller) and then against warring Griquas. He was involved in some fierce actions, culminating in his being appointed Acting Administrator of Griqualand West. He immediately offered to take 500 troopers to the assistance of Lord Chelmsford in Zululand, following the disaster at Isandhlwana. But it was considered not wise, and Warren remained in Kimberley.

It was as Lieutenant Colonel that Charles Warren returned to Britain, leaving behind a town bearing his name – Warrenton. He took up the position of Instructor of Surveying at the School of Military Engineering at Chatham.

When the British explorer,C.E. Palmer, Professor of Arabic at Cambridge University, went missing in Arabia, who else but Captain Charles Warren was qualified to search for him? Warren did not attempt the journey alone – with him went his wife of a few months, and a large retinue.

Warren found Palmer's body, and the search brought Warren the reward of a KCMG.

But soon it was back to South Africa – this time to sort out the boundary dispute and to arbitrate over two small renegade independent Boer diamond republics – Goshen and Stellaland – which were causing serious political repercussions to both the British Government and the Dutch Republic of the Transvaal. They had split from mainstream British control because of its stringent gem control.

In England again, he was made Commissioner of the London Metropolitan Police in 1886 – the time of Jack the Ripper, or the Whitechapel Murders, as they were officially known.

But Warren had been put in charge, too, of Queen Victoria's Jubilee Celebrations. The city had to be cleaned up, muggers and thieves apprehended. Warren's success culminated in him being awarded, by the Queen, the Knight Commandership of the Order of the Bath.

And a mention in the satirical magazine, *Punch*, to the melody of one of the most popular airs at the time, the Gilbert and Sullivan *A Policeman's Lot is Not a Happy One*, from *The Pirates of Penzance*:

"All honour to your management, my Warren,
All honour to the force you featly led!
And that honour, Punch opines, should not be barren,
(May we hear hereafter more upon that head).
'Midst the Jubilee joyous pageantry and pother,
(Though 'tis common of our Bobbies to make fun)
Taking one consideration with another
The policeman's work was excellently done."

But the "Ripper" was never caught, and Warren did not think the Home Secretary of the time had given him sufficient support – in fact, the opposite – and tendered his resignation. It was refused, but Warren later insisted, saying that he could no longer hold the appointment with due regard to the good of the force and his own credit.

But it brought him into close contact with Queen Victoria. The Queen's grandson was one of the "Ripper" suspects, and Victoria never forgave Warren for his presumption. Remembering this, she too later blamed Warren for "the loss" of Spioenkop.

The resignation was fully debated in the House of Commons on 14 November, 1888, where the same Home Secretary – Mr Joseph Williams - had this to say: " . . . Sir Charles Warren was a man not only of the highest character, but of great ability . . . By his vigour and firmness he has restored that confidence in the police which had been shaken . . . Sir Charles Warren has shown conspicuous skill and firmness in putting an end to disorder in the metropolis, and for that he deserves the highest praise . . ."

After some months of leisure, Warren was appointed to command the troops in the Straits Settlements in Singapore, which brought him in direct conflict with Sir Redvers Buller – at the time Adjutant General at the War Office.

Warren needed changes to suit conditions in his far-away station. Buller would not approve. It led to a long and acrimonious corespondence, and Buller dismissing a furious Warren's demands.

The two had met frequently over the years, and at times had been friendly towards each other. But each had kept his distance.

Warren retired in 1898 and moved to Ramsgate where he wanted to be left in peace.

It was not to be.

A year later the final act in the saga of this Victorian gentleman was about to be played out – in one of the most bitter battles of the Boer War, Spioenkop.

Let it be finally said that Warren was, and had been, a fighting man. When he was nominated to the command of the Fifth Division, everyone rejoiced, wondering only that he had not been among the first generals to be sent out . . .

SOURCES

1. *The Life of General Sir Charles Warren*, by Watkin Williams (Basil Blackwell, Oxford 1941), and *Sir Charles Warren and Spioenkop, A Vindication*, by "Defender" [D. Lambton] (Smith, Elder and Co., London, 1902). Also: *In the Shadow of the Temple*, by Nieir Ben-Dov; various papers by Jerusalem archaeologist, Dan Bahat, an authority on Charles Warren's Jerusalem.

CHAPTER THIRTEEN

War Games and Thoroughness

And a do-nothing policy . . .

Dapper Sir Charles arrived at Frere at about 10pm on Boxing Day 1899. He was pleased to be there, and reported his arrival at once to Sir Redvers.

Warren writes: "I found him rather reserved. The series of reverses to which he had been subjected and the loss of the guns might well alter a man for a while. I could not say what I wanted to say that night, though our conference did last two and a half hours; so we arranged to confer again in the morning. We slept in the railway carriage."[1]

At 6.30 the next morning Warren was with Buller. Cheerfully Sir Charles proposed, that as troops usually got out of sorts in a war if they had nothing to do, games be held – with Hlangwane as a pivotal point.

Hlangwane! It was a name Buller did not want to hear, and he turned angrily to Warren, who merely continued saying that Buller's proposed march to Potgieter's drift on the Tugela, which he had discussed with Warren the previous night, was dangerous, and he objected to it.

There, said Warren, the Boers could shoot at the British from safety at 2,000 yards.

Buller exploded.

"What," he shouted, "do you know about it!"

What he didn't know about it was that on the way by ship from England, and on the way to Durban, Warren and his staff had taken up most of their time playing war games.

And Hlangwane?

Warren writes: "Almost every drift was tried during the war games, and as a result of the discussion there was a general conclusion that the route by Hlangwane was the most passable, but it was not taken in the exercises because General Buller had given it up, and it was therefore assumed that there must be some unknown difficulty that way. But there were many opinions in its favour. The great difficulty with the British commanders was that they could not realise the tremendous mobility of the Boers; they kept thinking that Infantry moving 10 miles a day could outflank Boers moving 10 miles in two hours." [2]

So when Warren suggested Hlangwane to Buller, he was definitely not amused.

Warren writes: "But here was a fundamental difference which has existed for years between General Buller and myself. He has an aversion to the very type of action I think most necessary.

"He prefers to work in open country where the Boers can pick you off at 2,000 yards. As our men have no knowledge of distances beyond the barrack square, the cricket field or the end of the street, I prefer situations where our moderate-ranged vision can be of more service, such as those of mountain warfare and bush fighting. It is just these two kinds of fighting that General

Buller detests; I know it of old. I want to attack Hlangwane because there our men could get practice and be trained in fighting with the Boer more equally and I know the Boers dislike bush fighting.

"But there was nothing left for me to urge, so at 7.30am we returned to Estcourt and began to settle down in our camp." [3]

Warren's formula for keeping troops active was a sound one – and he acted on it as often as he could.

Most of his men, indeed, did not have any knowledge of what went on beyond the British barrack square, and that often enough meant Aldershot.

The South African veld was a very different battleground. The air was clear and clean, affecting the range of bullet and shell as commander after commander testified at the Commission; the distances were often misread.

Warren was trying to acclimatise his officers and his troops, and in the process saved lives. Practice, he said, often made perfect.

And Buller did not like it. Warren, he said, was wasting time.

Warren had not expected to be in Natal. His instructions were to take over command from General Lord Methuen after the British defeat at Magersfontein.

But Buller had countermanded them. It happened this way:

From Cape Town, Warren wrote, on December 14: "I most strongly urged . . . the necessity for keeping my Division intact and sending it to the relief of Kimberley, as I knew that country so well: and they (the authorities) are sending a telegram to Buller today . . ."

On the same day Landsdowne telegraphed to Cape Town: "On arrival, Warren is to be sent immediately to assume command of the forces under Methuen. Buller will be informed of this by telegraph."

Buller, however, immediately sent to Warren: "With reference to War Office telegram yesterday evening, do not proceed: order is cancelled."

But on December 15 came the battle of Colenso. After it, Buller sent, to London this telegram: " . . . I cannot agree with Commander in Chief and allow Methuen, who has done very well, to be superseded by Warren. Commander in Chief, comfortable at home, has no idea of the difficulties here. It would, I think, be a fatal policy to supersede every General who failed to succeed in every fight, but may I say that, as I myself have since failed, I offer no objection in my own case, if thought desirable . . ." [4]

But the government had had enough. On Monday, December 18, Buller was informed from London that Roberts was coming out as Commander in Chief.

The same day Warren arrived at De Aar junction after a railway journey of some 500 miles. There a Major in the Line of Communication sought him out and produced a telegram ordering him immediately back to Cape Town.

Colonel G.H. Sim, the commander of Warren's engineering force, wrote in his diary: "Our feelings may be imagined! However, there was no alternative and we got into the train again very despondent. No reason or object divulged for our return: perhaps it will transpire someday. Sir Charles is wonderfully cheery about our going back . . . " [5]

In London that night Lansdowne received this telegram from General Sir Frederick Forestier-Walker, who was in charge of the Lines of Communication in Cape Town: "I have to inform you that Warren has been stopped at De Aar junction, and as his Division is to proceed to Natal, he has received orders to return." [6]

And this telegram from Buller: "Warren's Division is, I hear, arriving at the Cape. I have telegraphed them to come on here and have told White to hang on if possible . . . I am frightened by the utter collapse of my infantry on Friday . . . When, however, I get Warren's Division I shall try to relieve Ladysmith by short stages . . ."

Again, later that night, Buller sent: "As to your telegram No 56, the directions which it contained have already been given, but after receiving your No 53, I ordered the Vth Division (less two battalions urgently required at De Aar Junction) to Natal. In my estimation it is the only way by which Ladysmith can be saved." [7]

Warren arrived back in Cape Town on December 20, and immediately went into conference with Sir Alfred Milner, writing in his diary later: "I had a long conversation with Sir A. Milner about my own services. He proposed that I should give up the Vth Division and organise the East District of the Cape Colony. But I said that I could not substitute defence for offence. I think I am in honour bound to go to Natal, and I cannot suggest to Buller that I should remain on this side." [8]

Every available moment of the four days' voyage to Durban in the steamer, *Mohawk*, was spent by Warren and his staff in war games.

The train reached Pietermaritzburg at 7pm on Christmas evening, and Warren went straight to Government House to dine with Hely-Hutchinson. Later, he wrote in his diary: "I was much perturbed by what I heard on all sides. I never met anything like it before anywhere. Usually in war, everyone is so reserved in expressing opinions on military subjects; but today everyone seemed of one mind, that I must go forward to restore confidence.

"It seems to have been their impression that General Buller has been telegraphing or talking about the dispirited condition of the troops, and this has got out and the troops are indignant. This is what came to me from all sources. I received local letters also to the same effect, and I feel that I must go up at once to see General Buller and clear up the situation in my own mind; and I hear too that he wishes to see me . . ."

On Boxing Day, Warren wrote: " . . . No one seemed to realise that our first objective was to beat and demoralise the Boer and to show him that the British soldier was the better man.

"In fact I did not find there was universal confidence that the British soldier was the better man: but I know that myself from experience.

"No one seemed to be the least disturbed by the fact that since Colenso (December 15 – nearly a fortnight) we have kept apart from the enemy and left them to strengthen their defences, whilst we did nothing.

"When I asked if our soldiers have had practice in skirmishing with the Boers, I was told that they have had plenty of exercise in athletic sports and racing at Christmas carnivals – and meantime our troops are shut up in Ladysmith and our soldiers untrained.

"What, I said, is most wanted is constant contact with the Boer; habit makes second nature." [9]

And so after travelling to meet Buller at Frere, Warren found himself back in Estcourt, ready to move wherever Sir Redvers wanted him to go.

Sim and Warren discussed Buller. Both were disturbed by his attitude.

Sim later wrote: "He [Buller] seems quite an altered man: the Colenso fight has told on him, so they say, and he has become very quiet and subdued since." [10]

And Warren wrote: "I was shocked to find how he had taken to his heart the reverse at Colenso. As an old friend I endeavoured to cheer him up and told him he would soon dispose of the Boers." [11]

Years later, when he was compiling his still unpublished account of the Relief of Ladysmith, Warren wrote:

"When I arrived at Durban on the 25th December 1899, Lyttleton [Sir Neville] begged me to come at once and buck up Buller, otherwise the army would go smash. Up to that point Buller was a counsel of despair: he could not see his way to relieve Ladysmith. My business was to tell him that it could be done and that I could do it. He must give up retiring.

"The fact of the matter is that there were two Bullers. The effects of shell-shock are at this day understood, but in those days few people recognised it as a complaint of persons subjected to danger. Years before when directing the excavations at Jerusalem in 1867-70 I had learned its effects on workmen in mines.

"And on arrival in Natal I recognised that General Buller ought to have had a month's rest after Colenso to recover from the triple shock of the failures of the 10th, (Stormberg) 11th (Magersfontein) and 15th December respectively.

"The first General Buller was my old friend, but the second General Buller was full of uncertainty and suspicion. At first I did not know how to meet this second General Buller, but by the 28th January I recognised that he was merely a phantom that required to be resisted, and when that was done, the real old General Buller took his place." [12]

Buller's temperament was to play a major role in what happened next . . .

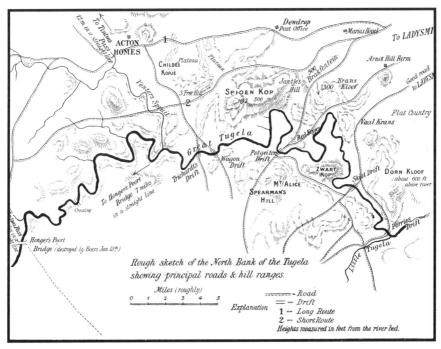

Contemporary map showing the north bank of the Tugela river as it was in January 1899. The crossing points are clearly marked – Trichard's Drift and Potgieter's Drift (misspelt on the map). Warren was ordered at the last minute to cross at Trichard's Drift, under the Spioenkop massif, under the noses of the Boers, while Buller was going to go into action at Potgieter's. He didn't. Buller's headquarters were at Mount Alice, clearly marked on this map. The road in rear of Spioenkop no longer exists, but some portions probably make up the current Natal Parks' Board road to the top.

117

Buller, says Bennet Burleigh had a choice of two routes to turn the Boer lines at Colenso.

"He may go eastwards via Weenen, or westward by Potgieters Drift or Springfield. At the moment the evidence points to his having selected the Springfield route.

"But General Buller has made it a custom rigidly to keep his own counsel in these matters. The double loops made by the Tugela at Potgieter's Drift are not inviting, nor is the gateway through which the troops must pass into the open, flat lands near Acton Homes. But it is said a succession of boldly-defined hills – Swartz Kop, Krantz Kloof and others – command the fords and roads into the plains west of Ladysmith.

"Possibly so, but maps and information supplied here have proved untrustworthy before today.

"The other road, by Weenen, is rougher going, and would bring us in on the east side of Bulwana, or Lombard's Kop.

"Springfield has advantages over that route. Both involve long detours, quitting the railway, and a big supply column, for we cannot start with less than six days' provisions.

"From Frere to Springfield is about 20 to 25 miles, and the distance to Weenen is little, if any less."

Burleigh also laments the non-action at Hlangwane: "More and more's the pity that, during the attack on Colenso, a determined effort was not made to carry Hlangwane, which completely turns the Boer works about Grobler's Hill and the Tugela Valley.

"It is rough country; but being upon this, the south side of the river, it would have served admirably for a safe and excellent artillery position, if not for launching our flanking assault along the shoulders of the ridges held by the Boers.

"Since then, they have done something to strengthen Hlangwane. But at best it is the weak spot in their lines, for with the Tugela in flood, as it is now after the rains, those left to defend Hlangwane would be completely cut off from rejoining their comrades over the river."[13]

Burleigh was not to know it, but on Friday, December 29, Buller visited Warren at Estcourt and discussed the next move – the advance to Potgieter's Drift.

Buller said he wanted to move on January 6, but Warren said it was too early – his artillery would not have arrived by then.

Buller had in fact already sent this telegram to Sir George White in Ladysmith: "*No 131, 30 December, Frere*: My intention is to start from here 6th January, by which time I hope the 5th Division will have arrived. My Point of attack will be Lancer's Kop [five miles south west of Ladysmith]. It will take me about six days to get there from the date I start from here. I will inform you later of my exact date of departure from here, and will endeavour to keep you informed of my movements, but my telegraph line may be cut."

White replied: "*No 38, P, 1st January*. Your Number 131, 30th December received today. If you will trust me with further details of your plan, I hope to be able to assist you in the later stages of your advance on Ladysmith; but to do this effectually I should require to know on which line or lines you intend to force passage of Tugela."

To which Buller sent: " . . . I adhere to the plan . . . of crossing Tugela river at Potgieter's. I expect a stiff fight when crossing the river, possibly a fight at the place I camp, between river and Lancer's Kop, and another fight there. If you can recommend me any better point to attack than Lancer's

Kop, please do so. As troops are not arriving up to time, I doubt if I can start until 8th January. I calculate it will take me seven days to reach Lancer's Kop."

White replied: " . . . As you intend crossing Tugela river at Potgieter's, Lancer's Hill becomes an essential point on your line of advance. If you can keep me informed of your progress, I can help you by attacking Lancer's Hill from the North, when you attack it from the south west. Communication by signalling from the hill above Potgieter's should be easy. Do not hurry on date of starting on our account if recently arrived troops need rest, as I am quite confident of holding my own here."

White was indeed. On January 6, the Boer forces assaulted Platrand and Wagon Hill, finally being driven off.

Anxiously, the British force at Frere waited for news, which came in a telegram early on the 7th, detailing the action and the excellent showing by the troops.

Later the same day, White telegraphed: "Our losses yesterday heavy. Officers killed, 14, wounded, 23. Men killed, about 100; wounded about 230 . . . Most of the troops here much played out, and a very large proportion of my officers have, up to date, been killed or wounded, or are sick."

Buller read the following sentences with consternation: "I would rather not call upon them to move out from Ladysmith to co-operate with you . . . Please do not allow our losses to be published in local papers, as they thus reach and encourage the enemy . . . "

He sent: "Sorry to hear of your severe list of casualties. Congratulate all the men, and say we shall strain every nerve to be with them soon."

To which White later replied: "Your reassuring telegram . . . much appreciated by troops . . . "

Warren raised objections to Buller's scheme to move to Potgieter's Drift because no arrangements had been made for checking Boer artillery fire from the high mountains of Spioen and Doorn Kop nearby on either side of the drift.

Nor were there any plans made by Buller to demonstrate - Warren calls it "demoralise" - the enemy.

Warren wrote: "It seemed to me most hazardous and unbusinesslike, because in that broad valley with high hills on either side we should be a target to the concealed Boers for three-quarters of a circle. I proposed to take Doorn Kop [between Frere and Springfontein, near Potgieter's farm] and Kloof but he objected to these 'alpine excursions'. So our advance was settled to be by Potgieter's Drift and I had to make all preparations for it . . ."

While waiting, Warren again manoeuvred his brigades each and got them partially expert in taking cover.

On 1 January, 1900, Sir Charles Warren wrote: "This was a great day for us, as we received a gracious message from H.M. Queen Victoria which greatly pleased us all. I made the most of the day. During the morning every soldier I met singly I stopped and shook hands with, wishing him a Happy New Year, and every picket and body of men I met on my rounds I made a little speech to . . ."

On January 4, Sir Neville Lyttleton saw Warren to discuss the advance to Potgieter's Drift and the possibilities of forcing the Boer position at - where? - Hlangwane, of course.

Warren, the next day, rode to see Buller and made two proposals: One, to advance via Hlangwane instead of Potgieter's and drive the Boers from the south side of the Tugela east of Colenso so as to give his troops practice and get them accustomed to the Boers; and two, that an order should be published on the subject of unauthorised retirement.

Buller refused to hear of the first, but accepted the second, and issued an order on the matter.

On January 5, 1900, Burleigh writes: "We are grievously perplexed. Three weeks have spun by since the Colenso affair of December 15, and neither Buller nor his staff has given any outward indication of the date of the next advance in force.

"Officers and men are wondering at our prolonged inaction, and they would not be free-born Britons were there not grumblings and rough-tongued remarks in the camps about the unwisdom of a do-nothing policy.

" . . . the vile weather has spoiled spirits . . . Last night it rained, thunder-stormed, and the wind blew icily from the Great Berg. Today the sky and the heat are of the tropics and we perspire in shirt-sleeves, whereas last night we shivered in greatcoats and blankets . . . "[14]

But movement was coming soon. Warren's troops began arriving at Frere on the 9th and on the 10th the army was on the move – to Springfield.

The second push was on . . .

SOURCES

1-12. *The Life of General Sir Charles Warren*, by Watkin Williams.
13-14. *The Natal Campaign*, by Bennet Burleigh.

Spioenkop – Part 1
Mud glorious mud:

An army on the march
The order Sir Charles knew nothing about

"None of us", wrote J.B. Atkins, "had ever seen such a sight. You looked down from any hill and the army was like a rope being drawn slowly across the country as far as you could see.

"Here and there it dropped into a spruit; but it rose again on the other side; here and there it disappeared behind a kopje, but you could pick it up again beyond.

"It seemed endless, this rope made of all the strands that hold an army together – infantry, guns, gunners, ammunition, horsemen, wagons with forage, rations and tents; wagons hung all over like a gypsy van with clattering utensils, Kaffirs plying whips like fishing rods, bakers, cooks, farriers, telegraphists, type-writers, paymasters and paymaster's clerks, post office clerks, telegraph wires and poles, sappers, chaplains, doctors, ambulance wagons, bearers, 'body-snatchers', signallers with flags and heliographs, sailors, naval guns, headquarters staffs, cobblers, balloons, aeronauts, limelight flashlights, traction engines with heavy lists to port or starboard, pontoons . . . " [1]

In total some 324 wagons (each of which made two trips) and 25,000 men stretched out some 15 miles along the 25 miles of road between Frere and heading towards Springfield.

Winston Churchill, back in the saddle after his escape from Pretoria, and now serving as an unpaid Lieutenant in the South African Light Horse as well as a highly paid war correspondent, was there.

He writes: "The vast amount of baggage this army takes with it on the march hampers its movements and utterly precludes all possibility of surprising the enemy. I have never before seen even officers accommodated with tents on service, though both the Indian frontier and the Soudan lie under a hotter sun than South Africa.

"But here today within striking distance of a mobile enemy whom we wish to circumvent, every private soldier has canvas shelter . . . The consequence is that roads are crowded, drifts are blocked, marching troops are delayed and all rapidity of movement is out of the question. Meanwhile the enemy completes the fortification of his positions, and the cost of capturing them rises.

"It is a poor economy to let a soldier live well for three days at the price of killing him on the fourth." [2]

Burleigh, as ever conscious of his deadlines, writes: "For several days before a start was effected, the destination of the army was discussed in a general way.

"How it was expected, with the district swarming with natives, and not a few Dutch farmers around us, that the news would be absolutely withheld from the enemy I failed to see.

"Nevertheless all pressmen were formally notified by Major Jones [the press censor] that no telegrams would be allowed to be sent by anyone during the next two or three days. The troops were going towards Springfield and the object was to keep the fact from the knowledge of the Boers . . . " [3]

J.B. Atkins, on the 9th, was riding back to Frere from Estcourt. Warren's division was marching on the same road.

"It was raining. The sky might have been – indeed it was – a shower-bath. The rain came through the still air in a steady, teeming, straight downpour that threshed in one's ears. I wore an oilskin coat, but it was useless; the rain found assailable chinks or else beat its way through . . .

"The hills seemed to melt down like tallow under heat; the rain beat the earth into liquid and the thick, earthy liquid ran down in terraced cascades . . .

"From Estcourt to Frere the division waded, sliding, sucking, pumping, gurgling through the mud; the horses floundered or tobogganned with all feet together; the wagons lurched axle-deep in into heavy sloughs and had to be dragged out with trebled teams of oxen . . . " [4]

The next day, the rain had ceased, but the floods were out and the army slithered its way towards Potgieter's Drift.

" . . . The passages through the spruits were nightmares – carts over-turned in the water, wheels off, mules mixed up, fighting and knotted in their harness and half drowning oxen, with their heads borne down under water and heaving with all their mighty strength to the opposite bank, a gun or a heavy wagon stuck and the river of traffic looping round it as water flows round an island . . . " [5]

Burleigh writes: "It was a prolonged and desperate scramble to get the men and about 400 wagons and non-descript vehicles down the steep, slippery bank, through the waist-deep stream, and up the sticky oppposite slopes. Three ox-wagons were run down into the river and converted into bridge-piers, planks being laid whereon part of the infantry were able to pass dryshod, but the planks and footing were insecure in places and it became like walking a greasy pole . . . for numbers of Tommies went hurriedly into the water in the most diverse and eccentric manner . . .

"The much laughed-at score of Aldershot traction-engines did not stick nor flounder in the mud, but lumbered about doing duty with comparative ease . . .

"A by no means overladen ox-wagon stuck in the middle of Blaauwkrants Drift, close to Frere Station. Eighty oxen were tried, and were unable to move the wagon an inch.

"It seemed as if the whole column must wait until the vehicle was carted off. A traction engine was requisitioned to try its powers; the enormous span of cattle were taken away, and a steel hawser was passed from the engine and made fast to the disselboom. Then the steam was turned on, and with a snort and whirr the steamer walked away with the wagon, conveying it some distance to a high and dry part of the roadway.

"Hours that day and the next passed by in weariness. The tracks, by profound flattery called roads, were utterly blocked. Hundreds upon hundreds of wagons were jammed together in mile-long lanes . . .

"With desperate hardihood the Tommies braved both mud and flood. Through and beyond they trod, heedless of boots or khaki uniforms. The smart soldier's clothes have lost their shine and neatness, and are now so bedraggled that a rag-picker might hesitate about appropriating them . . . " [6]

And keeping pace with them on the high ground on the Ladysmith Acton

Wagons sucked into a sea of mud on the way from Estcourt to Frere. Hours were spent trying to extract wagons sunk up to their axles. A huge backlog built up, watched by hundreds of troops who were called in to help. Finally the traction engines were called upon and got the line going again. (Picture: Author's collection.)

Homes side of the Tugela were the enemy. Secrecy of any kind was just impossible.

Surgeon Blake-Knox, in his book, *Buller's Campaign, With The Natal Field Force*, was also on his way to Spearman's, and had this to say: "Barbed wire in fences and in long loose coils scattered about in the tall grass bothered us at times; this constant source of annoyance to horses had been thrown about by the enemy in many places. Each mounted party had to be furnished with a pair of wire-clippers to overcome the nuisance."

As it was, the maelstrom was too much for a fretting Dundonald, who requested, and was given permission, to ride on with his Mounted Brigade to Springfield (Winterton), then consisting of only three houses and half a dozen farms.

Taking the bridge, he rode onwards, up the steep incline to Spearman's farm and Mount Alice, with Potgieter's Drift (today's main road between Winterton and Ladysmith) immediately below it.

Swartkop nearby was also taken.

The next morning he noted the ferry itself was moored on the far bank of the then raging Tugela. It wasn't there for long: Volunteers – Major Childe, Lieutenant Carlisle, Sergeant Turner, Corporals Cox and Barkley, and Troopers Howell, Godden and Collingwood – from the South African Light Horse stripped naked and swam across for it, under long-range Boer fire, eventually bringing it to the British side.

Most correspondents, including Burleigh and Churchill, rode ahead to Mount Alice where Buller would place his headquarters for the next move in the Natal chequer board.

Says Burleigh: "I rode to the top of Schwartz Kop and from there saw

Mount Bulwana and part of the position held by our troops around Ladysmith. To the left rose the grand outline of the Drakensberg from Mont-aux-Sources to the far north of Van Reenen's Pass. The peaks were silhouetted against the sky; waterfalls poured from their lofty, precipitous sides, and green foothills led in a series of Titanic stepping stones to their base.

"Away beyond were the dim crests of the Biggarsberg and the Impati Mountain, near which Dundee nestles. Boer tents, wagons and camps were ringed about Ladysmith from near Colenso and Onderbroek, where their main camp lies, and from Bester's Farm (near Ladysmith) bands of the enemy's troops, mounted and afoot, hurried towards the hills upon their side overlooking Potgieter's Drift. Already there were Boers to be seen at work in their shirt-sleeves, digging trenches, piling up stone walls, and constructing small semicicular forts.

" . . . Their objective was unmistakable – to draw line after line of trenches, and to erect forts which would command every inch of ground from the river front up to and beyond the crested ridges four miles north. Besides that, to the west they were crowning lofty Spioenkop with defences and gun positions . . . " [7]

Warren and his staff pitched their camp about three miles from Springfield Bridge.

Buller and his staff, riding on, arrived on January 12, at his camp between Spearman's farm and Mount Alice.

That day, Warren rode to see Buller.

Warren writes: " . . . from the signal station at Mount Alice he showed me the line of advance by Potgieter's. I did not like it. It was exposed to gun fire from three-quarters of a circle, to which we could not effectually reply, and it was exposed to rifle fire from unseen riflemen at 2,000 yards. Could there be a worse line of advance?" [8]

The next day Warren and Buller rode together to see General Talbot Coke's brigade at Springfield.

Says Warren: "The whole brigade had been employed in making splendid schanzes of the most up-to-date kind, a perfect defence.

General Charles Warren points across a donga during a reconnaissance near the Tugela while his officers and staff discuss the move. The picture was taken before Warren's crossing of the Tugela. (Picture: Cape Archives: J1191.)

"For some reason unknown to me, General Buller vigorously censured General Coke for his work, which he called folly. Of course it may be said that the Boers are not likely to attack a camp – but who knows? We have to be prepared for all eventualities, and in any case it is so important that the men should know how to built schanzes." [9]

Hard work was not new to Warren either. On the way to Springfield he had helped manhandle wagons in the mud. "At first I was not recognised, but eventually the men began to know me and look for my help in emergencies, and in three days I was known and welcomed throughout our force. This was an enormous advantage to me, because in starting out on the campaign I thus became well known to the men, though I knew none of them individually." [10]

Buller rode back later and sent this telegram to London: "*Spearman's Camp, 13th January 1900, 1.55pm:* The following is the situation here: – The river looked at from the south forms deep doubles. At the apex of one re-entering bend is Potgieter's Drift. The Boer position lies 6,000 yards off across the two salients, having command of from 200 to 500 feet; the intervening plain is without cover and flat; the enemy's flanks are unassailable; their defences are in two and three lines, the second line being out of sight of the plain with 8 guns.

"This position I do not think we can force. On the 14th we shall be concentrated here with 10 days' supplies which I am unable to increase . . .

"I propose that Warren – taking 36 guns, Field Artillery; 3 Brigades and 1500 mounted men – shall cross five miles to the west at Trichard's Drift; the mountain which forms the right flank of the enemy's defence will be turned by his advance, while we do the best we can here . . .

"He agrees to this, but as he can only take supplies for 3 days, and will have to march not less than 15 miles from the river, and as he will have difficulty in obtaining water, the operation is undoubtably risky. But this is the only possible chance for Ladysmith . . . " [11]

But Warren had not been consulted, and certainly had not agreed to the crossing at Trichard's Drift.

In Buller's evidence before the Commission he reiterated his statement: "The only road by which I could advance north of the river from that [Potgieter's] drift led into a re-entering angle of the enemy's defences. After a careful reconnaissance I discovered a far better crossing by Trichard's Drift, five miles to the westward.

"Having thoroughly discussed my plans with Sir Charles Warren, and ascertained his entire concurrence with them, I reported them to the Secretary of State . . . " [12]

Warren did not concur.

The first Warren knew of the change of plan was when he received, shortly after dawn on Monday January 15, secret instructions from Buller ordering him to command operations to cross the Tugela at Trichardt's Drift. [13]

Buller's evidence was not made public until 1902 and Warren had no idea either until then that he had "agreed" to Buller's change of plan as there was no way he was party to Buller's confidential telegrams to London.

The secret instructions to Warren read:

"1: The enemy's position in front of Potgieter's Drift seems to me to be too strong to be taken by direct attack. [Which is what Warren told him from the Mount Alice summit on the 12th.]

"2: I intend to try and turn it by sending a force across the Tugela from near Trichardt's Drift and up to the west of Spioen.

"3: You will have command of that force which will consist of the 11th Brigade of your Division, your Brigade Division, Royal Field Artillery, and General Clery's Division complete, and all the mounted troops, except 400.

"4: You will of course act as circumstances require, but my idea is that you should continue throughout refusing your right and throwing your left forward until you gain the open plain north of Spioenkop. Once there you will command the rear of the position facing Potgieter's Drift, and I think render it untenable." [14]

There were 13 items in the despatch.

In essence, while Warren crossed at Trichardt's, Buller's forces would cross at Potgieter's. Buller estimated there were some 400 men opposing Warren, and at least 7,000 in front of him.

Nowhere in the orders was it stated that Warren was to "surprise" the enemy.

Warren was to take a pontoon troop as well. "I do not think you will find it possible to let oxen draw the wagons over the pontoons. It will be better to draw them over by horses or mules, swimming the oxen; the risk of breaking the pontoons, if oxen cross them, is too great," he wrote.

It was a matter of later contention.

On January 14, Buller telegraphed to White: "*No 156 . . .* I find the enemy's position covering Potgieter's Drift so strong that I shall have to turn it, and I expect it will be four or five days from now before I shall be able to advance towards Ladysmith. I shall keep you constantly informed of my progress." [15]

Nothing about Trichardt's Drift.

White replied: "I can wait. Wish you best of luck."

And followed it up with this telegram: "*No 48. P. 16th January* . . . If you have considerable doubt of being able to get through to Ladysmith, would you put case to Roberts, and ask more troops. If you are repulsed now, Ladysmith will be in a bad way. If you are undefeated and ready to attack on any withdrawal of enemy's strength from your front, I could maintain this place till 15th February; but the sick would suffer badly . . . "[16]

When Warren got the secret instructions, he immediately set out to look for Trichardt's Drift.

Writes Warren: "I heard subsequently that this drift had already been reconnoitred on the 13th January for General Buller by Major Gough, Mounted Troops, and that General Buller had already on that day proposed to the Secretary of State that I should cross the river in command of a large force, and that I had agreed to this, and that the operation was undoubtedly risky.

"Of this at the time I was not informed. Until I was to to reconnoitre this drift on the 15th I fully supposed that my Division was to advance by Potgieter's, but I could see that General Buller was not now keen upon the subject . . .

"There were positions (at Trichardt's) where a bridge could be placed screened from the view of the distant hills . . . In this respect secrecy and surprise were important; but the surprise consisted in our getting to the spot unbeknown to the enemy; after that it must be a question of whether the enemy could get their long range guns and ammunition ready in time to oppose us.

"The time we should take to cross with 15 miles of wagons was well known beforehand. It was a mere matter of calculation, varying according to the dexterity of the persons employed. If done by Colonial experts we may put down two and a half to three and a half days for the crossing; if

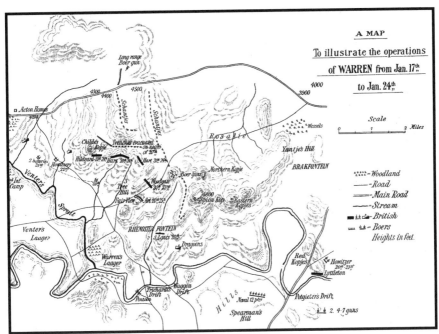

Contemporary map showing details of Warren's operations on the Tugela from January 17 to January 24. Fairview and Rosalie are clearly marked, as are the positions of the Boer long-range guns, one on Spioenkop.

done by European methods it might take a week. I selected the different paths leading down to the drift by which the wagons, pontoons and infantry would pass, and arranged so that they would not interfere with each other . . .

"When I returned to Springfield I reported to General Buller that it appeared to me that the crossing could be made, but if we crossed at Trichard's Drift we ought to take Spioenkop at once, and that if we had to take Bastion Hill (as he had told me) we ought to cross the river three miles further up, opposite to the Bastion as I objected to crossing the river with our 15 miles of wagons and then making a flanking march of 3 miles, parallel to and within a mile of the enemy's line of trenches: it seemed to be to be courting destruction . . .

"In any case I considered that I ought to have long range guns with me to oppose them [Boer long-range guns which Buller's intelligence had placed on Spioenkop]. I was so much impressed with the importance of the matter that I made a strong point of it to General Buller." [17]

Buller, however, waved aside Warren's objections.

At Spearman's Buller issued a proclamation in Army Orders to be read to the men on parade. The troops were warned not to allow themselves to be deceived by the enemy by means of the white flag trick. Should a white flag be displayed, it was to mean nothing, unless the force displaying it threw down their arms and held up their hands at the same time.

The troops were also to guard against being misled by false words of commands or false bugle-sounds, such as the enemy had been using earlier on in the campaign.

Men were not to be surprised by a sudden volley at close quarters: should such occur, there was to be no hesitation; they were not to turn from it, but to rush at it. [18]

Warren's operations were to begin at dawn on Wednesday January 17th.

It was a tough scramble, though. Warren had already issued maps of the Potgieter's Drift area. Now he had to make do with hurried pencil sketches of Trichardt's Drift.

Sir Charles Warren's force was in fact a flying column consisting of 1,500 mounted troops, 12,000 infantry and 36 field guns, carrying with it three and a half days' provisions (Buller's orders mentioned three days' provisions).

The wagons, guns and wheeled vehicles of this force (leaving all tents, camp equipage and stores behind) formed a massive column 15 miles in length, as he had calculated. [19]

There were 600 vehicles in all, of which 322 were ox-wagons; it would take 13 hours for this procession to pass any point on a level road, without any check in front.

The ox teams were a scratch lot which had recently come from the farms; the drivers were new and none of the teams had ever been over pontoon bridges before.

In his *Times History of the War*, Leo Amery says: "Apart from the actual execution of the plan, there was one thing accompanying its inception which went far to make success difficult and to invite failure. That was the extraordinary redistribution of the force, with its splitting up of command and its practical elimination of the commander-in-chief of the army and his whole directing staff . . . On the one side, Buller, with the entire staff of the original South African Field Force, was to sit apart, inactive, and wait events.

"On the other, Warren, with the ordinary staff of an infantry division was to attempt to carry on command of a large mixed force of all arms, including among its units a complete infantry division, with divisional general and staff, to look after a large convoy and superintend the crossing of a considerable river, and, not least, to plan and execute a series of important tactical operations over badly-mapped and unreconnoitred country."

A footnote to the above says: "Warren did apply to Buller for an increase of staff, a suggestion to which the latter only replied that he had got on quite well himself before his staff arrived, eventually, however, allowing Warren to take any regimental officers whom their commanding officers were ready to spare, with the result that none were to be procured." [20]

But Warren had been given a job to do, and he was going to do it.

On the evening of January 16, he was ready to march from Springfield Bridge to Trichardt's Drift.

"Our times were governed a good deal by our oxen which refused to alter their habits for the war! Critics on military subjects may lay down rules and say what they like, but when one has to deal with oxen, one's programme must be adjusted to meet their wants. They have no enthusiasm or patriotism to buck them up, and require their eight hours' browsing every day on the veld, so that travelling must be done at specific hours . . . Before sunset General Buller and Staff came to see us off . . . I sent an order out that there was to be no talking, smoking or lights amongst the kaffirs with the wagons and they behaved very well . . ." [21]

Surgeon Blake-Knox, following the movements with alacrity, and keeping a daily diary, tells how the troops moved from Springfield to what he thought would be Spearman's. But top secret orders arrived . . . where would they land up?

"On January 16th several important movements of troops took place; but before I attempt to describe them I must first remind the reader that our camp at Springfield was in full view of the Boer pickets on the surrounding high hills, and every move in camp could be seen by the enemy.

"Later orders were . . . the camp was to be left standing in full view of Boer outposts on Spioenkop. The main body at Springfield received sudden orders to parade at 5.45pm, and be prepared for a night march, all tents to be left in position; we were also told not to take heavy kits as we would probably be back the next day. The men left their greatcoats behind . . .

"A company of men from each regiment setting out was to stay behind to protect the camp. These were to bustle about in the morning and show themselves plainly to the enemy on the hills.

"A few buglers were left behind to blow bugle calls at the usual hours; others were to light fires; in fact those remaining were to show as much activity as possible. The result aimed at was to deceive Brother Boer in the morning as he looked from the hills and make him think the army was still occupying the camp, which in reality the main body had quitted under cover of darkness . . .

"It was dark, when we eventually marched off, and the route followed was so planned to keep the men in the shadows of the hills. After going for about seven miles, fresh orders were issued and instead of marching for Spearman's Hill as we originally expected, we moved off in a totally different direction.

"As we proceeded the column was joined by troops from different centres. The night was a glorious one for a [night] march. A full moon peeped out occasionally through heavy clouds, the atmosphere was fresh and dry, the light just sufficient to show up obstacles, the distant eminences clouded and silent, yet now and then one would ride into a barbed wire fence or stumble over an anthill.

". . . The column halted. A whispered conversation took place between the leaders; dark, mounted figures, silhouetted against the silvery clouds, galloped up and down the ranks, whispering orders to the officers.

"Strict silence was to be maintained, as the enemy were near. All pipes were to be extinguished; no matches were to be lit or lights shown. The Kaffir drivers were not to crack whips nor yell at their teams; no talking was to be allowed.

"In passing frowning hills and rugged valleys one now waited in watchful expectancy of a dose of Mauser hail; one imagined posts as men, bushes as guns; a click of a wheel seemed the cocking of a rifle, the thud of a hoof the booming of a gun.

"The main body came to a halt before dawn; behind and sheltered by a ridge of grassy, rocky hills, on which the artillery mounted their guns in the dark, and we were told to let the men eat their breakfasts.

"Our buglarboy, a lad of thirteen, fresh from Aldershot, hearing the order, started blowing the well-known 'Cook-house' call, as was his wont each morning on receipt of such an order.

"Fortunately he was stopped just in time, or the result might have been disastrous to the secrecy of the march . . .

"At dawn the infantry advanced in long lines across the kopjes and the white canvas hoods were ordered to be removed from the ambulance wagons, as they were deemed too conspicuous . . .

"We were heading for Trichard's farm."

Knox describes how a party of Boers were surprised, and fled across the Tugela and up over the hills. The Tugela crossing at Trichardt's was theirs.

". . . We now descended to the farm at Trichardt's Drift, which is worthy of description. It was built in the Colonial style – one-storyed, airy house, with spacious verandas and numerous corrugated-zinc-roofed outbuildings surrounded by well-tilled gardens and shaded by line and apricot trees.

"There was also an artificial pond, from which a small stream trickled to join the great Tugela, only some eighty yards away.

"When I arrived at the farm I learnt from some Kaffir hands that the owners had left on commando . . . but the farm was put under guard, as is usual, to avoid giving the owners any ground for afterwards stating that pilfering by our troops had taken place in their absence. The interior was well furnished – a walnut piano on which an officer was playing a popular air, numerous mahogany chairs and tables, all pointing to recent occupation by a well-to-do family." [22]

At dawn on Wednesday, January 17, Warren began to throw his pontoon bridge across the Tugela, while punts took the infantry across, first Woodgate's Brigade and then Hart's.

Warren was worried that if Buller's intelligence was correct and there were long-range guns on Spioenkop, he was in a death-trap, should they open up.

On the evening of the 17th the crossing of the 15 miles of wagons began. The banks on either side of the pontoons were steep and rugged and it was found necessary to outspan the oxen. The crossing went on throughout that night and the following day; Warren had one hour's sleep in 60 but he completed the actual crossing of his. 600 vehicles of which 322 were ox wagons (which experts said should take two and a half to three and a half days) in exactly 37 hours.

Warren writes: "I had now to get our wagons to a place of safety at Venter's Spruit (three miles to the west of Trichard's Drift) and to take the two Brigades by a flank march along the side of the hills to the neighbourhood of Bastion Hill, which I had been ordered to attack.

"This fitted in with my estimate of time. I wanted three days for the troops to practise their dress rehearsals. The 17th and 18th January were to be employed in accustoming the men to the presence of the Boer and to meeting him face to face . . . " [23]

It must here again be recalled that Warren's troops were green. They were used to the barracks of Aldershot and the Salisbury Plain, not the rolling veld of South Africa.

Warren explains: "All my life long I have watched events – and their results – and have become more and more certain that to do anything well you must have practice and rehearsals. We allow this for cricket and football and golf and theatricals, but no one now seems to realise that fighting the Boer was an operation which required practice and rehearsals, just as in the case of games.

"The men were trained to meet European troops, but meeting the Boers with their good weapons of precision and their powers of shooting and taking cover was a new experience to which our troops must get accustomed, while the advent of smokeless powder added to the intricacy of the operations . . .

"The troops I was taking into action were quite unfitted for immediately fighting the Boer. They had been kept entirely apart from him, till he had become rather a bogey. They had not seen him yet, dead or alive . . . It was my mission to introduce Mr Thomas Atkins to Mr Boer, face to face . . .

"I wanted three days for what I called Blooding the troops. I would no more think of taking troops, in the condition of our men as handed over to me, to assault a position, than I would take a team of cricketers, who had no experience of football, to compete in a football match; yet, after three days' contact with the Boer they were ready for action.

"The proof of the efficiency of my methods lies in the fact that subsequently General Buller told the men that the days at Spioenkop had given him the key to Ladysmith . . ."

And so Warren began the most controversial action of the Boer War . . .

Also ready for action was Surgeon Frederick Treves who had also been on the march with the men of his No 4 Field Hospital, and for the first – but not the last – time transportation was not by train, but by wagon.

"The hospital was equipped to accommodate a minimum of 300 beds and was made up of 60 tents and 10 marquees. The rank and file of the R.A.M.C. numbered 88 non-Commissioned officers and men; the staff was represented by three army surgeons, nine civil surgeons, the two army sisters who had worked at Colenso, and my remaining nurse, Miss McCaul. The other Nurse, Miss Tarr, who came out with me, was at Maritzburg, desperately ill with dysentery. She nearly lost her life and was scarcely convalescent when the time came to return to England."

Long after the soldiers had crested the left hand side of Mount Alice, and tramped down to their valley camp, the Treves caravan pulled into Spearman's Farm.

Says Treves: "At the back of the farm, and at the foot of a green kopje, was a quaint burial ground – little because it held but two graves, and quaint because these were surmounted by unexpected stone memorials, of a type to be associated with a suburban English cemetery. These monuments were fitly carved, and were distinctly the product of no mean town, and they were to the memory respectively of George Spearman and of Susan Spearman.

"For some undefinable reason these finished memorials, so formal and so hackneyed in their design, appeared inapporpriate and even unworthy of the dignity of the lonely graves at the foot of the kopje.

"Some more rugged emblem, free from artificiality and from any suggestion of the crowded haunts of men, would have covered more fittingly the last resting-place of these two pioneers. A few trees, almost the only trees within sight, shaded the little graveyard, and the trees and the monuments were enclosed by a very solid iron railing." [24]

It was in the shadow of this oasis that some of the dead from Spioen were to be buried.

SOURCES

1. *The Relief of Ladysmith*, by J.B. Atkins.
2. *London to Ladysmith*, by Winston Churchill.
3. *The Natal Campaign*, by Bennet Burleigh.
4. *The Relief of Ladysmith*, by J.B. Atkins.
5. Ibid.
6. *The Natal Campaign*, by Bennet Burleigh.
7. Ibid.
8. *The Life of General Sir Charles Warren*, by Watkin Williams.
9. Ibid.
10. Ibid.
11. *Commission on the War in South Africa:* Buller's Evidence.
12. Ibid.

13. *Commission on the War in South Africa:* Warren's Appendix 1.
14. *Commission on the War in South Africa:* Buller's Evidence.
15. *Commission on the War in South Africa:* Telegrams.
16. Ibid.
17. *The Life of General Sir Charles Warren,* by Watkin Williams.
18. *Buller's Campaign, with the Natal Field Force,* by E. Blake-Knox.
19. *The Life of General Sir Charles Warren,* by Watkin Williams.
20. *The Times History of the War,* edited by Leo Amery.
21. *The Life of General Sir Charles Warren,* by Watkin Williams.
22. *Buller's Campaign, with the Natal Field Force,* by E. Blake-Knox.
23. *The Life of General Sir Charles Warren,* by Watkin Williams.
24. *The Tale of a Field Hospital,* by Frederick Treves.

CHAPTER FIFTEEN

Spioenkop – Part 2

Just blame it on Sir Charles

"From General Sir R. Buller to General Sir G. White: *No 159 of 17th January* . . . I crossed one bridge at Potgieter's today, and am bombarding their positions. Warren, with three brigades and six batteries has crossed by pontoon bridge at Trichard's Drift, and will move to the north to try and outflank Boer positions. I somehow think we are going to be successful this time. We could not get reinforced in time to relieve you if we waited. Every man in this force is doing his level best to relieve you. It is quite pleasant to see how keen the men are. I hope to be knocking at Lancer's Hill in six days from now." [1]

It was a forlorn hope.

Safe atop Mount Alice, Buller sat back. It was Warren's show.

Or was it?

Warren always maintained that there were "two" Bullers – the benign, friendly Buller he had known well from their years of acquaintance, and the vindictive, morose Buller others, apart from Warren, had noticed.

The first failure – Colenso – had been indisputably Buller's, but at Spioenkop he was, by his own choice, not in command. He had handed over affairs to the man who had been, on account of his high reputation for conducting South African warfare, specially sent out from England to assist (and possibly supersede him even though Roberts was now in overall command) – so he, Buller, could not logically blame himself if anything went wrong. [2]

And it did.

But Warren had been specially chosen for his intimate knowledge, not of Natal, but of Griqualand West where he had surveyed for Her Majesty's Government in the 1870s. He knew the Free State almost as well.

Natal was another story.

Surgeon Blake-Knox, whose personal task – apart from treating the sick and wounded – was to keep a meticulous daily diary, described some of the events leading up to the Spioenkop battle, beginning with the action around its prelude, Bastion Hill.

Blake-Knox was an astute observer: "The enemy's guns had begun to shell Bastion Hill," he wrote. "The first few shells went over its summit, and skimmed into the valley below without doing any harm; the next a percussion shell, burst on the summit; the gunners had now found their range.

"This was soon followed by a time shrapnel, which exploded accurately just behind the British position on the crest. It was a searcher.

"The Boer gunner could not possibly see anyone here from his own post; he merely used his best judgement and fired on chance, but he succeeded. Major Childe, of the SA Light Horse, who led the party which took the hill earlier in the day, was sitting partly sheltered by the rocks, on this dangerous ground, and was instantly killed by a fragment which entered his brain. Half a dozen troopers who were close to him were seriously wounded.

"Major Childe's curious presentiment of impending death may be added to many other well-atttested examples. It is recorded that he discussed it with his brother officers on the night before, requesting as a word-play upon his own name that the inscription, 'It is well with the child? It is well' – 2 Kings iv. 26 – should be placed over his grave. This was done. [Childe is buried at what is today known as the Rangeworthy cemetery].

" . . . Very soon [on Tabanyama] I noticed . . . specks, solitary ones and slightly larger, moving out. My glasses showed these to be stretcher bearers . . . they went forward, solidly and unflinchingly, to the very firing line, and could be seen bending over the fallen, tending and removing the wounded with a devotion so faithful and a coolness so superb, amidst a hail of bullets and shells, that unfortunately many paid dearly for their self-sacrifice.

"The Boers fired on them without the least hesitation; either they could not or would not see the Red Cross brassard worn on their left arm. From experience gathered later on at Spioenkop . . . I have come to the conclusion that the Red Cross, which is a small one, fitting into a circle of an inch and half in diameter, could not be seen by the enemy at the range within which these men were shot down, and it may have been difficult to recognise a khaki-coloured stretcher . . .

"But Warren, refusing his right – he had no other course because of the hills – became, as he had earlier told Buller, boxed in by the range. There was no way through.

Spioenkop – also as we had earlier suggested to Buller – was next.

Blake Knox continues: "On the morning of January 23, General Warren

The deceptive top of Spioenkop, looking from Twin Peaks. This is the route the Boers rushed up when they heard the news the Tommies were coming. On the day of the battle, however, the summit was closed in with cloud. Only when it dispersed did the British troops realise they had not in fact reached the top, and the commandos were able to pick them off. (Picture: Author's collection.)

together with some of his staff went out early to reconnoitre Spioenkop. Two ways were seen to lead to the summit, one on its southwest face and one on its south eastern from the direction of Trichard's drift. The former was visible to the enemy, the latter not being exposed either to the view or fire of the Boers, appeared to the General the more suitable.

"At midday General Woodgate sent for Colonel W.H. Bloomfield who commanded the Lancashire Fusiliers, and told him that Spioenkop was to be taken that night, and, as he 'must have tried troops' for such a hazardous operation he had determined that the Lancashire Fusiliers should lead the way.

"At 3.40pm the following orders were issued by the Brigade Major of the Eleventh Brigade:

"1: The G.O.C. has decided to seize Spioenkop this night.

"2: The following troops will compose the forces: Royal Lancaster Regiment 96 companies, 2nd Lancashire Fusiliers; T.M.I. (Thorneycroft's Mounted Infantry), 180 men; half company of 37th company R.E.

"3: The above troops will rendezvous at White's Farm about half a mile north east of pontoon bridge at 7pm.

"4: Extra ammunition will be carried on the mules supplied by the 10th Brigade.

"5: One day's complete rations will be carried. Wagons with supplies of greatcoats will be brought up as soon as possible without exposure; also water carts and machine guns.

"6: The South Lancashire Regiment will hand over six mules three to each battalion for water carrying purposes.

"7: Pack mules will be utilized for carrying water in waterproof sheets.

"8: Twenty picks and twenty shovels to be carried in regulation stretchers.

"9: Password, *Waterloo.*

"But [says Blake-Knox] Order 7 was found impracticable, waterproof sheets being useless as waterbags; accordingly biscuit-tins were tried as improvised tanks. They were not a success as, owing to the steep nature of the hill, the tins were tilted to all sorts of angles . . .

"General Warren's original plan was that the attack should take place from the south eastern slopes. But as late as 7pm that evening General Woodgate announced that he had decided to attack Spioenkop from its other side – that is from the south western aspect. Colonel Thorneycroft immediately on hearing of this change of plan, rode on ahead, made a sketch, and took bearings as full as the very brief African twilight allowed, of the landmarks and the best route by which to ascend the hill.

" . . . The rendezvous was a long rocky ravine at the north of White's Farm . . . here the column was joined by some additional troops, two companies of the South Lancashire Regiment having been detailed as reinforcements . . .

"The men were warned not to talk, no pipes were to be lit, nor were any kinds of lights permitted . . .

"There was some discussion as to who should lead the column and finally Colonel Thorneycroft, who appears to have been one of a few, if not the only one present, who had seen both the eastern and western sides of this unknown mountain, was selected for the very difficult and responsible position of taking this force of 1,600 men up an unknown mountain in the dark, along an ill-marked sheep path . . .

"It was drizzling too. Occasionally Thorneycroft would stop and go on with a chosen band (Lieutenants Farquhar and Gordon Forbes and Privates Shaw and Macadam) for 100 or 200 yards to feel the way, and then come back and lead the column forward . . .

"Never were orders of a night attack better obeyed; yet the noise of the men's nailed boots on the rocks must have awakened any Boer, had the wind not been in our favour. Slowly but surely they clambered up. Nothing was now visible save the glowing embers of the fires in the British camp in the valley and the 'dash-dot' twinkle from a signaller's lamp on Three Tree Hill saying that all was well below.

"In many places the men had to go on all fours. As they neared the top, the Lancashire Fusiliers were now in four successive lines . . . with 100 yards or so between each. Several more halts were necessary owing to the mist . . ." [3]

As the men neared the top, they were challenged by a Boer picquet. One man was bayonetted to death, the others fled – to warn of the impending attack.

Within an hour, the battle had begun . . . and when it was over, Warren was damned . . .

Spioenkop is a catalogue of errors, and I have treated them in chronological order, firstly with Roberts and Buller's damning despatches, and the answer to them by Sir Charles.

But one important factor must be noted straight away. At no time – even after the *Spioenkop Despatches* were published in the Easter Parliamentary recess of 1900 – until the Commission, was Sir Charles allowed by Roberts to speak out publicly in his own defence.

Warren wrote four letters, one to Lord Roberts and three to the War Office, in which he replied in detail to the allegation made in the despatches against his conduct in the campaign, and requested that his statements might receive the same publicity as had been given to the original despatches.

These letters were never published, and Warren was strictly prohibited by Lord Roberts from taking any action in publishing them on his own account.

Of Buller's three despatches of January 30, Warren did not see the first two until after he had left Natal in April, and was entirely unaware of the existence of the third until its publication, with the full S*pioenkop Despatches*, in 1902.

An upset Warren wrote later: "He [Buller] used to come over to lunch with me, or I lunched with him, and on these occasions, both to myself and also to my staff, from the character of our conversation he appeared to be most friendly towards me.

"The impression as to our friendship was so widely spread that officers of all ranks outside my Division used to come to me to bring matters to Sir R. Buller's notice, on the assumption that I was the only officer in the force he would allow to speak out to him; and I was fully under the impression that, rough as his tongue was, he would in his Despatches do me the justice of ascribing the successful relief of Ladysmith in a great measure to my exertions.

"When I left Natal we parted on excellent terms, he assuring me that he had spoken well of me. I had received hints that he was against me, but I did not believe them." [4]

Just how against him Buller was is reflected in the following reports taken from official despatches and the Commission.

"From Field Marshal Lord Roberts to the Secretary of State for War.

"Army Headquarters, South Africa, Camp, Dekiel Drift, Riet River, 13, February 1900.

"My Lord – I have the honour to submit, for your Lordship's information, Despatches from General Sir Redvers Buller, describing the advance across the Tugela River on the 17th and 18th January, 1900, and the capture and evacuation of the Spioenkop position on the 23rd and 24th January, as well as certain minor operations between the 19th and 24th January on the right or eastern line of advance.

"2: The plan of operations is not very clearly described in the Despatches themselves, but it may be gathered from them and the accompanying documents themselves that the original intention was to cross the Tugela at or near Trichard's Drift, and thence by following the road past Fair View (a farm) and Acton Homes (a village) to gain the open plain north of Spioenkop, the Boer position in front of Potgieters Drift being too strong to be taken by direct attack.

"The whole force, less one brigade, was placed under orders of Sir Charles Warren, who, the day after he had crossed the Tugela, seems to have consulted his General and principal staff officers, and to have come to the conclusion that the flanking movement which Sir Redvers Buller had mentioned in his secret instructions was impracticable on account of the insufficiency of supplies.

"He accordingly decided to advance by the more direct road leading north-east and branching off from a point east of Three Tree Hill.

"The selection of this road necessitated the capture and retention of Spioenkop, but whether it would have been equally necessary to occupy Spioenkop, had the line of advance indicated by Sir Redvers Buller been followed, is not stated in the correspondence.

"As Sir Charles Warren considered it impossible to make the wide flanking movement which was recommended, if not actually prescribed, in his secret instructions, he should have at once acquainted Sir Redvers Buller with the course of action which he proposed to adopt.

"There is nothing to show whether he did so or not, but it seems only fair to Sir Charles Warren to point out that Sir Redvers Buller appears throughout to have been aware of what was happening.

"On several occasions he was present during the operations. He repeatedly gave advice to his subordinate commander, and on the day after the withdrawal from Spioenkop he resumed chief command."

The *Spioenkop Despatches*, as they were known, were published in the *London Gazette* of April 17, 1900, three months after the battle of Spioenkop, and provoked a fury of debate in the House of Commons and the House of Lords. (I have reflected these debates further on.)

Five pages out of 45 printed pages were released for public consumption.

What was not published was Buller's report of 30 January, marked specifically "Not necessarily for publication".

Also not published, but by directive of the Government, were secret despatches Buller had sent to Roberts on Warren. Until 1902, Warren had absolutely no idea these despatches existed.

The publication of the *Spioenkop Despatches* in the parliamentary Easter recess of 1900 took the world by surprise – so much so, indeed, that a story was current that it was due to a mistake on the part of a War Office clerk.

In short, it came as a shock. The largely patriotic British public suddenly found out that their trusted Generals – Buller and Warren – did not get on, and had been castigated by Roberts, the Commander-in-Chief of forces in South Africa.

More than that, the officers were still serving in the field!

The political mistake in publishing the despatches was speedily demonstrated by the debates that took place when Parliament reassembled, a mistake compounded by the non-publication of ALL – not just some – of the secret despatches. While this would have made little difference to those censured, it would have enabled the public to understand the Spioenkop operation, which could not be understood from the incomplete documents, and would have prevented Warren from living under the shadow of unjust accusations.

What was worse, when the full despatches were published in 1902, it was discovered that Buller had broken with army tradition. He had not shown Warren what he had secretly sent to Roberts.

Regulations stipulated that if a subordinate was to be criticised, he was to be given a chance to repudiate whatever accusations had been made against him.

Warren was never given this chance.

Buller's secret despatch to Roberts of January 30 marked "Not necessarily for publication" would have remained that way. Instead it was published with the rest.

Until that time, Buller could have rested assured that what was marked as not to be published would not have seen the light of day.

But Buller was not the only General to include secret despatches on Spioenkop. Roberts's next paragraph was also not included in the abbreviated 1900 publication, by order of the Government.

It reads:

"3: In his note on Sir Charles Warren's report, accompanying despatch of 30th January 1900, Sir Redvers Buller expresses a very adverse opinion on the manner in which Sir Charles Warren carried out the instructions he had received.

"Without knowledge of the country and the circumstances, it is difficult to say whether the delay, misdirection, and want of control, of which Sir Redvers Buller complains, were altogether unavoidable; but in any case, if he considered that his orders were not being properly given effect to, it appears to me that it was his duty to intervene as soon as he had reason to believe the success of the operations was being endangered. This indeed is admitted by Sir Redvers Buller himself, whose explanation of his non-interference can hardly be accepted as adequate.

"A most important enterprise was being attempted, and no personal considerations should have deterred the officer in chief command from insisting on its being conducted in the manner which, in his opinion, would lead to the attainment of the object in view, with the least possible loss on our side."

But the following was published in 1900:

"As regards the withdrawal of the troops from the Spioenkop position, which though occupied almost without opposition in the early morning of the 24th January, had to be held throughout the day under an extremely heavy fire, and the retention of which had become essential to the relief of Ladysmith, I regret that I am unable to concur with Sir Redvers Buller in thinking that Lieutant Colonel Thorneycroft exercised a wise discretion in ordering the troops to retire. Even admitting that due preparations may not have been made for strengthening the position during the night, reorganising the defence, and bringing up artillery – in regard to which Sir Charles Warren's report does not altogether bear out Sir Redvers Buller's contention – admitting also that the senior officers on the summit of the hill might have been more promptly informed of the measures taken by Sir Charles Warren to support and reinforce them, I am of the opinion that Lieut. Colonel Thorneycroft's assumption of responsibility and authority was wholly inexcusable.

"During the night, the enemy's fire, if it did not cease altogether, could not have been formidable, and, though lamp signalling was not possible at the time, owing to the supply of oil having failed, it would not have taken more than two or three hours at most for Lieutenant Colonel Thorneycroft to communicate by messenger with Major General Coke or Sir Charles Warren, and to receive a reply.

"Major General Coke seems to have left Spioenkop at 9.30pm for the purpose of consulting with Sir Charles Warren and up to that hour the idea of a withdrawal had not been entertained.

"Yet almost immediately after Major General Coke's departure Lieut. Colonel Thorneycroft issued an order, without reference to superior authority, which upset the whole plan of operations, and rendered unavailing the sacrifices which had already been made to carry it into effect.

"On the other hand, it is only right to state that Lieut. Colonel Thorneycroft appears to have behaved in a very gallant manner throughout the day, and it was doubtless due, in a great measure, to his exertions and example that troops continued to hold the summit of the hill until directed to retire.

"5: The conduct of Captain Phillips, Brigade-Major of the 10th Brigade, on the occasion in question, is deserving of commendation. He did his best to rectify the mistake [of the British troops withdrawing] which was being made, but it was too late. Signalling communication was not re-established until 2.30am on the 25th January, and by that time the naval guns could not have reached the summit of the hill before daybreak. Major-General Coke did not return and Lieut. Colonel Thorneycroft had gone away. Moreover most of the troops had begun to leave the hill, and the working parties with the half-company of Royal Engineers, had also withdrawn.

"6: It is to be regretted that Sir Charles Warren did not himself visit Spioenkop during the afternoon or evening, knowing as he did that the state of affairs there was very critical, and that the loss of the position would involve the failure of the operations. He was consequently obliged to summon Major-General Coke to his headquarters in the evening in order that he might ascertain how matters were going on, and the command on Spioenkop thus devolved on Lieut. Colonel Thorneycroft; but Major General Coke was not aware of this.

"About midday, under instructions from Sir Redvers Buller, Sir Charles Warren had directed Lieut. Colonel Thorneycroft to assume command on the summit of the hill, with the temporary rank of Brigadier-General, but this order was not communicated to Major-General Coke who, until he left the position at 9.30pm, was under the impression that the command had devolved on Colonel Hill as senior officer after Colonel Crofton had been wounded. Omissions or mistakes of this nature may be trivial in themselves, yet may exercise an important influence on the course of events; and I think that Sir Redvers Buller is justified in remarking that there was Want of organisation and system which acted most unfavourably on the defence.

"7: The attempt to relieve Ladysmith, described in these Despatches, was well devised, and I agree with Sir Redvers Buller in thinking that it ought to have succeeded. That it failed, may in some measure, be due to the difficulties of the ground and the commanding positions held by the enemy – probably also to errors of judgement and want of administrative capacity on the part of Sir Charles Warren.

"But whatever faults Sir Charles Warren may have committed, the failure must also be ascribed to the disinclination of the officer in supreme command [Buller] to assert his authority and see that what he thought best was done, and also the unwarranted and needless assumption of responsibility by a subordinate offcer.

"8: The gratifying feature in these Despatches is the admirable behaviour of the troops throught the operations . . ." – Roberts.

And Buller? Sir Redvers Buller's Memorandum "Not Necessarily for publication", Spearman's Camp, 30th January 1900 reads:

"Secretary of State for War – In forwarding this report, I am constrained to make the following remarks, not necessarily for publication.

"I had fully discussed my orders with General Warren before he started, and he appeared entirely to agree that the policy indicated of refusing the right and advancing the left was the right one. He never, though, attemped to carry it out. From the first there could be no question but that the only practicable road for his column was the one by Fair View. The problem was to get rid of the enemy who were holding it.

"The arrival of the force at Trichard's was a surprise to the enemy, who were not in strength. Sir C. Warren, instead of feeling for the enemy, elected to spend two whole days in passing his baggage. During this time the enemy received reinforcements and strengthened his position. On the 19th he attacked and gained considerable advantage. On the 20th, instead of pursuing it, he divided his force, and gave General Cleary a separate command.

"On the 21st I find that his right was in advance of his left, and that the whole of his batteries, six, were crowded on one small position on his right, while his left was unprotected by artillery, and I had to come out to tell him that the enemy on that flank had received a reinforcement of at least 2,500. I suggested a better distribution of his batteries, which he agreed to, to some extent, but he would not advance his left, and I found that he had divided his fighting line into three independent commands, independent of each other and apparently independent of him, as he told me he could not move any batteries without General Clery's consent.

"The days went on. I saw no attempt on the part of General Warren either to grapple with the situation or to command his force himself. By the 23rd I calculated that the enemy, who were about 600 strong on the 16th [earlier, Buller had said 700 strong] were not less than 15,000, and General White confirmed this estimate. We had really lost our chance by Sir C. Warren's slowness. He seems to me a man who can do well what he can do himself, but who cannot command, as he can use neither his Staff nor subordinates.

"I can never employ him again on an independent command. [Remember those words!]

"On the 19th I ought to have assumed command myself; I saw things were not going well – indeed, everyone saw that. I blame myself now for not having done so. I did not, because I thought that if I did I should discredit General Warren in the estimation of the troops; and that if I were shot, and he had to withdraw across the Tugela, and they had lost confidence in him, the consequences might be very serious.

"I must leave it to higher authority whether this argument was a sound one. Anyhow I felt convinced that we had a good chance on the 17th and that we lost it – Redvers Buller, General."

That was the report Warren never saw, nor knew had even been penned, until 1902.

Buller's official report was datelined Spearman's Hill, 30th January 1900. It was addressed to the Secretary of State for War, and was among the published *Spioenkop Despatches*.

It reads: "Sir C. Warren is hardly correct in saying that he was only allowed three and a half days' provisions. [Warren's full report, to which this mysterious message alludes, follows in the next chapter.] I had told him that transport for three and a half days would be sufficient burden to him, but that I would keep him filled up as he wanted it. That he was aware of this is shown by the following telegram which he sent on the day in question. It is the only report I had from Sir C. Warren: – To Chief of the Staff: Left Flank, 19th January.

" 'I find there are only two roads by which we could possibly get from Trichard's Drift to Potgieter's, on the road north of the Tugela – one by Acton Homes, the other by Fair View and Rosalie; the first I reject as too long, the second is a very difficult road for a large number of wagons, unless the enemy is thoroughly cleared out. I am therefore going to adopt some special arrangements which will involve my stay at Venter's Laager for 2 or 3 days. I will send in for further supplies and report progress – C Warren.'

"The reply to this was that 3 days' supply was being sent.

"2: I went over to Sir C. Warren on the 23rd. I pointed out to him that I had no further report and no intimation of the special arrangements foreshadowed by his telegram of the 19th; that for four days he had kept his men continuously exposed to shell and rifle fire, perched on the edge of an almost precipitous hill; that the position admitted of no second line, and the supports were massed close behind the firing line in indefensible formations, and that a panic or a sudden charge might send the whole lot in disorder down the hill at any moment.

"I said it was too dangerous a situation to be prolonged, and that he must either attack or I should withdraw his force. I advocated, as I had previously done, an advance from his left. He said that he had the night before ordered General Coke to assault Spioenkop, but the latter had objected to undertaking a night attack on a position, the road to which he had not reconnoitred, and added that he intended to assault Spioenkop that night.

"3: I suggested that as General Coke was still lame from the effects of a lately broken leg, General Woodgate, who had two sound legs, was better adapted for mountain climbing.

"4: As no heliograph could, on account of the rifle fire be kept on the east side of Spioenkop, messages for Sir C. Warren were received by our signallers at Spearman's and telegraphed to Sir C. Warren; thus I saw them before he did, as I was at the signal station. The telegrams Sir C. Warren quotes did not give me confidence in its sender, and, at the moment I could see that our men on the top had given way, and that efforts were being made to rally them. I telegraphed to Sir C. Warren: Unless you put some really good hard fighting man in command on the top you will lose the hill. I suggest Thorneycroft."

The next brief paragraph was not published in 1900.

"5: This was a mistake. Colonel a 'Court [Buller's ADC who had been sent up to the top by Buller as an observer] was sent down by General Woodgate almost as soon as he had gained the summit."

The following was published:

"6: I have not thought it necessary to order any investigation. If at sundown the defence of the summit had been taken regularily in hand, entrenchments laid out, gun emplacements prepared, the dead removed, the wounded collected, and, in fact the whole place brought under regular military command, and careful arrangements made for the supply of water and food to the scattered fighting line, the hills would have been held I am sure.

"7: But no arrangements were made. General Coke appears to have been ordered away just as he would have been useful, and no-one succeeded him. Those on the top were ignorant of the fact that guns were coming up, and generally there was a want of organization and system that acted most unfavourably on the defence.

"It is admitted by all that Colonel Thorneycroft acted with the greatest gallantry throughout the day, and really saved the situation. Preparations for the second day's defence should have been organised during the day, and have been commenced at nightfall.

"As this was not done, I think Colonel Thorneycroft exercised a wise discretion.

"Our losses, I regret to say, were very heavy, but the enemy admitted to our doctors that theirs were equally heavy, and though we were not successful in retaining the position, the losses inflicted on the enemy and the attack generally have had a marked effect on them . . . – Buller." [5]

Damned, indeed, was Warren.

SOURCES

1. *South Africa: The Spioenkop Despatches.*
2. *Buller's Campaign, With the Natal Field Force,* by E. Blake-Knox.
3. Ibid.
4. *South Africa: The Spioenkop Despatches.*
5. Ibid.

CHAPTER SIXTEEN

Spioenkop – Part 3

What really took place on top

And Sir Charles? This is his initial battle report, as sent to Buller and attached for London. Also included, but *never* published until the full *Spioenkop Despatches* were in 1902, were reports from General Woodgate, who was killed at Spioenkop, Thorneycroft, Coke and other officers, who were caught up in the maelstrom of bullets on the top.

Many of these despatches vindicate Sir Charles. But, I reiterate, they were never published until 1902.

"Report by Lieut.-General Sir Charles Warren, KCB, upon the capture and subsequent evacuation of Spioenkop.

"Capture and evacuation of Spioenkop: . . . Under the original instructions of the General Officer Commanding-in-Chief [Buller], of 15th January, 1900, I was to act as circumstances required but according to instructions, was generally to continue throughout refusing my right and throwing my left forward until I gained the open plain north of Spioenkop.

"1: Upon the 19th January, on arrival at Venter's Laager, I assembled all the general officers, Officers Commanding Royal Artillery and Royal Engineers of Divisions, and Staff Officers together. I pointed out to them that, with three and a half days' provisions allowed, it was impossible to advance by the left road through Acton Homes. In this they unanimously concurred. I showed them that the only possible road was that going over Fair View through Rosalie, but I expressed my conviction that this could not be done unless we sent the whole of our transport back across the Tugela, and attempted to march through with our rations in our haversacks – without impedimentia.

"The hills were cleared on the following day, and very strong entrenchments found behind them. The Commander-in-Chief was present on the 21st and 22 January, and I pointed out the difficulties of marching along the road, accompanied by wagons, without first taking Spioenkop.

"Accordingly, on the night of the 22nd, I ordered General Coke to occupy Spioenkop. He, however, desired that the occupation might be deferred for a day in order that he might make a reconnaissance with the Officers Commanding battalions to be sent there.

"2: On 23 January the Commander-in-Chief came into camp and told me there were two courses open – to attack, or to retire. I replied that I should prefer to attack Spioenkop to retiring and showed the Commander-in-Chief my orders of the previous day.

"3: The Commander-in-Chief then desired that I should put General Woodgate in command of the expedition and detailed Lieut. Colonel a'Court to accompany him as a Staff Officer.

"The same evening General Woodgate proceeded with the Lancashire Fusiliers, the Royal Lancaster Regiment, a portion of Thorneycroft's Horse and half company Royal Engineers, supported by two companies of the Connaught Rangers and by the Imperial Light Infantry, the latter having just arrived from Trichard's Drift.

[There is no mention of Woodgate having changed the direction of the attack from east to west, as reported earlier by Knox.]

"The attack and capture of Spioenkop was entirely successful. General Woodgate having secured the summit on the 24th, reported that he had entrenched a position and hoped he was secure, but that the fog was too thick to permit him to see. The position was rushed without casualties, other than three men wounded.

"Lieut-Colonel a'Court came down in the morning and stated that everything was satisfactory and secure, and telegraphed to the Commander-in-Chief to that effect. Scarcely had he started on his return to headquarters when a heliogram arrived from Colonel Crofton (Royal Lancaster). The message was: Reinforce at once, or all lost. General dead.

"He also sent a similar message to headquarters. I immediately ordered General Coke to proceed to his assistance, and to take command of the troops. He started at once, and was accompanied by the Middlesex and Dorsetshire Regiments.

"I replied to Colonel Crofton: I am sending two battalions, and the Imperial Light Infantry are on their way up. You must hold on to the last. No surrender.

"This occurred about 10am.

"4: Shortly afterwards I received a telegram from the Commander-in-Chief ordering me to appoint Lieut.-Colonel Thorneycroft to the command of the summit. I accordingly had heliographed: With the approval of the Commander-in-Chief, I place Lieut.-Colonel Thorneycroft in command of the summit, with the local rank of Brigadier-General.

"For some hours after this message I could get no information from the summit. It appears that the signallers and their apparatus were destroyed by the heavy fire.

"I repeatedly asked for Colonel Thorneycroft to state his view of the situation. At 1.20pm, I heliographed to ascertain whether Colonel Thorneycroft had assumed command, and at the same time asked General Coke to give me his views of the situation (copy attached). He stated that, unless the artillery could silence the enemy's guns, the men on the summit could not stand another complete day's shelling, and that the situation was extremely critical.

"At 6.30pm I asked if he could keep two battalions on the summit, removing the remainder out of reach of the shells; also whether two battalions would suffice to hold the summit. This was in accordance with a telegram on the subject sent to me by the Commander-in-Chief. Later in the evening I made arrangements to send two (Naval) 12-prs, and the Mountain Battery Royal Artillery to the summit, together with half a company Royal Engineers (and working parties, two reliefs of 600 men each) to strenghthen the entrenchments and provide shell cover for the men. I may here mention that the 17th Company Royal Engineers proceeded at the same time as General Woodgate's force, and were employed until daylight upon the entrenchments, then upon road making and water supply.

"Sandbags were sent up early on the 24th instant.

"While Colonel Sim was, with this party, ascending the hill, he met Colonel Thorneycroft descending, having evacuated the position."

This next paragraph was cut from the published despatches: "For the remainder of the account of the proceedings I attach the reports made to me by Colonel Thorneycroft and by General Coke, together with reports on the supply of food and water rendered by officers thus engaged. The supply of ammunition was ample."

The next five paragraphs were published. They read: "I wish to bring to notice that I heard from all but one expression of the admirable conduct and bravery shown by officers and men suffering under a withering artillery fire on the summit of the slopes and also of those who, with so much endurance, persisted in carrying up water and food and ammunition to the troops during this day.

"5: During the day a Staff Officer of headquarters [a'Court] staff was present on the summit and reported directly to the Commander-in-Chief.

"At sunset I considered that the position could be held next day provided that guns could be mounted and effective shelter provided. Both of these conditions were about to be fulfilled, as already mentioned.

"In the absence of General Coke, whom I ordered to come to report in person as to the situation, the evacuation took place under orders, given upon his own responsibility, by Lieut.-Colonel Thorneycroft.

"This occurred in the face of the vigorous protests of General Coke's Brigade-Major, the Officer Commanding the Middlesex Regiment and others.

"6: It is a matter for the Commander-in-Chief to decide whether there should be an investigation into the question of the unauthorized evacuation of Spioenkop. – Charles Warren, Lieut.-General."

NONE of the following reports were published in 1900.

"*(Copy of a letter from General Woodgate to Sir C. Warren)*: Dear Sir Charles,

"We got up about 4 o'clock, and rushed the position with three men wounded. There were some few Boers who seemed surprised, and bolted after firing a round or two, having one man killed. I believe there is another somewhere but have not found him in the mist.

"The latter (the mist) did us well, and I pushed on a bit quicker than I perhaps should otherwise have done, lest it should lift before we get here. We have entrenched a position, and are, I hope, secure. But fog is too thick to see, so I retain Thorneycroft's men and Royal Engineers for a bit longer.

"Thorneycroft's men attacked in fine style.

"I had a noise made later [the men on the hill raised a cheer which carried to the headquarters] to let you know that we had got in – E. Woodgate."

"*(Copy of a letter from Lieut.-Colonel Thorneycroft to Sir C. Warren)*: "Spioenkop, 24th January 1900, 2.30pm – Hung on till last extremity with old force. Some of Middlesex here now, and I hear Dorsets coming up, but force really inadequate to hold such a large perimeter. The enemy's guns are north-west, sweep the whole of the top of the hill. They also have guns east; cannot you bring artillery fire to bear on north-west guns? What reinforcements can you send to hold the hill tonight? We are badly in need of water. There are many killed and wounded – Alec. Thorneycroft.

"If you wish to really make a certainty of hill for night you must send more infantry to attack enemy's guns."

Major-General Talbot Coke wrote: "3pm. I have seen the above and have ordered the Scottish Rifles and King's Royal Rifles to reinforce. The Middlesex Regiment, Dorsetshire Regiment and Imperial Light Infantry have also gone up, Bethune's Mounted Infantry (120 strong) also reinforce. We appear to be holding our own at present."

But then came this from Thorneycroft: "The troops which marched up here last night are quite done up – Lancashire Fusiliers, Royal Lancashire

Regiment and Thorneycroft's Mounted Infantry. They have no water and ammunition is running short. I consider that even with reinforcements which have arrived, that it is impossible to permanently hold this place so long as they enemy's guns can play on this hill. They have the long range gun, three of shorter range and one Maxim-Nordenfelt which have swept the whole of the plateau since 8am. I have not been able to ascertain the casualities but they have been very heavy, especially in the regiments which came up last night.

"I request instructions as to what course I am to adopt. The enemy, at 6.30pm, were firing heavily from both flanks with rifles, shell and Nordenfelt, while a heavy rifle fire is kept up in front. It is all I can do to hold my own. If casualties go on occurring at present rate I shall barely hold out the night. A large number of stretcher bearers should be sent up, and also all water possible. The situation is critical – Alec. Thorneycroft, Lieut.Colonel."

And then: "Note from Colonel Thorneycroft to Sir C. Warren: Regret to report that I have been obliged to abandon Spioenkop as the position became untenable. I have withdrawn the troops in regular order, and will come to report as soon as possible. – Alec. Thorneycroft, Lieut-Colonel."

Later, in his official report, which was also not published, Thorneycroft's reasons for abandoning Spioenkop were:

"1: The superiority of the Boer artillery, inasmuch as their guns were placed in such positions as to prevent our artillery fire being brought to bear on them from the lower slopes near camp, or indeed from any other place.

"2: By my not knowing what steps were being taken to supply me in the morning with guns, other than the mountain battery which, in my opinion, could not have lived under the long-range fire of the Boer artillery, and their close-range rifle fire.

"3: By the total absence of water and provisions.

"4: By the difficulty of entrenching on top of the hill, to make trench in any way cover from artillery fire with the few spades at my disposal, the ground being so full of rocks.

"5: Finally I did not see how the hill could be held unless the Boer artillery was silenced and this was impossible."

Colonel D. Phillips was the man on his way up when he met the men streaming down after receiving the order from Thorneycroft and from Brigade Major William Bonus, of the Imperial Light Infantry – "Withdraw, and at once. 2am."

Phillips tried, to no avail, to stop them. He sent this message to the "Officers Commanding Dorsetshire and Middlesex Regiments, Scottish Rifles, Imperial Light Horse. This withdrawal is absolutely without the authority of either Major-General Coke or Sir Charles Warren.

"The former was called away by the latter a little before 10am.

"When General Coke left the front about 6pm our men were holding their own, and he left the situation as such, and reported that he could hold on.

"Someone without authority has given orders to withdraw and has incurred grave responsibility. Were the General here, he would order an instant reoccupation of the heights."

Phillips sent this message to "General Officer Commanding Three Tree Hill: Summit of Spioenkop evacuated by our troops, which still hold lower slopes. An unauthorized retirement took place. Naval guns cannot reach summit before daylight; would be exposed to fire if attempted to do so by day."

And this message to "Regimental Transport Officers: All vehicles should be withdrawn to a place of safety, either towards Wright's farm, or up the gully across the drift. By Order, D. Phillips."

Colonel J.H. Sim was Warren's Commanding Royal Engineer officer. It was up to him to make zigzag roads up the steepest part of Spioenkop for mules to carry up water and to make things easy for the Mountain Battery.

Sim reports (and this was not published either): " . . . I went to the top with Captain Hedley, R.E., and with Lieutenant Neill, R.E., crossed the valley and started work at dawn from the bottom of the slopes. I went to the top with Captain Hedley to choose out the best places, and on arrival we found the first half company, under Major Massey, R.E., had almost completed their intrenching work, and he sent back all but a sub-section to assist in the road making . . .

"I also found water from small springs halfway down the hill, and some men were sent to collect it on the side of the hill that was not exposed to fire. Broad slides were also made down some of the boulder slopes up which guns might be dragged by hand . . .

"At 10.30 Captain Buckland, R.E., was sent to 17th Company to get sandbags taken to the hill. These (about 2000) were taken by a small cart to the drift, and thence a rear company of a battalion going across (Dorsetshire Regiment) and the company native drivers of the 17th Company Royal Engineers, carried about 1,000 up the hill, the remainder were left as a reserve at the drift to be taken up later . . .

"At 12.30 Captain Buckland went to Venter's Spruit to procure three coils of a 3-inch cable from 17th Company wagon, to enable the Naval guns to be hauled up the hill at night. This was deposited at 17th Company camp about 2.30 to be ready for the guns when passing that way.

"About 5pm General Officer Comanding [Warren] showed me a letter from Sir R. Buller of which the following is an extract: 'If you send up either mountain guns or 12-pr. they should make some very strong epaulments, 8 feet thick, covering the gun from the line of its extreme fire [Here there is a drawing]. If this is done, any gun to attack it must come in front of it.'

"General Officer Commanding ordered me to be ready to do this, and also to take working parties at night to deepen the trenches on Spioenkop, so that they might screen the defenders from shell fire, being made 4 feet deep and sloping backwards inside, in the same form as the Boer Schanzes are made.

"I arranged with Officer Commanding 17th Company for the tools and for the half company that was now on Spioenkop to remain there, so that the officers and non-Commissioned officers might superintend the working parties. At 9pm, General Officer Commanding ordered me to proceed and make epaulments for two Naval guns (12-pr), each to be 23 feet diameter and to give 4 ft 3 inches cover; also epaulments as above for the Mountain Battery, and to improve the trenches.

"He also gave me a letter to Colonel Thorneycroft, urging him to hold the hill, and explaining the work I had been ordered to do. To carry the tools across a party of 200 Somersetshire Light Infantry was detailed and two reliefs, of 600 each, for the work were to be drawn from the reserves battalions on Spioenkop rear slopes.

"About 12pm [he means midnight] when I (with Captain Buckland, RE) had led the tool-carrying party about quarter of the away up the slopes of Spioenkop, we met Colonel Thorneycroft coming down, having ordered a retirement. I gave him General officer Commanding's letter, and he said it was too late, as the men, unsupported by guns, could not stay. He ordered me to take my party back. I sent them back with Captain Buckland, and then went forward to ascertain if the retirement was general. Finding it so, I walked up the valley to warn the officer in command of the naval gun of the altered situation, and prevent him risking his gun by moving it up to the evacuated hill top . . . – JH Sim, Lieut.-Colonel, RE, Commanding Royal Engineer, 5th Division."

One of Thorneycroft's points for abandoning Spioenkop was "the total absence of water and provisions".

But this is what Major H.N. Sergeant, DAAG (B), 5th Division, had to say. It was also *not* published.

"With regard to the water supply on Spioenkop, I have the honour to report that the arrangements made were as follows: All the available pack mules which could be procured – viz, 25 – were utilised in carrying biscuit tins, filled with water, up the hill, the tins being refilled from water carts placed at the foot of Spioenkop. Each tin contained 8 and a half to 9 gallons of water. An Officer was placed in charge of the water carts, and had a plentiful supply of spare tins, in addition to those carried by the mules. The mules were divided into two sections, each under an Officer. These two sections of mules conveyed to the troops up the hill at each trip 425 gallons of water.

"The water supply was kept going continuously during the day and late at night, with the exception of one break, caused by an order being given for one section of mules to bring up ammunition. In addition, the water conveyed on mules, there was a spring at the top of the hill, under Royal Engineer charge, which yielded a fair supply.

"I superintended generally the water supply myself, and made frequent enquiries as to whether the troops were getting sufficient quantity on top of the hill, and was told they were. A little delay was occasioned in the early part of the morning in looking for packalls, which I was told were in the camp, but which could not be obtained.

"With regard to the food supplies, as soon as ever the drift near Spioenkop was made passable for our wagons, I collected the regimental wagons at the foot of the hill and instructed the regimental officers in charge to communicate with their units as to getting the supplies up the hill, which was done, and the boxes of biscuits and meat were taken up by hand. – H.N. Sergeant, Major, DAAG (B)."

This was followed by a report from Major E.J. Williams, DAAG to Warren. Also *not* published.

He wrote: "I have the honour to report for your information that, on the 24th January, I undertook to take water to the troops engaged at Spioenkop hill. I guided 12 mules loaded with water to the trees near the top of the hill, arriving there about 12 noon. It was my intention to take the water to the field hospital on the top, but just as I arrived it was destroyed by shell fire, and the medical officer requested me to deposit the water where it was.

"The mules then made a second trip, and a water depot was established. After this all mules were seized to convey ammunition to the firing line. The Royal Engineer company dug for water, which was found three-quarters of the way up the hill; it was thick but fairly plentiful. At 3pm I impressed some more mules and from that time to 8pm I continued to hurry up water to the water depot; also men were sent up with filled water bottles for distribution to the firing line . . .

"Supplies of all kinds were plentiful at the foot of the hill, and in conjunction with the water, I impressed all mules, horses and straggling men to carry up rations before darkness came on, but it was impossible to say if these actually reached the front line, as it was impossible to see what was going on, owing to the troops going up and the stretcher bearers coming down – E.J. Williams, Major D.A.A.G."

But the most telling *unpublished* report came from Colonel A.W. Morris, AAG, 5th Division, who wrote: "Accompanied General Coke up Spioenkop about 11am. About half way up the hill, just by the trees on the Kop, we came across a depot water supply, under a non-Commissioned officer; I should say there were some 20 tins of water under this non-Commissioned officer's charge. Numbers of men asked this non-Commissioned officer for water, but he said it was reserved for the wounded. On this, General Coke ordered a certain number of tins be placed aside for the non wounded men, and this the non-Commissioned officer did at once . . . However when I got further up the hill, I saw several men bringing up by hand tins of water for the firing line. When I arrived at the firing line mules, loaded with ammunition, came up and the General ordered the ammunition to be unloaded and the mules were sent back to the water supply depot to bring up more water tins . . .

"Personally I don't think the men were suffering very badly from want of water. I consider that, under the circumstances, nothing could have been better than the very difficult arrangements made for water supply; it was not plentiful, but sufficient for the purpose required. – A.W. Morris, Colonel, AAG, 5th Division."

There are more than just a few inconsistencies in these reports. And remember, the British public had no knowledge of the intricacies of the battle of Spioenkop, and had no idea they were being kept in the dark.

For instance, by 5pm – and the battle had been raging since early morning – Buller had been able to compile a sketch plan for the naval gun epaulments and send it in a letter to Warren who showed it to Sim.

If Buller was so anxious at the way the battle had been going, why had he then given his blessing to the use of the naval guns which had not even arrived, to the extent of drawing diagrams how they should be situated?

According to the evidence above, too, there appears to have been lots of water and amunition.

Warren now turns to the panic message, the first intimation of severe trouble on top of the hill: "*Reinforce at once, or all lost. General dead.*"

On February 2, 1900, Buller wrote to the Secretary of State for War: "I forward this. It is certain that General Warren did receive the message in the terms he quoted. I saw it myself and he also repeated it to General Lyttleton, who has quoted it in his report. The signal station was not in or very near the firing line . . . – Redvers Buller, General Officer Commanding."

Neither Buller's letter nor the letters that follow were published.

Warren wrote: "With reference to my despatch on the Capture and Evacuation of Spioenkop already sent to you, I have now to forward a statement made by Colonel Crofton, Commanding 2nd Bn. Royal Lancashire Regiment, regarding the message which was signalled to me from the summit of Spioenkop, and which (as I have already reported) reached me in these words: '*Reinforce at once, or all lost. General dead*'.

"It seems certain that no message was written down at the transmitting station on Spioenkop and the only written record is that of the message received at the receiving station with me. – C. Warren, Lieut.-General, Commanding 5th Division."

This is what Crofton had to say: "From Colonel Crofton, Commanding 2nd Bn., Royal Lancashire Regiment, to the Brigade-Major, 11th Brigade: . . . . I beg most strongly to protest against the message reputed to be sent by me from Spioenkop on the 24th stating, 'All is lost'. Such a message was never sent by me, nor did it ever enter my thoughts to send such a message, as the circumstances did not call for it.

"My message, given to the Signalling Officer (Lieutenant Martin, Royal Lancashire Regiment) was: *'General Woodgate dead; reinforcements urgently required.'*

"This I considered necessary as the Boers were increasing in numbers every minute, and I had no means of ascertaining the numbers of reserves they had to draw upon.

"I very much feared some error had occurred from the returned message, directing me under no circumstances to surrender, and I felt most deeply being superseded during the engagement by an Officer very much my junior . . . – Malby Crofton, Colonel, Royal Lancaster Regiment."

Attached was another letter from General Arthur Wynne, who was the AAG, commanding 11th Brigade, who wrote: "Officer Commanding Lancaster Regiment: It would strengthen your case if you attached the message handed to Lieutenant Martin for despatch, and also called upon the signallers who signalled the message wrongly sent in your name to account for having despatched a message not properly authenticated by signature."

Crofton did. He wrote to Lieutenant Martin: " Be good enough to let me have a full report hereon of the message I gave to you to send from Spioenkop on the 24th relative to General Woodgate's reported death, and asking for reinforcements."

Martin replied: "On 24th instant, soon after firing began, I was looking for some signallers, you met me and said, 'I must have a signaller.' I said, 'I am looking for them.'

"You replied: 'Get them at once and send a message to Sir Charles Warren and say General Woodgate is dead, and ask for reinforcements at once.'

"I called for signallers and two men of 2nd Bn. Lancaster Fusiliers ran up. We went to a spot I selected, and found there was already a signaller there, Private Goodyear of the West Yorkshire Regiment (he was with Lieutenant Doomer, R.A., observing the effect of artillery fire).

"I said to Private Goodyear: 'You might send a message for me whilst the helio is being put up'.

"I told him to call up G.O.C. the station I wished to communicate with and say, 'General Woodgate is killed; send reinforcements at once'.

"I did not write the message down as I had no paper. — A.R. Martin, Lieutenant 2nd Bn. Lancaster Regiment."

But the signaller jumbled it up, and what Buller and Warren got was: "Reinforce at once or all is lost. General dead."[1]

There was no panic, according to Crofton, there was plenty of water and ammunition.

Sending such a message, emphasised Crofton, would not have "entered my head".

When Woodgate was mortally wounded, the Spioenkop command devolved upon the next senior officer present, Crofton.

Warren next telegraphed to Lyttleton at Potgieter's Drift: "Give every assistance you can on your side; this side is clear, but the enemy too strong on your side, and Crofton telegraphs that if assistance is not given at once all is lost. I am sending up two battalions, but they will take some time to get up."

At 10.20am Warren went over to General Coke to discuss the whole situation with him, and finally directed him to move up to Spioenkop and take personal command of the troops there, as the greater portion of his Division was now on top.

Coke left for the summit at 11.10am with full knowledge of all the arrangements Warren had made for food, water and guns, and with the engineers and supply officers all working under him.

But shortly after Coke's departure, Buller, watching the action through a telescope from Mount Alice, saw a rearward movement of some British troops on the summit and, says Warren's biographer, Watkin Williams "was at the same time able to recognise the energetic and courageous actions of one single officer of exceptional stature, who could be none other than Col Thorneycroft."

Accordingly at 11.45am Buller sent the following message to Warren: "Unless you put some really good hard fighting man in command on the top you will lose the hill. I suggest Thorneycroft."

Instead of telling Buller to mind his own business and stop interfering, Warren, the gentleman, acceded to his request, and flashed to Crofton: "With the approval of the Commander-in-Chief, I place Lt-Colonel Thorneycroft in command of the summit, with the local rank of Brigadier-General."

Because of Buller's direct inteference the following situation evolved. Warren received no reply to his message to Crofton (who as reported earlier was annoyed because he was superseded by a junior officer) nor any further communication from the summit for some hours because the signalling station had been destroyed by a Boer shell. The message, however, was received on the top, but the orderly who was detailed to take it to Thorney-croft was killed while trying to reach him.

But Lieutenant Rose, Thorneycroft's orderly officer, who had seen the message, crawled towards him and shouted: "Sir Charles Warren has heliographed that you are to take command. You are a General."

Coke had gone to take command and Warren presumed that once he reached the top, he would be told of Thorneycroft's appointment. He was not because Thorneycroft was at the head of the firing line, in personal command of his own force, while Coke remained towards the back of the hill.

Thus there were during the afternoon, writes Watkins, four officers on Spioenkop holding some form of General Officer's rank – General Talbot Coke commanding the 5th Division, Colonel Crofton, commanding the 11th (Woodgate's) brigade, Colonel A.W. Hill (Middlesex Regiment) commanding the 10th (Coke's) brigade, and Colonel Thorneycroft, who, though junior to the last two, in command of the summit. [2]

Warren was criticised for not, himself, going to the top. But why should he have done so with four highly experienced (with the exception of Thorney-croft) generals?

At 12.50pm Coke sent Warren the following messsage: "I am now on the plateau of Spioenkop slopes. The top of the hill is reported crowded with men, and as these are exposed to shell fire and suffering, but holding out well, I have stopped further reinforcements beyond this point. But troops engaged know that help is near at hand. Ammunition is being pushed up."

Warren was thus reassured at 2pm that Coke was well on his way up and in actual command, that there were sufficient men on top and that ammunition was on its way up, and no further pressing need was reported.

Half an hour later a panicky message from Thorneycroft was received by Coke: " . . . What reinforcements can you send to hold the hill tonight? We are badly in need of water. There are many killed and wounded . . ."

At 3pm Coke sent Thorneycroft's message to Warren, as already reported, with this endorsement: "I have seen the above, and have ordered the Scottish Rifles and King's Royal Rifles to reinforce. The Middlesex Regiment,

Dorsetshire Regiment and Imperial Light Infantry have also gone up, Bethune's Mounted Infantry (120 strong) also reinforce.

"We appear to be holding our own."

About that time, Lyttleton, who had been watching things from Potgieter's, launched his successful attack on Twin Peaks (two mounds separate from the Spioenkop massif, but part of the massive hillside) driving away Boer guns and gunners.

Immediately Buller saw Lyttleton's advance, he ordered its recall. But the men were committed and before the recall order reached them, they had carried the peaks.

Then at 4pm, Buller sent Warren what Watkins describes as this "cheery note": "I think it is want of head in the C.O. rather than want of strength which makes the difficulty. They tell me that Colonel Crofton is not much good. I have telegraphed to you to put Thorneycroft in command. There has been no attack on it from our side, but our Naval guns cleared the N.E. shoulder where all the rough stones are, I scarcely think you can see it, and drove down about 30 Boers.

"The Mountain Battery left Springfield for Trichard's at 11am. They will have a devil of a march; you must give them rest before they go up. I have got two Naval 12-prs. up the hill to my camp from across the river and can send them on if you want them; the Navy say they can get them up.

"I doubt whether you are wise to keep four Battalions on the hill. I would entrench two strongly and bring the others down. Too many are a mark for shells. I believe we have just stopped one Boer gun, and I telegraphed to the R.A. guns to say we thought the other guns were to the left of where they were firing, some little way. a'Court says that two Battalions can defend the entrenchments, though there is the shellfire . . . Pray tell C of S if I can help you and how, but above all put a good fighting man in command on top." [3]

An hour later, Buller sent up his sketches of the gun epaulments.

So from the top of the hill, Warren was urged to send up reinforcements, and from Buller, the opposite!

But for the men on top, the situation was, indeed, becoming critical . . .

SOURCES

1. *Spioenkop Despatches.*
2. *The Life of General Sir Charles Warren,* by Watkin Williams.
3. *Spioenkop Despatches.*

CHAPTER SEVENTEEN

Spioenkop – Part 4

Sir Charles refutes the charges

"The shallow trenches were full of dead and wounded; but the living crouching among them, overwrought as they were with fatigue and heat, with hunger and thirst, and the continual bursting of the shells amongst their crowded shelters, yielded no ground, and endured their unanswerable punishment in silence. But it was plain that the efficiency of the defence was fast dwindling. Many of the soldiers were so exhausted that they fell asleep in the sangars, and were shot as they slept. Towards sunset, the enemy redoubled the shell-fire and swept the plateau from end to end, and from side to side, with a searching stream of projectiles." [1]

Coke, too, became alarmed. With Colonel Hill he wrote this despatch to Warren: "The situation is as follows: The original troops are still in position, have suffered severely, and many dead and wounded are still in the trenches. The shell fire is, and has been, very severe. If I hold on to the position all night is there any guarantee that our artillery can silence the enemy's guns, otherwise today's experience will be repeated, and the men will not stand another complete day's shelling. I have in hand Bethune's Mounted Infantry and the Dorset Regiment intact to cover a withdrawal. If I remain I will endeavour to utilise these units to carry food and water up to the firing line. The situation is extremely critical . . . Please give orders, and should you wish me to withdraw cover retirement from Connaught Hill – J Talbot-Coke, Major-General."

Down below Sir Charles had been busy with arrangements for sending up at night all that was necessary to enable the position to be held next day.

The mountain battery and naval 12-pr guns, however, only arrived at Trichardt's Drift near 6pm, the mountain battery going straight on to the foot of Spioenkop.

At 6.30pm Thorneycroft, still out on his own, wrote to Warren: "I request instructions as to what course I am to adopt . . . It is all I can do to hold my own. If casualties go on occurring at present rate I shall barely hold out the night. A large number of stretcher bearers should be sent up, and also all water possible. The situation is critical."

Coke left the firing line shortly after 6.30 pm and returned to his reserves, having personally handed over the command to Colonel Hill. Coke still had not been told that Thorneycroft, who was at the firing line, was in overall command.

Darkness fell at 7pm.

Warren had received no news from the summit, nor had he any means of knowing whether the messages and information which he had repeatedly sent up during the afternoon had been received.

And Warren was quite unaware of the restraint which Buller had placed upon Lyttleton's supporting measures, after the successful Twin Peaks attack.[2]

The *Official History* states: "Sir C. Warren, by a train of unfortunate circumstances, could gather no true idea of the situation, for his messages remained unanswered, and those he received, if confusing, were still not of an alarmist nature . . .

"If a dangerous situation had arisen, all that could be done in the way of reinforcements had, he thought, been done, and was still being done. So, too, in the matters of water, tools, and sandbags for the troops engaged, and guns with which to reply to the enemy's overmastering artillery."[3]

At 7.30 the mountain battery arrived completely tired out from their long march, and it was arranged that they should rest there until midnight, as Buller had suggested, when the moon arose, and there would be plenty of time for them to ascend and get their guns into position on the top before daybreak.

Notice of this was sent to Thorneycroft by the hand of a scout.[4]

At 9pm, Warren sent Sim up with orders to construct the epaulements for two naval guns and the mountain battery, and to improve the trenches.

Sim, as has already been stated, had with him 200 men of the Somerset Light Infantry, who carried tools, and orders to draw, on arrival, two reliefs of 600 men each from the battalions which Coke had in reserve. He also bore a note from Warren to Thorneycroft urging him to hold on to the hill at all costs.

At the same time, Lieutenant James, in command of the naval guns, received orders from Warren to take one of his guns up in readiness for the next day. The second gun and the mountain battery were to follow later.

Warren was anxious to discuss with Clery (who had come down off the left flank feeling ill and was now at headquarters) and Coke various important details of orders for the following day, and he was also dissatisfied at the indecision caused by the lack of news from the summit and the confusion of what little news he had received. He therefore signalled Coke at 9.10pm, calling him down to his headquarters at Three Tree Hill.

Coke was loath to leave the top. "Is it not possible", he wrote in a message he wanted to be signalled to Warren, "to give orders without my presence?"

But the message could not be sent because the oil in the newly established signal post had run out.

Coke had no option but to begin the dangerous return to headquarters in the pitch dark.

He left at 9.30pm, satisfied, as Warren was, that nothing untoward could occur during his absence at night, because he had sufficiently fresh troops, despite the carnage, to hold the hill for the present. Food, water and ammunition was continuously being sent up, and guns and engineers would follow.

Coke did not know it, but the last act was about to begin.

First, Thorneycroft had made up his mind that the hill was untenable. In his report he states: "When night began to close in I determined to take some steps, and a consultation was held. The officer commanding Scottish Rifles and Colonel Crofton were both of opinion that the hill was untenable. I entirely agreed with their view, and so I gave the order for the troops to withdraw on to the neck and ridge where the hospital was." [5]

Thorneycroft, then, had decided "when night began to close in". It got dark at 7pm, so Thorneycroft must have decided as early as 6 or 6.30pm to withdraw.

But Coke was very much on the hill then, as were other general officers. Thorneycroft's report says he (Thorneycroft) tried to find Coke, but could not.

D. Lambton, the "anonymous"-for-years author of *Sir Charles Warren and Spioenkop*, says: "By seven o'clock orders were issued for the troops to retire on the hospital sangar, and the collecting of the men and bringing in the wounded commenced.

"It is said that Colonel Hill had a warm discussion with Lieutenant-Colonel Thorneycroft, who, however, asserted his right as brigadier-general commanding the summit to order a retirement.

"He neither sent word to Major-General Coke, nor to Sir Charles Warren . . ." [6]

By the time Coke left the hill, the preparations for retirement had been in full swing for three hours.

But no one knew it.

As Sim prepared to go up, he met Thorneycroft coming down, and there was no way Thorneycroft was going to remain on top.

No messenger was sent down to acquaint Sir Charles of the intention to retire taken as early as say, 6.30pm; no heed was paid to the vigorous protests of either Colonel Hill (the very man whom Coke had left in charge) or Captain Phillips who had endeavoured to stop the flow of men down the hill, (as explained earlier); and Sir Charles Warren's positive instructions received on the way down by the hand of Colonel Sim were treated with scant respect – in fact were ignored.

"And so it came to pass that Major-General Coke, summoned by Sir Charles Warren at 9.30, and Lieut.-Colonel Thorneycroft, unsummoned, arrived together at Sir Charles Warren's headquarters about 2.30am on the 25th, and for the first time he [Warren] heard of the abandonment of the hill after the retirement had been completed, and found all his plans swept away." [7]

Poor Coke. He could not find the wagon Warren was using as his headquarters. During the previous afternoon, Boer gunners had spotted the wagon and shelled it, wounding an orderly who was lying beneath it, and killing a horse.

Warren had ordered the wagon moved some yards to one side in a position of safety. Such was the darkness of the night, and the difficulty of the ground that, although Coke arrived somewhere near Three Tree Hill shortly after midnight, he lost his way and it took him some two hours stumbling about before he located Warren's wagon.

A few minutes later, Phillips, still on the summit, had found some lamp-oil and had signalled to Warren: "Summit of Spioenkop evacuated by our troops, which still hold lower slopes. An unauthorised retirement took place."

Says Watkin Williams: "It will be realised that at this time Warren knew nothing whatever of the retirement of the Boers [they too, had begun to withdraw]; his only present source of information was Thorneycroft – Thorneycroft who said it was impossible to hold the position any longer against the terrific fire and overwhelming numbers of the Boers, and who in the course of his retreat had caused the supplies of water, food, ammunition, working parties and guns to be likewise withdrawn.

"Moreover, Thorneycroft was Buller's choice as commander. and it was fair to all parties that Buller should have the chance of taking charge of the situation which his interference had indirectly created . . ."

Warren "tried to get through to Buller by telephone . . . but the line appeared to be out of order, so he at once sent a mounted orderly with the following report: '2.30am, Warren, to Chief of Staff, pressing. Colonel Thorneycroft has on his own authority abandoned the position of Spioenkop, and the troops are evacuating the place; can you come at once, and decide what to do? An immediate decision must be arrived at . . .' " [8]

Spioenkop today, an eerie, mystical place. Here is the grave of one of the Thorneycroft heroes – Lieutenant Thomas Flower Flower-Ellis, of Johannesburg, and beyond him one of the smaller mass graves that mark the summit. Today, too, the area forms part of the Spioenkop Nature Reserve, and the top is exposed to many more visitors than in previous years. However, the sanctity of the top needs to be preserved and protected, and it is up to the Natal Parks Board to do just this (Author's picture.)

By the time Coke and Thorneycroft reached Warren, Spioenkop was empty of life apart from one Boer hospital attendant. Only the dead remained grotesquely unburied.

For the Boers were even in a worse plight than the British.

Deneys Reitz writes, in *Commando*: "Long before nightfall we were holding the blood-spattered ledge with a mere handful of rifles . . . When at last the sun set I do not think there were sixty men left on the ridge . . .

"We fully believed that the morning would see them (the English troops) streaming through to the relief of Ladysmith, and the rolling up of our Tugela line."

The *Official History* states: "By nightfall every laager and most of the guns were on the move to the rear, the stormers of Spioenkop, utterly exhausted, slipped away one by one . . . and there arose signs of a panic throughout the whole federal force."

At 3.30am General Louis Botha received positive information from some burghers who had climbed the hill in search of the body of a comrade that the position had been completely abandoned by the British.

In the grey light of early dawn, Botha himself toiled up the hill and reoccupied the summit at 4.30am.

The hill of death was theirs.

Warren, angry, set to again, preparing for all eventualities. There were three possible alternatives – to reoccupy Spioenkop, to attack on the left (Buller's original plan, put forward in his telegrams to London before the Magersfontein defeat of December 11), or to retire completely.

But it was not until 6am that he was to know. The mounted orderly he had sent in search of Buller lost his way and never reached the Mount Alice headquarters. Instead, at 5am, he met Buller who had already started for Warren's headquarters.

The orderly told Buller of the withdrawal. It was the first Buller knew of it.

In Warren's unpublished account of the Spioenkop diary, he writes: "Thus when General Buller arrived at 6am I was able to tell him – 1: We have guns trained on Spioenkop and if you want to re-occupy you can do so at any time. The Boers cannot hold our side of the hill. 2: If you wish to attack on the left, as you wished me to do on the 23rd, it is all ready now for assault. 3: If you wish to retire, we can move off our wagons at a moment's notice."

But Buller, says Watkin Williams, was already forming plans for trying a new line, and committed himself, yet again, to retirement. He took personal control of the whole force and, once more treating Warren as his second-in-command, entrusted to him the details of arrangements for recrossing the Tugela.[9]

The entire force, including baggage train, which had previously crossed the river in 37 hours, this time recrossed in 47.

There is no statement in any despatch to suggest that Warren, who was in charge of the first crossing, did in fact organise the second too.

It was almost as if Buller had wiped Warren off the slate. His name almost disappears from official military despatches from then. Buller had, at last, found someone else to blame.

But was there? Warren followed Buller in giving evidence at the Commission of Inquiry. There he was told: "At the request of Sir Redvers Buller, we sent you yesterday (the date was Wednesday, 18th February, 1903), on the first opportunity we had of doing it, the statement which he had submitted to us with regard to events of the 17th to 27th January 1900; that you have had before you?"

It was the *first time* since arriving home on April 15, 1900 that Warren realised what Buller had done.

WARREN: "I received that last night. I had scarcely more than time to look through it, and I have written the following letter to the Secretary of the Commission, if I may submit it – Sir, I have the honour to acknowledge the receipt of your letter of 18th containing a statement made yesterday by General Sir Redvers Buller.

"I have read over this statement; it appears to me to be very incorrect and very misleading and I ask that I may have facilities and opportunities of refuting it. I beg to call attention to the correspondence between Field Marshal Lord Roberts and the Secretary of State for War and myself on the subject of General Buller's charges. I would also ask for telegrams to be produced which passed to and from Spioenkop on 24th January 1900, and the staff reports of 15th January to 28th February, 1900, of 5th Division.

"I point the following as salient mistakes in Sir Redvers Buller's statement: 1 – All baggage was left behind at Springfield. The contents of wagons I passed over Trichard's Drift consisted of artillery and ammunition, machine guns and ammunition, warlike stores, ambulances, great coats, cooking utensils.

"2 – Of the two days which Sir Redvers Buller states I wasted in passing over baggage, he was with me all one day, viz. 17th January, and wrote me a letter in the evening altering his orders somewhat (I have a copy of that letter here).

"3 – There is a statement . . . which clearly indicates the route Sir Redvers

Buller wished me to take;

"4 – Sir Redvers Buller has never yet stated definitely what his orders were intended to convey to me. I have to ask that he may be called on definitely to state the line of action he intended should be taken according to his present views. All the facts, I maintain, go to show that I carried out my instructions so far as they were then understood.

"5 – I beg to state unhesitatingly that the system I adopted of demoralising the enemy with artillery fire was the only one that could be carried out with our small force, that it effected its object, and would have been entirely successful in relieving Ladysmith had not Sir Redvers Buller interfered constantly with my operations, and finally withdrawn the force in the hour of success i.e. when the Boers were absolutely demoralised after Spioenkop."

Warren was told to submit a statement – "that", said the chairman, "is an opportunity which we should wish to give to any officer whose conduct is impugned . . ." [10]

Yes, the Boers had been demoralised. Captain Charles Levita, of the Royal Horse Artillery, who was Warren's AAG at Spioenkop writes in his diary: "When Buller came into camp the morning after the evacuation of Spioenkop, I personally told him that the Boers had gone, although we had evacuated Spioenkop. I had this information both from native intelligence and from reports from patrols I sent to Spioenkop, the accuracy of which has since been confirmed by reports from Ladysmith. The engagement at Spioenkop would have been a success and Ladysmith relieved had not Buller insisted on retreating across the Tugela River, saying that he had the Key to the position."

Michael Davitt says: "Botha's small force had fought every day, and had worked at trench building every night, from the 17th to the 24th, almost without cessation, and with very little food.

"They were utterly exhausted after so prolonged a struggle and it was simply impossible to order men so worn out to forgo sleep and rest on the eighth night in order to attack an enemy so enormously stronger in numbers, even on retreat.

"At 9 on the evening of the 24th, while the firing still continued, an officer wishing to see General Botha was told that he was in the tent of Major Wolmarans, writing his report of the day's battle for President Kruger. On entering the tent, the general, his secretary, and Wolmarans were found with a half-written report before them, and with heads leaning on the table, in sheer exhaustion, overcome with sleep." [11]

In his reassessment of Buller's campaigns, written in 1963, Julian Symons has harsh words to say about Warren.

He asks: "What was Warren to do? It has been said that there were still 1,600 troops on the slopes of Spioenkop, and that Warren might easily have issued an order that set them climbing up again to the summit.

"To suggest this, however, is to attribute to him far greater vision, mental agility, and indeed knowledge, than he possessed. It seemed to him that there was no reversing what had been done, or at least that he could not reverse it. Now, in time of trouble, he made the characteristic gesture of British Generals in the Natal campaign, that of trying to shift responsibility onto somebody else. He tried to telegraph Buller, but was unable to get through to the telegraph clerk. He sent a mounted orderly with the message that Thorneycroft had abandoned Spioenkop on his own authority, and that the hill was being evacuated.

"'Can you come at once and decide what to do?' he forlornly asked. It was the first request he had made for Buller's presence since he had been given his command . . .

"The orderly sent by Warren to Buller added one final touch to the tale of bungling by losing his way. He did not arrive at Buller's headquarters at 5 o'clock in the morning. An hour later Buller was with Warren . . ." [12]

Symons and Williams differ here on several points. While Williams may be partisan (he was after all Warren's grandson), he had access to Warren's papers. Symons obviously did not.

And I would be inclined to believe Williams, who was a lot closer to the source.

Symons says Warren tried to send a telegraph message. Williams says he tried the telephone; Symons says the messenger found Buller at his headquarters; Williams says Buller was on his way to Warren when he was found by the orderly.

Symons alledges Warren lacked vision and mental agility. But the reverse is surely true. Warren's carefully-thought-out and planned manoeuvres Buller later admitted "gave him the key to Ladysmith". Not only that, but also the lifting of the siege.

And why shouldn't Warren have turned the unauthorised evacuation of Spioenkop back on Buller, who did, whatever way you look at it, insist that Thorneycroft, the man who ultimately abandoned it, be placed in overall command?

Buller had got him into it, now Buller could get him out.

But criticism of Warren has come from many sources. This is not surprising. The non-publication of the *Spioenkop Despatches* saw to that, and Warren's denied request to Roberts that he (Warren) be able to publicly refute Buller's allegations meant that not until the full publication of the despatches and the release of the Commission itself in 1903, a year after the war had ended, was his side of the story able to be read – albeit as an appendix to the complete report.

Most historians have used the Buller despatches. None have used Warren's answers.

Warren was too slow after crossing Trichardt's Drift, they write; Warren had the element of complete surprise which he lost; Warren recalled the impetuous Dundonald to Trichardt's just when his Lordship was about to break through onto the Ladysmith Road (I will come back to this point later); Warren did this; Warren did that.

Careful reading of the despatches gives the lie to most of these allegations. How is it possible for anyone to keep troop movements a secret when there are hundreds of wagons stretching 15 miles crossing at Trichardt's Drift.

How was it possible to keep secret the movement of 25,000 troops from Frere to Springfield? And from Springfield to beneath the towering masiff of Spioenkop?

Truth is, it was impossible.

But the myth persists.

For instance, one recent magazine writer is a case in point. The author, fired with enthusiasm over the Spioenkop Nature Reserve and the hill, writes that (from Trichardt's) " . . . three British infantry brigades and Dundonald's cavalry crossed the Tugela almost unopposed. It was perhaps the most brilliant movement of the war so far." [13]

It was not. Warren explains why later.

The magazine writer also says: "General Sir Charles Warren had had some small-scale campaigning experience in Africa in years past, but it had never been his lot to be in charge of an army even half the size of his new command."

The corollary to that is, neither had Buller.

But Warren's service was a lot more recent, was of wider scope and showed his unquestionable leadership under severe pressure.

The Spioenkop myth is being perpetuated, too, in "official' literature, such as that available at the Spioenkop Nature Reserve camp. It is time for it to stop.

In his report to the commissioners which forms an annex to his evidence, Warren successfully refutes all these allegations.

Warren's preamble sets the tone . . . : "In forwarding this statement, I have to observe that it would have been comparatively a simple task to reply to, or explain, facts that actually occurred. I find myself however confronted with a series of fanciful episodes based on misconceptions and misapprehensions so numerous, that it is difficult to refute them or put them right in any limited space.

"Sir Redvers Buller does not state what are his sources of information concerning events of which he was not an eye-witness, and his criticisms teem with eroneous assumptions, based apparently on an imaginary aspect of affairs. The account of operations given in his telegrams to the War Office of 15 to 27 January, 1900, are in the main correct, but it differs so essentially from that given in Despatches of 30th January, 1900, and in his evidence before the Royal Commission, that the two accounts might be supposed to refer to totally different operations . . .

"But what is most required is a really correct narrative of events; if this were promulgated his adverse cricitisms would at once fall to the ground, as they are founded on an eroneous view of affairs. I find that I cannot give such a narrative without occupying too much space, and I therefore must fall back upon the shorter method of taking Sir R. Buller's criticisms *seriatim* and traversing them, giving here and there short abstracts of events, so as to connect the whole together and placing important telegrams, letters etc. in an appendix. By these means I may succeed in compressing my statement into a comparatively short space." [13]

And Warren, indeed, was able to put the record straight . . .

SOURCES

1. *Official History.*
2. *The Life of Sir Charles Warren*, by Watkin Williams.
3. *Official History.*
4. *Sir Charles Warren and Spioenkop*, by "Defender" (D. Lambton).
5. *Spioenkop Despatches.*
6. *Sir Charles Warren and Spioenkop*, by "Defender".
7. Ibid.
8. *The Life of Sir Charles Warren*, by Watkin Williams.
9. Ibid.
10. *Commission on the War in South Africa.*
11. *The Boer Fight for Freedom*, by Michael Davitt.
12. *Buller's Campaign*, by Julian Symons.
13. *Getaway magazine*, Cape Town, January 1992.
14. *Spioenkop Despatches.*

Spioenkop – Part 5

Now the truth comes out

Under the heading *Sir Redvers Buller's Original Orders and Plan of Attack*, Warren writes: "He [Buller] states in his secret report of 30 January 1900: 'I had fully discussed my orders with General Warren before he started, and he appeared entirely to agree that the policy indicated of refusing the right and advancing the left was the right one. He never attempted to carry it out.'

"Sir R. Buller is entirely incorrect in the first portion of this paragraph; he is confusing two distinct subjects. There never was any full discussion concerning the order to me of 15th January.

"The discussion that took place was concerning the attack originally contemplated via Potgieter's Drift; see orders of 9th January. Until 15th January the Second Division was to cross at Potgieter's and engage and drive back the enemy, and then the Fifth Division was to pass the defile between Krantz Kloof and Vaal Krantz; the discussion was concerning the method of carrying this out. I had previously proposed to take Doorn Kloof [a drift between Chieveley and Springfield] which Sir R. Buller negatived.

"The proposal to attack at Potgieter's was suddenly abandoned on 15th January, and I was sent to reconnoitre Trichard's Drift, with a view to crossing there. On my return on the morning of the 15th January, I reported that the crossing could be made, but that there was likely to be hard fighting subsequently. Sir R. Buller then drew up his orders, which I received on the 15th January and then I had to draw up my orders for the night march on the following day; there was no time for any full discussion, and as there were no correct plans of the ground, there could be no real discussion as to the form of attack.

"Sir R. Buller pointed to Sugar Loaf (Bastion) Hill on the Farm Map, which he said terminated the Boer lines, and told me to swing round my line from the west of Spioenkop, as a centre, and envelop Bastion Hill, so as to roll up the Boers. As to refusing the right and advancing the left, it was a natural consequence on the nature of the ground; I could not advance without doing so. The attack was commenced under the eye of Sir Redvers Buller on 17th January and was carried out according to the orders he himself gave to General Woodgate, as will be shown."

Warren's next heading was: *Was Trichardt's Drift the Best Place to Cross for the Attack contemplated?*

He writes: "This is a matter requiring consideration before the criticisms of Sir R. Buller on the carrying out of his instructions can be referred to.

"Trichardt's Drift was a convenient place to cross for an attack on the hills immediately in front of it, via Spioenkop and Three Tree Hill; but an attack on Three Tree Hill entailed the capture at the same time of the whole range as far west as Bastion Hill and would have required four brigades.

"Spioenkop, however, was taboo [this is explained later] by order of Sir R.

Buller; though it commanded the crossing with long range guns and rifle fire and under such circumstances the crossing (for the attack to be delivered in the shortest space of time) should have been made three miles higher up the river, so that the attacking line would cover the crossing, and no flank march be required in contact with the enemy's guns and rifles.

"As matters stood, the phrase 'refusing the right and advancing the left' used by Sir R. Buller meant a flank march along the front of the enemy's position, within the range of their guns and of their long range rifle fire. It could not have been intended that such a march be made, while leaving the artillery and munitions of war to pass over unguarded and uncovered.

"During the crossing a brigade was required to guard our left flank on the south side and furnish working parties to hand haul the vehicles over the pontoons, and two brigades were required to cover the crossing and feel for the enemy.

"Had four brigades been sent at first an attack could have been delivered 24 hours earlier, and had the crossing been made three miles higher up the river there would have been an advantage in time, but we should have been away from the support of our naval guns."

Warren's next heading was: *It was not intended that the column should pass round by Acton Homes.*

He writes: "There is not an indication of any kind in Sir R. Buller's instructions or remarks that the column should go round by Acton Homes; but his frequent allusion to attacking the left of the Boer position has given rise to the assumption that such a course was contemplated, and Lord Roberts appears to assume it in his despatch of 13 February, 1900.

"Sir R. Buller puts the matter beyond doubt in saying: 'From the first there could be no question but that the only practicable road for a column was the one by Fairview. The problem was to get rid of the enemy who were holding it.'

"I have, however, been blamed for not going round by Acton Homes.

"Such a course, with only three brigades, would have involved the destruction of the Natal army. At that time the Boers were elated with the check they had given our troops at Colenso, and any advance of a force into the hills without beating the enemy would have had disastrous results.

"The first essential in our advance was not to divide our comparatively small force. Therefore any breaks in our whole line by pushing my section far beyond Spioenkop was tactically wrong. My guiding rule in crossing at Trichardt's Drift was to keep touch with the troops at Potgieter's Drift; so long as we did so my right was more or less protected, and the long range guns could help us. Had we done otherwise and passed off to the left, our communications would have inevitably been cut off. General Lyttleton's telegrams to me all point to the same view. I am sure that anyone with military knowledge, and aware of the inexperience of our officers and men in Boer warfare, will realise that (so long as the Boers were jubilant) our strength and safety lay in our keeping together and beating them as near to the river as we could get them to fight.

"That the Boer intention was to lure us on to Acton Homes I do not doubt. The valley there is a cul de sac where battalions could have been annihilated by small bodies of Boers placed in the hills surround it on three sides. Sir R. Buller on 17 January himself informed me, that according to reports, the intention of the Boers was to lure us away to the west, and he advised me to be careful in advancing my left too far to the west; he also subsequently sent me telegrams desiring me not to get away too far to the left, and pointed out that the road to Clydesdale [on the Acton Homes and

Ladysmith road] was not suitable for advance, being full of dongas and rugged hills."

Warren's next heading was: *Can Sir Redvers Buller's Instructions for 15th January be defined?*

"Originally they seemed simple enough, though absolutely undefined. 'You will act as circumstances require, but my idea is that you should continue throughout refusing your right and throwing your left forwards till you gain the open space north of Spioenkop.'

"First I will allude to the discretion given me. It is distinctly stated that *I am to act as circumstances require*, if there is any meaning attached to the words, this means that the responsibility for the form of attack rested with me, and I claim to be judged according to that responsibility and not according to the 'idea' of Sir R. Buller which was only put forward as a general guide. Either I had the responsibility or I had not. If I had, then Sir R. Buller cannot state that I disregarded the instructions in exercising the discretion he gave to me.

"With this preamble I proceed to point out what Sir R. Buller's instructions actually were intended to convey. Bishop Baynes (in *My Diocese during the War*) gives the idea in a few words, as derived from General Lyttleton. I was, when in line, to swing my left forward, with my right resting on Spioenkop as a pivot. This is the only meaning that can be attached to the proposals. My left was to envelop Barton Hill; [one of the hills towards Bastion-Rangeworthy hills, now unidentified]. This was stated to me verbally, both at Spearman's and at Trichard's Drift, by Sir R. Buller.

"So far the meaning appears simple enough, and Sir R. Buller in his secret paper also points out that the only practicable road was by Fair View and that 'the problem was to get rid of the enemy who were holding it'. Thus it is evident that from the first Sir R. Buller had views only concerning the initial operations involving the taking the outer line of the Rangeworthy Hills. It was still a problem in his mind how the further advance was to be made . . .

"Thus far there is no apparent difficulty. But on 17th January, Sir R. Buller wrote me a letter – received 18th January – stating that, when watching the attack on the enemy's lines by General Woodgate, he did not consider that General Woodgate had kept his left sufficiently disengaged. This letter adds to the instructions and complicates them, for instead of attacking in line, and swinging around the left, he now proposes that when the line is in contact with the enemy, and cannot advance, it is to *turn half-left!* He says: 'If you can make a direct advance, it will be in line, but if you are checked, the next advance must be by moving half-left; I mean that to get on your left will creep outward and forward, and your right follow.' It is clear from this that I was to search for an opening where I could attack, commencing from the west of Spioenkop and moving to the left.

"It will be seen from General Buller's telegrams of 17th to 27th January, 1900, that these instructions he gave me were adhered to so far as they could have any meaning attached to them. But in fact, the terms 'to refuse the right and advance the left' without any limitations or explanation, is merely a kind of oracular statement. It can always be said afterwards that it was carried out too far or not far enough. If it meant swinging round the left on a pivot, it would depend on the length of the line, how far it extended, and if it meant moving off diagonally to the left, with the enemy's lines continuous, it meant going to the Drackensburg. There seems to be only one reasonable conclusion as to which was intended, namely the attack on Rangeworthy (Bastion) Hills.

"MY PLAN OF OPERATIONS.

"Sir R. Buller states: 'I was dissatisfied with Warren's operations, which seemed to me aimless and irresolute.'

"I can say that I had very clear and certain plans in my own mind, keeping in view Sir R. Buller's instructions; and I may say also that I had had particular facilities for knowing the Boer method of warfare, having served with Boer burghers against Kaffirs in 1878–9 and having commanded an expedition against Boers in 1884–5.

"I had heard many methods of relieving Ladysmith discussed, but not one that I considered likely to have been successful. The general idea was to send a large body of cavalry (some 3,000) to make a dash at the Boer lines around Ladysmith, either by Acton Homes or Weenen. Our cavalry and mounted men were not then fitted for such enterprises in mountain countries, and such an attempt would only have resulted in their being surrounded in the mountains. They were not numerous enough, experienced enough, or well enough armed to succeed in such a business so long as the Boers were jubilant.

"Only two methods of relieving Ladysmith were possible, and in each case it would consist of *breaking up*, and not merely *breaking into*, the Boer lines. (1) On the one hand, by an overwhelming assault of infantry on a position of the Boer lines, combined with a general advance of our whole lone line; or (2) on the other hand, the pounding away with our artillery at the Boers in their trenches until they were demoralised, and nearly on the run, and then launching an infantry assault. We were not strong enough to sweep over the country by sheer force of numbers, and our only prospect of success lay in the second method, of preparing a way with artillery bombardment of the Boer lines . . . This is what I proposed (in a telegram to Lord Roberts of 12 February 1900) in the final advance to relieve Ladysmith and in that way we did relieve Ladysmith.

"My plan, therefore, was to demoralise the Boers with artillery fire, and to assault their lines with infantry fire, and this would take some time . . .

"My instructions in the main seemed clear to me, and even without them, very little change in the course pursued could have been made, given the crossing at Trichard's Drift. Spioenkop being taboo, the only possible place for attack was the Rangeworthy Hills as far as Barton Hill; beyond that the valley of Acton Homes runs between two ranges of hills, and was swept with the fire of long-range guns, to which we could not reply, having none ourselves.

"At the time of receiving my instructions, the topography of the country was unknown, and I had to reconnoitre to find out how the roads ran, and feel for the enemy and elaborate a plan of attack.

"THE NIGHT MARCH WAS A SURPRISE TO THE ENEMY:

"Sir R. Buller states: 'The arrival of the force at Trichard's Drift was a surprise to the enemy, who were not in strength.'

"It was intended that the crossing should be commenced as a surprise, and the hills immediately commanding the crossing occupied by our troops; but the hills beyond could not be reached so rapidly by our troops as by the enemy who were camped immediately behind Spioenkop, and within two hours of sunrise on 17th January the Boers could have had from 5,000 to 10,000 men ready to oppose us.

"The enemy did not oppose us strongly at Trichardt's Drift because, in doing so, they would have been more or less exposed to the fire of our Naval guns situated near Potgieters and they wanted to turn us away from the help of these guns . . . "

But Warren was ultimately proved right. Boer troops came to Trichardt's within half an hour of Warren's wagons.

Eminent Boer archivist historian, J.H. Breytenbach, in volume 3 of his *Geskiedenis van die Tweede Vryheidsoorlog*, says only a few Commandos occupied the area where Warren's troops showed up. He says the British could have got on and through to Ladysmith.

But could they? Warren was worried about Acton Howes, which was on the road to Ladysmith, and therefore used by "a large portion of Free State Boers" on the move all the time.

Had the British taken the initiative they, says Warren, stood a good chance of being cut off and isolated, without supports.

Sir Charles now describes the countryside around the Rangeworthy hills position and says: "There are two roads over the Rangeworthy Hills; the more southerly by Fair View to Groote Hoek, immediately west of Spioenkop. It is about five miles from Trichard's Drift to Groote Hoek by this road; the more northerly road runs nearly east-and-west through Acton Homes . . .

"No advance could be made by Acton Homes without first securing the hills north, east and west. Thus, strategically Acton Homes could not be considered as a route for advance, except with an overwhelming force.

"The road by Acton Homes, however, was known to be the line of communication of a large portion of the Orange Free State boers, and the question would naturally arise whether it was desirable to hold and secure it.

"The answer is clear. For a large and overwhelming attacking force Acton Homes was a point to secure, but for a small attacking force such as that with Sir R. Buller, the Acton Homes position was to be avoided. For the relief of Ladysmith it was strategically a mistake to attempt to cut off the Boers from the Orange Free State at a time when they were desirous of proceeding there to resist Lord Roberts's threatened advance. The true strategy lay in inducing the Orange Free State Boers to retire into their own country, so as to diminish the preponderating Boer force then in Natal."

Warren's next heading was *Sir R. Buller's Views as to Crossing the Tugela*, including a description of how Warren masterminded the river crossing at Trichardt's Drift with his wagons across dangerous pontoon bridges.

Then he moves on to: *Consideration I Had Given to Crossing the Tugela.*

"We were aware on leaving Cape Town for Natal that the Boers had made the north bank of the Tugela their line of defence. It was a formidable obstacle, as it is about 100 yards wide, has a rapid current, and in wet weather is impassable by any of its fords.

"On board ship I instituted war games to consider the crossing, and I came to the conclusion that the best point to cross at (failing Hlangwane) was opposite to Doornkloof, near the junction of the Greater and Lesser Tugelas; and that it was necessary that we should at once establish a post on the north side of the Tugela, with a pontoon bridge, so as not to depend on the rise and fall of the river.

"On January 15, I issued projects to the senior officers of the 5th Division calling on them to state how they would cross over an imaginary river defended by one long-range gun, with a view to causing the officers under me to think the matter well over.

"On January 15 I issued plans of the country about Potgieter's (from the farm map) but had to withdraw them at once, and make and issue plans of the ground about Trichardt's Drift, and on January 17th I issued a more complete plan divided into numbered squares, so that officers could signal to each other and to me concerning particular spots of ground they wished to refer to."

Under the heading *We make a Record Crossing of the Tugela* and *The Time That Sir R Buller estimated the Crossing Would Take*, Warren explains how it was possible to cross the river in the record time he did, and under severe pressure.

Then he writes: "Sir R. Buller states in his telegram to the War Office on the morning of January 18 the time he expected the crossing to take. 'Four miles higher up (Trichard's Drift) Warren has crossed the river by pontoon bridge 85 yards long, and hopes that his force will, by the evening, have advanced five miles from the river. To his right, the enemy are busily entrenching.'

"Now this information must have been derived from his personal observation when with me all the afternoon of January 17th overlooking the crossing; and it is thus plain that he then expected that I should have got over my vehicles by evening of the 18th, and advanced five miles." (What then of the element of surprise?)

"Now what was the actual result of our crossing? By the evening of January 18th I had crossed all my vehicles and troops, and was ready to march my infantry and artillery before sunrise on the following morning; part of my cavalry had proceeded about nine miles from the river, and encountered the enemy near Acton Homes, and required all the remaining cavalry to support them, and General Woodgate had arranged for a night attack on the enemy's position in front, it being considered too strong to attack by day.

"This is a copy of General Hart's note to General Woodgate: 'The operations you propose might be done by night with the moon. It would, probably, I think, result in severe repulse by day . . .'"

Under this heading: *While The Artillery and Vehicles were Being Passed Over the Tugela the Infantry and Cavalry were Engaged in Feeling for the Enemy*, Warren writes: "Sir R. Buller states: 'Sir C. Warren instead of feeling for the enemy elected to spend two whole days in passing his baggage. During this time the enemy reinforced and strengthened his position.'

"'He met with very slight opposition, but remained that day and the 18th passing over his baggage' (*Evidence, Royal Commission*).

"'At that time we had a fine chance. After the 17th our advantage was fast vanishing' (*Interview with London Daily Mail*, February 18, 1902).

"The manner in which these facts are misrepresented in these paragraphs gives a very wrong complexion to affairs. It has led the public to suppose that I took with me all kinds of camp equipage that should have been left behind.

"There was no baggage with my column in the ordinary acceptance of the term, and Sir R. Buller has given a wrong impression in speaking of artillery and munitions of war and food for the march under that name; although I would observe that the term was used generally for the whole impedimentia of the column.

"In my force orders of January 16th is the following: 'The only baggage that will be taken with the column will be the greatcoats of the men, camp kettles and a certain proportion of regimental tools, with 20lbs per officer, including their canteens. All other baggage, blankets and waterproofs, and other gear will be packed in separate wagons and will proceed to Spearman's Hill.'

"Thus the vehicles with the column contained only what was required for the first line – great coats, food, and munitions of war, besides the artillery, engineer and medical stores and vehicles. It was, I believe, the lightest equipped column of a mixed force that was at any time sent out during the war in South Africa.

"Thus my force has been pictured as luxuriating in all kinds of comfort during those eight days north of the Tugela, while the men had nothing but their great coats, not even waterproof sheets, and were sleeping out in the rain in the open.

"Again, Sir R. Buller states that I did not feel for the enemy as soon as Lord Dundonald reported himself to me on January 17th. The horses did not like the hollow noise of the pontoons and they went over by the drift (with some difficulty to the smaller horses). They did not complete their crossing till the evening of the 17th and they bivouacked that night within the infantry lines.

"This crossing took place immediately under the eye of Sir. R. Buller, who was watching it all the afternoon. On morning of the 18th the cavalry went west and north-west and Lord Dundonald reported to me that the Range-worthy Hills were occupied in force by the enemy. That afternoon he came into collision with the enemy, and asked for reinforcements which I sent him.

"Two brigades of infantry under Generals Woodgate and Hart crossed the Tugela on the morning of January 17th and at about noon Sir R. Buller met General Woodgate at the ferry, and gave him orders relative to the attack, told him not to hurry, and to give the men their dinners before he started. The hills immediately commanding the pontoon were cleared of the enemy about 3.30pm for, say, 2,000 yards from the river. Beyond that there was a dip in the ground.

"Sir R. Buller witnessed the attack . . . On the morning of the 18th January, General Woodgate proposed to advance, but General Hart considered it too dangerous by day and a night attack was arranged which did not come off. On the afternoon of January 18 I reconnoitred the position on Rangeworthy Hills, and saw that if we took them we could not take our wagons by the Fairview Road without first taking Spioenkop also, or rendering it harmless. I therefore thought it necessary to reconnoitre the Acton Homes road, which I did the next day.

"Thus the two days (17th and 18th) which Sir R. Buller states I occupied in passage of my baggage, without feeling for the enemy, on one day (17th) the work was carried out under his own eyes; he gave orders himself to my subordinates, and he claimed my attention all the afternoon, instead of allowing me to be occupied fully with my own arrangements. If matters were not being carried out in accordance with his views, it is strange that he should not have notified this to me verbally or in writing . . ."

Much has been made in other works and publications of the rapidity by which Lord Dundonald and his cavalry was able to get going, finding the way to Ladysmith apparently open, but being recalled by Warren at the instant of success.

Various reports have Warren and Dundonald in acrimonious exchanges, with Dundonald insisting the way was clear, and Warren insisting Dundonald had overstepped his mark. Warren's biographer disputes the alleged tiff.

This is what Warren has to say, under the heading: *Lord Dundonald Feels for and Engages the Enemy on January 18:* "A great deal of confusion has arisen as to the position of Lord Dundonald's engagement, because the maps of the country issued in the daily papers showed Spioenkop *to the WEST of Acton Homes* and the engagement is depicted in some maps of taking place on the Boers lines of Rangeworthy Hills.

"Nothing of the sort ocurred.

"Lord Dundonald himself reported that the engagement took place two miles WEST of Acton Homes, and Sir R. Buller in his telegram to the War Office of January 18th says it took place to the WEST of Acton Homes.

"The facts, as related by Lord Dundonald are briefly as follows: At about 3pm to 4pm on January 18 a party of 200 to 300 Boers were seen by the advanced cavalry to be going WEST along the Acton Homes road, in the direction of the Orange Free State. They were successfully ambuscaded by Major Grahame at a point where the road crosses the Venter's Spruit near the Frere's store, at 25 miles from Ladysmith. Some of the Boers were shot down, most of them fled, but several got away to the west of Frere's store, and took up a position amongst some rocks, probably near the farm Nooitgedacht; they numbered about 30 altogether.

"This exploit was seen by Lord Dundonald from his signal station at Earthcote, and he sent me an 'express' saying he was heavily engaged, and required all the cavalry to assist him. This I received about sunset. I sent all the cavalry at once and detached General Hildyard's Brigade to march at 4.30am next morning to Venter's Spruit to support him.

"This was a serious mishap, as it appeared at the time, altering all my plans, but next morning I learnt how trivial the engagement had been, though it was successful.

"Later in the night I learnt more of the engagement, but it was not until about 10am on the following day that I ascertained that Lord Dundonald could hold his own without further assistance . . .

"Thus a skirmish of Lord Dundonald with a few Boers riding along a road west of Venter's Spruit and Acton Homes has been changed by Sir R. Buller into a forward movement of the cavalry *eastward* towards Ladysmith. In this affair, the cavalry got too far away to the west, and quite out of the direction of Ladysmith.

"Sir R. Buller tells the *Daily Mail* (April 18, 1902): 'But for Warren, Lord Dundonald, after winning Acton Homes, would have pressed forward and probably ended the matter by entering Ladysmith. Warren effectually stopped Dundonald by refusing him further supplies.'

"Lord Dundonald never had the slightest prospect of getting past Acton Homes to Ladysmith; if he had attempted to do so, he would certainly have been captured." [1]

Confirmation that Warren was right came unexpectedly by telegram from Sir George White in Ladysmith. On January 19, he telegraphed to Buller: "A force of 1500 to 2000 Boers moved from Clydesdale towards Acton Homes, 5pm today, by main road." [2]

Warren continued: "I found it necessary when he [Dundonald] got so far away from me to remind him of Sir R. Buller's orders, and said: 'Our objective is not Ladysmith; our objective is to effect junction with Sir R. Buller's force, and there to receive orders from him.'

"To this he replied: 'I quite understand your general plan, and that we have to unite with Sir R. Buller.' At this time, Lord Dundonald was corresponding direct with Sir R. Buller, I presume by his [Buller's] orders.

"Lord Dundonald never gave me the slightest indication that he would push forward by east or north-east to Ladysmith, or that he found any opening in that direction; so far as I know he was never able to make any reconnaissance of the Boer Lines in that direction. In any case, he never sent me any information up to January 19th, except the following: 'Silbourne, who took the flag of truce into the enemy's lines last night, reports the heights on either side of main road

(Acton Homes to Ladysmith) to be very strongly defended,' and a verbal report that the enemy were concentrating at Acton Homes.

"In his report subsequently he states that on the afternoon of January 18 (i.e. on his arrival at Acton Homes) he sent out patrols to the west and north-west and saw that large numbers of the enemy were continually arriving from the east, to concentrate and resist an attack by him on the Acton Homes to Ladysmith road, and he had made no attempt to meet them.

"So far from the cavalry having pushed up in any way to the enemy's lines on the Rangeworthy hills, the tendency was entirely in the other direction, and the position taken up west of Acton Homes was an anxiety to me on that account."[3]

And that disposed of Lord Dundonald.

SOURCES
1. *Spioenkop Despatches.*
2. *Commission on the War in South Africa.*
3. *Spioenkop Despatches .*

CHAPTER NINETEEN

Spioenkop – Part 6

Warren tightens the screw
Buller's statements of a man in a dream

Then Sir Charles moved on to an intriguing item he labelled: *Sir R. Buller depicts an engagement on January 19 which did not take place.*

"The events on January 19th are briefly as follows: The troops and vehicles of the force were all on the march from Trichardt's Drift to Venter's Spruit Laager early in the morning.

"General Hildyard's brigade started at 4.30 am to assist Lord Dundonald, if it should be necessary. General Woodgate's and Hart's Brigades covered the flank march of the vehicles which were in six parallel columns. In doing so, General Woodgate was directed to search for any weak point in the Rangeworthy hills defence, and to make a reconnaissance up the slopes of Three Tree Hill, where I considered we could attack. In the mean time I reconnoitred towards Acton Homes and saw that it would be impossible to take troops in that direction with wagons without occupying the hills beyond, and for this we were too weak.

"I then settled to attack the Rangeworthy hills on the morning of January 20th, sending our wagons back again to Potgieter's as we could not take wagons by either of the two roads.

"I then saw Lord Dundonald, who was still in possession of the site of his engagement of the 18th, but could not assist by any advance. I then communicated my plans for the next day to the Generals and Staff Officers concerned.

"There was NO engagement on the 19th, except the flank march of the brigades, and reconnaissance made.

"These are Sir R. Buller's criticisms on the work of January 19: 'On the 19th he attacked and gained a considerable advantage; on the 19th I ought to have assumed command myself. I saw that things were not going well – indeed everybody saw it.'

"'On the 19th Lord Dundonald, with Warren's cavalry moving northwards, had taken the right flank of the Boer position, whereas General Warren had advanced to the westward, and was crossing Venter's Spruit. I was dissatisfied with Warren's operations, which seemed to me aimless and irresolute.'

"'Dundonald's movement was a decided success, and should have been supported by artillery, while Warren's infantry should have attacked the salient which Dundonald's success had left exposed. On that night I debated with myself whether or not I should relieve Warren of his command."' (*Evidence to the Royal Commission*).

Warren writes: "These are the statements of a man in a dream. No such occurrences ever took place as far as I know. Lord Dundonald was with me on the afternoon of the 19th, and his reports never mention any such occurrence.

"If Lord Dundonald had really taken the right flank of the Boer position would not Sir R. Buller, who was in direct communication with Lord

Dundonald, have asked me for a report, and telegraphed it to the War Office?

"In these statements Sir R. Buller finds fault with me for going down to the water at Venter's Spruit; in his letter to me of January 17th he tells me to do so in these words: 'If your direct road is blocked, we must go forward by moving off to the left, and this will have the further advantage that it will keep you near the water at Venter's Spruit.'

"The only possible solution I can suggest to this extraordinary misconception is that Sir R. Buller imagines that Lord Dundonald's attack on Bastion Hill, on January 20, took place on January 19 against some position further north than Bastion Hill, and that he was subsequently withdrawn from it. But as Sir R. Buller was on the ground on the 21st, 22nd and 23rd, I cannot understand his falling into such errors."

Relentlessly, Warren moves on.

Under the heading: *Sir R. Buller's inconsistent statements concerning the capture of the Rangeworthy hills on 20th January,* he writes: " 'Telegram to War Office, 20th January – General Clery, with part of Warren's force has been in action from 6am to 7pm today. By judicious use of his artillery, he has fought his way up, capturing ridge after ridge for about three miles. Troops are now bivouacing on the ground they have gained, but main position is still in front of them.'

"'Telegram to War Office, 27th January – Sir Charles Warren, as I have said, drove back the enemy and obtained possession of the southern crest of the high tableland, which extends from the line Acton Homes, Hunger's Poort to the western Ladysmith hills.'

"This is how this successful engagement was depicted in the Despatches of 30th January and subsequently: 'On the 20th, instead of pursuing it (his imaginary advanatage of the 19th) he divided his force and gave General Clery a separate command.

" 'On the 20th I went over and saw Warren. He had that day attacked the salient and taken it, but instead of supporting Dundonald, he had induced him to fall back from the position which he had occupied on the 19th.' Again he states he wished to relieve me of the command. (*Evidence to the Royce Commission*).

"These later statements are simply a mass of misconceptions. There was no advantage gained by Lord Dundonald on the 19th January, and I could not have induced him to abandon a position he never occupied. I did not divide my force and give General Clery a separate command.

"Further, Sir R. Buller did not come over to see me on the 20th January as stated by him before the Royal Commission. It might be supposed that he had simply made a mistake of dates, but he says: 'On 20th I went over to see Warren. He had that day attacked the salient and taken it.' He states that on this day he found that his own plans were hopelessly wrecked, and that then he left me to carry our my own plans, sending me the reinforcements I asked for. This is all wrong, as will be shown (under the next heading). He did not come over on the 20th, but he came and interfered with my operations on 21st, 22nd and the 23rd."

The next heading reads: *General Buller states that on 20th January he left me to carry out my own plan of operations, and yet he elsewhere states that on 21st, 22nd and 23rd January he urged me to adhere to his plans, which he states had already been hopelessly wrecked.*

Warren writes, quoting Buller: " 'I continually proposed to General Warren that he should attack the enemy's right, which was *en l'air* and not strong, and which was part of the original programme to try and turn, but I never suggested doing this hurriedly or without adequate forethought and preparation".

" 'On the 20th I went over to see Warren. I saw . . . that my own plan of operations had been hopelessly wrecked . . . I concluded to leave Warren to pursue his work, merely suggesting to him certain changes in the posting of his troops for the greater security of the position. I then returned to my former position to watch for my change.'

"Thus Sir R. Buller, though considering my operations to be aimless and irresolute, concludes on the 20th January to leave me to carry them out. Yet while considering his own plans hopelessly wrecked, he, on the 21st to the 23rd, continually urges me to adhere to the original programme of attacking the enemy's right (we had already taken it). Yet again he states that by the 23rd, the enemy against us was 15,000 strong, and that the right was too strong to attack. 'The enemy's right was too strong to allow me to force it.'

"It will be seen that while I was in command Sir R. Buller speaks of the force in front of me as being insignificant, only 600, but when he took command it amounted to 15,000. He makes no suggestion as to where these 14,400 men were located in the interval. As it only took three hours for a party of Boers to get from their extreme left to their extreme right, from Colenso to Acton Homes, they must always have been close at hand."

Warren goes on in the next section to detail the Boer forces and from whence they came.

Then he says, under the heading: *Sir Redvers Buller did not give me the assistance in my attack that he could have given.*

"(a) Had General Barton been directed to attack and harass the enemy at Hlangwane and Colenso, he might have kept a considerable number of Boers off me, but owing to his receiving no instructions to do so, the Boers left his front to a great extent.

"(b) Had Sir George White been communicated with he might have made some demonstration . . .

"(c) Sir R. Buller made no use of the 10th Brigade at Potgieter's, although he states in his instructions: 'I shall threaten both the positions in front of us, and also attempt a crossing at Skiet's Drift, so as to hold the enemy off you as much as possible.' This he did not attempt to carry out.

"(d): Sir R. Buller kept the balloon with him when it was comparatively useless, and never gave me any information about the enemy from 17th to 23rd January, except what he got from Sir G. White. The balloon with us would have been invaluable.

"(e): Sir R. Buller kept all the long range guns with him, though these were urgently required by us, and yet he did not use them to advantage.

"He could have enfiladed the whole length of the Boer lines opposite to me and made havoc among the enemy's entrenchments with lyddite shells. I was not aware at the time that his guns had so long a range, and he may not have been aware of it either.

"(f): Sir R. Buller did not send me the 10th Brigade and the 5in. howitzer Battery until 22nd January; if they had been sent at first operations would have been expedited.

"(g): Sir R. Buller allowed me no extra staff to assist me in the work of an independent command, and would not permit me to take any regimental officers to assist me unless the commanding officers concurred. All said that they could not spare any officers."

Sir Charles continues: "Sir R. Buller states that I swung round my left on January 21st and subsequently he states that my right was in advance of my left, and that I refused to advance my left.

"Telegram to War Office, January 21, 9pm: 'Warren has been engaged all day, chiefly on the left, which he has swung round about a couple of miles. The ground is very difficult, and as the fighting is all the time up hill, it is difficult to say exactly how much has been gained, but I think we are making substantial progress.'

"'On the 21st I find that his right was in advance of his left.' He then proceeds to state that my artillery were crowded on one small space, and that I had divided my fighting line into three, independent commands, independent of each other, and independent of myself.

"This statement about independent commands independent of me is purely imaginary.

"With reference to the artillery, it is still a question how far guns should be concentrated and how far they should be distributed; in this case I exercised my own judgement, in which General Clery and the Commandant Royal Artillery concurred. As for putting artillery on the left, the 15-pounders were of little or no use then, except against infantry; what we wanted was long-range guns to reply to those of the Boers on the left.

"I urged strongly on Sir R. Buller the necessity of long-range guns, and he sent me the 5in howitzers, which were very useful, but still not sufficient range.

"In the morning, however, I heard from Colonel Kitchener [brother of Horatio Kitchener] that a force of Boers were moving down against our left from Acton Homes, thus requiring the 15-pounders on my left. Upon which I telegraphed to General Clery, 9.35am: 'A Boer force is coming round beyond left from Acton Homes. I am taking two batteries down there at once to support the left which is very weak near Bastion Hill.'

"It will thus be seen that I acted on my own initiative in putting guns on the left; in fact I had spoken to General Clery on the subject on the previous day that it might be necessary . . ."

Warren now moves to January 22, and under the heading *Sir R. Buller proposed an attack on January 22nd on our left, and also desires me not to execute any enterprise further to the left, as he anticipated a counter stroke from the enemy,* says: " 'The days went on, I saw no attempt on the part of General Warren either to grapple with the situation or to command the force himself.'

"The 10th Brigade had only arrived during the forenoon of this day, and the 5in howitzer battery the previous evening and this morning, and Sir R. Buller had sent me a telegram at 5am: 'I think it possible the enemy may try a counter stroke; they are concentrated, while your troops are widely extended, and do not support each other. I should be cautious how I attempted any enterprise further on the left at present.'

"Sir R. Buller arrived in the morning and told me he wished me to attack the position in front of Bastion hill on our left on the Rangeworthy Hills if I thought it desirable, and that I must consult my generals on the subject, otherwise he proposed to withdraw the force.

"I went over the positions with Sir R. Buller and again I pointed out to him that unless Spioenkop was taken, or neutralised we could not march our wagons over the hill road, and I had proposed to send them back, but that I hoped to capture the position in front of us after a few more hours' fire when we had got the howitzers into work.

"He replied: 'Of course you must take Spioenkop.' I then arranged that if we decided not to attack on the left, we would take Spioenkop that night."

So much for the theory, made much of, that the attack on Spioenkop was a spur-of-the-moment decision taken willy-nilly by Warren without due consideration.

It was proposed by Warren. And seconded by Buller.

"I was myself," writes Warren further, "desirous of going on with the bombardment, and then assaulting the position in front of Three Tree Hill. At this time, the trenches of the Boers had only been under fire for one day, the 21st, and the howitzers had not yet commenced.

"At the meeting of the Generals, General Clery was most emphatic against an assault on the left from Bastion Hill, and I concurred with him, because I could see no particular object in possessing this position at great loss, as there were other positions behind it. The best position to capture was evidently that in front of Three Tree Hill, but it was not yet prepared for assault.

"Next to this was Spioenkop. The advantages of an attack on Spioenkop over that on the left was that we should there have the fire of all our guns from both sides (i.e Three Tree Hill and Potgieter's) and very few Boer guns could be trained on it. While in regard to the position on the left, we could get but few of our guns on it and it was under fire of a great number of Boer long-range guns to which I could not reply."

Now Warren moved onto his item 22: *Sir R. Buller came over and said to me (January 23rd) 'Attack or retire'. In saying this he referred only to attacking Spioenkop, so far as I understood him.*

"Sir R. Buller states that he calculated that at this time there were 15,000 against us, or more than twice the number there were against him at Potgieter's, when he hesitated to attack. He states that for four days I had kept my men continuously exposed to shell and rifle fire, etc.

"All this conversation related in paragraph 2 of his Despatch of January 30th was new to me when I read it.

"It certainly was never addressed to me, and the paragraph is written as though Sir R. Buller had had no report from me from January 19 to January 23rd. At the time of this alleged conversation we had held the position for bombarding purposes on 21st and 22nd and the 5in. howitzers had only been in use on the 22nd, so that the position was not prepared for assault. Sir R. Buller said the assault must take place that night, or he should retire the force, and accordingly I arranged for the capture of Spioenkop. He refused to allow General Coke to go in command of the assaulting party, and ordered me to place General Woodgate in his place.

"Now General Coke I knew was well acquainted with throwing up earthworks [Warren and Buller saw as much when they visited him at Springfield, and Buller was annoyed at the effort] but I was not aware that General Woodgate was so acquainted.

"I had proposed to lead the assaulting column myself, but Sir R. Buller said I must not do this, but must occupy a central position all the time, so as to command the attack on Spioenkop, and be ready to provide against a counter stroke on our left, which he expressed some anxiety about. I quite saw the wisdom of this remark."

Under the heading: *From the first, Sir Redvers Buller appears to have had misgivings as to the practicability of the attack on the Rangeworthy Hills*, Warren says: "I consider that the pessimistic views of Sir R. Buller respecting our advance were most injurious to our successs; nothing could be more depressing to a force for the Commander-in-Chief to hold such views on the subject, as he has since expressed.

"Sir R. Buller was with me all through January 17th watching the enemy, and yet he says to the (London) *Daily Mail* (April 18th, 1902): 'After the 17th our advantages were fast vanishing, for the enemy was fast concentrating before us. By the 19th, through Warren's dilatoriness, it was all but gone. I might have saved the situation, but after the 19th I could not well have done so.

" 'On the 20th I went to see Warren. I saw that the advantages I had hoped for had been let slip, and that my own plan of operations had been hopelessly wrecked'.

"It is thus apparent that so early as 18th Sir R. Buller was contemplating the possibility of a retirement. Yet all this time, Sir R. Buller gave me no hint of his entertaining such views."

In item No 24, *Sir Redvers Buller gives two very inconsistent views of the position occupied on the Rangeworthy Hills from January 20th to 25th*, Warren goes further. " 'Telegram to War Office, January 23rd: Warren holds the position he gained two days ago. In this duel the advantage rests with us, as we appear to be searching his (the enemy's) trenches, and his artillery fire is not causing us much loss.'

" 'Telegram to the War Office, January 27th: The actual position held was perfectly tenable, but did not lend itself to advance, as the southern slopes were so steep that Sir C. Warren could not get an effective artillery position, and the supply of the troops with water was a difficulty.

" 'His force was in a good position, and might be successful. In any event, whether successful or not, the troops would spent some little time under fire in fairly close contact with the enemy, and would then gain comparatively cheaply that battle training in what I knew them most deficient.' "

Again, Buller corroborates what Warren had been trying to do all along – acclimatising his fresh-from-Britain troops to the harsh realities of the South African veld, and the merciless onslaught of the well-trained Boers.

Warren goes on, quoting Buller: " 'General Warren's disposition had mixed up all the brigades, and the position he held was dangerously insecure.

" 'For four days he had kept his men continuously exposed to shell and rifle fire, perched on the edge of an almost precipitous hill. I said it was too dangerous a situation to be prolonged, and that he must either attack or I should withdraw his force.'

" 'His position was insecure' [all the above quotations are from Buller].

"The question of the security of the position must be a subject of opinion depending on many circumstances, but I was quite satisfied with it, and felt convinced that the Boers would not attack us from the front, though we were always liable to attack from the Spioenkop side.

"As to mixing up my brigades, they had already been mixed up by Sir R. Buller. The 10th Brigade had left two battalions behind in Cape Colony, and had two temporarily attached and was now a corps brigade attached from 5th Division, while General Lyttleton's Brigade had been attached to the 5th Division, though it belonged to the 2nd Division, and General Hart's Brigade had been attached to the 2nd Division so that the brigades were all mixed, but not by me.

"If Sir R. Buller means that the battalions of the brigades were all mixed up, I can state that there was less mixing up of battalions on this occasion than in any other engagement I witnessed in Natal.

"So far as I know the only mixture was the York and Lancaster on the left and the Connaught Rangers on the right; but such changes are inseparable from modern warfare, where an advancing line, if it intends to hold what it gets, must remain on its ground.

"These dispositions were made by General Clery, of whom Sir R. Buller has stated that 'with a thorough knowledge of his profession, he thoroughly understands how to lead his troops in the field'.

"Any battalion, coming on to the Rangeworthy Hills from General Hildyard's Brigade were attached to General Hart's Brigade, in accordance with the following memorandum from General Clery: '8.30pm, January 21st. I will be glad it if was made clear that all troops coming up the ridge occupied by General Hart would come under his orders. If you approve, please instruct General Hildyard.'"

SOURCES
Spioenkop Despatches.

Spioenkop – Part 7

Warren justifies Spioenkop

It is Item 26 in Warren's reply to the charges and insinuations by Sir Redvers Buller. Under the heading: *The Capture of Spioenkop*, Warren writes: "The misstatements concerning the engagement on Spioenkop have been so numerous that it would require a volume to refute them all.

"As an example I may point out that the late Colonel Henderson, the official historian of the war, in a preface to Count Sternburg's work, states that a force of 4,000 held a position where there was not room for 500, while Colonel Thorneycroft reported on the ground that with six battalions the force was really inadequate to hold so large a perimeter.

"On the one hand I have been blamed for crowding the troops on top, and on the other hand for not sending sufficient reinforcements.

"The principal charge made against me by Sir Redvers Buller in his Despatches is that I did nothing to assist the troops there. He states that I made no arrangement, and that Colonel Thorneycroft exercised a wise discretion in abandoning his post; and he comes to the conclusion after he (Sir R. Buller) had issued an order that there was to be *no retirement*, after I had telegraphed 'No surender' and after I had written to Colonel Thorneycroft a letter (which he received) stating that it was of *vital importance* that the position should be held.

"I am quite convinced that throughout the war there was no occasion when matters were more fully considered and provided for, considering the short space of time permitted. I have further to mention that Sir R. Buller states that I ought to have done certain things at sundown, such as clearing the trenches, deepening them, arranging for artillery on the top. These were all divisional matters, which must be superintended by the officer commanding on the spot. So far as I was concerned I sent to Spioenkop everything I possessed that would have been of use.

"Sir R. Buller had debarred me from going myself. [NB: This clarifies Warren's statements earlier that Spioenkop was taboo.] In any case the retirement commenced at sundown, and no intimation of this reached me until 2.30am."

Sir Charles continues under the heading: *Engineer Operations on Spioenkop:* "The 17th Company Royal Engineers only had been sent with my force, the 37th Company Royal Engineers being kept by Sir R. Buller at Potgieter's.

"I sent half the 17th Company Royal Engineers, under Major Massey, up Spioenkop with General Woodgate's column, provided with entrenching tools, and at 3.30am on the morning of January 24th I sent the remainder of that company, and also Colonels Wood and Sim, Royal Engineers, and their staff officers, to do all that was necessary on the slopes and summit of Spioenkop.

"They were employed there most of the day. The work they carried out was very considerable, and consisted of (a) entrenchments on summit, (b) gunslides on the slopes of Spioenkop, completed at 3.30 pm, for naval guns should they arrive, (c) making mule path up Spioenkop slopes, and wagon road over the drift at foot, (d) making dam for water at foot of Spioenkop for carts to fill and take up mule path.

"For these purposes not only the Engineers, but also their batmen and kaffir drivers and boys turned out and helped; every man was employed on the works, and they worked well.

"During the day I sent up to the summit of Spioenkop every pick, shovel and crowbar, and sandbags (2,000) we possessed. They were taken up by the Middlesex and Dorset Regiments. I also had three coils of 3 inch rope brought up from Venter's Spruit laager to the Engineer bivouac, to be ready in case Sir Redvers Buller should send over any long-range guns to reply to those of the Boers.

"At 4.30pm I telegraphed to 37th Company, Royal Engineers, to be sent over to relieve the 17th Company during the night. They arrived at Trichardt's Drift at 8.25pm, arriving at the foot of Spioenkop at 12.30am on January 25th. They were about to ascend to relieve the 17th Company Royal Engineers when they were stopped by the retirement."

Warren's Item 28 is headed: *Artillery Operations on Spioenkop:* "The 4th Mountain Battery started from Chieveley by train for Spioenkop on morning of January 23rd, and commenced march from Frere at 5.30pm, but did not make much way in the darkness. It marched all day of 24th, reaching Trichardt's Drift at 2.30pm. Sir R. Buller told me it must have rest before it went up Spioenkop, and the ascent was commenced at 12.30am, but progress was arrested by the retirement of the force from Spioenkop.

"I constantly asked Sir R. Buller for long-range guns. At 4pm on January 24th I gathered from a note from Sir R. Buller that he was sending two Naval 12-pounders, and I at once sent Captain Hanwell, R.A., up Spioenkop to report to officer commanding, and look out for sites for these guns, and I detailed Lieutenant Otto Schwykkard as guide to these guns.

"I detailed Colonel Sim, R.E., to go with a fatigue party of 600 men to make the epaulements for the guns, and two relaps of 600 each from regiments as reserve were ordered. Lieutenant James, R.N., arrived with the guns at about 8.30pm, and left with Colonel Sim about 9.30pm. They arrived about midnight at the foot of Spioenkop, and met the force retiring.

"Lieutenant Doomer, R.A. was sent to foot of Spioenkop on the night of January 23rd to report on the practicability of getting up guns and to signal effects of artillery fire. He was on Spioenkop from 7am till 5pm, signalling information to Commandant Royal Artillery. He reported it impossible to get 15-pounder guns up the slopes. The naval guns could, however, have been got up readily, and could also have been used on the slopes in reply to pom-poms etc. Attempts were made to get up machine guns without avail. Lord Dundonald offered to get up one of his machine guns during the night of the 24th, and this offer I accepted; he would have done it but for the retirement."

Warren goes on now to describe the *Water Supply on Spioenkop.* He writes: "Most elaborate arrangements were made for the water supply for troops. It would have averaged one gallon per man for the troops originally sent up.

"Every pack mule in the force was employed, 25 mules in all, and Major Sargent, Deputy Assistant Adjutant General, and Major Williams, Provost Marshal, were employed all day supervising.

"Everything was done that could be done, but the men were suffering from artificial thirst, due to their having just arrived in a very hot climate and having been exclusively fed on tinned meat."

[The tinned meat was salty through preservatives – author.]

"Water was brought up in water carts from the dam to the Spioenkop depot, and from there it was loaded up on mules in biscuit boxes. Of course a good deal of water spilled from the biscuit boxes, but they were the only receptacles we had. There were East India pickul bearers [a *picau* is the Maori word for haversack – author] in the force which Sir R. Buller had at Potgieter's, and they were asked for, and eventually sent, but they arrived without their pickuls."

Under Item 30, *Supplies of All Kinds on Spioenkop*, Warren writes: "Supplies of all kinds were plentiful at the foot of the hill. All the regimental supply wagons of the battalions of the 5th Division and other corps on our side engaged were congregated there in the afternoon, and the troops had exactly the same supplies available then, as they had had during the whole period of the expedition. Moreover at 5pm nearly all the 11th Brigade who had gone up during the night had come down for water and food. General Coke states the men brought down eight or 10 water bottles to fill and took them up again. There was a limited amount of water on the hill in springs, which had been developed."

Under the heading *Ammunition on Spioenkop* Warren writes: "There was a plentiful supply of ammunition. In fact, the Dorset Regiment were employed all night in bringing it down after the retirement."

Then came *The Abandonment of Spioenkop*. This is what Warren had to say: "The retirement from Spioenkop is a unique episode in our military history, and seems unaccountable (taking place as it did, at nightfall, when there were at least 10 hours of rest before dawn the next day) unless the retirement of the King's Royal Rifles from the Twin Peaks may have influenced Colonel Thorneycroft's proceedings."

(Buller recalled them after Warren had asked Lyttleton to endeavour to clear the hillocks from where rapid and heavy fire emanated.)

"In order that some misconceptions concerning Spioenkop may be cleared up, I give the following brief account:

"I had telegraphed at 11.50am to Colonel Crofton that Colonel Thorneycroft was placed in command of the summit with rank of Brigadier-General, and it was Colonel Crofton's duty to communicate to Colonel Thorneycroft this order, together with my former message to him of 11.50am, telling him to 'hold out to the last; no surrender', and that I was sending him three battalions to support him.

"That this heliograph of 11.50am was written out correctly and communicted to Colonel Crofton there can be no doubt, as it was subsequently picked up by a Boer on Spioenkop and published in the (London) *Daily Mail.*

"How it reached Colonel Thorneycroft I don't know, but as Colonel Crofton continued throughout the day to command the 11th Brigade, he must have been in communication with Colonel Thorneycroft at intervals. Either Colonel Crofton retained the command, or he handed it over.

"Sir R. Buller states: 'The officer who was placed in command on the top of the hill made several efforts to communicate his situation to General Warren, but received no reply' (*Evidence, Royal Commission*, February 18, 1903).

"This is a very grave mis-statement, as I will show. At 1.25pm, I heliographed to Officer Commanding Spioenkop: 'Please say where Thorneycroft is; has he assumed command'?

"Reply: 'Colonel Thorneycroft is not here.' At 1.35pm, I again said to

Officer Commanding Spioenkop: 'Is General Coke on Spioenkop?' It was received but I got no reply.

"At 1.40pm I said to Officer Commanding Spioenkop: 'Please give me your views on Spioenkop, and inform me what you can do, and if anything can be done to advance the tactical situation.'

"It was received. At 1.50pm I said to Officer Commanding Spioenkop: 'What battalions have you got on Spioenkop?' At 2.15pm I said to Officer Commanding Spioenkop: 'Is General Coke on Spioenkop?'

"All these heliographs were seen by General Buller, who states that he was at the signal station, and saw all the messages I sent or received.

"About 2pm the sun began to be obscured, and it was difficult to send heliographs.

"It seems certain that these messages must have been sent on to Officer Commanding Spioenkop, and that either Colonel Crofton or Colonel Thorneycroft knew that General Coke was coming up.

"At 2.30pm Colonel Thorneycroft wrote the only report he sent during the day, and which was, I believe a reply to my heliogram of 1.40pm. This report was seen by General Coke at 3pm, who said on it: 'I have seen the above and have ordered the Scottish Rifles and King's Royal Rifles to reinforce. The Middlesex and Dorset Regiments and Imperial Light Infantry have also gone up . . . We appear to be holding our own at present.' This was received by me at 4.30pm, and so far there seemed to be no anxiety. At this time there were seven battalions on and about the summit.

"At 3.30pm, or an hour before I received this report, I received a telegram from General Buller stating there were seven battalions on Spioenkop (giving their names) and saying that Colonel Hill seemed to be in command. General Buller's remark on the tactical situation was, 'We hold the saddle on our right.'

"At 3.40 I received a heliograph from General Coke sent after he had endorsed Colonel Thorneycroft's report saying: 'The hill is being cleared of the Boers; the necessary reinforcements have been sent up; Scottish Rifles just reached the top etc.'

"About 3.30pm Colonel Sandbach, Assistant Adjutant General to Sir R. Buller, arrived from Spioenkop on his way to Sir R. Buller, and gave a good account of affairs.

"Thus the period during which I received no messages from Spioenkop was from noon to 3.40pm; but I had several times communicated with with Spioenkop during that time up to 2.15pm, so that had Colonel Thorneycroft or Colonel Crofton or Colonel Hill any messages to send they would have sent them.

"At about 4.30pm, I was making arrangements for sending the naval guns and working parties for the epaulements, and sent Captain Hanwell out to select sites for the guns on Spioenkop, and I assume that the latter reported his arrival to Colonel Thorneycroft. I received no further communication from Spioenkop till about 7.30pm, the heliograph being not now available; but at 6.30pm I sent by oil light a message to General Coke asking whether two battalions would be sufficient to keep on top of Spioenkop, saying that the others might be kept over in reserve.

"After 7.30pm I received General Coke's review of the situation, written at 5.30pm, and soon after a further report from General Coke, brought by Major Williams, taking a more cheerful view of affairs. Then I received a report from Lieutenant Winston Churchill, who had left me at about 4pm for the summit. I received no further communication from Colonel Thorneycroft till *after* he had reported the retirement to me at 2.30am.

"Sir R. Buller states I could not be found because I changed my camp. My divisional wagon had been moved because it had been shelled and a man had been severely wounded under it and a horse killed close to, but my bivouac was only changed a short distance, and the position was known at artillery headquarters. The fact is the night was so dark from mist at times, that it was easy to lose your way, even in a few yards.

"Sir R. Buller states in his evidence that I appealed to the nearest brigadier for reinforcements on Spioenkop on the morning of 24th January. He had directed me to apply to General Lyttleton for any assitance from Potgieters, because Sir R. Buller was so often away from there, and I was in constant contact with General Lyttleton from 17th to 25th January. I was under the impression that Sir R. Buller had seen my telegram, and that all my telegrams to General Lyttleton were duplicated and sent to Sir R. Buller.

"The taking of Twin Peaks by King's Royal Rifles by General Lyttleton was exactly what was required, and General Buller would not have done better himself.

"General Buller could readily have recalled the troops General Lyttleton sent if he had wished to do so, as he was at the Signal Station looking on all the time."

(Buller did later recall them, but read on).

"At 10am I asked for assistance and the hours at which the troops crossed the Tugela are as follows:

"Bethune's, 11.45am.

"Scottish Rifles, 12.30pm

"King's Royal Rifles, 1pm.

"At 1pm, General Lyttleton told me what he had done [sent his KRR up the Twin Peaks in a successful bid to get rid of Boers firing regularily at the top of Spioenkop, which they were able to enfilade] and said he would send further assistance if occasion offered, and General Buller was looking on. It is not intelligible that for three hours he [Buller] was not aware what General Lyttleton was doing, immediately under his eyes.

"Unfortunately General Buller did retire the Kings Royal Rifles during the afternoon. Had it not been for this I doubt if Colonel Thorneycroft would have retired from Spioenkop . . .

"I would here mention that when I received notice of the retirement from Spioenkop at 2.30am on January 25th I sent off at once duplicate messages by telegraph [Warren's biographer says telephone] and mounted messenger to Sir R. Buller . . .

"Sir R. Buller received the message at 5am and arrived at my bivouac at 6am."

So it was over. People had to be told.

On January 25th, Buller telegraphed to White: "Warren took Spioenkop the 24th and held it all day, but suffered very heavily; General Woodgate dangerously wounded, 200 killed and 300 badly wounded, and his garrison abandoned it in great disorder at night. I am withdrawing to Potgieter's and mean to have one square try to get with you, but my force is not strong enough I fear . . . "

Again, Buller the hesitant. The unwilling.

He had told White the same thing before Colenso.

On January 26th Landsdowne telegraphed to Buller: "Would it not be feasible, in case you should think it possible that your next endeavour to relieve Ladysmith may not be successful, for White to break out at night with all his mounted men, and as many others as he could carry in carts, together with some of his guns at any rate, and cross the Tugela River? The most likely moment for this endeavour would seem to be when you were engaged on the Tugela River, or immediately after, if you did not have decisive success.

"I am authorised by the Secretary of State for War to say that the Government is quite prepared to give you every support if you adopt this suggestion; but please understand that no restraint is placed on your entire freedom of decision."

Roberts, too, stepped in. In a telegram to Lansdowne, he wrote: "The following has been sent to Buller: 'I should be glad to have the earliest information of the reply you propose to send to Commander-in-Chief. It seems to me that White's action depends entirely upon the time he can hold out . . .

"It would be a desperate venture for White to break out and it would be a severe blow to our prestige throughout South Africa, and would in no small degree embarrass our future operations should he abandon the position he has so long defended and the sick and wounded."

A forceful Roberts, perhaps reading Buller's hesitancy.

Early on January 27th, White replied to Buller's telegram of the 25th:

" . . . We must expect to lose heavily in this campaign, and be prepared to face it. If you try again and fail, Ladysmith is doomed. Is not 7th Division available to reinforce you?

" . . . I put it to you and the government whether I ought not to abandon Ladysmith and try and join you. I could, I think, throw 7,000 men and 36 guns into the fight. If you would commence preparing an attack and draw off the enemy, say in the afternoon of a day to be settled between us, I would attack that night and do my best to join you.

"The attack from here ought to have great effect, but I fear my men are weak, and in some instances morally played out. The fall of Ladysmith would have a terrible effect, especially in India. I am deeply impressed with the gravity of the situation, and trust you will repeat this to the highest authoritiess.

"Deserters report Boers lost severely on the 24th, and were quite disheartened by your artillery fire, [which is what Warren continually advocated – author]. If we stick to them we may effect a junction but my proposal is a desperate one, and involves abandoning my sick and wounded, naval guns and railway rolling stock . . ."

The same day, Buller replied to London: "It has been one of my great difficulties that White has all along stated that he could help me very little, as when I originally planned his relief I fully expected to be met halfway. I fear that it would scarcely be possible for him to break out . . .

"Luck is dead against me, this last time cruelly so, but the enemy had 16,000 against me, or not less than the force that I could put into the field.

"The fact is that two set battles are required to relieve White. I have always thought that I could make a certainty of the first, but have been defeated. I am stopped by the necessity for the second. If, for example, I succeed here and then fail later, I shall be left with a demoralised force, short of water, perhaps 3,000 wounded and 16 miles from anywhere. Our officers expose themselves so unnecessarily that one loses them, and then the battalion is thereby demoralised. In a couple of days, however, I shall wire further particulars."

Obsequiously, Wolseley, Buller's friend, wired: "War Office . . . It is possible that my telegram of yesterday might be misinterpreted. Please understand that it is not intended to suggest that it is the best course for White to cut his way out. On the contrary, it is only when all the expedients for extricating him have failed that this plan, if practicable at all, should be adopted. The telegram, however, had better be considered as cancelled in view of Lord Roberts' subsequent communication to you."

While the tone of Wolseley's telegram may have placated Buller, he needed to tell White what went on at Spioenkop. White could hear shelling and firing all day from the hillock, as it is seen from Ladysmith. Now Buller telegraphed, on January 28th: "We had awful luck on the 24th; I had got two naval guns and a mounted battery half-way up Spioenkop when the troops came down. If we had had the luck out of all the Colonels up there to have found a really good fighting man, we should have been in Ladysmith in four days."

(Not a word, one notes, about the "fighting man" whom Buller ordered in supreme command. No mention of Thorneycroft at all.)

"As it is we are no better off, and some regiments here have had a severe shake. On the other hand, the Boers themselves admit very heavy casualties and that they are tired out."

(The Boers in fact lost 335 burghers).

"We have held them in their trenches at a distance of from 1,000 to 1,400 yards for a week and our artillery fire has been very good. We have lost, say, 1,400. I cannot think their casualties less than 1,000. The question is, can I get within a day's fight of you? At the present time they have the position at Potgieter's. I think I can certainly take that, but it will leave them on my left in the Acton Homes–Spioenkop position. They may not remain there, but if they do, I doubt if I can get to the Roodepoort position, which is, I hear, heavily entrenched."

(Roodepoort is a small hill a few kilometres from Lancer's Hill, between Ladysmith and Spioenkop.)

"I propose about Wednesday to attack Potgieter's. If I get through I shall be able to arrange with you for a simultaneous attack, you on Lancer's Hill and me on Roodepoort, and that I think offers the best chance of success. Believe me, I will leave nothing untried.

"Your No 55 (telegram) received since above was written. I agree with you that breaking out is only a final desperate resort. I shall try and force this position, and then we shall see.

"Some old Boers, who were very civil to our doctors on Spioenkop, told them that there were 16,000 of them in front of us, and not more than 4,000 left at Ladysmith.

"I have no means of knowing how true this is, but deserters say that most of the men are here. Lord Roberts says he cannot reinforce me, but that if you will wait till end of February, he will by then be in Bloemfontein and will have relieved Kimberley, which will, he says, reduce the pressure on Ladysmith.

"I doubt Roberts' forecasts coming off, and think I had better play my hand alone, and as soon as I can. What do you think?"

White replied the same day: " . . . It is most provoking about losing Spioenkop. I think it would be better if you stick to bombardment, and slow progress by something like sap rather than commit yourself to another definite attack. Information which I believe is correct says Boers are discouraged by superiority of your armament, and say they cannot stand it. Keep them therefore in their trenches and bombard them as heavily as you can. I don't think they will stand it long. I trust to your preventing them from throwing their strength on me . . . Boers can, however, come here from Potgieter's in 90 minutes. In this lies their great strength, you must not let them leave you and throw their strength on me."

White kept on advocating what Warren had been saying all along – bombard the Boers, and keep at it!

But what of Sir Charles? In a further statement, to the commisioners of the Royal Commission Inquiry, he writes under the heading *Retirement Across the Tugela*: "The abandonment of Spioenkop might have been reduced to a mere episode in our advance to the relief of Ladysmith had not Sir R. Buller committed himself to the plan of retirement in order to try a new line of attack at Vaalkrantz, almost from the first day of our crossing . . .

"Had we reoccupied Spioenkop on the morning of 25th January, we should have been masters of the situation, but Sir R. Buller could think of nothing but retirement from our positions so well gained.

"I had constantly brought before his notice that the Boers were getting shaken, and the Orange Free State Boers wished to be off as early as 21st January."

Under the heading *The Retreat of the Boers from Spioenkop and the Complete Victory of our Troops on the evening of 24th January*, he says, among other points: "Intelligence report, C32, 27th January: Natives tell scouts that day after Spioenkop fight large numbers of Boers and wagons trekking towards Berg (westward) thus confirming our suppositions. They however are now returning. Natives show great disappointment at unlooked-for result of battle, after apparent victory (A.W. Campbell, Lieutenant RA).

"Some Boers who had been on Spioenkop told my Aide-de-Camp Lieutenant Lowther in May 1900 that the Boers who were in full retreat from Spioenkop on evening of 24th January, and that our victory was complete."

Whatever Buller may have thought, Warren would not go away. In his final comments to the commissioners, under the heading *Sir R. Buller's Orders and his Suggestions*, Warren writes the most telling last few paragraphs.

"I have to call attention to the unfair position taken up by Sir R. Buller regarding my action. Either I was responsible for what I did, or I was acting under orders; but Sir R. Buller makes my position depend on after results.

"He states that he only suggested to me putting General Woodgate in command of the attacking column, instead of General Coke. It was most decidedly an order, for he stated he would not have General Coke in command.

"He states that he only suggested to me putting Colonel Thorneycroft in command of Spioenkop, and yet he says, in a letter of 24th January: 'I have telegraphed to you to put Thorneycroft in command.'

"On the other hand in respect to his suggested attack from our left, he says that I refused to carry out his instructions in not attacking there. Yet he told me to consult my generals as to doing so, and telegraphed to me at 7pm on 22nd January: 'If you mean to attack there, I should organise the attack thus – shell with howitzers stop howitzers as you open machine guns . . . and then attack. One battalion to attack, and all to open fire on the other schanzes.'

"If I had (against my own judgement and the judgement of the generals I consulted) attacked on this occasion, and failed, is it to be supposed that Sir R. Buller would have accepted the responsibility for the action he states that he constantly urged on me?"

And, under the heading *Sir R. Buller's Secret reports and charges against me*, he says: "I have to call attention to the adverse reports and charges Sir R. Buller has made against me, while (so far as I know) he was on the most friendly terms with me.

"He gave me no hint of any kind that he was reporting against me, and was, apparently, on such friendly terms that I often was asked by officers of other divisions to bring matters for them before him. I had myself for many years had a friendly feeling towards him, and though on several occasions after the war commenced, I was warned that he was not friendly, I did not credit it, and did not realise the manner in which he had treated me, until I saw copies of the *Spioenkop Despatches* in May, 1900, on my way to Griqualand West (*The Abridged Despatches*).

"Sir R. Buller gained his information in an informal manner, and not according to the usual routine, and he did not seem to have a good knowledge of topography or any mental prospective as to the value of the various items of information he received from so many different sources.

"The result was that he was apt to have an incorrect and distorted view of matters, which it was difficult to correct. If the correct view could be put before him he would suddenly grasp it and treat it as if he had always known it.

"Sometimes I succeded in putting a correct view before him, but, as a rule he would not permit me to proceed with what I had to say.

"As an instance of the manner in which he secretly reported wrong information, without informing me, I relate the following: On 12 February 1900, on looking at some telegrams in Sir R. Buller's book relative to the relief of Ladysmith, which Lord Roberts wanted me to see, I caught sight of a telegram from Sir R. Buller to Lord Roberts stating that I had had an acrimonious dispute with my staff relative to Spioenkop.

"I called Sir R. Buller's attention to this, and requested an explanation, and he assured me that he found he had made a mistake, and had explained to Lord Roberts that the dispute was between Colonel Thorneycroft and Colonel Hill.

"This instance will give you some idea of the random manner in which Sir R. Buller wrote about me, and how terribly handicapped I was in my dealings with him.

"I claim that, as I was in independent command (according to all the usages of war) I should have been informed of all the statements concerning my conduct made against me, and given an opportunity at the time of replying to them.

"Under such a system as that adopted by Sir R. Buller the reputation of no officer was safe."

And now for the *coup de grace*.

"Sir R. Buller states: 'I can never employ him (Warren) in an independent command.

"Yet after Vaal Krantz, on the 7th February, Sir R. Buller suddenly left the field, leaving me in independent command, to extricate the force from the position, and he sent me a very complimentary telegram on doing so.

"After Vaal Krantz I was always in command of at least three brigades up to the relief of Ladysmith, and I pushed the advance through, my command being always to the front.

"On the last day (Pieters) I organised the successful advance, and commanded the whole line north of the Tugela and east of Onderbroek, while Sir R. Buller was south of the Tugela.

"I received several congratulatory telegrams and verbal thanks, given before my staff, but on most days Sir R. Buller omitted to mention my name in the accounts of the actions given in his Despatches."

— Charles Warren, Lieut.-General, April 18, 1903.

The man who masterminded the final push to the relief of Ladysmith.

SOURCES

Spioenkop Despatches.
Commission on the War in South Africa.

CHAPTER TWENTY ONE

The Spioen Kop Despatches

The silence that shocked a nation

It was the Easter Parliamentary recess. The weather in London on Tuesday, April 18, 1900 was showery, but generally fair. Spring was in the air.

But the news wasn't. It was distinctly stormy, and Londoners awoke to a shocking headline in the *Daily Mail*: "Roberts on Spioenkop – Drastic Criticism of British Officers."

Alongside were the headlines: "Lord Roberts apportions responsibility; Officers censured; Buller's 'disinclination to assert his authority'; Sharp Criticism of Warren and Thorneycroft." [1]

It was like the burst of a Creusot shell in the middle of Piccadilly. What on earth had gone wrong? they wanted to know.

The fact that Spioenkop had happened almost four months earlier, almost forgotten now in the euphoria over the lifting of the siege of Ladysmith, suddenly mattered not.

It had never happened, in the long turgid, proud history of Britain's armed forces, that a senior officer – nay, not just a senior officer, but "Our Bobs" – had openly criticised two generals and a colonel. And not only that. They were still proudly serving their country!

The *Spioenkop Despatches* had been published, minus of course the section Buller had clearly marked "not necessarily for publication", and the sections withheld from publication by the Government. While the public clamoured for more, parliamentarians wanted – no demanded – to know why.

For days the *Mail* and every other British newspaper, continued to publish comment, speculation and reports on the *Despatches.*

It was a sensation!

No-one (apart from the War Office) had any indication that a feud existed between Buller and Warren. Certainly no one had any indication of how serious it really was.

The next day, the *Daily Mail* thundered in a leading article: "The sensation produced by the publication of the *Spioenkop Despatches* . . . (is a) painful fact that can have only one significance.

"It must surely mean that, in the interests of the nation and Army, Lord Roberts will be allowed, if he wishes, to send home those officers whose mistakes have had such tragic results.

"Any other measure would render the washing of this dirty linen in public quite incomprehensible.

"It is no doubt a painful and disagreeable task to remove from his command men who went out with so great a reputation . . .

"It is being said, indeed, that the relief of Ladysmith has expiated the blunders of Colenso and Spioenkop, and that Generals Buller and Warren will still be left in authority.

"But in these matters victory in the war and the welfare of the troops must be placed before any personal regard for officers, however distinguished.

"It is plain that General Buller and his second in command are far from being on the best of terms, and under these circumstances cordial co-operation is impossible . . .

"So many grave errors have been committed by our Army in the present war that it is of the utmost importance that incompetence, in whatever rank, should make way for talent . . .

"Lord Roberts is in a better position to judge of his subordinates' merits than the War Office authorities at Home, none of whom have seen anything of warfare against a white enemy under modern conditions!" [2]

But worse was to come. People began calling it a conspiracy of silence. Why, they wanted to know, had the Government kept the *Spioenkop Despatches* a secret for four months?

Why had they not been told what was going on? Also they wanted to know, how much *hadn't* they been told?

The clamour grew to a furore, and questions were asked. The first was on April 27, 1900, in the House of Commons, from Mr Swift MacNeill (Donegal): "I beg to ask the Under Secretary of State for War when did the comments and strictures of Lord Roberts on the operations at Spioenkop, dated 13th February, reach the War Office, and why were those comments and strictures withheld from the public until the (evening of) 17th April, and published when Parliament was not sitting?"

The Under Secretary of State for War (Mr Wyndham, Dover), replied: "Lord Roberts's despatch covering all the documents bearing upon Sir R. Buller's second attempt to relieve Ladysmith was received on the 9th March. The interval which elapsed between its receipt and publication was occupied by the printing of the documents, the consideration of their contents, and the telegraphic correspondence which took place between Lord Roberts and the Secretary of State on the question of publication," he said.

Which brought this rejoinder from Mr Swift MacNeill: "The delay is so great that we want Joshua's sun." [3]

But Wyndham's remark unleashed yet another furore. What did he mean by saying "telegraphic correspondence between Lord Roberts and the Secretary of State?" If there had been, what about Buller and Warren?

And three days later, Mr Swift MacNeill asked this question: " . . . Whether, between 9th March, the date of the receipt of the *Spioenkop Despatches* and Lord Roberts's comments thereon on 17th April, the day of the publication of those documents, any communications were held between the War Office and Sir Redvers Buller with reference to those *Despatches* and their contemplated publication?"

Wyndham replied: "No sir. No communication passed between the War Office and Sir R. Buller directly between the dates mentioned, but communications did pass between Lord Roberts and Sir R. Buller with regard to the publication of the *Despatches*." [4]

What did this mean? Was the public getting the whole truth?

In the meantime the British papers went to town. On April 19, for instance, the *Daily Mail*'s headlines read: "Consternation caused in military circles: Changes possible and probable; Reported recall of Sir Charles Warren.

"Something like consternation reigned yesterday throughout the military clubs and, indeed, in all military circles at the publication of Lord Roberts's comments upon the *Spioenkop Despatches*.

"It is impossible," said an officer of standing, "to see why these adverse strictures are published at all, and why, in particular, just now!

"Lord Roberts' despatch is rather more than two months old. It was penned by him when the deplorable events with which it deals were quite recent, and must have impressed him, who was but just arrived in the country, very forcibly. Here was his principal lieutenant engaged in the most crucial operation of the war failing from what seemed perfectly avoidable causes.

"Buller undoubtably neglected to keep his hand upon events, and left Warren to control them in a way that he disapproved. Warren's conduct throughout evinced a very mediocre gift of leadership, to call it by no stronger name.

"All this must have presented itself strongly to Lord Roberts, and encouraged him to speak out strongly, possibly to prevent further mishap by a timely reproof, or if necessary, removal.

"But a great deal has happened since Spioenkop . . . For what occult reason has the despatch been disinterred, reviving wretched memories . . . ?

"One plausible explanation has been offered . . . it has been suggested that a further change in command at the front is visible and that no better way could be found of removing Sir Redvers Buller or getting him to resign. If this is the intention it is an unworthy one and cannot be too strongly condemned . . ."

The *Mail* quotes another anonymous officer: "It seems that the officers likely to be affected by the *Despatches* are General Sir Redvers Buller, General Sir Charles Warren, Major-General Talbot-Coke, Colonel Thorneycroft and Colonel Crofton.

"The view is largely entertained that Sir Charles Warren will come home, and possibly General Buller."

A few paragraphs down the column is the headline: "Reported recall of Warren." The story reads: "The *Evening Standard* yesterday published the following: 'A reliable correspondent sends us this message: It is reported that Sir Charles Warren has been recalled from South Africa and ordered home. It is also further reported that the order commanding Sir Charles Warren to return was cabled to South Africa this morning.'"

Scenting blood, later in the evening the *Central News* announced: "The reported recall of Sir Charles Warren is not denied by the War Office." [5]

The reason Sir Charles was recalled (after the lifting of the Ladysmith siege) is given later.

On April 21, the *Mail* wrote: "The ferment which the publication of the *Spioenkop Despatches* has caused shows no sign of abating . . .

"So far Colonel Crofton alone has been retired. We have expressed the opinion that he was only culpable in a very minor degree: the most that can be said against him is, it would seem, that he sent a true, but very alarming message from the top of the hill, and that he did not show quite the vigour of organisation which was to be expected from a British Officer in his position."

(It was not a true message Crofton had sent from *Spioenkop*, as we have already seen, but no-one was to know that then,)

"It would be well, however, if we recalled the terrible state of things on Spioenkop. The place was a simple shambles, crowded with troops, who were being torn to pieces by shell fire. No severer trial could be inflicted upon mortal man . . .

"Colonel Thorneycroft . . . erred from no fault of courage. By the unanimous testimony of all his comrades in the field, his demeanour was superb and heroic. But a responsibility was thrust upon him which he was not fit to bear. Upon the shoulders of the two generals rests the true blame. They were not harassed by the horrible sights and sounds of that blood-stained summit . . .

"Where generals go wrong their errors have such far-reaching results, such disastrous consequences that it is best to grant them honourable retirement . . . .

"Those who have failed in the war must come home, in bare justice to the men they lead, that lives may not be wasted or defeat piled upon defeat, but they will be received by the nation, which they have done their best to serve, with regard and sympathy."

In the same issue of the *Daily Mail* appeared this headline: "Natal papers praise Lord Roberts' candour": referring to the *Spioenkop Despatches*, the *Advertiser* (now the *Daily News*) says: 'Lord Roberts' remarks will cause a sensation; and general regret will be felt at the necessity for administering what can only be regarded as a severe rebuke to men who, whatever their errors of judgement, are brave and high-minded soldiers.

"In the case of Sir Charles Warren this regret is intensified to those who know how hard he has worked during the campaign, and especially during the operations which culminated in the relief of Ladysmith . . . "

The *Natal Mercury* commented: " . . . Lord Roberts' censure really confirms some unpleasant stories about the blundering at Spioenkop on the part of the officers of high rank who were regarded as among the best in the British army . . . " [6]

And, according to the public, they were. That Redvers Buller could be censured was an impossibility.

But more was to come.

In the Commons on May 1, Mr Swift MacNeill was at it again: "I beg to ask the Under Secretary of State for War whether Lord Roberts' *Report on the Spioenkop Despatches*, dated 13th February, was originally meant for immediate publication or was regarded by him as a confidential document; what was the difference, with reference to the responsibility of publication, between Lord Roberts and the War Office, the settlement of which involved delay from the 9th March, the day after receipt by the War Office of the report of Lord Roberts, and the 17th April, the date of the publication of that report; and whether, having regard to the public interest in this matter, the telegraphic correspondence between Lord Roberts and the Secretary of State and correspondence and communications between Lord Roberts and Sir Redvers Buller with reference to the publication of the Spioenkop reports, will be laid upon the Table of the House before the discussion . . . on Friday next." The Under Secretary of War: "Under the exceptional circumstances of the case I propose to lay upon the Table of the House the telegraphic correspondence between the Secretary of State and Lord Roberts with reference to the publication of the Spioenkop reports. That being so, I must ask the hon. Member to allow me to postpone my replies to his other questions until Friday next."

(Four questions later came this one: Mr John Ellis (Nottinghamshire): "I beg to ask Mr Chancellor of the Exchequer what the total cost of the war in South Africa was to the National Exchequer up to 31 March?"

(Mr Hanbury: "My right hon. friend has asked me to reply to this question. The latest figures which are yet available of the war expenditure up to the 31st March are . . . about £23 million." [7]

(And that was a lot of money over a six-month period.)

But there was a scandal somewhere. The public sensed it, and the newspapers attempted to break it. There were hints of telegrams between Lord Lansdowne and Lord Roberts over what was published – and, horror of horrors, what was not.

Lansdowne, it was hinted, said he could not publish all the *Despatches* and had asked Roberts to edit the ones he could publish. This would mean getting Buller to re-write his reports on the *Spioenkop* action.

Buller, it was said, refused.

How true were these rumours?

Members of the House of Lords and Commons were soon to know, when they were issued with a full report on Friday, May 4, 1900.

The debate began in the House of Lords at exactly 4.15pm, with the Earl of Portsmouth proclaiming: "My charge against the noble Marquess (Lord Lansdowne) is that he has transgressed the rules of honourable tradition by publishing in those *Despatches* confidential reports of a privileged character, compiled in the discharge of official duty, intended solely for the information of the superior authority in the public interest, and accepted in that character by the officers reported upon as well as by the officers reporting.

"Before I proceed any further I must make some allusion to the extraordinary attempt which has been made by the noble Marquess to shuffle the responsibility of the publication of these *Despatches* on to the shoulders of Lord Roberts. The paper which has been placed in your Lordships' hands this morning appears to me – and I have now been in Parliament for over 20 years – to be the most extraordinary piece of Parliamentary literature that has ever been presented!

" . . . I am bound to say that, having regard to the character of the *Despatches* the noble Marquess felt he could publish, one cannot help feeling some curiosity as to what there is behind those which he felt he could not publish.

"He (Lansdowne) telegraphs to Lord Roberts, and uses these words: 'I do not feel justified in thus editing the papers unless you concur, and you may perhaps think well to refer to Buller.

" 'I suggest, as an alternative, that we should treat your despatch of 17th February and all its enclosures as confidential, and that Buller should send through you a full narrative of the operations. This you could forward to me with any observations you desire to make for publication.'

"That, my Lords, in my opinion, seems to point to this, that Sir Redvers Buller was invited to re-write his despatch; that inasmuch as the account which he had originally given to Lord Roberts had received from Lord Roberts adverse criticism, an opportunity – a temptation – was offered to him to re-write his despatch, and, as it were whitewash himself, changing his account so that Lord Roberts might be able to pronounce a different opinion in his covering despatch.

"It is certainly a serious matter that confidential communications should be published at all, but it is far more serious, to my mind, in the public interest that the Secretary of State for War should, so to speak, invite *Despatches* to be made to order so that they may be palmed off upon the public as genuine expressions of opinion by responsible officers.

"Sir Redvers Buller declined to take part in any such proceeding. He said: 'I do not at all like the idea of re-writing a despatch for publication. I much prefer to leave it in the hands of the Commander-in-Chief and let him select for publication whatever he thinks proper.'

"We know what followed. The Secretary of State for War telegraphed to

Lord Roberts asking him whether he should publish the *Despatches* as they now stand, and Lord Roberts simply replied that he agreed to their publication.

"Lord Roberts had nothing to be ashamed of in the *Despatches* he had written, and it must not for one moment be supposed that because Lord Roberts acquiesed in their publication it can be urged that he approved of that course." [8]

So there it was. The confirmation the public had sought. Oh yes, it was a scandal all right, a right royal scandal!

Lord Portsmouth continued: "Having endeavoured to show that the Secretary of State and Her Majesty's Government are responsible, I must, with the permission of your Lordships, quote that portion of Lord Roberts' despatch which seems to me singularly unfortunate in publication.

"Lord Roberts says: 'The attempt to relieve Ladysmith described in these *Despatches* was well-devised.

"'That it failed may in some measure be due to the difficulties of the ground, and the commanding positions held by the enemy probably also to errors of judgement and want of administrative capacity on the part of Sir Charles Warren; but whatever fault Sir Charles Warren may have committed, the failure must also be ascribed to the disinclination of the officer in supreme command to assert his authority and see that what he thought best was done, and also to the unwarrantable and needless assumption of responsibility by a subordinate officer.'

"You published a despatch reflecting on Sir Charles Warren for a want of judgement and administrative capacity, but I have recently seen that you have appointed him Governor of an enormous territory in Griqualand West.

"It does not seem to me that it was necessary to make that appointment ridiculous. You could have appointed Sir Charles Warren to this position without publishing these words in the despatch." [9]

Warren took up his position of Governor of Griqualand West in Kimberley late in 1900.

"Then as to Sir Redvers Buller, upon him you pronounce a sort of public censure. You imply that he has neither the power nor the capacity to assert his own authority. I cannot conceive any language, if published, more detrimental to discipline, and if you publish it to the world as you have done, more unjustifiable, unless, as you have not done, you recall him from his command . . .

"Because the noble Marquess has thought fit to publish these *Despatches* . . . he should also publish all the Despatches that tell againt himself or against some favoured officers who are responsible for blunders at Magersfontein, Reddersburg, Karee Siding, at Koorn Spruit, and, alas I fear, at many other places . . ."

There was a concurrent debate running on why General Lord Methuen had not been censured and brought back to Britain after his loss at Magersfontein. One MP suggested it was because of his "high" – and therefore protected – position in the House of Lords.

Lord Lansdowne followed: " . . . I now come to the present campaign. Since it began we have published with regularity Despatches descriptive of each of the engagements and operations which have occurred. We have published eight such Despatches . . .

" . . . the *Spioenkop Despatches* certainly did not reach us in a shape at all corresponding with what is laid down in the Queen's Regulations. They covered some 45 pages of print and . . . 20 different documents of one sort or another, many of them being clearly of such a kind that their inclusion in a Despatch would not be in accordance with the Queen's Regulations . . .

"That was the position we found ouselves in and we had to decide what we should do. The alternatives open to us were limited in number. We might have published nothing at all; and I gather that is the course which would have found favour in many quarters.

"But if we had done that it would have been a new departure of a very abrupt kind. We should have been affirming a new principle – the principle that we might publish so long as a Despatch contained nothing but praise, but that the moment we received a Despatch containing blame, that Despatch was to be held back from publication.

"I strongly suspect that if we had taken that line the public would have endeavoured to insist upon publication; and I doubt extremely whether we should have been able to offer a successful resistance.

"Why, my Lords, that action at Spioenkop cost us over 1,600 casualties. I doubt whether there was any engagement in the campaign that aroused a deeper public interest than the battle of Spioenkop, and do your Lordships think that it would have been possible for us, if asked whether there were any Despatches about that engagement, to have said that we had such Despatches, but that we intended to keep them to ourselves; or that that answer would have been accepted as sufficient and satisfactory by the public?

" . . . I say with confidence that there was such an impression in men's minds as to the management of the Spioenkop operations that if we had held back the Despatches the impression created would have been more damaging to the generals concerned than the publication of the Papers which we have laid on the Table of the House.

" . . . Just one word as to the alleged disastrous results of this publication. As regards the public, the public wanted to know the truth, and the truth was given them. They know how Lord Roberts apportions blame for the miscarriage which occured; they know that neither Lord Roberts nor the military authorities in this country desire to hush up the truth . . ." [10]

Stirring words. But not quite true – NOT all the despatches were published, and the public did not know that.

What was published was confusing enough, given those bare facts. Lansdowne knew what was in the unpublished despatches; the public did not.

But he went on: "Now, what was the censure passed by Lord Roberts on Sir Redvers Buller? I must say, in the first place, that it is not so much, to my mind, the publication of the censure that obliges you to recall an incompetent general officer; it is the fact that he has been censured for incompetance.

"Whether you publish the censure or not, if the general is incompetent or not you ought not to leave him in charge of the lives of the men and the reputation of the Army.

"But what was the censure on General Buller? Did Lord Roberts say that he considered him unfit to lead an army, or that he had lost the confidence of his troops? Nothing of the kind. Lord Roberts' censure is contained in a very short and very pregnant sentence at the end of his despatch. He begins by distinctly expressing a favourable opinion of Sir Redvers Buller's plan of operations. He goes out of his way to say that, as far as the conception of the plan goes, Sir Redvers Buller had shown himself not as an incompetent, but a competent general, and then he says: 'That it (the plan) failed, may, in some measure, be due to the difficulties of the ground and the commanding positions held by the enemy . . .'

"No censure in that. '. . . probably also to errors of judgement and want of administrative capacity on the part of Sir Charles Warren. But whatever faults Sir Charles Warren may have committed, the failure must also be ascribed . . .' not to Sir Redvers Buller's bad strategy, incompetence, or ignorance of his profession, but '. . . to the disinclination of the officer in supreme command to assert his authority and see that what he thought best was done . . .'

"That is the whole censure upon Sir Redvers Buller. The censure amounts to this: Sir Redvers Buller trusted too much to his subordinates and did not take measures to satisfy himself that his orders were being carried out. That strikes me as a very mild reproof indeed. And more than that, Lord Roberts himself, by his own conduct, showed conclusively that he had not withdrawn his confidence from Sir Redvers Buller, because Lord Roberts left Sir Redvers Buller in charge of a large army.

"He entrusted to him the charge of the most critical and difficult operation of the campaign, an operation which Sir Redvers Buller has brought to a successful conclusion . . . " [11]

The parliamentary debate, of course, preceeded Warren's statement to the Commissioners. Also, it was Warren who organised the relief of Ladysmith, not Buller. And later, not very much later, Lansdowne was to rue his defence of Sir Redvers, as would others who spoke out in favour of Buller.

It was the Earl of Rosebery who put the spanner in the works, so to speak. Speaking on the "re-writing" of the *Despatches,* he said: "These were . . . desperate straits to which the War Office and the Commander-in-Chief in South Africa were put in order to meet the desire of the War Office to publish these *Despatches;* and as it were, after suggesting numerous alternatives to the unhappy Lord Roberts and the even less happy Sir Redvers Buller, the War Office at last determined to publish everything that was damaging, everything that was critical, everything that was censorious, to satisfy a public curiosity of which no outward sign existed.

"Now there are two results of this policy. One is that you have been compelled to wash some dirty linen in the presence of the world. The conduct of your military operations has not been uniformly successful, and it has not been free from the criticism of Europe; but so far as I can infer from what reaches us of the Continental press, all comment which they have hitherto passed on our operations in the field is low as compared with the stupour of astonishment with which they have received the publication of these *Despatches.*

"Then there is the second effect, which has a far greater influence on Sir Redvers Buller himself. Some of these generals have been punished, some have not.

"Sir Charles Warren has been removed [to Griqualand West governership]; a colonel who was on top of Spioenkop . . . has suddenly been placed on half pay [Crofton]. The highest of all has been left to bear the stigma you have placed upon him in the presence of his victorious troops. The noble Marquess thinks it is no stigma at all . . ." [12]

But it was left to the erudite Mr Wyndham, the Under Secretary of State for War, to try and play down the whole thing.

He said: ". . . there have been criticisms to the effect that the *Spioenkop Despatches* were withheld for some time; that they were then published to meet popular demand, and published without any reference to Lord Roberts or Sir Redvers Buller.

" . . . (But) why did the Government publish the criticism on Sir Redvers Buller if it was intended to leave him in so important a command? It is desirable that this cobweb of suspicion of base motives . . . should have evaporated and disappeared, and that we should be arraigned upon a specific and legitimate charge – the charge that, in the exercise of the discretion vested in the Government we have made an error of judgement . . .

"For in relation to the tragic incident of Spioenkop it is natural to desire some simple and plain explanation which would remove all the evil consequences of that disaster. That cannot be the case. You cannot lose 1,600 men in a battle, you cannot evacuate a position won by the heroism of British troops, you cannot lose the fruits of their heroism, you cannot see the Army discouraged by this unexpected failure, and expect to have no evil consequences.

"All you can do is to choose between such evil consequences as follow from defining and explaining the nature of the case which led to that disappointment and the evil consequences which follow if you withhold altogether from the public a reasoned account of these disasters and the causes which led to them . . .

"What have we done? Briefly in the course of this war we have published 10 *Despatches*; we published seven in the *London Gazette* of 26th January, two in the *Gazette* of 16 March and one in the *Gazette* of 17th April . . . in that we published the *Spioenkop Despatches.*

" . . . The (Queen's) regulations say that a despatch containing a concise description of every action of every specific military operation, irrespective of its magnitude, will invariably be written by the senior officer actually present on the occasion.

"To enable him to do this, reports describing the action taken by their respective commands will be furnished to him by officers commanding divisions or brigades, and by such officers as he may specially call upon.

"These reports will not accompany the despatch, the senior officer being alone responsible for rendering the Secretary of State for War an account of the operation and therefore the account will invariably be written by the officer in chief command . . .

"If we take the alternative – to publish not only the report of the senior officer, but all the documents upon which he has based his judgement, then I find that in publishing the *Despatches* of Sir Charles Warren and Sir Redvers Buller we ought also to have published everything that was written by all the other officers . . . "

Had they, the truth about Warren would have been exposed.

"The charge has been made that, as we wished to remove misconception, we ought to have made a clean breast of it and to have published the 45 pages of printed matter which came back in connexion with the Spioenkop operations."

HON MEMBERS: "No!, No!"

MR WYNDHAM: "Then I hope the charge will not be made we have kept anything back."

Wyndham continued: "On 9th March we received the Magersfontein despatch, the Stormberg despatch and the Spioenkop despatch. The Spioenkop despatch filled to the letter the conditions prescribed in the . . . Queen's Regulations . . . (where) it is laid down that where the senior officer in command is present, but does not assume actual command, then one of two things is to happen – either he, which in the case of Spioenkop would be Sir R. Buller, is to write the single narrative account, or the officer in actual command, in this case Sir C. Warren, is to write the account, which the senior officer, Sir R. Buller, is to accompany by a covering despatch, in which he is to express his own opinion of the manner in which the operations have been carried out.

"By that mail we received not only the report of Sir C. Warren on the whole of the operations with regard to the taking and evacuation of Spioenkop, but two covering Despatches from Sir R. Buller and Lord Roberts, and we received besides 20 considerable documents, making together 45 pages of printed matter."

How astute are the ways of politicians. Wyndham admits receiving 45 pages of documentation, but does not disclose what they contained. Neither does he query Buller's statement against the statements by Warren, Crofton, Thorneycroft and others. Having in his hand the entire Spioenkop *Despatches*, he is determined to keep the status quo.

But only five were published. And thereby Buller's "not necessarily for publication" stricture was honoured.

He went on: "It will hardly be argued that the Commander-in-Chief is not to comment upon such Despatches. What course, then, was open to the government? There was only one possible course . . . to publish all these documents, many of which were not Despatches, and were never intended to be treated as Despatches, [to publish them the way they were published – five pages] or to get Sir R. Buller, with advantage, to pursue the alternative course, namely to write one definite, connected account of the whole situation.

"That seems to have excited a good deal of surprise; but for my part I think there is a good deal to be said for it.

" (Further) . . . To suggest that . . . The *Spioenkop Despatches* could be covered over and left in the hope that they might be dropped is contrary to all precedent. It was the right course to publish what they did – that and nothing more . . .

"To say that Sir Charles Warren failed in a large independent command is not to say, as some of the public seem to think, that he is not a good soldier or an able man.

"Are we to forget his past services? Does it follow that he is not, perhaps, the very best man for performing some other task – and even some other military task? I would like to take this opportunity of pointing out to the Committee and . . . to the public, how captious and arbitrary many of our judgements must seem to the officers who are serving in South Africa . . .

"I say that charges are brought against officers for incompetence which are couched in such general language as to be understood in South Africa to mean that those officers are incompetent and careless men who have not done good service to their country . . .

"As to Sir Redvers Buller, I feel that to attempt an apology in his behalf would be the greatest insult to so great a man, who has deserved so well of his country . . . I am quite certain that Sir Redvers Buller – that man who in 1885 brought back and saved from destruction the column which failed to relieve Khartoum, and who did relieve Ladysmith turning 'the winter of our discontent' into an explosion of national rejoicing – I am sure he will never be erased from the administration of his country."

Buller was. But that is another story altogether. [13]

SOURCES

1. *Daily Mail,* April 19, 1900.
2. *Daily Mail,* April 21, 1900.
3. *Hansard: House of Commons Debates,* 27 April, 1900 (p. 116).
4. *Hansard: House of Commons Debates,* 30 April 1900 (p. 271).
5. *Daily Mail,* April 19, 1900.
6. *Daily Mail,* April, 21, 1900.
7. *Hansard: House of Commons Debates,* May 1, 1900. (p. 416).
8. *Hansard: House of Lords Debates,* May 4, 1900 (p. 708).
9. Ibid.
10. Ibid.
11. Ibid.
12. Ibid (p. 732).
13. Ibid (pp. 785 ff).

CHAPTER TWENTY TWO

The House of Commons Debate

The failure of the Government reply

The House divided. There were 116 votes against the publication and 215 for. Which meant that the Government had a majority of 99, and the truncated *Spioenkop Despatches* were printed.

But it was not yet over.

In a leading article, the *Daily Mail* says: " . . . Not the least painful part of the affair is the curious correspondence with Lord Roberts and General Buller published yesterday. From this it appears that even now the full facts have not been revealed, and that something has been kept back.

"We are told that the *Spioenkop Despatches* originally filled 45 pages. What is there in the 40 or so which have been supressed? So that the Government excuse that Lord Lansdowne and the War Office always take the public entirely into their confidence is absurd . . .

"In view of these facts and of the manner in which the war has been conducted, it cannot be said that Lord Lansdowne retains the confidence of the nation. The feeling against him is deep and strong. He is the responsible minister and it is his own organisation which after five years of office has broken down.

"If the Government is wise it will remember that War Ministers are open to censure as well as generals, and that the public has already pronounced sentence.

"To conclude the war, to support the Army properly and fully, to organise victory, we need a stronger and greater War Minister then we possess.

"This is the true moral of yesterday's painful debate, and if it is not realised Lord Lansdowne may drag down the Government with him in his ultimate fall." [1]

The debates had another sequel – the publication of *Sir Charles Warren and Spioenkop*, a Vindication by 'Defender' published in London in 1902.

'Defender' is unknown, although the South African Library say it was written by one D'Arcy Lambton.

What 'Defender' has to say – stung by the rebuke to Warren – is worth recording.

"It is now more than two years since the operation took place on the Tugela River in Natal, that ended in the capture and unwarrantable abandonment the same day of the position of Spioenkop. The lapse of time since these events occurred naturally caused a loss of interest in this chapter of the history of the war in South Africa; but the recent publication of portions of the *Despatches* omitted in the (London) *Gazette* of 1900, and also of other documents received at the time by the War Office but not disclosed, has again brought the subject into prominence, revived public interest in it, and offered an opportunity which we gladly seize to vindicate the conduct of an officer who has been condemned without being heard.

"Whether Sir Charles Warren will be allowed any opportunity of defending himself against the strictures passed upon him . . . either now or when the war is over is doubtful; but at length having before us all the documents received at the War Office, it is proposed to show . . . that in spite of the difficult circumstances in which he found himself, Sir Charles Warren did his duty, and that, had Spioenkop not been recklessly abandoned by a subordinate, there is every reason to suppose that he would have gained great success.

"The publication of the *Despatches* on Spioenkop in the parliamentary Easter recess of 1900 took the world by surprise – so much so, indeed, that a story was current that it was due to a mistake of a War Office clerk . . .

"It did not commend itself as either a useful or desirable proceeding to publish to the whole world the strictures passed by the general in command in Natal upon his second-in-command in South Africa upon both, especially as those officers were still serving their country in the field. To this course, however, Sir Redvers Buller would not consent. He prided himself on his integrity in resisting such a proposal, and has been much praised for refusing to write a despatch for publication, having already written one, which was mainly an indictment of his second-in-command, on whom he threw the responsibility for the failure of the operations.

"It is the custom of the Service – and a very fair and proper custom it is – that an unfavourable confidential report made upon a junior officer by his superior shall be communicated to him before it is sent forward, so that he may have an opportunity either of excusing himself or of amending his conduct, and may have no reason to complain that advantage has been taken of a confidential communication to make unfavourable reports behind his back, of which he remains in ignorance.

"Sir Redvers Buller does not appear to have been mindful of this custom, when, instead of writing a simple account of what he proposed to do, and how it failed of accomplishment, he used the opportunity to criticise most unfavourably the conduct of the distinguished officer, his second-in-command, still serving under him in the face of the enemy, and left him in complete ignorance of the accusations made against him.

"This ignorance he knew must last in any case until the *Despatches* were published, and, if they were not published, would never be removed. But Sir Redvers went beyond this, for he attached to his despatch a separate memorandum 'not necessarily for publication' in which he reiterated his complaints of the conduct of Sir Charles Warren and accused him of such incapacity as unfitted him for independent command.

"But not a word of this reached Sir Charles Warren, whose exertions in the field during the succeeding month under Sir Redvers Buller contributed so greatly to the victory of Pieters and the relief of Ladysmith; and it was not until he saw the *Despatches* in the newspapers, long after this campaign was over, that he knew of the secret stab his reputation had received at the hand of his commander.

"Two years later the recently published omissions have informed him how seriously the attack upon his reputation as a soldier was intended.

"A correspondence between Mr Henry Norman, MP [one of the commissioners] and the Right Hon. A.J. Balfour, First Lord of the Treasury, published on 21st February last, contains some observations by the latter very much to the point on the want of any narrative of the *Spioenkop Despatches* in Sir Redvers Buller's Despatches.

"Mr Balfour points out, as was done two years before in the parliamentary debates, that the General in command 'in accordance with the Queen's Regulations, with the best precedents, and with public convenience', should have furnished a simple narrative, unencumbered by controversy, of the operations which took place.

"To this Sir Redvers Buller objected, in a letter published on the 28th March last, that he was not in command, that he was not present, and that therefore it was not his duty to write such a narrative.

"(An extract) of the reply from Mr Balfour to Sir Redvers Buller, in a letter dated 10th March, 1902, reads: 'You say that, not being in chief command, you were not the proper person to write an account of what took place. But can this be sustained?

"I find that on 15th January you ordered Sir Charles Warren to cross the Tugela to the west of Spioenkop; on the 21st and 22nd you gave him personal instructions as to the disposal of his artillery; on the latter day you agreed with him, after discussion, that Spioenkop would have to be taken; on the 23rd you definitely decided upon the attack; you selected the officer who was to lead it, detailing one of your staff to accompany him; it was by your orders that on the 24th Lieut.-Colonel Thorneycroft assumed command on the summit of Spioenkop after General Woodgate was wounded, and all heliographic messages between the officers in the fighting line and Sir Charles Warren passed through your camp, and were seen by you before they reached their destination.

"As you were thus in constant touch with the troops actually engaged on the top of the hill, so also you kept general control over the movements of the co-operative forces under General Lyttleton, with whom you were in communication during both the morning and the afternoon of the 24th.

"It is of course true that you were not present at the actual Spioenkop engagement. But if this was a reason for not writing an account of it, it was a reason equally applicable to Sir Charles Warren, whose headquarters, as I am informed, were very little nearer to the scene of action than were your own . . .

"You were responsible for the general plan of action; you intervened frequently in its execution; you were not prevented either by distance or any other material object from intervening more frequently still, had you deemed it expedient to do so . . .

"We have never been able to understand why the orders given to Sir Charles Warren were not published with the *Despatches* two years ago. True they were called secret instructions, but of course the secrecy was a temporary matter, and they ceased to be secret when the operations were over.

"Without them there was no way for the public to learn officially, except in the most general way, what the General in command in Natal desired to do, and probably owing to the wording of Lord Roberts' despatch, a misconception arose, widely entertained in the army and highly prejudicial to Sir Charles Warren.

"The political mistake made by the Government was speedily demonstrated by the debates that took place on the reassembling of Parliament; but it now appears a greater want of judgement was shown than was supposed, and that having decided, rightly or wrongly, to publish the *Despatches* the Government would have done better to have published them in full. And this for several reasons – it would have made little difference to those censured, would have enabled the public to understand the Spioenkop operations, which could not be understood from the incomplete documents, and would have prevented a distinguished officer lying for two years under the shadow of unjust accusations.

"Much capital was made by the Opposition in Parliament out of the suggestion of the Secretary of State for War that Sir Redvers Buller should rewrite his despatch, or rather should write a separate despatch for publication; but anyone who has tried to get to the bottom of the business from the material available must have felt that Lord Lansdowne was perfectly right in suggesting that what was wanted was a simple statement from Sir Redvers Buller of what he intended to do, and how it was done or not done.

"Instead of this there were Despatches giving formal cover to other Despatches from Sir Charles Warren, and then criticising that officer's actions unfavourably.

"No statement was to be found anywhere indicating what Sir Redvers Buller had intended to do, and as the instructions he issued were not published, the operation which Sir Charles Warren was directed to execute could only be gathered from the references he made to them in his reports. These reports were evidently written to his chief in the belief that the General commanding would write a full account of what he had proposed to do, and how far his orders had been successfully carried out, or otherwise.

"To most men, conscientiously compelled to censure in an official despatch those employed under them, the suggestion from the War Office that such censure should be confined to a confidential communication, and that some account of the operation and the cause of failure should be written for publication, would have come as a welcome relief; and had Sir Redvers Buller seen his way to comply with it and at the same time send copies to Sir Charles Warren of the confidential Despatches, he would have placed himself in an unassailable position, he would have given Sir Charles Warren an opportunity of confidentially justifying himself, if he could do so, to the Secretary of State for War and the Commander-in-Chief, he would have enabled his countrymen to know more about the operations than was otherwise possible, and the world would have been spared a very painful exhibition.

"The misconception was that Sir Redvers Buller instructed Sir Charles Warren to make his turning movement by way of Acton Homes, instead of which Warren obstinately preferred the route by Groote Hoek. It is supposed that by the first of these two routes the force might have marched a long way round but would have got into Ladysmith with little difficulty, whereas the (hypothetical) substitution by Warren of the Groote Hoek road had necessitated the capture of Spioenkop.

"The publication of the instructions upsets this theory. The Acton Homes road is never mentioned. The only references to the direction of the turning movement are vague – 'to the west of Spioenkop – acting as circumstances require' – 'refusing your right and throwing your left forward' – and it now appears that Sir Redvers Buller intended Warren to go by the Groote Hoek route." [2]

Sir Charles Warren, finally, has been vindicated.

SOURCES
1. *Daily Mail,* May 5, 1900.
2. *Sir Charles Warren and Spioenkop.*

CHAPTER TWENTY THREE

Vaalkrantz

The third failure

Spioenkop aftermath: January 25 and onwards

Surgeon Frederick Treves had walked from his hospital behind Mount Alice at Spearman's Farm and, looking out from the height, wrote: "The Tugela glistened in the sun like a band of silver, and over the plain and in and out among the kopjes and round the dongas the brown road wound to Ladysmith.

"The road was deserted, and the few homesteads which came into view showed no signs of life. At the foot of the hill was Potgieter's Drift, while above the ford was a splashing rapid, and below was the pont which our men had seized with such daring.

"The face of the hill towards the river was covered with mimosa trees and with cactus bushes and aloes, and this unexpected wealth of green almost hid the red and grey boulders which clung to the hillside. Among the rocks were many strange flowers, many unfamiliar plants, and creeping things innumerable.

" . . . The quiet of the place, when the guns had ceased, was absolute, and was only broken by the murmur of the numerous doves which occupied the mimosa woods.

"The whole place seemed a paradise of peace, and there was nothing to suggest that there were some thousands of grimy men beyond the river who were busy with the implements of death . . . " [1]

The later editions of some of the London papers of Friday, January 26th, and all the editions of the 27th, bore this brief announcement at the head of the leading column of their page of war news:

"The Following telegram from General Buller was received at the War Office at 6am today: 'Spearman's Camp, January 25, 12.5pm. Warren's garrison, I am sorry to say, I find this morning had in the night abandoned Spioenkop.' " [2]

Warren and Buller met later in the day. Warren writes: "When I met Sir R. Buller . . . he used some words in disparagement of General Coke. I replied that General Coke had carefully carried out his instructions and that the failure was not due to him . . . Later, General Buller said I ought to write a report against General Coke, as he had heard that he had been asleep during the action of Spioenkop. This I declined to do. I had not heard that General Coke had been asleep, and I said I thought that as General Coke had been up all night he might choose his own time to get a little rest . . .

"Before this, however, Sir R. Buller appears to have secretly written to the disadvantage of General Coke, on inadequate information, without informing either General Coke or myself that he had done so." [3]

But Buller mentioned nothing of these matters when he handed this statement to newspaper correspondents on January 27: "General Woodgate who commanded the summit being wounded, the officer who succeeded him decided on the night of the 24th and 25th to abandon the position, and did so before daylight 25th.

"I reached General Warren's camp at 5am, 25th, and decided that a second attack on Spioenkop would be useless and that the enemy's right was too strong to force it.

"I accordingly decided to withdraw the force to the south of the Tugela and try some other part. At 6am we commenced withdrawing the train, and by 8am on the 27th the whole of Sir C. Warren's force was concentrated south of the Tugela without loss of a man or a pound of stores. The fact that the force could withdraw from actual touch (in cases the lines were less than 1,000 yards apart) with the enemy, in the perfect manner it did, is I think sufficient evidence of the morale of the troops, and that we were permitted to withdraw our enormous ox and mule transports as we did, across a river 85 yards broad, with 20 foot bank . . . unmolested, is I think proof that the enemy had been taught to respect our soldiers' fighting powers."

Neither Warren nor his troops had any reason to doubt that the tenor of this statement was the same as that which had been sent to the War Office.

This was strengthened on January 29th when Buller addressed the troops, extolling their conduct and pluck, told them that their work had not been in vain, and said they had given him "The key to Ladysmith".

Three years later, in his evidence before the Commission, Buller said: "I believe at this moment that those six days' operations at Spioenkop really relieved Ladysmith." [4]

And General Coke? He told the Commission on March 19, 1903: "I maintain that I did all that was possible to improve the state of affairs after I reached Spioenkop . . . Sir C. Warren appeared to be quite satisfied with what I had done and requested that there might be an Inquiry into the unauthorsed evacuation.

"But Sir R. Buller's conduct was certainly most extraordinary. He neither saw me nor said one word to me regarding the action, though I met him daily.

"Lord Roberts, in his report of February 13th, 1900 on the Spioenkop operations, whilst freely blaming many of the officers concerned, passed no censure on the part I took.

"Sir R. Buller subsequently three times favourably mentioned me in Despatches, and personally thanked me in the field for my action in holding on to the position of Van Wyk [June 6, 1900, after the siege had been lifted] and the capture by my brigade of the strong position of Alleman's Nek (June 11, 1900), by which the Boers were driven out of Natal.

"Yet after he returned to England he most unaccountably made an adverse report after the lapse of many months, and after favourably mentioning services in Despatches, is contrary to the best traditions of our Army, and, if allowed to form a precedent, will strike deeply at the honour and good understanding existing amongst officers, the maintenance of which is essential to the success of our arms in future wars.

"The way in which I have been treated is entirely at variance with the public statement made by the Secretary of State for War to the House of Commons, to the effect that no officer could suffer without a full Inquiry into his case, for I have had no such Inquiry, in spite of my many appeals for justice, and I have so far been denied any opportunity of replying to and disproving what has been alleged against me by Sir R. Buller . . .

"I brought all my correspondence with the War Office. It is rather a personal matter, but I should rather like to remark that I have addressed this file of papers to the War Office, and I have entirely failed in getting the very slightest injury.

"I saw the Commander-in-Chief, Lord Roberts, and he was very polite and told me he could not in any way listen to anything; that is all I got out of him, and so far I have not had the slightest Inquiry . . ."

The Commission told Coke his appeal would be noted . . . [5]

Like Warren, he was not permitted to speak out . . . to clear his name.

The descriptions of the horror of mangled bodies on top of Spioenkop are legion. Treves, the caring humanitarian, describes what he had to contend with at his hospital behind Spearman's hill: "Many of the wounded . . . came in after sundown. The largest number arrived at night. It was very dark. The outline of the tents and marquees was shadowy and faint. The camp was but a ghost of a camp. Here and there a feeble light would be shining through the fly of a marquee, and here and there an orderly, picking his way among the tent ropes by the aid of a lantern, would light up a row or two in the little canvas town.

"In the front of the camp was the flagstaff, high up upon which were suspended the two white lights which marked the situation of the hospital. These lamps only sufficed to illumine a few of the tents in the first line.

"It was a weary journey to the hospital, and one can imagine with what eagerness the tired, hungry, aching wounded would look ahead for the two white lights. Rocking in pain on a crawling ox wagon, or jolted in the rigid fabric of an ambulance, the way must have seemed unending . . .

"How many times a tired head must have been lifted up from the straw to see if there were yet any sign of the two white lights . . ."

"The volunteer ambulance corps and the coolie bearers did excellent service. The large number of the wounded were on the top of Spioenkop. The path down was about two miles, was steep, and in places very difficult. The carriage of the wounded down the hill had all to be by hand. From the foot of the hill to the hospital the carriage was by ambulance wagon, and in some cases by bearers. All the stretchers had hoods . . ." [6]

Among those "coolie" stretcher bearers was a man who was to become the greatest pacifist of all – Mohandas "Mahatma" Gandhi.

Many of the wounded were later sent by train to Durban and taken aboard a plush, well-fitted-out American hospital ship called the *Maine*.

It was a private American charitable venture, conceived by the American wife of a South African mining magnate who interested Lady Randolph Churchill in the project.

The ship was an old cattle vessel of 3,000 tons, donated by Mr Bernard N. Baker, founder of the Atlantic Transport company of Baltimore. Lady Churchill formed a committee of American women in London and raised £41,000 for what turned out to be "the most complete and comfortable hospital ship that has ever been constructed. It had accommodation for 218 patients and had X-ray equipment and an operating room. It also flew three flags – American, British and the flag of the red cross." [7]

Surgeon Blake-Knox, however, had a disturbing encounter on the top of Spioenkop, which he recounted in his diary a few days later on his way to Colenso.

When he left camp just after midnight on the morning after the Spioenkop battle, to seek and attend the wounded who still lay at the top, he says: ". . . As I expected to get back before dark, I had put on the lightest of clothes, thin drill khaki and a flimsy vest in anticipation of the usual terrific heat from the mid-day sun; now however the cold air . . . began to make itself apparent, and I felt almost frozen.

"We had neither blankets nor greatcoats; our only substitute was empty canvas bags which the troops fill with clay for entrenching purposes; many of these lay about and afforded some warmth when placed under our tunics and held in place by the tightening of our belts.

"Just before daybreak a heavy dew came on, accompanied by a further fall in temperature. The dawn breaking lit up the ghastly faces of the patients around and I gave orders for a fresh supply of Bovril and coffee to be served to them . . ."

Blake-Knox had established a hospital collecting point, and it was here on the side of Spioenkop that the orderlies brought the injured.

He says: ". . . Immediately (after breakfast) I sent all the wounded down the hill to the drift. I then got all the stretcher parties I could muster, and visited the ill-fated plateau.

"On this spot not a living soul, either Briton or Boer was moving. A death-like silence reigned. Terrible indeed was our work here. In the still, obscure morning light we set to work in the trenches; wounded, dying and dead lay intermingled, and as we sorted them some unwounded men were found in a state of utter collapse and exhaustion from their ordeal on the previous day.

"We had been but a short time engaged when the silence . . . was interrupted by a hoarse cry to our front; I could not catch the words at once, but on its repetition it was more audible – 'Hands up!'

"On looking up I found we were surrounded on all sides; we were prisoners. As I was the only unwounded officer with the party, I advanced to parley; explanation was useless.

"I said I was a doctor but the man to whom I spoke laughed and pointed to my sleeve. I glanced at it; my brassard was gone.

"We were marched off under an armed guard to the back of the plateau, where some more Boers were standing . . . Very soon more came up, and I spoke to one who wore a brassard; he was, he told me a Boer doctor with an Edinburgh qualification. I satisfied him as to my identity and he sent a message to his commandant for our release.

"General Louis Botha and his Staff now arrived; the former was pointed out to me – a good-looking man, with closely clipped beard and moustache, dressed in a brownish suit and wearing smart top boots and spurs.

" . . . I explained my object on the hill to the General, and showed him the crested buttons on my tunic and some letters I had in my pocket, which satisfied him as to my identity.

"He immediately ordered my release – on parole not to leave the hill without his permission; he then very kindly gave me a cigarette and sent to his camp close by for coffee . . .

"By 6am on the 25th some 500 Boers had collected on the plateau; they were well dressed and clean. Most of them wore tweed suits, leggings and spurs, and soft hats with the Transvaal colours round the brim; each had three or four well-stocked bandoliers containing some sixty cartridges apiece.

" . . . About 10am Colonel Allin, Principal Medical Officer of the Field Force, arrived on the hill and succeeded in obtaining leave to have our wounded removed. The work was carried out at once and within an hour's time every injured man was at the field hospitals."

There is a footnote which reads: "The identification of soldiers killed in action is very laborious, and quite often impossible. The present identi-fication-ticket is sewn in a special pocket in the soldier's tunic; men often take off their coats in action, and they are temporarily mislaid, or their coats may be taken off to dress their wounds. Should such men be killed or die, all means of identification may be lost; such cases have occurred. If every man wore a metal disc bearing his name, number and corps on a chain or cord around his neck, identification would at all times be certain . . ."

Then he went on: " . . . A melancholy scene was being transacted on the plateau of Spioenkop. Early in the morning of the 25th, three army chaplains, the Rev. A.A. Gedge, the Rev. L.J. Matthews and the Rev. Mr. Wainman, with a burial party of 25 men from the Natal Volunteer Ambulance Corps proceeded . . . to fulfil the last sad duties connected with the burial of the dead.

"On the plateau they were joined by the Rev. R.C. Collins, who had been there since daybreak.

"Two large graves were at once made; in one, 12 bodies were placed, and in the other, 42. As the working party was small, and as the ground was as hard as iron, rendering it almost impenetrable to spades and pickaxes, many of which were broken in the attempt, advantage was taken of the shallow trenches thrown up by our men in the engagement the day before; these were deepened, and another 85 bodies interred, thus bringing up the total buried on this day to 139.

"Though the enemy watched the proceedings and showed due respect and reverence, they rendered no assistance; and as darkness came on, Father Collins and the Rev. Mr. Gedge, seeing other bodies unburied, made arrangements with the Boer Commandant to come up on the following morning to finish their task.

"Early on the morning of the 26th, nothing daunted, up the hill they went again with a small 'scratch' burial party to resume the interments.

" . . . The summit was attained about 2.30pm. Here they were met by a Boer who stated that there were over 100 more bodies to inter. In a soft piece of ground that seemed like a filled-in trench, 25 of these were placed, but as fog came on and light failed, no further work was done that day . . .

"After breakfast (on the 27th) Father Collins and the Rev. Mr. Sorsbie and four officers and 100 men of the 2nd Dorset Regiment, left camp near Trichardt's Drift with a pontoon party to complete the burials on Spioenkop. The hill was searched in all directions for any dead that remained, and 84 bodies were buried . . . bringing the total to 243.

"The casualties recorded from January 17 to 24 gave a total of 1,733, and comprised 27 officers and 245 men killed, 53 officers and 1,050 men wounded, and 7 officers and 351 men missing." [8]

A week passed peacefully in camp after the Natal Field Army retired across Trichardt's Drift to the south bank of the Tugela. During this time the force was strengthened by the arrival of Horse Artillery, two siege guns, two squadrons of the 14th Hussars and fresh drafts for infantry battalions, amounting in all to 2,400 men.

Thus, allowing for the losses of killed and wounded during the Spioenkop campaign, it was, in addition to the guns, stronger by about 1,000 men than it had been before.

Colonel Arthur Wynne, who had up till now been Buller's Chief of Staff, was appointed to command the 11th brigade in Warren's Division in succession to General Woodgate.

But then it was time to move on.

On February 3rd, Buller held a conference of his generals and issued his orders for the operations at Vaalkrantz. On this occasion the 2nd and 5th Divisions were, to exchange the duties which had been allotted to them during the operations at Spioenkop.

The 4th Brigade, under Lyttleton, was detailed for the assault, with the 2nd (Hildyard's) and the 5th (Hart's) in support, the whole being under the command of General Clery. A demonstration at Brakfontein was to be undertaken by the 11th (Wynne's) and the 10th (Coke's) in reserve.

J.B. Atkins (writes: "Again the troops prepared for battle. For more than a week, they had lived in tents, slept their fill, and tasted fresh meat. It was now Sunday, February 4th, and all through the hot, slow, sleepy, silent afternoon two caterpillars of infantry, scarce distinguishable from the hillsides . . . crawled along the line of hills to the east of Spearman's Farm . . .

" . . . In that sleepful week just past Sir Redvers Buller himself had said that the key was found. None had it in his heart to doubt it. Do not suppose that the troops thought of defeat; the daily signals from Ladysmith were an intolerable incentive; the sound of guns and the knowledge that sickness struck its roots deeper every day into the splendid garrison smothered the memory of Colenso and Spioenkop.

"On Saturday night I had been at a concert given by the South African Light Horse in the flare of bonfires on the open veld, and then Colonel Byng and 'Bimbashi' Stewart had vowed in speeches that they would do their best to lead their men into Ladysmith, and the men had sworn that they only had to be led to follow. Not a man but felt, and feels, that Ladysmith must be helped; its need overcomes all the considerations of modern warfare which forbid us to assault the hills of Northern Natal . . ." [9]

If Ladysmith was to be helped, what was Buller going to do about it?

He told the Commission: "Every attempt which I had made to force the Boers' positions during my operations for the relief of Ladysmith had been confronted by one great and commanding difficulty.

"We could never be sure that, after taking from the enemy the position immediately before us, we should find there a secondary artillery-position to aid us in forcing the enemy's second line of defence, which we knew, though we could not see it, must lie behind.

"The position west of Spioenkop would have been very easy of capture could we, after taking the crest lines of the hills, have found further artillery positions.

"This we could not do, and our infantry were consequently contained in the positions which they had first captured.

"The position which I now decided to attack offered a hill, Vaalkrantz, which (so far as was ascertained by reconnaissance) seemed likely, when captured, to afford a most eligible secondary artillery position.

"I had ascended a hill (Swart Kop) immediately opposite to it on the south side of the Tugela, and had been assured by an English farmer (Mr Harding) who passed under Vaalkrantz every time he went into Ladysmith, that I should find the hill to be an exact duplicate of Swart Kop." [10]

Says J.B. Atkins: "The ascent to Swart Kop at the back is almost like a ladder placed against a house. Guns had been hauled up onto the plateau – a pleasant grass plat, fit to play cricket on, placed, characteristically of South Africa, on precipitous walls. How the guns reached the top is the sailors' secret. The naval gunners might be Boers for their skill in hauling guns on to half-impossible peaks. Mules rolled heels over head down that steep path, but the guns went steadily up drawn by steel ropes; and when all we at the top, I counted six naval twelve-pounders, a battery of six mountain guns, and two field fifteen-pounders.

"Lieut. Ogilvy R.N., and Lieut. R. James, R.N. had their guns behind the heavy screen of cactus and mimosa, but the stems of the trees had been cut almost through and when the guns were needed on Monday sudden vistas crashed into existence before the muzzles of the guns." [11]

Buller, in evidence, continued: "Before attacking Vaalkrantz the two best artillery officers with me had drawn up a scheme for the placing of our guns, with a particular eye to the command of those positions from which the enemy might bring enfilade or raking fire to bear upon us. But in a mountainous country an advance often discloses positions which more distant reconnaissance could not possibly have appreciated." [12]

Atkins writes: "The plan was this. There was to be every appearance of a frontal attack on Brakfontein hill opposite Mount Alice; no less than six batteries were to move forward across the open ground; but while the appearance of the attack was being sustained the batteries were to be withdrawn one by one and were to move to our right for the real attack on Vaalkrantz.

"While the intermittent bark of guns was rising to a cannonade there were Mounted Infantry behind Mount Alice still saddling up or moving off to our all-important right at the walk. You might expect the sound of guns, mounting to a climax, to sting every one into instant furious action. I have seldom seen anything that appeared so cool and slow as the squadrons walking off behind Mount Alice . . .

"The river lies in the valley like the folds of a serpent. General Lyttleton was now moving to our right – it was he who was to assault Vaalkrantz – and he had to cross the river twice. For his first crossing the bridge was made, for the second the bridge was in the making, and five sappers were wounded before that half-hour's job was finished." [13]

In the early stages of the operation everything went according to plan. At 6am on February 5th, Wynne's brigade emerged from Maconochie's Kopjes and, covered by the artillery, advanced on Brakfontein. But Brakfontein awaited them in silence, and the Boer guns did not open fire until 11.45am.

At 12.20 Wynne's artillery moved off to support Lyttleton, whose advance on Vaalkrantz, having begun at 7am, ended with the occupation of the summit shortly before 4pm.

Lyttleton's infantry entrenched on the summit of Vaalkranz, under fire, on the evening of February 5th; but during the night the Boers, realising the significance of the capture of the summit, speedily altered the position of their guns and men, so that by daybreak on the 6th they had 10 guns and about 5,000 men in commanding positions overlooking the British lines.

But Buller had done it again. And this time there was no Warren to blame.

"On the morning of the 6th writes Arthur Conan Doyle in [*The Great Boer War*] the position of the British force was not dissimilar to that of Spioenkop. Again they had some thousands of men upon a hill-top, exposed to shell fire from several directions without any guns upon the hill to support them . . ."

Atkins, on Swart Kop, watched as the guns behind him opened up. Then . . . "A three-inch Boer gun was firing from Spioenkop. And now there came from east of Brakfontein the hateful hollow sound of the Vickers-Maxim – pom-pom-pom-pom-pom – and the little shells fell and spluttered along the ground in a string. They seemed to rake the whole line of the 78th Battery . . ." [14]

Early in the morning Lyttleton reported to Buller that even with the help of the artillery it was impossible to attempt to seize Hill 360, a strongly held Boer position close at hand, from which, says Watkin Williams "the most devastating of their shell fire came". [15]

Says Atkins: "A third gun opened up on our batteries. At once little squirts of dust were threshed up all around the 78th Battery, just as when the first few drops of a heavy storm are flung upon a pond. Afterwards came the peculiar unmistakable wail. It was shrapnel. I saw the gunners through a drifting cloud. Again and again the shells fell before, behind, between and to the right and left of the guns.

"Presently a few gunners appeared more clearly. They were coming back. Three or four guns stood deserted. The rest were worked as busily as ever. Behind all the batteries, under the shelter of a slight ridge, horses and limbers were wheeling into formation. They were going to bring home the guns. Forward they went, six teams in perfect row, galloping towards the imperilled treasures in the open veld. Was there anything finer than British gunnery or so extravagantly dangerous?

"I could see an officer at the guns waiting for the rescue. He sat stock still on his horse . . .

"The six teams passed in front of the first row of guns, wheeled round like horses driven on the curve of a drive, and pulled up at the guns. Men were busily twitching and hauling at the couplings. Again the shrapnel dust flew from the ground and a large shell fell between two teams . . .

"(Then) the first line of guns was back under shelter. The shells began to fall among what had been the second line . . . but soon these guns too had been brought home . . ." [16]

Buller told the Commission: " . . . During the fighting at Vaalkrantz, the enemy, contrary to our expectation, was able to enfilade us with one gun so placed as to be defiladed from our fire and hidden from our sight." [17]

Says Atkins: "A large Creusot gun on the top of Doornkloof was dropping 100lb shells here and there all over the field with impartiality . . .

"Twenty guns were firing at the hundred-pounder. It used black powder and the shaft of white smoke that it belched up out of its mouth would not have done discredit to the whole of our mountain battery. The ground near it smoked like a lime kiln from our shells, but the gun itself smoked away too, with no hitch in its regularity.

" 'There it is; it's up again!' was the cry, for the gun was on a disappearing carriage. Its barrel, plain against the sky, vacillated till it settled on its object . . .

"The white cloud spouted forth . . . The gun rose from its den, pointed, fired, and disappeared in twelve seconds. Our shells from the nearest guns took eighteen seconds to reach it, so they were always six seconds too late."
[18]

Says Buller: "Vaalkrantz was attacked and carried on February 5th. That evening I made preparations for further advance and for the occupying of the hill with artillery. The position had been captured by General Lyttleton's Brigade, and, in consultation with him, I learned that I had been deceived as to the configuration of Vaalkrantz, and that, though I had been able without much difficulty to get guns on to its counterpart, Swart Kop, on the south side of the river. [That is not what Atkins says] It would be impossible to get guns on Vaalkrantz. To make a further advance I should, therefore, have had to use my infantry alone without the support of the artillery." [19]

Williams states that during the course of the morning Buller and Lyttleton became convinced that the sides of Vaalkrantz were so steep, so thickly strewn with boulders [they are: It takes some three hours to get to the summit] and so completely exposed to Boer fire, that it was impossible to mount even two field guns on the summit.

Buller turned to Roberts for advice and sent: "After fighting all day yesterday, though with but one small loss, I have pierced the enemy's line, and hold a hill which divides their position, and will, if I can advance, give me access to the Ladysmith plain, when I should be 10 miles from White, with but one place for an enemy to stand between us.

"But to get my artillery and supplies on to the plain, I must drive back the enemy either on my right or on my left.

"It is an operation which will cost from 2,000 to 3,000 men, and I am not confident, though hopeful, I can do it. The question is how would such a loss affect your plans, and do you think the chance of the relief of Ladysmith worth the risk? It is the only possible way to relieve White; if I give up this chance I know no other."

"Lord Roberts replied [Buller told the commission] that Ladysmith must be relieved at any cost. 'Tell your troops,' he said 'that the honour of the Empire is in their hands, and that I have no possible doubt of their being successful.'"

[What Roberts actually said was: "Ladysmith must be relieved even at the loss you expect. I should certainly persevere, and my hope is that the enemy will be so severely punished as to enable you to withdraw White's garrison without great difficulty. Let troops know that in their hands is the honour of the Empire, and that of their success I have no possible doubt."] [20]

Buller, in evidence, continued: "I confess that I was puzzled by this telegram. In all his communications to me, Lord Roberts had, from the first, advocated the status quo as a general principle. Only eight days before the date of this telegram, he had telegraphed that, unless I saw a reasonable prospect of success, he thought it better for me to remain on the defensive until the effect of his advance should have been seen.

"Only seven days before he had shown me that he had counted upon me to retain the enemy's force in Natal. Only on the previous day I had received from him a letter saying that if I were not confident of forcing my way to Ladysmith, it would be better for me to abandon the attempt until he was in the Orange Free State.

"I was therefore at a loss to account for this sudden exhortation to sacrifice two or three thousand men in a venture wherein, as I told him, I was not confident of success." [21]

Buller, however, decided to hold on to Vaalkrantz in the hope that some reconnaissance could be made of the ground beyond its further slopes. During the afternoon of the 6th a Boer counter-attack was repulsed by the Durham Light Infantry and the King's Royal Rifles, and Lyttleton's weary troops were relieved by Hildyard's brigade at nightfall.

On the morning of the 7th it was a deadlock. Hildyard's men had spent the night improving the defences and trenches. The heat was intense, and water and food could only be obtained at the risk of life.

February 7th was Warren's 60th birthday. He was able – for the first time since arriving in Natal – to spend the day relaxing. Buller had borrowed his two brigades to take part in another demonstration with which Warren was not directly concerned.

Says Warren: "I went up to the firing line . . . as Buller had taken my brigades and I had nothing to do. I heard him lamenting that no-one had looked over the top of Vaalkrantz to see what the country was like on the other side, so I volunteered to do this.

"He said, Be sure you don't get killed, and I rejoined 'Righto'. I took with me Major Kelly, A.D.C., and Lieutenant Schwikkard of the Colonial Corps.

" . . . First we went over a great plain where the artillery were firing and being shelled. Then we rode over a plain where few shells were falling, to the Tugela, where pontoons were. Here it began to get exciting; all the men and horses were kept well under cover, and shells and bullets were abundant. We left our horses to be held and then crossed the pontoons . . .

"On the other side, shells were falling in both directions, a very nasty crossfire, and the only shelter was a donga crowded with men . . . not a soul was to be seen outside the donga. We had to make short dashes from place to place, till we got to the foot of Vaalkrantz. There we ascended a donga full of men, and had to walk on some of them . . . When we began to ascend it was more exciting as the shells were coming both ways all about us, and we made dashes from cover to cover . . . Eventually we got up to Colonel Kitchener (West Yorks) . . . and took a perilous tour over a lot of boulders, from point to point, with bullets and shells flying about.

"After this, Kitchener left us, pointing out our way to cross the open. We now got pretty well out of the shell zone, and had only to face bullets coming over the hill . . . we crawled and rushed and at last got to the firing line on top of the hill . . . then by lifting my head fitfully, as the least movement caused a patter of bullets, I looked out and reconnoitred the country, and made little sketches and notes about the ground, which I took back to Sir Redvers Buller . . . who was pleased and said, 'See what it is to be an Alpine climber.'" [22]

In the afternoon, Warren received an urgent message from Buller requesting him to attend a meeting of Generals at 4.30pm. The Council of War was to be held at Clery's camp as he was laid up with a bad knee and unable to move.

Buller told the Commission: " . . . I assembled all my Generals in Council of War, placed the facts of the case and General Roberts' telegram before them, and asked them whether they advocated persistence in an attack from our present position.

"With one exception, they advised a withdrawal, Sir Charles Warren recommending withdrawal only on the condition that I knew of some other point where I could attack . . ." [23]

Warren wrote: "I was very anxious that my report should be confined to topographical detail, as I did not wish to be asked my opinion on the operations as a whole, which I had already told General Buller I believed to be all wrong. Fortunately he, knowing my strong views against this line of advance, only asked me my views on the topographical subject. I replied from a scout's point of view only, describing the country east and north-east of Vaalkrantz, and said that the advance could be made, but with considerable sacrifice of life.

"Then the Generals were asked their views on the question 'Attack or retire'. They all voted for retiring except Hart and myself. Hart was splendid. Nothing would induce him to retire except a direct order . . . I said we must go on unless General Buller could suggest a better line of advance.

"He at once asked me if I knew of any better line, and I replied – by Hlangwane." [24]

And there it was. The proposal that Warren had made a special study of on board ship on his way to South Africa, the way Warren had suggested when he first met Buller at Frere.

The real key to Ladysmith, to which Buller could have turned in December 1899 – but which he refused to even consider.

Warren writes: "Hlangwane must have been pressing on all our brains, because the moment I mentioned the word, there was a murmer of assent. General Buller looked quite relieved, and there was unanimous agreement.

"And so, Hlangwane it was." [25]

Buller told the Commission: " . . . I thought we should stand a better chance now if we attacked Hlangwane and tried to cross the Tugela from that position, afterwards attacking Bulwana, and that I believed this to be preferable to any attack from our present position.

"I added that in December I had carefully studied that line of advance, that it would involve fighting in bush and in very difficult ground, but that the men had advanced so extraordinarily in their training for war, that I now judged it safe to entrust them with the enterprise.

"The council, one and all, expressed themselves as ignorant of the line of approach which I indicated, but as perfectly satisfied to trust my opinion . . ." [26]

Now that's not what Warren said. And as for the Generals to be ignorant of the line of approach at Hlangwane it is just rubbish. They fought near it, they discussed it, Charles Long's guns were lost near it. No, they knew it well . . .

Only too well!

Immediately after the Council of War, Buller sent this telegram to White: "The enemy is too strong for me here, and though I could force the position it would be at great loss. The Bulwana big gun is here, and a large force. My plan is to slip back to Chieveley, take Hlangwane, the Boer position south of the Tugela and east of Colenso, and the next night try and take Bulwana Hill from the south. Can you think of anything better? I find I cannot get my guns and trains through these mountains. I hope to be at Hlangwane on Saturday. Keep it dark."

But White replied: "Gun opposite you was formerly on Telegraph Hill. Bulwana gun still in position here. Cannot offer suggestions as do not know the country or where you propose to cross the Tugela. I could help at Bulwana. The closer to Ladysmith you can establish yourself the better chance we shall have here."

Then to Roberts, and the Secretary of State for War in London, Buller sent: February 7th. "I found the Boer positions on my right and left so superior to mine, and I was so outclassed by their big guns, which I could not silence, that I have decided that it would be useless waste of life to try and force a passage, which, when forced, would not leave me a free road to Ladysmith.

"I propose to try by a forced march to get back east of Colenso, and seize the Boer position south of the Tugela River, whence I mean to make a desperate effort to take Bulwana hill, the garrison of which has been much weakened, at least so my information says. My view is that I have a forlorn hope chance at both places, but if I get through here I am not at Ladysmith by a long way, while if I get through there I relieve the place." [27]

Warren writes: "Now anyone conversant with the facts will say to me at once, 'Then how is it that you, knowing all this, were the only one except Hart who propsed to go on and not retire? Others could not see the difficulty; why did you, who saw it, propose to advance?' I saw it at once: because at the moment I spoke I knew we were going to succeed." [28]

Atkins writes: "That night several corps of Mounted Infantry and some guns passed my tent on the road to Spearman's farm. 'A reconnaissance' someone said, 'to see if the Boers are still holding their right.' But I awoke in the night, and the tramping and grinding were still on the road. Day and the truth dawned together. We were retiring . . . " [29]

And from Bennet Burleigh: "At 6pm, Wednesday, orders were issued for the retirement of the supply column . . . that evening the Boers were shelling the column, and the hospital. Throughout Wednesday night and Thursday the retirement of the whole army continued, the Boers shelling the wagons and troops in all directions – as usual doing, I assure you, very little hurt.

"Our naval guns . . . replying whilst the pontoons were taken up. The guns removed from Swartz Kop all all our baggage and stores were hauled back . . .

"Today (Friday) the last of the stores and troops have been withdrawn from Spearman's and are encamped around Springfield . . .

"What next? Well, within three days General Buller means to make an attack, with not a brigade, but with his whole army, over the old Colenso ground, which I have all along maintained we should never have left, as it is upon our best line of communications – the railway.

"Before Monday you will have startling news, I hope, and hear that Ladysmith has been this time in reality relieved . . ." [30]

That wonderful descriptive observer, Surgeon Treves says: "On the afternoon of Thursday, February 8, the news came to the hospital at Spearman's that the army was once more to retire . . . At the same time an order arrived to the effect that all the wounded were to be moved at sunrise, on the following day, to Frere. Our stay at Spearman's – extended now to three weeks – had therefore come to an end.

"Among those left in the hospital were 150 patients whose condition was more or less serious. They had been kept under care as long as possible to avoid or postpone the danger of the long journey to the base. It was determined that these 150 men should be carried down to Frere on stretchers and by hand. And this was done . . .

"It was no light undertaking, for the distance was twenty-five miles, and the road was dusty . . . Every step had to be tramped under a glaring sun, and the heat that day was great.

"Allowing twelve men to a stretcher, 1,800 men would be required. This number was forthcoming at sunrise, and they accomplished the march, reaching Frere at sundown . . .

"When all was ready the stretchers were lifted off the ground in order, and the bearers filed out of the camp on to the dusty track. The morning was like that of a summer's day in England . . ." [31]

The army was on the move.

But Buller was in trouble again.

SOURCES

1. *The Tale of a Field Hospital,* by Frederick Treves.
2. *Life of General Sir Charles Warren,* by Watkin Williams.
3. Ibid.
4. *Commission on the War in South Africa.*
5. *Commission,* Evidence of General Coke.
6. *The Tale of a Field Hospital,* by Frederick Treves.
7. *The Great Anglo-Boer War,* by Byron Farewell (Harper & Row).
8. *Buller's Campaign, with the Natal Field Force,* by E. Knox-Grant.
9. *The Relief of Ladysmith,* J.B Atkins.
10. *Commission on the War in South Africa.* (page 179).
11. *The Relief of Ladysmith,* J.B. Atkins.
12. *Commission on the War in South Africa.* (p. 179).
13. *The Relief of Ladysmith,* J.B. Atkins.
14. Ibid
15. *Life of General Sir Charles Warren, by* Watkin Williams.
16. *The Relief of Ladsymith,* J.B. Atkins.

17. *Commission on the War in South Africa.* (p. 179).
18. *The Relief of Ladysmith*, J.B. Atkins.
19. *Commission on the War in South Africa.* (p. 179).
20. Ibid (page 628).
21. Ibid (page 180).
22. *The Life of Sir Charles Warren*, by Watkin Williams.
23. *Commission on the War in South Africa.* (p. 180).
24. *The Life of General Sir Charles Warren*, by Watkin Williams,
25. Ibid.
26. *Commission on the War in South Africa.*
27. Ibid.
28. *The Life of General Sir Charles Warren*, by Watkin Williams,
29. *The Relief of Ladysmith*, J.B. Atkins.
30. *The Natal Campaign, by* Bennet Burleigh.
31. *The Tale of a Field Hospital*, by Frederick Treves.

CHAPTER TWENTY FOUR

The Beginning of The End

The battle of Pieters

Buller slipped back with his staff as far as Springfield without seeing Warren again. But he left him a message to the effect that he entrusted to him not only the retirement from Vaalkrantz but also the withdrawal of the whole force from Spearman's to Springfield and then to Chieveley.

Warren's diary reads: "The troops were not at all pleased with the retirement. The gist of their views that came to me was that they were fairly mad when they heard of it; after losing a lot of men in taking positions, they would rather go on and risk their lives than retire and leave what they had won.

"They were in an exasperated condition, and I had to restore them to equanimity. They recovered their spirits, however, during the retreat.

"I let it get out to them that I staked my credit on our going on, but this time to a place where they could get at the enemy more readily.

"I spoke of the bush, and the hills of Hlangwane, where there would be no long range rifle firing at 2,000 yards, and not so much chance of the Boer long range guns being effective.

"For three days whilst retiring I was absolutely in command, and I did my best to encourage the men to have games of skill with the Boer; we had many exciting adventures and really good fun, and they delighted in it.

"Crossing the Tugela naked, with nothing but their rifles and ammunition, and turning the Boers out of some schanzes quite took their fancy. These schanzes had been constructed on the north side of the Tugela to cover our retreat from the Kopjes and to form a bridge-head to the pontoon whilst being dismantled.

"As soon as the pontoon had been dismantled, the men occupying the bridge-head were ferried over; but they had omitted to raze the schanzes that they had constructed for their defence, and it was immediately observed that the Boers were creeping down to occupy them.

"Volunteers were at once called for, who stripped naked but for their ammunition and rifles, and half waded and half swum across. They demolished the schanzes before the Boers could get to them, and returned in safety.

"In our final clear-up I lingered behind to see that nothing was left and noticed a large fire on some table land, and approaching it found it was the stores of our camp, which they could not remove in time and had tried to burn up.

"A large quantity of pots of very good jam were still untouched by the flames, so I sent the last companies of infantry round by that fire, with instructions that every man could take a pot of jam for his tea. There was a fine scamble and the men marched off well-laden with jam, sardines and potted lobster!" [1]

Buller and his staff left Springfield early on Friday, February 9th, and reached Chieveley that same evening. Warren and the troops followed about two days' journey behind.

On the evening of the 11th, when Warren was at Pretorius's farm, on the last lap, he received this telegram from Buller's Chief of Staff: "The General Commanding desires me to express to you his appreciation of the excellent arrangements you have made for the evacuation of Spearman's Camp, which have resulted in the retirement being so promptly effected."

Buller was back at his old headquarters, familiar ground – like being home, perhaps.

But it was here that he had failed the first time. And he would not be at Hlangwane on Saturday. It was going to be Monday now.

"From General Sir R. Buller to General Sir G. White: No 191, 8th February. My No 190 of yesterday. For 'Saturday' read 'Monday' ".

He spent some time looking out over the sweeping, descending valley to Colenso, turning right to, from where he was standing, the hillock called Hlangwane.

He was depressed, says Symons.

And the telegrams he sent to Roberts (who passed them on to Lansdowne) were as well: "The operations of the past three weeks have borne in upon me the fact that I had seriously miscalculated the retentive power of the Ladysmith garrison.

"I now find the enemy can practically neglect that and turn their whole force on me.

"I am not consequently strong enough to relieve Ladysmith. If you could send me reinforcements and if White could hold out till they arrive, I think it might be done; but with a single column I believe it to be almost an impossibility.

"I shall continue attacking it, as it keeps the enemy off Ladysmith, but I think the prospects of success are very small. Can you send me the other half batteries of 5-inch guns. I have two here, and should like the full batteries available."

The second telegram read: "It is right you should know that, in my opinion, the fate of Ladysmith is only a question of days, unless I am very considerably reinforced. Where I go the enemy can anticipate me with superior force.

"I turned yesterday from Vaalkrantz, and am moving towards Colenso; the enemy have left Vaalkrantz and are now at Colenso. They do in six hours and seven miles what takes me three days and 26 miles.

"When I said I should try and save Ladysmith the 5th Division had arrived at the Cape, and the 6th and 7th were likely to come and were expected to be at my disposal; but two days after you were appointed, and directed that all troops arriving after that date were to be kept at the Cape. I understand from you that you expect to occupy Bloemfontein by end of February, and so relieve the pressure on Ladysmith.

"I hope the forecast will prove correct, but I cannot help feeling that to relieve Ladysmith as it is for such a chance is a great risk, and it is right that I should say so.

"As for myself, I am doing all I can, and certainly have reason to think that I retain the confidence of all who know my difficulties; but if it is thought that anyone can do better, I would far rather be sacrificed than run the risk of losing Ladysmith. I should like you to forward this to the Secretary of State." [2]

Who but Buller could do better? Warren? Of course not. He had "failed" at Spioenkop, hadn't he? Therefore no-one. Buller was best.

Buller craved approval. It is in all his telegrams, certainly those of Colenso and before Spioenkop. Look, he says, what I am doing is right, now get me out of here! Send me more men.

But Roberts wasn't having any of it.

He sent the following telegram to Lansdowne: "10 February, 1900, 8.15pm. Following is copy of telegram I have sent to General Buller: 'Your cypher telegrams No 193 and No 195 of 9th February open out such a large question that it seems necessary to recall what has taken place since my appointment to the chief command in South Africa.

"My views on the general military situation were communicated to you in my cypher telegrams No 1, dated London, 23rd December, and No 3 dated Madiera, 26th December, in the first of which I pointed out the importance of concentrating all our available force in Cape Colony, with the object of advancing on Bloemfontein, and in the second informed you that pending the landing in Cape Colony of the 6th Division the status quo in Natal did not appear altogether disadvantageous.

"On my arrival at Cape Town on 10th January, you did not ask for further reinforcements. In your telegram No 157 cypher, dated 15th January, you informed me that you had collected stores more quickly than you anticipated and were concentrating your troops for an advance, adding that you would probably be unaided as White had told you to expect very little help from him.

"In your cypher telegram, 158, dated 17th January, you repeated a message from White reporting that his force was much played out, and suggesting that you might apply for more troops if you felt any serious doubt of being able to get through to Ladysmith.

"On this you remarked that you questioned if you could do better with a larger force, the difficulties of supplies on the Tugela river without roads being enormous.

"You reported your withdrawal from Spioenkop in your cypher telegram No 169, dated 25th January, to which I replied in my telegram, No 26, dated 26th January.

"In this I informed you of my intention to collect sufficient transport and invade the Orange Free State early in February, and I suggested that you should postpone further attempts to relieve Ladysmith until the effect of the operations which I contemplated had become apparent.

"On 28th January, in your cypher telegram No 179, you repeated a message of the same date from White in reply to a question from me in which he stated he could hold out for six weeks longer.

"Even then you did not ask for reinforcements, and as you disregarded my suggestion that you should act on the defensive until I had time to lessen the hostile pressure in Natal by advancing on the Orange Free State, the natural conclusion to be drawn was that you felt yourself strong enough, with the troops at your disposal, to make a further attempt to relieve Ladysmith.

"As for your remarks about the 6th and 7th Divisions, it is true that had you been holding chief command in South Africa, you could have diverted them to Natal, but their original destination was Cape Colony, and, though you knew that I proposed to employ them in that Colony, you did not ask for their services, nor did you leave anything on record showing that you wanted their services.

"From the foregoing references, it will be seen that by the middle of January you were acquainted with White's position, resources and inability to afford you material assistance, and that on 26th January I have your specific information of my intentions, which involved the employment in offensive field operations of every soldier in Cape Colony that could be spared from defence duty within the Colony.

"It will also be seen that, from the date of my assuming chief command until yesterday, I have had no reason to suppose that you considered reinforcements necessary for the relief of Ladysmith.

"Sending you large reinforcements now would entail the abandonment of the plan of operations, the objects of which was explained to you on the 27th January, and in the prosecution of which I am convinced lies our best chance of success both in Natal and on the North of Cape Colony.

"Such a course would involve endless confusion, and protracted delay, and as Cape Colony is weakly held, might not improbably lead to a general rising of the disaffected Dutch population.

"I must therefore request that while maintaining a bold front, you will act strictly on the defensive, until I have time to see whether the operation I am undertaking produces the effect hoped for.

"The repeated loss of men on the Tugela river without satisfactory result is that which our small army cannot aim at. I will gladly meet your wishes as regards the remaining half-batteries of 5-inch guns, but I can do nothing more. Your two telegrams under reply, and my answer to them is being repeated to the Secretary of State for War." [3]

Buller had stirred up a real hornet's nest. Roberts, it appears, had had enough.

The next day Roberts sent this telegram to London and Buller from Modder River, dated February 11/12, 1900.

"In continuation of my cypher telegram . . . of yesterday, and with reference to your telegram . . . of the 9th instant, in which you give it as your opinion that fate of Ladysmith is only question of days, unless you are very considerably reinforced, I should like to have the views of your second in command on this question, which is one of vital importance to our position in South Africa, that it is very necessary I should know whether Sir Charles Warren shares your views.

"Show him all your and my telegrams on this subject, also White's telegram of 28th January to me, in which he states he could hold out until Middle of March.

"I wish also to know why, as stated in your telegram . . . of 25th January, you considered it necessary to take command of operations which resulted in withdrawal from Spioenkop.

"Please send very early replies to these telegrams." [4]

Fate was catching up with Buller, the tired, unwilling general. Was it possible he had lost his nerve?

It is important to remember that when Roberts sent this telegram he had not yet received Buller's Spioenkop despatches. But it is obvious from the tone of the telegrams that he was not happy – not at all happy – with the way things were going.

He had reservations about Buller's interference in the Spioenkop action – he was not sure whether Buller was right – and regarded Warren as an authority whose opinion was of the utmost importance to him. And rightly so. Warren, as Buller's second in command, was the third senior officer in South Africa.

It is not recorded what Buller felt when he received these telegrams. But he was stung into action and replied at once to Roberts: " . . . Pray do not think I wish to lay my troubles on you. I quite admit that that I miscalculated the retentive power of Sir George White's force. I thought he would hold at least 10,000 off me. I doubt if he keeps 2,000, and I underrated the difficulties of the country.

"I don't know your plan or where your troops are, and the last thing I wish to do is involve your plans in confusion.

"I merely state the fact that I think Ladysmith is in danger, and that I find myself too weak to relieve it. But as you value the safety of Ladysmith, do not tell me to remain on the defensive. To do that means to leave the whole Boer force free to attack Ladysmith.

"Sir George White has repeatedly telegraphed: 'I trust to you preventing them throwing their strength on me.' And again, 'The closer to Ladysmith you can establish yourself, the better chance we shall have.'

"I feel sure this is the right policy, and I hope you will not say I am to rest supine and leave Ladysmith alone. During the late operations I am confident the Boer force has been reduced by two men to every one I have lost, and for three weeks our operations have practically caused the cessation of the bombardment of Ladysmith. As I have said, I will do all I can, and you may rely that I will not compromise my force."

As to Warren, Buller tells it this way in his evidence before the Commission: "Sir Charles Warren, being absent, I replied at once to the second issue raised in the telegram: 'Warren comes in tomorrow, and shall send you his opinion after having read all the telegrams. My report of operations west of Spioenkop was posted to you 30th January, and should reach you before this, so I will only say I was not in command of the operations which resulted in withdrawal from Spioenkop.

"During these operations I had gradually, at Warren's request, reinforced him until he practically had with him my entire force, except the, as I thought, too weak garrison of Spearman's.

"After he reported the abandonment of Spioenkop I decided that we had lost our chance, and took command. His whole Division was there; one of his brigades had no commander, and I thought, in the circumstances, his presence with his division was essential."

But only Warren's 5th Division was committed to Spioenkop. Thousands of idle troops stood by with Buller at Mount Alice.

Says Buller: "Warren came in that evening. I gave him all the telegrams . . . and he wrote a long telegram which I sent to Lord Roberts . . . One sentence of the telegram summarises it. Warren said, addressing me: 'The matter involves an immense number of considerations and innumerable details, on which I may or may not shares your views; but on the main and important subjects I think that my views closely coincide with yours.' " [5]

For Warren that was a strangely passive statement. Why not, having been given the opportunity, blast Buller? Put before the Commander-in-Chief those matters that had aggravated him? Why didn't Warren tell Roberts how Buller had constantly interfered?

Again, Roberts had not received the Spioenkop despatches, with its damning "not necessarily for publication" report. And again, Warren had absolutely no idea that he had been so mishandled by his commanding officer.

Symons suggests Warren's reply could only have confused Roberts even further.

But Warren says: "On the 12th February I was for the first time shown all the telegrams between Lord Roberts and General Buller and had to make up my mind immediately. The outcome of my perusal of them was this:

"Lord Roberts had the idea that if General Buller's advance on Ladysmith was delayed somewhat, till Bloemfontein was occupied, Ladysmith would automatically be relieved. This was the idea of all thinking persons, provided that time was no object.

"There can be no doubt that the occupation of Bloemfontein would have materially aided in relieving the pressure on Ladysmith, but the effect would not have been instantaneous, and Ladysmith was only good for a certain number of days.

"I was satisfied that Lord Roberts was too optimistic as to the very rapid rate of his advance on Bloemfontein, and if he were to be delayed, or failed, Ladysmith was doomed.

"What guarantee was there that Lord Roberts would automatically raise the siege of Ladysmith before its last ration was eaten? None whatever!

"As a matter of fact Lord Roberts did meet with very serious delays, and Bloemfontein was occupied some fortnight after the garrison of Ladysmith ate their last ration; and if Lord Roberts' view as to waiting for him had been followed, Ladysmith would have fallen.

"General Buller, on the other hand, considered that he could not . . . relieve Ladysmith without very great reinforcements. But although time was so pressing, it might be done if my methods of continued attacks and artillery bombardment were adhered to.

"Under one set of circumstances, therefore, I entirely agreed with General Buller . . . and under another set of circumstances I entirely disagreed . . .

"These are the considerations I laid before General Buller: You have stated in your recent telegram that you cannot relieve Ladysmith without considerable reinforcements. In this I disagree with you; you have not given a fair trial to my methods. If you trust to Lord Roberts relieving Ladysmith automatically, you are trusting to a broken reed; he cannot do it in time.

"I know that because I know intimately the country that he has to go over. If you do not use my methods, Ladysmith is lost, and I must say so to Lord Roberts.

"But if you agree to support my methods, and we get more long-range guns, there is a good chance of winning in, and I can tell Lord Roberts that I agree with you, but I shall feel obliged to say that I think the reinforcements are more wanted on Lord Roberts' side.

"In using my methods you have always interfered and reduced their effectiveness; yet you have told the men who served under me on the Spioenkop campaign that they have given you the key to Ladysmith.

"You had the troops for several weeks before I came: why did they not show the same prowess then?

"Hitherto you have systematically kept the soldier aloof from the Boer, and have just made two little dabs at the enemy, at Colenso and Vaalkrantz. What our men want, to make them heroes, is what they got in the Spioenkop campaign – to be continually in face of the Boer, day by day, hour by hour, night and day. The Englishman wants active warfare; he is a fighting animal. You have kept him sitting down for weeks doing nothing, not even practising for warfare.

"Sir Redvers is not altogether a man to interfere with, says Sir George White. And usually he peremptorily stopped a subordinate saying what he had to say. But this was a special case; it was a matter of life and death to thousands. I was bound to speak plainly, and General Buller was bound to listen.

"But instead of getting angry he took up the matter eagerly; it seemed a new light to him, and he appeared to be quite relieved from anxiety.

"When I ventured to insist on his giving my methods fair play before I replied to Lord Roberts, he then and there gave me his assurance that he would support me in my methods until the relief of Ladysmith, and he honestly tried to keep to his engagement.

"This being successfully arranged, the question remained, how was I to word my reply to Lord Roberts?

"I did not want to be asked to take over the command myself: I was quite satisfied to act as General Buller's second in command, so long as I had his support.

"But if he was going to adopt my methods, how was this sudden *bouleversement* on his part to be accomplished without attracting too much attention?

"I proposed, as the only method of dealing with the matter, a piece of bluff which I trusted Lord Roberts would see through and understand.

"It was to save General Buller's face. He could not possibly have telegraphed to say that he had given up all his views and subscribed to mine. But as he had actually done so in private, I worded my reply to the effect that my views coincided with those which he expressed to me on the 12th February, and then proceeded to enumerate them in detail.

"This reply of mine has never been understood because it seemed so contradictory. The official histories apparently thought it too hard a nut to crack, and barely touch on it.

"No-one except perhaps the Chief of Staff knew that General Buller had changed his tactics." [6]

What did Warren write? Roberts sent this telegram to Lansdowne from Enslin, in the Northern Cape, on February 14, at 7.55pm: "Following received from Buller, dated Chieveley, 13th February: 'I have received following from General Warren: Secret. With reference to Field Marshal Lord Roberts question of 11 February . . . as to whether I share your views expressed in your telegram . . . of the 9th February, the matter involves an immense number of considerations and investigation of details on which I may or may not share your views, but on the main and important subjects I think that my views closely coincide with yours as follows:

" 'A-In my estimation the force now in Natal is not sufficiently strong to effectually relieve Ladysmith if the Boers have long-range guns well directed, with good shells, except by getting hold of some position where we are able to get our artillery to pound away at the Boers in their trenches, and then worry and harry till they are tired out." [7]

It was this tactic at the forthcoming battle of Pieters, in fact, that finally enabled Ladysmith to be relieved. Warren was right.

The telegram continues: "'B-I consider that an attack on Bloemfontein and the occupation of the Orange Free State would materially assist in relief of Ladysmith by drawing off Orange Free State Boers, because, immediately the Orange Free State is declared British territory, the Orange Free State Boers in Natal must either return home or lose their farms.

" 'C-I agree with you and General White that it would be fatal to Ladysmith merely to remain on the defensive until operations are carried out in the Orange Free State. I consider that the General officer commanding, Natal, (Buller) is bound to continue closely attacking the Boers, even though he should know that he cannot effect relief of Ladysmith, by doing so, arranging, of course, that it may be done with as little loss of life as possible.

" 'D-General White first stated that Ladysmith could only hold out to 15th February, but can now hold out to 15th March. This gives us nearly a month more. I consider that 10,000 would be much more effectually employed in

Orange Free State and Transvaal in giving assistance to Ladysmith; at the same time I am of opinion that the Natal force is just so weak, without its proper complement of artillery, as to act with difficulty against positions held by the Boers, which are practically forts with fortifications.

"On the whole, I think that the most effectual arrangement is for the force here, kept up by drafts to full strength, to pound away with their artillery and hang on, and to worry the Boers to the utmost while a rapid advance is made on Bloemfontein, with the object of occupying Harrismith and Van Reenen's Passes, and at the same time for a proclamation to be issued stating that the Orange Free State is British territory, and must call on the Boers to return home or lose their farms.

"'E-You have shown me your proposals as to attacking Hlangwane near Colenso. I think this will much assist General White, and that if sufficient long-range guns can be got up, it is possible that the Boers may be worried by artillery until a passage is forced through to Ladysmith; at any rate, it is necessary constantly to pound away to keep the Boers off Ladysmith until they are drawn by Lord Roberts' advance.

"The only point I would suggest is that, when a frontal attack is necessary, it should be done, if it is practicable, by sappers, so as to save life; but I have not met with a place in the recent operations where a sapper would be useful, as the Boers dread being killed in anything like equal proportion to our men. There are a considerable number of minor points I should touch on, but these five . . . are the most essential." [8]

Roberts's answer is significant in that it again castigates Buller: "15th February: . . . My reason for asking you to maintain strictly defensive attitude while still showing a bold front was because you informed me that you felt too weak to relieve Ladysmith without reinforcements, and considered its fall merely a question of days.

"As I am unable to spare reinforcements for Natal, it appears to me to involve useless waste of life for you to again undertake an enterprise which you regarded as hopeless until it could be seen whether my operation in Orange Free State would lessen forces opposed to you and make your task easier.

"At the same time I have no wish that you should adhere to a passive defence, provided that care is taken to avoid complications which may result in heavy loss of life. Subject to this condition I abundantly agree that the more you can harass the Boers the better.

"I therefore leave it to you to do what you think best, and rely on your assurance that you will not compromise your force . . .

"As regards Warren's telegram, I am glad to find his views coincide in the main with yours, and also that he agrees with me in thinking that a rapid advance on Bloemfontein will materially assist in relieving Ladysmith by causing many of the inhabitants of the Orange Free State to return to their farms." [9]

Warren's account of his meeting with Buller ends with the following observation: "The most important result of this conference with General Buller, next to my methods being approved, was the privilege I gained of being allowed to suggest, each afternoon during the advance on Ladysmith, the proceedings that I proposed for the following day, instead of receiving orders formulated by some junior officer, or due to what General Buller could see through his spyglass.

"It was arranged that I should each day send to the Chief of Staff my proposals for the following day; then General Buller could either approve, and issue the orders in his own name, or, if he did not approve, I could ride over and explain matters and get them settled directly with him. It was fortunate that there was such a sterling good Chief of Staff as Colonel Miles to help cordially in this matter.

"As soon as the arrangements resulting from the conference were settled at Headquarters, I sought out General Lyttleton and arranged with him many details, so that we could work together in unison.

"Now that General Clery was on the sick list for some time, General Lyttleton was in command of the 2nd Division. One of the most important matters to secure was that, of the two Divisions, one should lead and the other be in support on alternate days. This was carried out as far as circumstances would allow.

"The troops under General Lyttleton were his two brigades, the 2nd (Hildyard) and 4th (Norcott's) and a brigade division of Field Artillery. The troops under me were my two brigades, the 10th (Coke's) and 11th (Wynne's) with the 6th (Barton's) brigade attached, and a brigade division of Field Artillery. The 5th (Hart's) brigade was sometimes attached to my division and sometimes worked independently.

"Thus, with my proposals accepted by General Buller and confirmed by Lord Roberts, we started on the 14th February our last – and successful – attack on the Boers in the relief of Ladysmith . . ." [10]

SOURCES

1. *The Life of Sir Charles Warren,* by Watkin Williams.
2. *Commission on the War in South Africa.*
3. Ibid.
4. Ibid.
5. Ibid.
6. *The Life of Sir Charles Warren,* by Watkin Williams.
7. *Commission on the War in South Africa.*
8. Ibid.
9. Ibid.
10. *The Life of Sir Charles Warren,* by Watkin Williams.

CHAPTER TWENTY FIVE

The Juggernaut Begins to Roll

Battle of Pieters – Part 2

It was Tuesday, February 17, 1903. Sir Redvers Buller had got into his stride now, sitting in St Stephen's Hall in London. His mind went back three years, almost to the day.

The rustle of papers quietened as he said: "On the 14th (of February, 1900) I moved to Hussar Hill, and commenced the occupation of positions for attack on Cingolo, Monte Christo and Hlangwane mountains.

"During the 13th and 15th Sir George White reported continual and increasing concentrations of the enemy in front of me.

"On the 15th Lord Roberts replied . . . to my telegrams . . . that he had no wish that I should adhere to a passive defence, and left it to me to do whatever I thought best, relying on my assurance that I would not compromise my force . . .

"On the 12th I reconnoitred the approaches to Hlangwane. I found as I thought, not more than 1,500 men, with two or three guns in the position, but the ground was fearfully rugged, covered for the most part with dense bush, and would evidently be very difficult to approach.

"On the 13th the day was so intensely hot that I did not allow the infantry to move . . . " [1]

Bennet Burleigh would have no doubt have said something about the soldiers and the heat. But he, disgusted at the Vaalkrantz retreat, had left to join Roberts. There was more news there, he said.

But J.B. Atkins stayed.

"Success is comparatively dull," he wrote. "Here were we making a fighting march along the range of Monte Christo, flanking the enemy, taking him at a complete tactical disadvantage, making his whole line bulge and crumple because we were pushing hard on it at one end, and yet there was never a moment when one was thrilled as by the impotent heroism of Colenso, Spioenkop or Vaalkrantz.

"Your own successes in war may be dull to watch; it is not dull indeed to your heart, but warming and genial; if your heart has been frozen, and sickened with failure.

"The fighting march, as I may call the battle of Monte Christo, was dull to see because it was gradual, the events of a day seemed trifling, and the fighting was more than half invisible.

"But the accumulated events made it the best achievement so far of Sir Redvers Buller's column.

"And what a pleasant irony was success here and now! A month before we had left this place – these close-tangled, knotted hills – to find a way round. We were back here with our knowledge of geography strengthened. There was no way round . . ." [2]

Briefly, the advance was to take place in three stages: the Boers were to be driven from the heights of Hlangwane, Cingolo and Monte Cristo, and cleared out of the whole area on the south side of the Tugela.

In the second, the troops were to cross the river and attack the hills north of Colenso in preparation for the final advance; and in the third stage, the advance was to be made by way of Pieters and along the relatively level country from Nelthorpe to Ladysmith.

But there was one great advantage: Hlangwane was on the south, British side. The Boers would have to cross the Tugela to defend it.

Some of Winston Churchill's descriptions of the final push are perhaps among the most vivid of the war, along with E. Blake-Knox. Churchill writes: "On the 12th orders were issued to reconnoitre Hussar Hill, a grassy and wooded eminence four miles to the east of Chieveley, and the direction of the next attack was revealed . . .

"If Buller goes in and wins he will have accomplished a wonderful feat of arms, and will gain the lasting honour and gratitude of his country. If he is beaten he will deserve the respect and sympathy of all true soldiers as a man who has tried to the best of his ability to perform a task for which his resources were inadequate.

"Hussar Hill – so called because a small post of the 13th Hussars was suprised on it six weeks ago and lost two men killed – is the high ground opposite Hlangwane and the mountainous ridges called Monte Christo and Cingolo, on which the artillery must be posted to prepare the attack. Hence the reconnaissance of the 12th.

"At 8 o'clock – we never get up early in this war – Lord Dundonald started from the cavalry camp near Stuart's Farm . . . we soon occupied Hussar Hill, driving back a small Boer patrol which was watching it, wounding two of the enemy . . .

"At noon, Sir Redvers Buller arrived and made a prolonged reconnaissance of the ground with his telescope. At one o'clock we were ordered to withdraw . . ." [3]

Buller says: "On the 14th we occupied Hussar Hill and on the 15th I threw my right forward to turn the enemy's left. But the heat was so great and so trying to the men in the waterless bush that I halted the troops when the movement was about half completed, and ordered them to bivouac where they stood."

Natal's February heat is stupefying. It is bad enough walking the battlefields today in T-shirt and shorts. Everything shimmers. It must have been absolute hell in any kind of uniform. On February 13, White had telegraphed: "Considerable movement yesterday, among Boer camps. All those north of Potgieter's moved, some towards Potgieter's Drift and some eastward. We anxiously await news from you." [4]

Buller had news.

On the same day, he telegraphed to White: "Field Marshal desires me to communicate the following to you: . . . I have entered Orange Free State with a large force, specially strong in cavalry, artillery and mounted infantry. Inform your troops of this and tell them from me I hope the result of the next few days may lead to pressure on Ladysmith being materially lessened." [5]

On the 15th, White sent: "Following movements of enemy observed today: about 50 wagons and 600 Boers from Roodipoort to Surprise Hill; 55 wagons and about 400 Boers from Dewdrop to Underbrook [Onderbroek]."

[Dewdrop was a farm near Clydesdale between Acton Homes and Ladysmith on the Bergville road].

And on the 16th: "Considerable move northward took place yesterday afternoon and evening. Not less than 2,000 men, with large proportion of wagons, moving north up valley towards Cundycleugh . . ." [6]

Cundycleugh is a small village in the Biggarsberg.

But there was even better news. The siege of Kimberley had been lifted. As Roberts entered the small Free State town of Jacobsdal, General French – the man who had caught the last train out of Ladysmith before it was closed in by the encircling Boers – had ridden hard into Kimberley.

Says Buller, referring to the Boer movement northwards, and the lifting of the siege of Kimberley: "This was great news, and I felt certain we were going to be successful." [7]

But there was no movement again on the 16th. Says Buller: " . . . being again a blazing hot day, we did not leave our positions".

While the troops didn't move, the artillery carried on. And Buller's immobility came in for some pretty harsh, saracastic, words in *The Times History*: "In five days, Buller had covered just five miles in his desperate dash for Bulwana. The weather during these five days was undoubtedly hot. But it was no less hot on the dusty plains of the Free State, and it was during these same days that Roberts' army did some of its hardest marches, trudging and staggering along to victory under the impulse of a clear directing brain and a keen will. It was the absence of these impelling factors, and not the heat, that was the real cause of the present futile performance. The heat was but an excuse for indecision and feebleness of purpose." [8]

Warren sums up the situation as follows: "In the attack on Hlangwane there was immediate need for celerity of action; and yet a whole Division was kept stationary on Hussar Hill for three days, doing nothing – exposed to shell fire and the sun's rays without any cover . . .

"In this campaign General Buller never seemed to know when to make a dash and when to hold his hand. He could have cleared the Boers out of Hlangwane when he made his reconnaissance on the 11th February; but he chose to retire . . .

"Both the *Times History* and the *German History* contrast the inertness of General Buller on the four days, 13th to 16th February, with the long marches made by Lord Roberts during the same period: but in this they are wrong.

"The climate of the Orange Free State in the very hottest weather is delightful for working in, compared with the heavy summer weather of Natal around Ladysmith."

But he goes on: "The weather on these four days was very hot, but what I insist on is this: when you are living in the open air without shelter from the sun, the most disagreeable phase of life is to be forced to sit down and do nothing; but to be forced to sit down and do *nothing* and be heavily shelled all the livelong day, is putting a limit on human endurance."

Later he says: " . . . The task that I had imposed on myself was not yet over: I was determined to devise some means of impressing on all that we had to stick on Hussar Hill, shells or no shells (their bark was worse than their bite.) So I directed the excellent Ayton [Warren's batman], always ready to heat me some water and put it in my Mackintosh bath."

The Mackintosh bath was portable, and like the raincoat of the same name, waterproof. It unfolded, but did not have side supports.

" 'But where, sir?' Oh, in one of those small (shell) holes. So the water was heated, and I proceeded to have my bath, with the men all about, curious and rather amused, and the shells dropping galore.

"As luck would have it, General Buller sent for me to give me some orders just as I was getting into my bath. So I sent a humble petition to the

Commander-in-Chief, asking if he would come and give me the orders as I was not dressed.

"Shortly there appeared General Buller with a large Staff on horseback, who surrounded me, whilst I covered my nakedness with a bath towel, and I felt like an Eastern potentate receiving homage.

"General Buller gave me his instructions and then rode off, and I felt I had done what I could for the day to amuse the men – for there was a great crowd of men peeping on, at a respectful distance, and the incident got into the the English and Continental papers!"

More than that. There are artists' drawings of Sir Charles in the bathtub – drawings, incidentally, that confused the Boers. Was this the way the English spent their time?

Warren continues: "Next day, the 16th February, the shelling of Hussar Hill was still more vigorous on the part of the Boers, and the shells got well into my H.Q. Bivouac. Our pots and pans got knocked to pieces, and cooking duties became unpopular . . . the shelling looked an amazing holocaust, but it was really not so terrible in its effects – the men must get used to it. There would be no grousing now that I had had my bath in the midst of it, with the Commander-in-Chief's Staff all closing round . . ." [9] While Leo Amery contrasted Roberts's march with Buller's dallying, young Winston Churchill enthused: "Not since I wrote the tale of my escape from Pretoria have I taken up my pen with such feelings of satisfaction and contentment as I do tonight" [the date was February 19].

"The period of doubt and hesitation is over. We have grasped the nettle firmly, and as shrewdly as firmly, and have taken no hurt. It remains only to pluck it. For heaven's sake no over-confidence or premature elation; but there is really good hope that Sir Redvers Buller has solved the Riddle of the Tugela – at last!

" . . . The water question presented some difficulty, as the Blue Krantz (Blaauwkrants) river was several miles from Hussar Hill and the hill itself was waterless.

"A system of iron tanks mounted on ox wagons was arranged, and a sufficient though small supply maintained." [10]

And J.B. Atkins had this to say: "For three days the hill was like a standing flywheel which winds everything up to it. The chief need was water, and to get water we must spread out. All Thursday and Friday we were edging crabwise along the ridge south-eastwards; little white bursting globes of smoke went first, probing the bush, teaching us the way; the mounted infantry came next, and the whole column was beckoned on, as by the white arms of a syren, by the silver band which was curved in the valley at the end of the ridge. That was the Blaaukrantz; that was water.

"It was slow work moving. The troops lay about for the greater part of the day, and craved water. The sun was uncovered; the heat was mordant. 'We are just laying and drying up,' I heard a solider say in a phrase, I thought, of unapproachably descriptive quality.

"Meanwhile the Boers sat among the mimosas and in their elaborate sand-bagged trenches on Hlangwane, and on all the ranges between there and Monte Christo . . .

"On Saturday February 17, our bombardment waxed to a higher power. The naval gunners on Hussar Hill were splendidly protected by sandbag works, and though they were shelled with precision, lost no men.

"With one of the five-inch garrison guns, it was otherwise. They were not protected. Why not protected? 'It's not our way,' the army gunner says.

"Major Caldwell sat in a deck chair near the five-inch guns – the type of the cool, scornful British artillery officer – and kept saying, 'Number One gun, *fire* . . . Number Two gun, *fire*' while I talked to him about the Domokos, which we had seen together in Greece . . ." [11]

On the 16th, too, Buller, says Churchill, "resolved to plunge, and the orders were issued for a general advance at dawn. Colonel Sandbach, under whose supervision the Intelligence Department has attained a new and a refreshing standard of efficiency, made comprehensive and, as was afterwards proved, accurate reports of the enemy's strengths and spirit, and strongly recommended the attack on the left flank.

"Two hours before dawn the army was on the move . . ."

The target was Cingolo and Monte Cristo.

Buller's evidence is sparse. He told the Commission: "On the 17th I occupied Cingolo hill, and threw my mounted men well to the right, sweeping the country between the Blaauwkrantz and the Tugela Rivers. On the 17th I reported to Lord Roberts that I had been engaged all this week in trying to force my way nearer to Ladysmith, that my losses were very small, but that I expected a heavier engagement on the morrow." [12]

Warren wrote: "On Saturday the 17th the British line began to wheel to the left with Hussar Hill as its pivot; Lyttleton's Division attacked Cingolo and Monte Christo, and the right of Barton's brigade was also engaged, while Coke's brigade was in reserve and Wynne's in support all day.

"On the 18th there was a general move forward of attack; Lyttleton's Division captured Cingolo and Monte Christo, and Barton's brigade captured Green Hill (north of Hussar Hill and midway between Hlangwane and Cingolo)." [13]

Churchill watched, from close-up, the battle for Cingolo, taken and held ("The Boers who were much disconcerted . . . showed themselves ostentatiously on the turned back ridge of their position as if to make themselves appear in great strength, and derisively hoisted white flags on their guns. The Colonial and American troopers – for in the South African Light Horse we have a great many Americans and one even who served under Sheridan – made some exceeding good practice . . .") and Monte Christo: "The musketry swelled into a constant crackle like the noise of a good fire roaring up the chimney, but in spite of more than 100 casualties, the advance never checked for an instant, and by half-past ten o'clock the bayonets of the attacking infantry began to glitter among the trees of the summit.

"The Boers, who were lining a hastily dug trench half-way along the ridge, threatened in front with an overwhelming force and assailed in flank by the long-range fire of the cavalry, began to fall back. By eleven o'clock the fight on the part of the enemy resolved itself into a rearguard action.

"Under the pressure of the advancing and eveloping army this degenerated very rapidly . . . and I have never seen an enemy leave the field in such as hurry as did these valiant Boers . . ." [14]

Warren says: "This was a real rout of the Boers – the first one we had had – and if we had been permitted to go on we certainly would have prevented them getting their wagons across the Tugela. I was with the Royal Scots Fusiliers when they were recalled, and I saw the Boers were in a state of real panic . . . if General Buller had seen what I saw I think he might have pursued . . .

"The enemy retired hurriedly, leaving their camps standing, also thick blankets, coats, waterproofs, entrenching tools and a great quantity of ammunition in their trenches." [15]

They also found ponies, reins, saddles, Mauser cartridges, "pom-pom" shells, flour, biltong and bibles.

But there is that word again: Recalled.

The *German Official account* says: "It seemed as though the Boers could no longer escape the certain annihilation with which the pursuit of the British Infantry threatened them.

"But suddenly an order was received from Buller that the troops were to halt in the positions they had taken and were to press forward no further.

"Whether it was attributable to the great heat, or whether to the fear of another retirement which should hazard the retention of what had been so far gained, this fateful order saved the Boers from certain destruction and reduced to half its value this the first success of the British arms. Pursuit, which would have carried the British across the Tugela at the same time as the Boers, would have made it impossible for the latter to take up a new position and, it may fairly be assumed, would have effected the Relief of Ladysmith . . ." [16]

Buller is silent on the reason.

He is not silent on the taking of Monte Cristo. "On the 18th I assaulted and took Monte Christo and manoeuvred the enemy out of the Hlangwane position," he told the Commission.

But it was Warren who took Hlangwane – the hill he was so familiar with. On Monday the 19th, Hart's brigade advanced from Chieveley to Colenso and took up position next to Warren's division on the extreme left of the line. On the same day, Warren moved his three brigades towards the south bank of the Tugela, and with Barton's brigade, which was in advance of the other two, attacked and captured Hlangwane.

Warren writes: "I was directed to take Hlangwane Hill with the 6th brigade supported by the 2nd Division. The southern portion of the hill had been hastily evacuated by the enemy.

"I proceeded there in advance of the brigade and gave General Barton instructions to occupy the whole of the hill – this was done with the exception of the northern extremity, where the enemy succeeded in keeping a lodgment during the whole day and were not turned out, their object being to cover the retirement across the river . . ." [17]

On Tuesday 20th, Warren completed the capture of Hlangwane and advanced Barton to a point a mile beyond the northern slopes of the hill. He placed Coke's brigade on Hlangwane itself, and arranged for a new road to be made direct from Hussar Hill to Hlangwane.

But he did more than that.

The small disputed town of Colenso had been bypassed by the British. Now Warren sent a reconnaissance party there. It was deserted, although a few shots were fired from the hills on the far side of the Tugela.

Later, Warren sent Wynne's brigade to a point immediately east of the town, one company held Colenso during the night.

The capture of Hlangwane, fittingly by Warren's division, brought to a close the first stage in the advance to Ladysmith.

It also constituted the turning point of the campaign.

The *Times History* says: "The Boer wagons streamed away in unbroken lines over the shoulder of Bulwana, and with them went a considerable number of burghers." [18]

Buller told the Commission: "On the 19th Lord Roberts informed me that the moment was favourable for an attempt to relieve White, as Cronje was almost surrounded by his troops. He added some information as to the withdrawal of Lucas Meyer, with some 3,000 men, from Ladysmith to help Cronje.

"This did not accord with my own intelligence. On this day we cleared the Boers from the south bank of the Tugela and I advanced my left from Chieveley to Colenso. General White reported more wagons trekking north." [19]

Deneys Reitz in *Commando* states sadly: "During the last two days . . . we heard a constant rumble of gun-fire coming from the direction of Colenso, and, on reaching our Pretoria camp, we were met with the disturbing news that the English had broken into our defences there to the extent of capturing Hlangwane Hill, a commanding position that was considered the key to the Tugela line . . . when we neared the river at daybreak we found a critical situation. Not only had Hlangwane been taken, but every Boer trench on the north bank for a distance of several miles had been evacuated, and, what was far more serious, there was a feeling of discouragement in the air that dismayed us . . . we knew . . . Hlangwane had been taken, we did not know that the fighting spirit of the men had gone with it." [20]

But it hadn't. There was to be one more battle – perhaps the most vicious of the war.

Buller has the last word: "On the 20th I ascended Monte Christo and made careful reconnaissance for a route for my further advance. It was clear that I must occupy Colenso, and, attacking from there, take a hill on the north bank of the Tugela between Onderbrook and Langewacht Spruits before any further advance in the direction of Bulwana Hill could be possible." [21]

Surgeon Blake-Knox however, really had the gift of descriptive writing. Consider this: "I had an opportunity of walking over Green Hill, Monte Christo and Cingolo . . . and examined the Boer position. Green Hill I first visited; its grassy slopes were 'pock-marked' with holes from our shells, the ground being one mass of pieces of shell in the form or iron splinters, copper driving bands, and shrapnel bullets.

"A Bull in a China Shop, speaking figuratively, could scarcely make such a litter. The trees, bushes, rocks, and ground were distorted by lyddite. Here a tree cut across, its trunk stangely twisted and stained yellow; there a boulder, large enough for for men to hide behind had been struck and split into segments, separated by great brimstone-smelling fissures.

"The path of lyddite could easily be traced for eveything within some distance of its explosion is stained a canary yellow colour.

"The Boer trenches on Green Hill and the adjacent hills, which we had taken, extended over an area of two miles.

"They were a marvellous example of the ingenuity, cunning and patience of the enemy with which we had to deal. Looking at the entrenchments from the British side, even with a powerful telescope, one would be deceived, so artfully were they concealed by a facing of bushes or sods, so well put together and matching the surrounding ground that it was almost impossible to detect any irregularity of surface.

"On close examination, these trenches proved so interesting that I think them worthy of a short description.

"As the surface soil was extremely shallow – not 6 inches in places – and as the trenches were sunk to the depth of about five feet, they had for the most part to be hewn out of the solid rock. This seemed to have been done entirely by manual labour, as marks of picks were apparent on the stone.

"The sites selected were chiefly just along the skylines, but if a means of communication existed from the side of a trench with the back of a kopje, two, or even three rows of trenches might be present, one above the other.

"Although there were some two miles of trenches, none of them were straight, but cut in zigzag fashion to avoid enfilading fire; many had traverses also for this purpose, and in some the traverses were tunnelled in such a way as to allow of communication between one trench and the next.

"The width of the trenches at the top was never more than two and a half feet, and they widened out at the bottom to nearly four feet, being in fact, so hollowed out as to afford excellent shelter against shellfire.

"The clay and rocks removed to make the excavation were thrown up in front in the form of a solid embankment, which was in many cases surmounted by sacks full of clay, with sods, cut grass and bushes in front to conceal the ridge.

"The bottom of the trench was strewn with hay or straw for comfort, enabling the occupants to sleep there at night, and many were roofed over with beams of wood, having sacks of clay between, to protect the occupants from shell-fire, or with sheets of corrugated zinc, torn from the roofs of our colonists' houses in Colenso, to afford shelter from the sun."

Later, Blake-Knox observed: "On Hlangwane being taken . . . the trenches south of the Tugela were now all in our hands.

"At the rear of Hlangwane we found a big Boer camp which was captured. Among the tents standing I noticed one, a rather large marquee; this had been looted from the British hospital equipment which was captured from us by the enemy at Dundee, after the battle of Talana Hill, and had been used by them as a headquarters tent for General Botha.

"A considerable quantity of food was also found – flour, potatoes, bags of rusks and meat, some of the latter in pots on still smouldring fires; to all apprearances the Boers were provided with good food.

"I never saw such a variety of rubbish as lay about both in the laager and in the trenches; old clothes, old boots, and tin cans were strewn everywhere . . . The Boers also left behind about 1,700 new picks and shovels and about 60 horses.

"The amount of Mauser ammunition abandoned by them was considerable, and I had an opportunity of picking out from amongst it specimens of the following illegal articles: soft-nosed, flat-nosed, split-nosed rifle bullets; also the cupped man-stopping revolver ammunition.

"All these bullets are but varietes of what are called 'expanding bullets', often erroneously described . . . as 'explosive bullets'.

"The wounds they produce are of such a barbaric and ghastly nature that their use in war is forbidden by international law."

But more on that, later . . . [22]

SOURCES

1. *Commission on the War in South Africa.*
2. *The Relief of Ladysmith,* J.B. Atkins.
3. *London to Ladysmith,* by Winston Churchill.
4. *Commission on the War in South Africa.*
5. Ibid.
6. Ibid.
7. Ibid.
8. *The Times History* (Vol. 3).
9. *Life of Sir Charles Warren,* by Watkin Williams.
10. *London to Ladysmith,* by Winston Churchill.
11. *The Relief of Ladysmith,* by J.B. Atkins.
12. *Commission on the War in South Africa.*

13. *Life of Sir Charles Warren*, by Watkin Williams.
14. *London to Ladysmith*, by Winston Churchill.
15. *The Life of Sir Charles Warren*, by Watkin Williams.
16. *German Official Account*, Vol. 2.
17. *The Life of Sir Charles Warren*, by Watkin Williams.
18. *The Times History*, Vol. 3.
19. *Commission on the War in South Africa.*
20. *Commando*, by Deneys Reitz.
21. *Commission on the War in South Africa.*
22. *Buller's Campaign, with the Natal Field Forces*, by E. Blake-Knox.

CHAPTER TWENTY SIX

Hill of Hideous Whispering Death

Battle of Pieters – Part 3

Winston Churchill, too, climbed Monte Christo. From the captured ridge, he wrote: "We could look right down into Ladysmith. Only eight miles away stood the poor little persecuted town, with whose fate there is wrapt up the honour of the Empire, and for whose sake so many hundred good soldiers have given life or limb – a twenty-acre patch of tin houses and blue gum trees, but famous to the uttermost ends of the earth.

"The victory of Monte Christo has revolutionised the situation in Natal. It has laid open a practicable road to Ladysmith . . ."

And later: "The Monte Christo ridge is the centrepiece to the whole battle. As soon as we had won it I telegraphed to the *Morning Post* that now at last success was a distinct possibility.

"With this important feature in our possession it was certain that we held the key to Ladysmith, and though we might fumble a little with the lock, sooner or later, barring the accidents of war, we should open the door." [1]

But the door was not going to be easy.

For his objective in the second stage of the advance, Buller had chosen a hill just north of the Colenso Falls, where the Onderbroek spruit meets the Tugela.

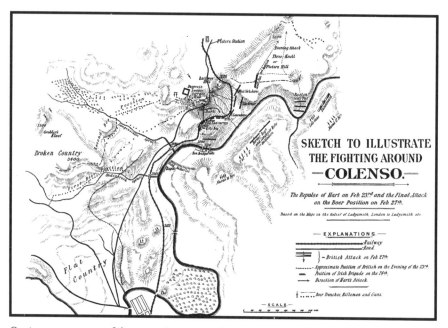

Contemporary map of the operations around Colenso, and the final push to Pieters.

Afterwards it became known variously as Hart's Hill, Terrace Hill and Inniskilling Hill.

Warren describes this choice as a "masterly stroke". But *The Times History* did not, criticising Buller's hesitation in pursuing the Boers across the Tugela.

Warren writes: "General Buller, for this hesitation, has been most unmercifully criticised and blamed. Critics who were incapable of realising his position were all ready to find solutions to the difficulties, without knowing what the difficulties were, and the solutions all differed . . .

"By a stroke of genius he hit upon the only solution that seemed to me possible – the occupation of Hart's Hill as an objective. Only those who were with General Buller in his reconnaissance knew the lie of the land sufficiently to form any certain opinion; but map reading is part of my profession, and I thought that we ought to get hold of that bunch of hills near the corner of Colenso Falls.

"But General Buller was in front of me; he saw the ground itself and plumped for Hart's Hill. Whatever may be said of his dispositions, there is this fact, that immediately he saw the lie of the land he chose the true objective . . .

"In my opinion General Buller had a stupendous task in this advance on Ladysmith, and I know of few generals except Lord Wolseley who could have done it so well.

"The warfare on the western side could not bear comparison in any way the difficulties encountered and surmounted in Natal."[2]

In his evidence before the Commission, Buller said: "During the night of the 20th-21st, the whole of the immense Boer laagers between us and Ladysmith, as well as those visible from Monte Christo to the north of Ladysmith were broken up and removed." [3]

What Roberts had predicted was coming true. The Boer forces were heading to help in the Free State. Not only that, the 25,000 men opposing them, the British juggernaut, was on the roll.

Earlier, Thorneycroft's Mounted Infantry had crossed the river and, after a short, sharp action, taken the kopjes on the other side easily enough. In the evening of the February 19 Colenso station was again puffing with trains.

At daybreak on Wednesday the 21st (writes Watkin Williams) the Royal Engineers, covered by Barton's brigade constructed a heavy pontoon bridge, 110 yards (metres) long, across the Tugela to the west of Hlangwane. In spite of being shelled, they were able to complete their work at 12.45pm.

J.B. Atkins writes: " . . . the pontoons were floated on the river, swung nose to stream, jerked and strained at their moorings, and were stationary at regular intervals like a line of deployed infantry.

"The planks were laid across the the infantry began to walk over. The Somersets and Middlesex – of General Coke's brigade – and the Lancaster Regiment were first over.

"Once again, we had crossed the Tugela."

Also on that day, White sent this telegram to Buller: "We have observed reinforcements for enemy disembarking at Modder Spruit Station, and about 700 mounted men have been seen during last two days moving south via Bulwana."

But Buller telegraphed to White: "I am now engaging in pushing my way through by Pieters. I think there is only a rearguard in front of me. The large Boer laager under Bulwana was removed last night. I hope to be with you tomorrow night. . ."

White replied: "We can detect no signs of the enemy retreating: all indications point the other way."[1]

Warren, in his diary, wrote: "On the 20th, when the Boers were still really scared, we were preparing for an attack by them, and on the 21st, when the Boers had stiffened up again, they were treated as though they were retreating, and we were told it was a rearguard action and we seemed to have ceased to take precautions. The real point [of the contradictory telegrams] was that those Boers who were scared and affected the others had departed, and the residue were stiff-necked, and ready to die for their cause. There was no doubt that the Transvaal Boers remaining had made up their minds to fight stiffly." [4]

But on the 20th there was also a scare. Blake-Knox, whose account of the final push will be extensively used, wrote: "Shortly after daybreak while the men were preparing their breakfasts, an alarm was given to the effect that a considerable force was advancing on our outposts from the direction of Chieveley.

"At the same time the 6-inch gun at Chieveley fired, and a shell burst close by in the village. Our glasses, however, showed that the advancing men were clothed in khaki and that they were not burghers.

"As they neared we could make out the scouts, advance guard, flankers and supports, and in the van rode an officer, with polished straps and sword glittering in the morning sun. This was General Fitzroy Hart, and the troops were the gallant Irish Brigade . . . " [5]

After breakfast, writes Blake-Knox: "I had a walk around Colenso and its environs south of the Tugela, which were historically interesting on account of the action of December 15.

"The village had been shamefully looted and polluted. What had once been a picturesque little hamlet was now a mass of foetid ruins . . . the enemy had dragged their dead horses into the interior of the houses and they lay in the rooms among broken furniture and debris."

A footnote says that some Boer prisoners were afterwards employed by the officer in charge, while waiting for their train to a Durban prison camp, to drag these putrid horses away and bury them.

Blake-Knox says: " . . . In front of the village lay the lines of trenches from which on the date of the battle there had come that deadly hail of bullets which had caused the loss of our two batteries.

"The donga from which Major Babtie, R.A.M.C. had sortied and gained his Victoria Cross was still littered with the accoutrements of our men and artillery horses . . ." [6]

Early in the afternoon of the 21st, writes Watkins, Warren crossed the pontoon with Coke's brigade, and his brigade division of artillery, and, under cover of the guns, advanced towards the low hills on the south side of the junction of the Onderbroek spruit with the Tugela.

Says Blake-Knox, who crossed with the troops: "During a halt near Fort Wylie I was able to examine this hill. It was honeycombed with trenches, delved out of the rocky hillside, and affording perfect shelter from shell-fire, this accounting for the enemy enduring so much of it. Miles of trenches also lined the river-bank, and, owing to the presence of a network of dongas, which joined the river at right angles, the entrance and exit of Boers could not be seen.

"Another rural camp lay behind Fort Wylie, composed of huts, partly made of loose stones, sods and bushes, with dry ox-hides spread over them; some were roofed with loose sheets of corrugated zinc, others with doors torn from buildings; all sorts of house-hold utensils and furniture lay about – chairs, sofas, pianos, tables and beds.

"One of the last-named, a double one, I saw set up under a tree, with its late occupant's portmanteau open upon it – he had evidently left in a hurry. Food and ammunition were strewn everywhere.

"Some Royal Engineers were already engaged in repairing the railway line, a train for this purpose having arrived at Colenso from Chieveley.

"The Colenso railway-bridge was a perfect ruin, the whole five spans of ironwork having been blown to pieces with dynamite by the enemy, and one stone pillar entirely demolished.

"A temporary trestle bridge was about to be erected; the material for this was on its way from Durban.

"The telegraph line had also to be repaired, and to effect this object Corporal Adams, of the Royal Engineers, swam the river, taking with him the wire, which was as least 200 yards long. It was the same corporal who swam across the Little Tugela for a similar purpose. . ." [7]

But Warren's army met with stern opposition, though the Somerset Light Infantry, with the Dorsets in support, managed to capture a portion of the hills. But they suffered heavy losses and were, during the day, unable to make much progress.

After dark, Warren withdrew Coke's brigade a short distance and, bringing Wynne's brigade across the pontoon, drew up the two brigades in a line to the north-west of the Colenso kopjes, and established a firm position on the nothern side of the Tugela. [8]

"Thursday (the 22nd) was the ninth day of the fighting and the first serious day in the shell-trap," writes J.B. Atkins.

" . . . a howitzer fired and waited. The answer came. A shell buzzed down somewhere from the skies, and a geyser shot up in front of the battery. All our guns leaped to the rescue and fumed back . . . It is said we silenced some Boer guns.

"That means that the Boer gunners walked away from their guns for a time when the ground began to rock; but the guns were not hurt, and their tongues were loosed again soon enough." [9]

Blake-Knox was in a good position to see everything. He writes: "From a high kopje which we now occupied, I had a good view of the Boer front, and could from my position actually see, aided by my glasses, the enemy working a 15-pounder Creusot gun.

"It was in the open, near the far end of the road which ran up the valley [today's 'Back Route' between Colenso and Ezakheni African township at Pieters] being placed behind a stone wall, which had two openings for the muzzle.

"Before firing, the gunners ran it forward by hand, and after each discharge they ran it back in a similar manner.

"The gun was worked by only three men, and I could see neither gun team nor wagon in the vicinity. Its flash was very small, and it evidently fired smokeless powder, as no vapour was perceptible but it threw up an appreciable quantity of dust in its recoil.

"The position of this gun was reported to our artillery, who promptly dropped a few shells near it, and we had the satisfaction of seeing it hurried back over the hill crest, where it disappeared." [10]

Warren advanced Wynne's brigade and forced the passage of the Onderbroek spruit. He then attacked the Boer positions on the three-spurred hill (afterwards known as Wynne's Hill) which flanked, on the northern side, the junction of the spruit with the Tugela.

Says Watkins: "Wynne's Hill not merely stood in the way of Warren's advance, but was a necessary point of vantage which must be held before Hart's Hill could safely be attacked.

"At an early stage in the action Wynne was shot in the leg, and Warren made a special request for Colonel Kitchener [brother of Lord Kitchener, who was, of course, with Roberts] to be temporarily transferred from his battalion to command Wynne's brigade."

Watkins quotes Warren's diary thus: "I went forward with General Wynne, as I had only one brigade in action, and was with him when he was wounded in the leg. I assisted him till he was safely looked after, and then I placed Colonel Crofton as Senior Officer in Command.

"But it is not given to every officer commanding a battalion suddenly to take over a brigade in action, and we were in so ticklish a position that I felt that to carry the matter through successfully I must have a Brigadier specially qualified to act promptly in all things.

"Of course I was bound to have ready in my mind the one man I considered most qualfied – Colonel Kitchener, West Yorks. I had seen him at work on several occasions, the last time being at Vaalkrantz, and noted him for any vacancy." [11]

Kitchener was duly transferred that night – these days, what Warren wanted, Warren got – and took over command of the brigade before dawn on the 23rd.

But most of the Boer riflemen were still invisible – as invisible as they had been from the kopjes overlooking Colenso way back in December.

Wynne, says *The Times History*, pointed this out, before he was wounded. But he was told to go ahead anyway.

Says The *Times*: "Under a terrific volume of fire the three battalions . . . toiled up the lower slopes, the Boers falling back from the crest before them. But as usual, the real Boer defence lay behind, a line of sangars running along the northern ridge of the western and central portions of the plateau.

"Topping the crest, the British met a staggering fire, which promptly drove them to take cover below it . . .

"There was hardly a spot on the slope that was not exposed to long-range fire from the cloud of keen-eyed marksmen scattered over the surrounding heights and in the bed of the Onderbroek and Langvewacht spruits . . .

"A more insecure and useless position it would be difficult to imagine . . . as the hours wore on without any signs of improvement, the men began to get shaken.

"Towards dusk, the Ermelo men . . . increased their fire and began cautiously pushing forward. The advance companies of the Royal Lancasters were unable to hold . . . and suddenly ran back to the crest-line. This started a general wavering of the men under the crest. Up jumped a number of men and poured down the hillside in confusion. For a moment it seemed as if the whole force was going to be driven off the hill . . . but the troops were speedily rallied . . .

"The morning of the 23rd certainly furnished no indications of a Boer withdrawal. The (British) firing . . . reopened with full vigour at the first glimmer of dawn. The actual occasion of it was an attempt to rescue the company of the 60th in a sheep kraal in front of the Boer sangars.

"Lieutenant Wake had crawled out and made his way through the Boers . . . to the crest where he found Crofton and informed him of what had taken place. Crofton had sent Wake back with orders for the company to hold on until dawn when he would send a force . . . of two companies of East Surreys . . .

"These now moved forward across the plateau till they were nearly level with the kraal and lay down in open order while riflemen slipped out as quietly as they could . . . several coming out made a noise. A burst of firing came from the sangars and was taken up all along the line . . .

"The tremendous burst of fire proved too much for the overstrained nerves of some of the men, and there was a sudden panic . . . but the men were promptly rallied. But the company hung on doggedly . . ." [12]

In spite of the heavy casualties on Wynne's Hill, the position was held and a further stage had been carried out.

Warren described the advance under cover of the railway via Wynne's Hill to Hart's Hill as "the most risky proceeding of the whole Natal Campaign, except perhaps the Spioenkop expedition", and added: "I greatly admired General Buller for proposing it, and sticking to it resolutely. There was no wavering or vacillation in the proceedings, and it was a delight to find him so firmly resolved." [13]

But it had been a terrible battle. Churchill says: " . . . The Boers attacked heavily at nightfall with rifle fire all along the line [of Wynne's Hill] and in their eagerness to dislodge the troops, came to close quarters on several occasions at various points. At least two bayonet charges are recorded.

"Sixteen men of Stuart-Wortley's Composite Battalion of Reservists of the Rifle Brigade and King's Royal Rifles showed blood on their bayonets in the morning." [14]

Warren considered the position could become untenable on the morrow, unless it were fully entrenched, so he issued an order to Crofton that proper trenches must be made before daybreak, even though the men might have to work all night long.

He wrote: "This making of schantzes was our great difficulty. Men, tired and exhausted with their fighting since 2pm, were called upon to work all night – for their lives."

It is the second time Warren uses that expression – " for their lives". It indicates his fine grasp of the situation and perception of what was to come.

"It was difficult for them to realise at night what might be required in the morning. General Buller repeatedly said after an action 'the men did it'. So they did, if the term 'men' is allowed to include also the officers, urging on tired men *to work for their lives.* That is the point. The men could see it in the morning, when they were safely covered by secure schanzes. But at night it was not given to all officers or men to realise the necessity. However, those who did not take care of themselves got wiped out. And we gradually came to read our own special meaning in the phrase 'the survivial of the fittest'." [15]

But daylight showed victory rested with the British. Yet, there remained the main obstacle, Hart's Hill . . .

Churchill says he found Sir Redvers Buller and his staff in a somewhat exposed position, but from whence an excellent view could be obtained from a hill near Colenso.

The General, he said, displayed his customary composure and asked him how his brother's wound was (Churchill's brother was wounded in the leg on the day Churchill arrived).

He then told Churchill he had ordered General Hart's brigade, supported by two battalions from Lyttleton's division to assault Hart's Hill.

"I have told Hart to follow the railway. I think he can get around to their left flank under cover of the river bank," he told Churchill, "But we must be prepared for a counter attack on our left as soon as they see what I'm up to." [16]

Hart's brigade was immediately attached to Warren's division, but it had received Buller's instruction before it came under Warren's orders.

Warren wasn't happy. He felt the position had not been sufficiently prepared, but there was little he could do about it but wait.

It is left to Churchill to describe an operation he called "so tragic and full of mournful interest".

Its commander – General Hart – he called: "One of the bravest officers in the army."

This is what happened . . .

"At half past 12 on the 23rd General Hart ordered his brigade to advance. The battalions which were sheltering among stone walls and other hastily constructed cover on the reverse slope of the kopje immediately in front of that on which we stood, rose up one by one and formed in rank.

"They moved off in single file along the railroad, the Inniskilling Fusiliers leading, the Connaught Rangers, Dublin Fusiliers and Imperial Light Infantry following in succession.

"At the same time the Durham Light Infantry and the 2nd Rifle Brigade began to march to take the place of the assaulting brigade . . .

"Wishing to have a nearer view of the attack, I descended the wooded hill, cantered along the railway . . . and dismounting, climbed the rocky sides of the advanced kopje. On the top, in a little half-circle of stones, I found General Lyttleton . . . and together we watched . . .

"Nearly a mile of the railway line was visible, and along it the stream of Infantry flowed steadily. The telescope showed the soldiers walking quite slowly, with their rifles at the slope. Thus far at least they were not under fire . . .

"A mile away the river and the railway turned sharply to the right; the river plunged into a steep gorge, and the railway was lost in a cutting.

"There was certainly plenty of cover, but just before the cutting was reached the iron bridge across the Onderbrook Spruit [it was the Langvewacht spruit, actually] had to be crossed, and this was evidently commanded by the enemy's riflemen. Beyond the railway and the moving trickle of men the brown dark face of Hart's (Inniskilling, now) Hill, crowned with sangars and entrenchments rose up, gloomy and, as yet, silent . . .

"Before us the infantry were moving steadily nearer to the hill and the open ground by the railway bridge, and we listened amid the comparatively peaceful din for the impending fire storm.

"The head of the column reached the exposed ground, and the soldiers began to walk across it. Then at once above the average fusilade and cannonade rose the extraordinary rattling roll of Mauser musketry in great volume . . .

"I turned my telescope on the Dutch defences. They were no longer deserted. All along the rim of the trenches, clear cut and jet black against the sky stood a crowded line of slouch-hatted men, visible as far as their shoulders, and wielding what looked like thin sticks.

"Far below by the red iron work of the railway bridge – 2,000 yards at least from the trenches – the surface of the ground was blurred and dusty.

"Across the bridge the infantry were still moving but no longer slowly – they were running for their lives.

"Man after man emerged from the sheltered railroad, which ran like a

The railway bridge across the Langverwacht spruit, as it is today. It was then the mainline bridge to Ladysmith. And across it, British troops ran the gauntlet to reach Hart's Hollow. The left-hand side of the bridge was piled high with sandbags in an effort to minimise the Boer fire from Inniskilling (Hart's) Hill, a few hundred metres away. It was this area that Churchill called the valley "of whispering death" an allusion to the Mauser bullets that rained down. (Author's picture.)

covered way across the enemy's front, into the open and the driving hail of bullets, ran the gauntlet, and dropped down the embankment on the further side of the bridge into safety again.

"The range was great, but a good many soldiers were hit and lay scattered about the ironwork of the bridge.

"Pom-pom-pom, Pom-pom-pom, and so on, twenty times went the Boer automatic gun and the flights of little shells spotted the bridge with puffs of white smoke.

"But the advancing infantry never hesitated for a moment and continued . . . across.

"The enemy's shells . . . and a whistle of stray bullets from the left, advised us to change our position, and we moved a little further down the slope towards the river. Here the bridge was no longer visible . . .

"The artillery had seen the slouch hats too and forgetting their usual apathy in the joy of a live target, concentrated a most hellish and terrible fire on the trenches . . .

"At four o'clock General Hart ordered the attack, and the troops forthwith began to climb the slopes. The broken ground delayed their progress, and it was nearly sunset by the time they had reached the furthest position which could be gained under cover.

"The Boer entrenchments were about 400 yards away. The arete by which the Inniskillings had advanced was bare, and swept by a dreadful frontal fire from the works on the summit and a still more flanking fire from the other hills.

"It was so narrow that, though only four companies were arranged in the firing line, there was scarcely room for two to deploy.

"There was not however the slightest hesitation, and as we watched . . . we could see the leading companies rise up together and run swiftly forward on the enemy's works . . .

"But if the attack was superb, the defence was magnificent; nor could the devoted heroism of the Irish surpass the stout endurance of the Dutch . . .

"The whole summit of the hill was alive with shell from our artillery. Shrapnel flashed into being above the crests . . . again and again whole sections of the entrenchments vanished in an awful uprush of black earth and smoke, smothering the fierce blaze of the lyddite shells from the howitzers and heavy artillery.

"The cannonade grew to a tremendous thundering hum. No less than 60 guns were firing continuously on the Boer trenches. But the musketry was never subdued for an instant. Amid the smoke and the dust the slouch hats could still be seen . . .

"The terrible power of the Mauser rifle was displayed. As the charging companies met the storm of bullets they were swept away. Officers and men fell by the scores on the narrow ridge.

"Though assailed in front and flank by the hideous whispering Death, the survivors hurried obstinately onward, until their own artillery were forced to cease firing, and it seemed that, in spite of bullets, flesh and blood would prevail. But at the last supreme moment the weakness of the attack was shown. The Inniskillings had almost reached their goal. They were too few to effect their purpose; and when the Boers saw the attack had withered they shot all the straighter and several of the boldest leapt out from their trenches and, running forward to meet the soldiers, discharged their magazines at closest range.

"It was a frantic scene of blood and fury.

"Thus confronted, the Irish perished rather than retire . . .

"Yet the Irish soldiers would not leave the hill, and . . . they lay down on the ground they had won, and began to build walls and shelters, from behind which they opened a revengeful fire on the exulting Boers.

"In the two attacks both colonels, three majors, twenty officers and six hundred men had fallen out of an engaged force of scarcely 1,200.

"Then darkness pulled down the curtain, and the tragedy came to an end for the day . . ." [17]

The Times History is graphic, too, in its descriptions of the Hart's Hollow action: "Hart decided to attack . . . Off went the Irish battalions, the impetuous Hart repeatedly making his bugler sound the double and the charge to hurry them along.

"After pushing on for half a mile in the teeth of a heavy converging fire, they reached the railway . . . meanwhile the leading battalions were up and over the railway line, breaking down the barbed wire fence, scrambling down and up the cutting, through another fence, and then up the side of the hill.

"Immediately from every quarter, from Wynne Hill . . . the busy Langvewacht valley, from the line of sangars on the crest of the hill . . . and from Railway Hill, the Boers poured in a devastating fire . . .

"The Inniskillings . . . were the first at the foot of (Hart's) hill and went up the steep face with a rush that nothing could check. At their approach the Boers melted away from the forward crest.

"Exulting the men flung themselves over the low parapet into the trench – only to find before them 300 yards of loose boulders, interspersed with scanty thorn trees, sloping up towards the main Boer position in front of them . . .

"The attack simply withered away before the appalling magazine fire opened upon it . . . the line ran back and threw itself down behind a parapet.

" . . . (but) In the waning evening light the Irish regiments leapt over the parapet and rushed desperately forward . . .

"It was the supreme moment which the Boers knew was coming, and for which they had been husbanding themselves. From every nook and cranny along the flanks of the hill, and from the unbroken trench in front rifles crashed and roared . . .

"Halfway across .. it became beyond the power of human endurance. Those who could, turned and ran . . . the Boers leaping to their feet and emptying their magazines after them.

"Those who had got furthest forward threw themselves on the ground and waited till merciful night closed over them . . ." [18]

But it was not over yet. The troops stayed exactly where they were that night. Churchill says: "As soon as it was daylight I rode out with Captain Brooke to learn what had happened in the night . . . suddenly a shrapnel shell burst in the air above our heads with a sharp, startling bang.

"The hollow and slope of the hill were crowded with infantry battalions lying down in quarter columns. The bullets and splinters of the shell smote the ground on all sides. We were both mounted and in the centre of the cone of dispersion. I was immediately conscious that nothing had happened to me . . . I turned to Brooke . . . about to elaborate my theory that shrapnel is comparatively harmless, when I saw . . . no less than eight men . . . were killed or wounded by this explosion . . ." [19]

While these heroic troops lay within speaking distance of the Boers, Buller again was in trouble.

He had come to a dead stop. What was he now to do? He was certain the Boers meant to make a stand – perhaps a last-ditch stand.

Should Hart attack again? He sent Warren to tell Hart to do so, but by the time the plans had been made, it was already 4pm and Hart suggested the attack be postponed until the morning.

Sunday, 25th.

Buller agreed – and then decided to withdraw all his troops, wagons and guns from Wynne's Hill – the Boer bank of Tugela. Buller was to attempt another crossing, this time further down the river.

The Times says: "All this while a number of the wounded from the unsuccessful attacks across the Wynne Hill plateau and across the sloping top of Inniskilling hill had been lying out between the opposing lines, suffering unspeakable agonies from their wounds, from heat and thirst, and from the stench of the dead with whom they lay intermingled." [20]

And on that Sunday, Buller sent an officer with a request for an armistice. The Boers – Botha and Meyer – agreed not to fire upon stretcher-parties.

All remained quiet on Sunday, bloody Sunday.

SOURCES

1. *London to Ladysmith*, by Winston Churchill.
2. *Life of General Sir Charles Warren*, by Watkin Williams.
3. *Commission on the War in South Africa*.
4. *Life of General Sir Charles Warren*, by Watkin Williams.
5. *Buller's Campaign, with the Natal Field Force*, by E. Blake-Knox.
6. Ibid.
7. Ibid.
8. *Life of General Sir Charles Warren*, by Watkin Williams.
9. *The Relief of Ladysmith*, by J.B. Atkins.
10. *Buller's Campaign, eith the Natal Field Force*, by E. Blake-Knox.
11. *The Life of Sir Charles Warren*, by Watkin Williams.
12. *The Times History*, pp. 517-522.
13. *Life of General Sir Charles Warren*, by Watkin Williams.
14. *London to Ladysmith*, by Winston Churchill.
15. *Life of General Sir Charles Warren*, by Watkin Williams.
16. *London to Ladysmith*, by Winston Churchill.
17. Ibid
18. *The Times History*, pp. 525, 526.
19. *London to Ladysmith*, by Winston Churchill.
20. *The Times History*, p. 532.

CHAPTER TWENTY SEVEN

Victory on Majuba Day

Battle of Pieters – Part 4

Much has been written in other histories about the genial meeting, on that Sunday armistice day morning. How Boer and Brit exchanged tobacco, spoke about their families and the war.

Expressions of surprise and wonder came from the Boers, as the British sources have it, as to the life of the professional soldier, ready and willing to take the Queen's Shilling – and die for it.

In India. In Egypt. In the Soudan. And now on a rocky hillside in the searing heat of Natal.

Indeed it must have been a source of wonderment to some of the burghers. Not ignorance, because the burghers knew pretty well how to deal with professional soldiers. But more of a sense of wonder at the stupidity of it all.

Particularily, as Breytenbach says, when they emerged from their trenches on to the top of Hart's Hill and saw the slopes "sown" (*besaai*) with the bodies of the dead and wounded.

Many of the bodies had begun to reach a putrid stage.

Breytenbach says that neither Botha nor Meyer wanted an armistice, but Generals Fourie and Oosthuisen, off their own bat, agreed to it.

The conditions were that unwounded, but trapped, soldiers would be made prisoners of war, while the wounded could be moved to hospital, and the dead, buried. [1]

The British, however, came off the best. Of that there is no question. While the soldiers and officers mingled with the burghers, they were able to observe the position of the trenches.

Warren says: "There was a good deal to be done this morning. The truce did not preclude movements of troops, and all our wheeled traffic of the 5th Division and Hart's Brigade had to be moved across the Tugela to the south side, ready to cross over to the north side again (when the time arrived) by a new pont in another part of the river.

"Six weeks ago the proceedings in such a case were only understood by a very few men in the force. Now we were all well trained in such matters, and working a well-regulated piece of machinery. The drivers, oxen and mules all understood their work, and everything went like clockwork . . .

"By 10am our wounded were being attended to and the British and Boers were amiably confabulating between the two positions.

"About that hour I left my bivouac and went over to see General Buller at the pont. He told me that we should have to recross the Tugela, that I must get to Hart's Hill before 6pm and that I was to take command of all the troops north of the Tugela and east of Langvewacht spruit, as they came over the new pont . . .

"They had been collecting the dead all day, and when I arrived, at Hart's Hill, I saw 59 corpses closed up in blankets ready for interment . . ." [2]

For the Boers the massive withdrawal, yet again, of the the British troops back across the Tugela was a puzzle. Were they withdrawing, finally, as they had done all along the Tugela line?

At Vaalkrantz questions had been asked as the massive British army with all its wagons trundled across the veld to Springfield: Was this the end? Were the British finally pulling out and abandoning Natal?

Where were they going? It was felt that from Vaalkrantz the British would again try Spearman's, and with the Boer forces consolidated at Brakfontein, make a lightning strike through Acton Homes before they could move.

Or, were they going back to Frere? To be shipped urgently to Cape Town and back up the railway line to join Roberts?

And what about Ladysmith? There were some Boer officers who felt that Buller didn't have the guts for any more fighting – and was going to abandon Ladysmith to the Burghers.[3]

None of these things happened.

Instead J.B. Atkins was able to record: "All day I sat on a high rocky place above a cascade of the Tugela, and looked down on to the foot of Railway Hill, which begins to rise immediately across the river.

"In the river above the cascade was a platform of black and dripping rocks, half exposed, and the cascade seemed like the receding of the tide from a rocky coast. Above the rocks was a slight footbridge built by the Boers, and our men passed to and fro on it all day . . . I could see the bodies . . . some lay under the soldier's strip of yellow waterproof sheet, just as they had been left by the comrades who would risk more than a Boer flanking fire to linger behind to perform a cherished act of sentiment.

"At least once I plainly saw a man move up there; he was trying to crawl down the hill . . .

"The officers had bloodshot eyes and voices that trailed with weariness. I understood we have knocked our heads against a hard wall; the officers did not disguise their belief in its hardness; with the same trailing voices they told me how some of the wounded had lain thirty-six hours on the hill." [4]

The quiet of that Sunday lasted until 9pm. Then the Boers opened fire, says Churchill, to see if the British infantry was still in position on the Colenso, Wynne's and Hart's hill line.

It was returned.

They knew the British had not abandoned Colenso.

But they did not know that, as the dawn of the 26th broke, 76 guns were in position facing them – 70 downstream of the falls, six on one spur of Monte Christo. The breakdown is given in *The Times History* as 4 naval 4.7s, including two platforms brought from Chieveley; 8 naval 12-pounders, 4.5-inch guns RGA; 61st howitzers, 4th MB, "A" RHA, and 7th, 28th, 63rd, 64th and 78th RFA.

On the 26th, too, Buller, Warren and some staff officers rode the length of the right bank, then Buller called a conference.

Says Warren: "On arrival at our meeting place for the conference of officers . . . General Buller asked me what form of attack I would propose. From the position we were in, to the north of Monte Christo, we could see the whole range of hills that we were going to attack. I had my views in concrete form and at once delivered them to General Buller and those present.

"Three hills (Pieters, Railway and Hart's) were to be attacked in quick succession, commencing at Pieters, Pieters to be taken and the enemy's fire on it subdued before the assault on Railway Hill was consummated, and Railway Hill to be taken before the assault on Hart's Hill was consummated.

"I gave my reasons: the rifle fire from Pieters on Railway and Hart's Hills was so tremendous that Pieters must be crowned first.

"What I said immediately appealed to General Buller and he approved straight off. The method of attack by the four brigades under my command was then left to me to arrange, and the subject to be considered was the fire of the guns and the route to be taken by General Barton in approaching Pieters Hill." [5]

The *British Official History* describes in some detail how at this conference Warren twice disagreed with the proposals for the new site of the pontoon, and could only be persuaded of his mistake by making a personal reconnaissance.

Warren commented thus: "The *Official History* has little down for this day except an excursus on various alleged objections, imputed to me, as to the proposed site of the pontoon bridge which the engineers were putting up.

"The manner in which I am dealt with on these occasions by the historians is very amusing to me.

"Like Pantaloon in the pantomime . . . I am brought in for some silly speech or grotesque performance whenever there is nothing else to put on the boards.

"The talkers who gave the information to these historians could not make out my position in this *galere.*

"General Buller had said in his despatch of the 30th January that he would never again give me an independent command, and yet here he was always putting me to the front whenever he was in a tight place. Thus the only thing the historians could do was to make me the fool of the play.

"In this particular case they have got the matter absolutely wrong. I entirely agreed as to the line of road and position of the pontoon bridge leading over to Hart's Hill. In fact I had given so much help in the matter from my Division that General Buller had said to me:'You seem very fond of doing my work; this work should be done by Corps troops.'

"We had an amusing encounter over it . . ." [6]

It would be useful here to give the dispositions of the troops: Coke's 10th Brigade held Colenso and the kopjes west and north of Fort Wylie; Hildyard's Brigade held the low kopjes on the extreme left of the line; Hart's Irish Brigade and Norcott's Brigade held the slopes of Hart's Hill and the river gorge beside the hill; Barton's Fusilier Brigade and Kitchener's Lancashire Brigade, with the two remaining battalions of Norcott's Brigade, had crossed the river to the Hlangwane plateau; the 1st Border Regiment joined the main body from Chieveley; Dundonald's irregular cavalry brigade took up position on the nek between Monte Christo and Cingolo.

At 6am on Tuesday, February 27th, Warren issued his orders to his troops, which concluded with the quotation of a telegram just received by Buller from the Secretary ot State for War: "The whole country is watching with admiration your steady advance in the face of tremendous difficulties, the magnitude of which are fully understood here. The conduct of your troops is beyond all praise."

At the same time Buller received, and communicated to the troops this message from Queen Victoria: "I have heard with the deepest concern of the heavy losses sustained by my brave Irish soldiers. I desire to express my sympathy and my admiration of the splendid fighting qualities which they have exhibited throughout these trying operations."

Buller replied: "Sir Redvers Buller has, on the part of the Irish Brigade, to thank the Queen for her gracious telegram of sympathy and encouragement."

A pessimistic Churchill, however, had this to say: "All was now ready for the final attack on the left of the Pieters position, and in spite of the high quality of the infantry it was generally recognised throughout the army that the fate of Ladysmith must depend on the success of the . . . day's operations. The spirit of the army was still undaunted, but they had suffered much from losses, exposure and disappointment.

"Since January 11, a period of more than six weeks, the troops had been continually fighting and bivouacking. The peaceful intervals of a few days had merely been in order to replenish stores and ammunition. During this time the only reinforcements to reach the army had been a few drafts, a cavalry regiment, a horse battery, and some heavy guns.

"Exclusive of the 1,100 casualties suffered at Colenso in December the force, rarely more than 20,000 men, had had over 3,500 killed and wounded, had never had single gleam of success, and had hardly seen the enemy who hit them so hard.

"Colenso, Spioenkop, Vaalkranz, and the third day at Pieters were not inspiring memories, and though everyone was cheered by the good news of the entanglement of Cronje's army on the western side, yet it was felt that the attempt to be made . . . would be the last effort the Natal Field Army would be asked, or allowed to make. And oppressed by these reflections we went anxiously to rest on the eve of Majuba Day." [7]

Blake-Knox says: "The dawn of February 27, the anniversary of Majuba, broke cloudy. Almost before the dark outlines of the Pieter's range of hills were evident our artillery opened the day's work, battery after battery sending their messengers of death – lyddite and shrapnel – to herald the day, a day never to be forgotten in the annals of this war." [8]

Atkins is more descriptive: "The Tugela seemed to be ten thousand times in flood; never before had it such a mighty rushing voice. The Rifle Composite Battalion (reservists of the Rifle Brigade and the 60th Rifles, with 10 years' service at their backs almost to a man) and the Border Regiment were firing across the deep, narrow valley at the bottom of which the river runs.

"All the Maxims the battalions had between them were firing too till the water round the barrels boiled and boiled again; the Colts added their deep, deliberate rapping; and the river, drawing it all down, gave an impressive resonance to the continuous sweeping roar . . ." [9]

But the roar of the water and the guns was soon drowned by the The News – a "Clear the Line" telegram from Roberts: Cronje had surrendered at Paardeberg! And as each regiment heard it, cheer after cheer echoed through the morning air.

By 10.30am the new pontoon bridge had been put in place between Railway Hill and Pieters.

Says Blake-Knox: "General Barton's party was the first to cross the pontoon where some wag in the Royal Engineers had erected a signpost with a hand painted on it pointing north and *To Ladysmith* inscribed in capitals alongside . . . Barton's brigade, having crossed, turned to the right, and were marched down the river bed." [10]

Atkins says: " . . . The attacking battalions were creeping in one long thin line (their legs moving like those of a monstrous centipede) along the north bank of the river . . ." [11]

Says Blake-Knox: "The advance was very slow as all had to walk in single file, there being no path, and their course was strewn with rocks overhung by steep and rugged cliffs. In many places men had to wade knee-deep in the rapids, the reserve ammunition on mules and the signalling apparatus accompanying them in this fashion.

"Arrived at the foot of Barton's Hill (Pieters), they had a considerable delay to permit the tail of their column to arrive. Rest was not ill-timed as they had now to ascend an almost precipitous cliff of about 500 feet and then to assault and carry the hill tops." [12]

Atkins says: "I never saw infantry strain at the leash as they strained this day. The renascence of confidence and power and spirit and dash was complete. It was Majuba Day; the attack had been planned dramatically. None could say that it was planned vindictively by Sir Redvers Buller, who has a nice appreciation of the ridiculous military importance which the inconsiderable affair of Majuba Hill has acquired from the proximity of a political arrangement.

"But the private soldier has a strong sense of what is elementarily dramatic; and the General who has lives to save as well as to take would be wrong to neglect any one of the mediums through which he can work. On this day, too, the troops had been told that General Cronje had surrendered unconditionally, and one had traced the passage of the news as the squib of cheering and commotion spluttered along the lines." [13]

But on Pieter's it was 12.30 before the upward advance was made. The Scots Fusiliers were on the right, the Irish Fusiliers on the left, with the Dublin Fusiliers in support. The summit of Pieter's Hill consisted of three distinct kopjes. That on the left was taken at the first rush by the Irish Fusiliers with admirable precision; the whole brigade advanced against the next, and here, while crossing the open ground between the kopjes, the Irish lost two officers and 14 men killed, and six officers and 70 men wounded out of a total of three companies.

"Notwithstanding this heavy loss, the assaulting force drove the enemy from their post. The third or northern knoll on Pieter's Hill was for some reason not simultaneously attacked. During the delay the enemy had been reinforced at that place and soon opened a deadly fire causing more casualties . . .

"A dashing bayonet charge carried the position." [14]

But Barton had been wounded in the action, and the highest point of the Pieter's position was still in the hands of the Boers. Barton decided the hill had to be taken – and after a concerted rush by three companies of the Dublins and a company of Scots, it was. Every officer but one, however, had been hit.

And while the fighting was still going on in an apparently futile attempt to take this last obstacle, Kitchener was given the "go!"

Says Atkins: "The East Surreys and Rifle Brigade in front and South Lancashires on the east had all crept up . . . the South Lancashires lay on the near slope of the railway bank; if you had not seen them go there you would have said that they were heaps of ballast dumped at intervals.

"If a man put his head above the line the track flew up in dust. A mere handful of men squirmed over the line and chose their rocks on the other side.

"It was well, and they were a few yards further, but that did not make the taking of Railway Hill much the nearer. Another handful and another crept across. But still was it not critical? How were they to cross that ghastly open hillside? [from the river slopes to the crest of the hill.]

"I was still thinking it was critical, and it was nearly five o'clock.

"And then came the most extraordinary revolution, sudden, astounding, brilliant, almost incomprehensible. Across the railway the South Lancashires suddenly rose up out of the ground, stones rose up too, and turned out to be infantrymen – more must have passed over than I had counted – and all

The battle of Pieters – the bombardment. Inniskilling (Hart's) Hill is seen, left, with shells exploding over it. Another shell explodres in the valley, and still others towards the rise of Railway Hill. Lines of infantry are pictured climbing the steep sides of the hill in front. (Picture: Cape Archives J676.)

began to run, not in stiff lines, but with the graceful spreading of a bird's wings straight up the hill.

"Splendid, and always new is the rush of British infantry, but had not the Inniskillings done this before? Would this gain the hill now, that had not been gained before?

"I waited stricken with admiration and suspense. And then another revolution happened. Further on the right of Railway Hill came a second rush of infantry out of the invisibility, or at least, from the unobserved and wholly unexpected, and it converged on the first careering body. On a small stony kopje on the lower slopes of Railway Hill the sweeping wave broke.

"Two trenches were there – Boer trenches. And now out of the trenches and down the back of the kopje ran black figures – speeding before the infantry outstripped them.

"I have never seen a Boer run like this in the open before. Out of one trench an arm – just an arm – appeared waving a shirt or a towel – a grotesque of the arm that grasped Excalibur. Some soldiers stooped over the trenches – prisoners were made – and then on after the rest of the wave which had split on the kopje and mended itself again.

"The whole party joined the men who had charged on their left. The assault on Railway Hill was doubled.

"Up and up and up the South Lancashires went, seeming to drive and haul themselves up the side of the hill with arms and heads and legs. Now one man was on the top-most trench and waving his helmet on his bayonet, and down the sharp, stony, foot-destroying descent on the other side went a headlong, heedless flight of Boers.

"Shrapnel whipped and stung them home. On foot they went; there was no time to snatch their horses, or perhaps, as some say, their horses were, most of them dead, or, again, had been taken away from them." [15]

The hill was theirs.

And Hart's Hill?

A portion of it had already been stormed, not from the bottom as was the plan, but by a party of Royal Lancasters who, rushing towards Railway Hill, had suddenly turned left and headed at a rush to Hart's Hill, charging straight up to the summit, and unbelievably securing a foothold at the top.

It was a mistake, but no-one was arguing.

As the Lancs charged, so Hart and Norcott advanced their men. The Durhams still held the trenches captured by the Inniskillings just above Hart's Hollow, had the advantage of a useful start.

Soon the slopes of Hart's Hill were alive with British soldiers, assaulting it from three sides.

The Boers ran. But, says Blake-Knox, a huge fellow in a dark jersey was seen to go out boldly and try to rally them. Returning to the trench, he sprang on the top of a sangar and emptied his Mauser into the advancing army.

He was then hit by a 50-pound lyddite shell, which burst right upon him. And thus vanished the last defender of Hart's Hill.

"The infantry now occupied the crest line, and, having put up their sights, poured a heavy fire into the fleeing Boers . . . Many of the enemy held up their hands as a token of surrender, and were made prisoners.

"About 5.30pm Dundonald got orders to escort three batteries of artillery across the Tugela with all the men that he could collect, and thus assist Sir Charles Warren in pounding the enemy; but his force was stopped at the pontoon by Sir Redvers Buller in person, who considered it too late for anything further to be done that night in the rocky and broken country into which the enemy were retiring." [16]

Churchill says that when orders for Dundonald's cavalry came to cross the river, they mounted in high expectation knowing that behind the captured hill of Pieters lay an open plain stretching almost to the foot of Bulwana.

But would there be a counter-attack?' Buller thought so when he stopped the men crossing.

Blake-Knox was on Pieter's when Boer firing commenced.

"We all took cover. I lay down among some rocks alongside the infantry and suddenly felt what I thought was the flick of a whip on the back of my thigh. It was something a little more serious."

Blake-Knox had been shot.

"As I lay still, with my wound smarting and my limbs stiff . . . something white moved in a bush close by . . . At first it seemed to be a handkerchief, but as it moved again I thought it was a chicken, for I had seen the men carrying some . . . It moved again and I saw it was a dog. I whistled; it came up wagging its tail and we made friends. I spoke to it in English, but it did not heed me; I then tried Dutch, and it understood.

"It was a Boer dog – a white spaniel spotted with dark patches. It wore a collar bearing its owner's name and the Transvaal arms. It was very tired, and evidently very hungry. It had lost its master – probably he was dead; anyhow it nestled to me, and licked first my face and then the bandage on my damaged limb. I made up my mind to foster it. That dog has been with me ever since. It followed me on foot for close on 500 miles, through all four Colonies of South Africa, and it is now under my parental roof – at home." [17]

But Blake-Knox's ordeal was not yet over. As he moved, injured, he got in the way of some Dublin Fusiliers who were rushing by.

"They were charging along with fixed bayonets on their way to reinforce the Scots Fusiliers. What they took me for, I don't know, but one huge, hulking fellow evidently suspected me to be a crouching Boer, and drew back for the lung.

"I shouted at him, and, with the observation 'Right! Be aisy now!', he passed on and disappeared.

"Seeing that this was no place for me, I got up and made my way slowly and stiffly down the hill, leading my newly-annexed dog on the end of a piece of bandage.

"At the pontoon, I got a lift back to Sir Charles Warren's camp near Monte Christo. Here there were close on 100 Boer prisoners. A wretched, dejected lot they looked – some, old men with patriarchal beards, aquiline noses and cadaverous, pinched cheeks. Others, still boys, with smooth round, yellow shining faces and oval eyes, all clothed in ragged, patched civilian clothes, slouch hats with . . . coloured bands round them, different colours denoting different commandos . . .

"One haggard, middle-aged burgher who was near to me was waiting his turn to get a wound in his thigh dressed. A long, ragged splinter of shell, partly covered with khaki-coloured paint, protruded from his wound through his breeches.

"His face, hands and clothes were stained a canary yellow from a lyddite shell which had burst near him. Small, dry hard droplets of the half-burnt explosive hung from the threads of his torn garments and from his singed hair.

"I brought him a tin of Bovril . . . he told me that he alone was left alive from the occupants of one trench on the left of Barton's (Pieters) hill above the ravine . . .

"Questioned by me on the effects of Lyddite, he said it was useless, that unless one burst in an enclosed space, it was hardly so destructive as common shell . . . the fumes, he said, had different effects on different people. Some they made exhilaratingly drunk. For the moment such a man became absolutely reckless; his nerves were so stimulated that he felt equal to almost any deed.

"On others the fumes had a different effect, making them sick . . . the explosion made most people deaf, and gave them besides a headache . . .

"But what they feared most was shrapnel. There was nowhere to hide . . ." [18]

It was now evening. The battle of Pieters was won. After their evening meal, says Blake-Knox, the men, well satisfied with the day's work, sat in groups around the bivouac fires, singing songs like "Soldiers of the Queen" to the accompaniment of heavy Mauser rifle-firing in the Boer lines near Ladysmith. The cause, he says, remained unknown.

Atkins says: " . . . The low evening sun glittered on their front; and their backs were as black as the backs of silvery fishes. On every part of the hill troops climbed up into the sun and a golden, splendid property.

"On all the hills in front of me British troops bristled. A sudden realisation of the victory swept over the field; there was a cessation, almost a silence. Guns no longer crashed; and then from some part of the field there came a little unaided cheers, that asked assistance.

"Assistance came; cheer answered cheer, backwards and forwards across the river, till all cheers became the same cheer, and staff officers forgot that they were not as ordinary officers and threw up their helmets and shook hands with one another." [19]

Says Churchill: "We got neither food nor blankets that night, and slept in our waterproofs on the ground; but we had at last that which was better than feast or couch, for which we had hungered and longed through many weary weeks, which had been thrice forbidden us, and which was all the more splendid since it had been so long delayed – Victory!" [20]

And at 9pm that night, Sir Charles Warren received this message from Sir Redvers Buller: " I congratulate you on the day." [21]

SOURCES:

1. *Geskiedenis van die Tweede Vryheids Oorlog*, Vol. 3.
2. *Life of Sir Charles Warren*, by Watkin Williams.
3. *Geskiedenis van die Tweede Vryheids Oorlog*, Vol. 3.
4. *The Relief of Ladysmith*, by J.B. Atkins.
5. *Life of SIr Charles Warren*, by Watkin Williams.
6. Ibid.
7. *London to Ladysmith*, by Winston Churchill.
8. *Buller's Campaign: with the Natal Field Force*, by E. Blake-Knox.
9. *The Relief of Ladysmith*, by J.B. Atkins.
10. *Buller's Campaign: with the Natal Field Force*, by E.; Blake-Knox.
11. *The Relief of Ladysmith*, by J.B. Atkins.
12. *Buller's Campaign, with the Natal Field Force*, by E.; Blake-Knox.
13. *The Relief of Ladysmith*, by J.B. Atkins.
14. *Buller's Campaign: with the Natal Field Force*, by E.; Blake-Knox.
15. *The Relief of Ladysmith*, by J.B. Atkins.
16. *Buller's Campaign: with the Natal Field Force*, by E.; Blake-Knox.
17. Ibid.
18. Ibid.
19. *The Relief of Ladysmith*, by J.B. Atkins.
20. *London to Ladysmith*, by WInston Churchill.
21. *Life of Sir Charles Warren*, by Watkin Williams.

CHAPTER TWENTY EIGHT

Ladysmith

Thank God we kept our flag flying

Now for the next day. What was Buller to do? Could he avoid another action before getting into Ladysmith? What about the sombre mass of Bulwana, with its Long Tom Creusot on the top?

For once, Buller did not stop. He determined to reconnoitre the hills to the side of Bulwana, and to plan an attack on that position on March 1.

At daybreak Buller's cavalry consisted of two independent brigades, one under Burn-Murdoch and the other, mostly irregulars, including the Composite Mounted Infantry with Natal Carbineers, Natal Police, King's Royal Rifles, Dublin Fusiliers and Imperial Light Horse, under Dundonald.

With them was Hubert Gough.

Soon they set out, but came under fire. At once they spread – Burn-Murdoch in the open country on the right and Dundonald in the hills to the left.

Blake-Knox, ever observant, writes: "Over Ladsymith floated a balloon. Had we known what its occupants saw, the Boer retreat might, by a combined advance of infantry guns and mounted men, have been turned into a complete rout.

"It appears that the garrison of the town were depressed at not hearing our heavy guns in the morning; they thought that the relief force had again retired. When the balloon went up, the aeronaut, Captain Tilney, saw our infantry occupying Pieter's position, observed the cavalry reconnoitring, and then noted the Boers were in retreat along the road east of Bulwana; finally he saw that a gin had been raised over Long Tom of Bulwana, preparatory to moving that gun.

"He then gave Ladysmith the good news that the 'enemy were off at last'.

"Unfortunately, from our position south of Bulwana, we could not see what was taking place on the north side, as the mountain, a very high one intervened." [1]

But from Inniskilling Hill, the plain towards Ladysmith was thick with British and Boer troops.

Writes Blake-Knox: "While the cavalry were engaged with the enemy's rear-guard the infantry were inactive, resting on the most part on the hills which had been captured the day before.

"In the Boer trenches many items of interest met our eyes. Thousands and thousands of rounds of the enemy's ammunition lay everywhere, abandoned in their flight.

"As it was believed that they had buried several of their guns, the troops occupied their time in closely searching the trenches, some of which had been filled with earth by the fugitives in burying their dead before the arrival of our men.

"In one place, the soil being accidentally removed from two Boer graves with crosses and inscriptions while our men were digging fresh ones, many thousand rounds of split-nosed and flat-nosed ammunition were discovered.

"Evidence was also found of the presence of Boer women on the battlefield . . . This is said to be accounted for by the fact that some 400 women proceeded thither to join their husbands on Majuba Day. It has, however, been stated by newspaper correspondents with the Boers that during the fighting on the Tugela not only were several women present as spectators, but some actually took an active part in the fighting.

"Mrs Helena Herbst Wager, of Zeerust, spent five months in the trenches. Her husband went on commando at the commencement of the war, leaving her at home with a baby. The child died in January, and the mother donned her husband's clothing, obtained a rifle and a bandolier, and went off to join him.

"Failing to find him, she joined Commandant Ben Viljoen's forces, and went through Spioenkop, Vaalkrantz and Pieter's Hill. Later she heard that her husband lay wounded in Johannesburg Hospital, and she left the army temporarily to nurse him.

"That her husband recovered from his wound is borne out by the fact that many months afterwards I obtained at Pretoria a portrait of the happy pair (both in male attire) armed with rifles and bandoliers . . .

"There were two dead women in the trench, too. One was only about 19 . . .

"When I arrived at the infantry bivouacs on Pieters Hill about midday on my pony, I found the men still burying the dead. In one long trench alone . . . a non-Commissioned officer pointed out a heap of 98 dead Boers, who were being searched for the identification cards supplied by the Red Cross Society. Dozens of Mauser rifles lay about many of which had been smashed to render them useless . . ." [2]

Again, however, comes the issue of expanding bullets. It will be recalled in Chapter One how it was explained to the Commission that Dum-Dum bullets were to be Britain's main source of ammunition for the war.

But the issue was stopped and the bullets recalled when it was found that inexperienced riflemen had been subjected to blow-backs when the rifle barrels were found to be dirty. Hot summer conditions, too, seemed to affect the bullets.

In 1899, Britain had a stock of 172,000,000 expanding bullets of which some 66,000,000 had been delivered to British bases all over the world.

A lot apparently to Ladysmith.

Blake-Knox writes: "During the afternoon, Dr Krieger, General Lukas Meyer's staff surgeon, came into our lines with several ambulance wagons to take away the enemy's wounded . . .

"As to this visit, Mr Hillegas [in *With the Boer Forces*, by H.C. Hillegas, Methuen] relates: 'General Warren produced a Dum-Dum bullet which had been found on a dead Boer, and showing it to Dr Krieger, asked him why the Boers used a variety of cartridge which was not sanctioned by the rules of civilised warfare.

" 'Dr Krieger took the cartridge in his hand, and, after examining it, returned it to Sir Charles, with the remark that it was a British Lee-Metford Dum-Dum.

" 'General Warren seemed to be greatly nonplussed when several of his officers confirmed the physician's statement and informed him that a large stock of Dum-Dum cartridges had been acquired by the Boers at Dundee.

" 'It is an undeniable fact that the Boers captured thousands of rounds of Dum-Dum bullets which bore the broad arrow of the British Army, and used them in subsequent battles.'

"From this statement Mr Hillegas would wish us to believe that the Boers retained all the bullets captured at Dundee for use, and no others.

"The implication is too absurd in face of the fact that such bullets would not fit the Mauser rifle, though the missiles which inflicted the hideous lacerated wounds found on many of our soldiers were fired from those guns.

"The contention is therefore that the bullets were British and were fired from Boer guns is an impudent attempt to explain away the case.

"The Dum-Dum bullets captured by the Boers after the evacuation of Dundee by the British were left in the camp because their use had been prohibited by the British Commanding Officer.

"They had been brought there by the lately-arrived Indian contingent and since then it had been clearly laid down in Army Orders to all troops disembarking in South Africa that no Dum-Dum bullets were to be landed and none were.

"While it was impossible for the Boers to use Dum-Dum bullets in their Mauser rifles, they used many varieties of expanding Mauser ammunition.

"Mr Hillegas acknowledges: 'It was an easy matter, however, for the Boers to convert their ordinary Mauser ammunition cartridges into Dum-Dum by simply cutting off the point of the bullet, and this was occasionally done.'

"Another Boer writer says: 'The story that the Boers only used those they had captured from the English is quite inadmissable, for the Mauser rifle, which was exclusively used in the Transvaal, was largely provided with them. I will try to describe the patterns chiefly used: 1-Section in the nickel casing, leaving the extremity of the leaden bullet exposed; the lead, getting very hot, emerges partly from the casing, flattens at the slightest resistance, and expands.

" '2-Four longitudinal sections in the nickel casing allow the bullet to flatten at the moment of contact, and to exude the lead through the apertures.' " [3]

Churchill had this to say, about the same scene: "The trench was cut deep in the ground, and, unlike our trenches, there was scarcely any parapet. A few great stones had been laid in front . . . the bottom was knee-deep in cartridge cases, and every few yards there was an enormous heap of Mauser ammunition, thousands of rounds, all fastened neatly, five at a time, in clips.

"A large proportion were covered with bright green slime, which the soldiers declared was poison, but which on analysis may prove to be wax, to preserve the bullet . . .

"A field officer, recognising me, came up and showed me an expansive bullet of a particularly cruel pattern. The tip had been cut off, exposing the soft core, and four slits were scored down the side. Whole boxes of this ammunition had been found." [4]

But what of Dundonald? Churchill says: "When I rejoined the South African Light Horse and Irregular Brigade had begun to advance again.

"Major Gough's Composite Regiment had scouted the distant ridge and found it unoccupied. Now Dundonald moved his whole command thither, and with his staff climbed to the top. But to our disappointment, Ladysmith was not to be seen. Two or three other ridges hung like curtains before us.

"The afternoon had passed, and it was already after 6 o'clock. The Boer artillery was still firing and it seemed rash to attempt to reconnoitre further when the ground was broken and the light fading.

"The order was given to retire and the movement had actually begun when a messenger came back from Gough with the news that the last ridges between us and the the town were unoccupied by the enemy, that he could see Ladysmith and that there was, for the moment a clear run in.

"Dundonald immediately determined to go on himself into town with the two squadrons who were scouting in front, and to send the rest of the brigade back to camp.

"He invited me to accompany him . . ." [5]

But it was Major Hubert Gough who got there first, on his horse wet from its crossing of the Klip River. He met Sir George White in the middle of the dusty main road. "Hello, Hubert," said Sir George, "How are you?"

Blake-Knox says: "Those who took part in this memorable ride will never forget the scene that presented itself. As the neutral camp of Intombi was passed, men who could hardly stand were supporting others almost as weak . . .

"On and on the relief force galloped, passing Indians and Kaffirs who were mad with joy, until at the outpost lines, Lord Dundonald stopped to send a message to Sir Redvers Buller of Ladysmith's relief.

"As the welcome news spread to the town a mighty cheer arose and travelled from all sides to the Klip River, which divides the flat from the town. At the drift over the river General Brocklehurst met Lord Dundonald followed by a great concourse of hurrahing and cheering men; some were even crying and in the twilight looked ghastly pale and thin.

"In the meanwhile the advanced squadrons of Gough's regiment of Natal Carbineers under Major Mackenzie and Imperial Light Horse under Captain Bottomley were filing into the town.

"Women and children were seen weeping with excitement and gladness. As Sir George White turned back with the party to headquarters, he received an ovation from the great gathering which now filled the streets.

"At the post office the General stopped in response to the cheers and endeavoured to address the crowd. Struggling with emotion aroused by the prevailing enthusiasm, he could hardly make himself heard. He concluded his short address to the townspeople with the words: 'I want heartily to thank you for the very great assistance you have given me during this trying time.'

"Three cheers were now given for General White, Lady White, General (Sir Archibald) Hunter, the Staff, and the crew of the *Powerful* causing a temporary interruption, and General White then continued: 'This is indeed a happy moment. I thank God our flag has been upheld.'" [6]

Or as Kenneth Griffith he writes: Thank God we kept the flag flying.

That night, while troopers still guarded the Ladysmith perimeters, others partook of a feast of hoarded food. The morrow would bring wagons of food! But as we saw earlier, it took a lot longer for food to arrive.

The next day Blake-Knox wrote: "Shortly after daylight I visited Intombi Hospital which lay under Bulwana. I had put a few tins of tobacco and some eatables in the saddle-bags of my pony for distribution on arrival.

"The hospital was situated on the banks of the Klip River and after a somewhat tedious passage through a network of dongas and thick, thorny mimosa-bush the white canvas of the tortoise-shaped tents came in view.

"As I was the first arrival of the relieving force in that pest-stricken camp I got a very cordial reception from all sides. Notwithstanding the barren and grassless nature of the ground between the tents, I was struck by the remarkable cleanliness everywhere observable.

"After a conversation with the medical officers, with some of whom I had had previous personal acquaintance, I took a walk around the wards.

"There were about 800 patients; the features and limbs of one and all showed unmistakably what the ravages of disease and starvation will produce.

"Thin, gaunt haggard men – living skeletons – met my eyes everywhere, some in beds, others seated, others crawling rather than walking; listless, claw fingered beings in ragged hospital clothes whose only signs of life seemed centred in their eyes – large, round glistening eyes, set off by pinched, cadaverous, bearded faces. Such was Intombi. The medical staff themselves looked almost as bad; one of them, whom I had known as a stout well-groomed man about town at home, now had a pale, emaciated face, his tattered khaki hanging in folds about a wasted frame; he appeared rather a subject for medical aid than one fit to administer it.

"He pointed out what seemed to me be a small forest of short white stakes, glistening in the morning sun, between the hospital and Bulwana. I asked him what it was. It's the graves of 1,600 men, he said, the victims of enteric, dysentery and wounds . . .

"As I was anxious to get to have a look at the town itself, I mounted my pony and made off. A gallop over some two miles of flat plain, and I forded the Klip River and was in Ladysmith – at last.

"Again the barren nature of the ground impressed me – dry, hard, caked clay, no grass, no herbage, the few trees and bushes covered with red dust, hiding the verdure of their leaves.

"Squalid dusty streets, barricaded houses with broken windows, shops with shutters up; one with a signboard, 'Luncheons and Dinners' at any Hour' seemed rather a mockery in a beseiged town . . .

"Many of the buildings were absolutely empty; some showed signs of shell damage; here a large hole in the masonry, there a corrugated zinc roof, with the sun shining through many small round holes, each the size of a florin, produced by shrapnel.

"The clock tower of the town-hall showed a large gap in its side, just as if some monster had taken a bite out of it – so one did, Long Tom of Bulwana – for the clock was gone.

"Other strange and weird sights met my eye everywhere, even on this my first visit – for example the strange underground shelters in the banks of the Klip River, where the race again became dwellers in caves tunnelled out in rabbit fashion.

"The very inhabitants seem strange; talk to a man and he edges round; he does not like to turn his back on Bulwana; it has been his wont for a good while back to keep an open eye on this unwelcome landmark; he expects to see that white column of smoke rise . . .

"I heard on arrival that General Buller was expected in the afternoon, and that an escort of mounted troops had been sent out to meet him.

"These failed, however, in their object, as he did not come by the expected route, but took Intombi's Hospital on his way before visiting the town.

"The care of his troops, especially the comfort of his sick and wounded, had ever been a characteristic of General Buller in this campaign.

"He entered the lately-besieged town about 12 o'clock accompanied by a small personal escort. Some of his cavalry, who had come by the main road, had distracted the attention of the garrison and civil inhabitants then lining the streets, and the General's arrival was not expected so soon.

"News of it, however, soon spread and General White and his staff went out to receive him. The meeting was most cordial . . .

"One hour after his entry into Ladysmith the war correspondents . . . were able to telegraph home from Ladysmith a full account of the proceedings . . .

"The first message to be sent was to Her (late) Majesty the Queen announcing the relief of the town. Her Majesty sent the following reply to Sir Redvers Buller: "Thank God for the news you have telegraphed to me; congratulate you and all under you with all my heart – V.R.I." [7]

On March 3, General Buller published the following address to the Natal Field Force in Army Orders: "Soldiers of Natal – The relief of Ladysmith unites two forces, both of which have, during the last four months, striven with conspicuous gallantry and splendid determination to maintain the honour of their Queen and country.

"The garrison of Ladysmith have during four months held their position against every attack with complete success, and endured many privations with admirable fortitude.

"The relieving force has had to force its way through an unknown country across an unfordable river and over almost inaccessible heights, in the face of a fully-prepared, well-armed, and tenacious enemy. By the exhibition of the truest courage, the courage which burns steadily as well as flashes brilliantly, it has accomplished its object and added a glorious page to the history of the British Empire.

"Ladysmith has been relieved. Sailors and soldiers, colonials and home-breds, have done this, united by one desire, inspired by one patriotism.

"The GOC congratulates both forces on the martial qualities which they have shown; he thanks them for their determined efforts, and desires to offer his sincere sympathy to the relations and friends of those good soldiers and gallant comrades who have fallen in the fight. – Signed: Redvers Buller, General."

Buller told the Commission: "Early on March 2, I ascended Bulwana Hill. It was an extraordinary good day for seeing. Van Reenen's Pass was perfectly clear with the exception of some wagons at the extreme top, and there was not a soul to be seen in the direction of Sunday's River on the enemy line of retreat to Dundee and Newcastle.

"I moved my camp that evening to Ladysmith, and on the morning of the 3rd, sent the following telegram to Lord Roberts: 'I find that the defeat of the Boers is more complete than I had dared to anticipate. This whole district is completely clear of them and except at the top of Van Reenen's Pass, where several wagons are visible, I can find no trace of them.

" 'Their last train left Modder Spruit about one o'clock yesterday . . . and then they blew up the bridge. They packed their wagons six days ago, and moved them north of Ladysmith, so I had no chance of intercepting them, but they have left vast quantities of ammunition of all sorts, entrenching tools, camp and individual necessaries.

" 'They have got away all their guns but two. My troops want a week's rest, boots and clothing. The Ladysmith garrison wants a fortnight's food and excercise. I do not think there is any chance of the enemy making a stand this side of Laing's Nek." [8]

In a letter to his family from Ladysmith (as reported by C.H. Melville in his book the *Life of General the Right Hon. Sir Redvers Buller*), Buller unveiled his thoughts: "Here I am at last. I thought I was never going to get through here. We have had a hard busy time and I have not been able to write to you for the last three mails.

"I have really have not had time to eat and sleep, much less to write. However it is all over and well over, thank God. We began fighting on the 14th February and literally fought every day, and nearly all every night also, until the 27th, so we had plenty of it.

"I must say the men were grand; they meant to do it, and it was a real pleasure to command them. It has all seemed to me like a dream. Every day some new complications to meet, and every day the same roar of guns and rattle of musketry with, alas, every day the long list of killed and wounded, which is what I cannot bear.

"However, I thought if I got in it would cost me 3,000 men, and I hope I have done it under 2,000, which is something. Congratulatory telegrams of all sorts are pouring in upon me, and I feel that the great British public will like it none the less because there has been a butcher's bill. I fancy too they will like the idea of continuous fighting.

"As for me, I am filled with admiration for the British soldiers; really the manner in which these men have worked, fought and endured during this last fortnight has been something more than human. Broiled in the burning sun by day, drenched in the rain at night, lying not 300 yards off an enemy who shoots you if you show so much as a finger, they could hardly eat or drink by day, and as they were usually attacked at night, they got but little sleep, and through it all they were as cheery and willing as could be. I was interrupted here to attend a ceremony.

"I marched into LS at the head of my whole force; a ragged-looking lot of ruffians they are, poor fellows, but fine men at that.

"As I passed each company of the garrison who were lining the street they gave three cheers for Sir R.B., and in the middle there was a photographer fiend with his cinematograph, so I suppose it will all be at the Alhambra or some other house of entertainment as soon as may be. I dare say it was all right, but should have been glad to have dispensed with it.

"Halfway through there was a sudden alarm; the Boers had come back, and had occupied some hills which commanded the town. I did not believe a word of it, but was glad to get out of the show, so off I galloped. It was nothing, however, the LS scouts had been so accustomed to thinking everybody outside a given line a Boer that they had mistaken my cavalry patrols for them.

"The troops finished their march undisturbed and I escaped part of the boredom, so all was well that ended well. I am living here in the Convent, but the poor nuns have been shelled out, the house is honeycombed with shellholes having been hit during the bombardment by eight or ten 100-lb. shells from Long Tom.

"I wish you could have seen our fight of the 27th. It was intensely interesting and it is only in a country like this that once can stand 2,000 yards off and see a whole battle. There was a moment that I thought it was touch and go, but it was only a moment."

Then began the mop-up. The Boer forces, confronted by the British juggernaut had held a *krijgsraad*, council of war, and decided on a general retreat to the Biggarsberg. But the decison was not unanimous. Louis Botha, Erasmus and Lukas Meyer objected, entreating the others to hold their ground.

They did not. The retreat turned suddenly into a panic. When Botha and Meyer arrived at Modder Spruit, the Boer railhead, they found General Joubert and his 10,000 burghers had moved north.

The Long Tom on Bulwana was gone.

The fight for Ladysmith was over.

Buller, in his wisdom, had not pursued the reatreating army either.

He told the Commision: "All that I know worth knowing about rearguards I learned from the Boers whom I commanded in 1879; and I was, and am still, deeply impressed with the belief that unless there is some paramount object to be gained, an attempt to force a Boer rearguard is merely a waste of men . . ." [9]

Churchill writes: "My personal impression is that Sir Redvers Buller was deeply moved by the heavy losses the troops had suffered, and was reluctant to demand further sacrifices from them at this time.

"Indeed the price of victory had been a high one. In the fortnight's fighting, from February 14 to February 28, two generals, six colonels commanding regiments, a hundred and five other officers, and one thousand five hundred and eleven soldiers had been killed or wounded out of an engaged force of about 18,000 men . . .

"In the whole series of operations for the relief of Ladysmith the losses amounted to three hundred officers and more than five thousand men out of a total engaged force of about twenty three thousand . . .

"Nor had this loss been inflicted in a single day's victorious battle, but was spread over 25 days of general action in a period of ten weeks; and until the last week no decided success had cheered the troops.

"The stress of the campaign, moreover, had fallen with peculiar force on certain regiments: the Lancashire Fusiliers sustained losses of over 35 per cent, and the Dublin Fusiliers of over 60 percent . . .

"The ceaseless marching and fighting had worn out the clothes and boots of the army, and a certain number of the guns of the field artillery were unserviceable through constant firing . . ." [10]

Atkins writes, from the deck of RMS *Norman*, on his way home to England: "Reflection inclines me to attempt a valuation of the Boer as a fighting man. Briefly, our evidence for the estimate is this. Before the war the colonists told us that the Boer was a coward and could not shoot.

" 'The old Boer may have been able to shoot' they said, 'but he practised on big game, and there is not much big game left now. The young Boer cannot shoot.'

"They continued to say that after a couple of months in the field the Boers would fly incontinently home.

"Now there never was a greater misjudgment of a national character, and when the shock of realisation came there was a natural, indeed inevitable, tendency on the part of Imperial officers to rush to the other extreme . . .

"They (the Boers) are brave and their quickness in judging distances – in other words, of finding the range – is a lesson to riflemen or gunners anywhere in the world . . . As for the Boer gunnery, it is the astonishment of the world. People say the gunners are Germans. Well, there may be Germans among the gunners, as there may be French and Scandinavians, and Russians and Irish; but I say that most of these gunners must have had a long experience of this country.

"To have the range absolutely at the second shot in this dancing, deceptive atmosphere is beyond the scope of the simple imported European gunner . . .

"Where the Boers have an advantage probably over every other army in the world is that each man is an intelligent and thinking unit.

"Lastly, I must say something about the accusations against the Boers [and there were many] of improperly using white flags, ambulances and so forth. A judicial observer has said to me: 'Two-fifths of the stories are lies, two-fifths are accounted for by the mistakes and accidents of the battlefield, and one-fifth are true.'

"Wrong uses of the white flag certainly have been committed. It is sufficient to remember that Lord Roberts, whose name promises to become memorable for courtesy, leniency and humanity, has protested on this score . . .

"Some one has told me . . . that among many ignorant Boers there is a belief that there is a kind of local value in a white flag. If a man is wounded, for instance, they think they may legitimately wave a white flag while they carry him off, and then themselves rejoin the the firing line . . .

"The correspodent who tells us that the field was swept with a 'hail of bullets' also complains that ambulance staffs while working on that field were fired upon . . .

"There should be certain things which a regimental officer should never allow himself to do, and one is to halt his men in the neighbourhood of ambulance wagons. . ." [11]

In the *South African Despatches*, Buller wrote: "So was accomplished the relief of Ladysmith. It was the men who did it. Danger and hardship were nothing to them, and their courage, their tenacity, and their endurance, were beyond all praise."

But Buller wasn't . . .

SOURCES

1. *Buller's Campaign, with the Natal Field Force*, by E. Blake-Knox.
2. Ibid.
3. Ibid.
4. *London to Ladysmith*, by Winston Churchill.
5. Ibid.
6. Ibid.
7. Ibid.
8. *Commission on the War in South Africa.*
9. Ibid.
10. *London to Ladysmith*, by Winston Churchill.
11. *The Relief of Ladysmith*, by J.B. Atkins.

CHAPTER TWENTY NINE

Shocks for Warren

Revealed at last: the *Spioenkop Despatches*

There were to be no rewards for the man who master-minded the lifting of the Siege of Ladysmith. Not Buller. Warren. In Buller's despatches on the final operations, written from the Convent in Ladysmith, Sir George White's headquarters, in March 1900 – despatches that occupied six foolscap pages of the Blue Book – it is surprising to find that no mention whatever is made of the important part which Warren took in commanding the majority of the operations which led to the relief.

He is mentioned in an account of the capture of Green Hill on February 18 – the hill was taken as a prelude to Hlangwane: "General Warren throwing the 6th Brigade forward," and at the end of a page of description of the plans for the final attack on Februrary 27 he wrote: "The whole under the command of General Warren."[1]

Moreover, in Buller's detailed recommendations for meritorious service, there is no mention whatever of any member of Warren's staff, although that Staff had for fully half the period from January 16 to February 28 been doing the work of administration of a field force in addition to their divisional duties.

In the details of recommendation, over three pages are taken up with descriptions of the service of 61 undoubtedly excellent officers (including Lyttleton, Clery, Hildyard, Wynne, Miles, Kitchener, Dundonald and Thorneycroft).

At the end of this list appears a paragraph in which, shorn of all descriptive details, the names of 257 officers (most of them captains and subalterns) are mentioned, beginning with the statement: "I also recommend the following Officers for your consideration: Lieut-General Sir C. Warren, G.C.M.G., K.C.B., Major General G. Barton, C.B., Major-General A. Fitz Roy Hart, C.B., Colonel (local Major-General) J. T. Coke . . ." [2]

At the conclusion of his account of the operations for the relief of Ladysmith Warren states: "One of my chief objects in writing these pages has been to vindicate the work and character of the officers of the Vth Division, and incidentally the 4th and 6th Brigades, and to show that although they are not mentioned in the Despatches for meritorious service, yet it was on them that the brunt of the work happened to fall during our six weeks campaign.

"The names of my Staff were: Major T. Capper (A.A.G.), Major N.H. Sargent (D.A.A.G), Captain C.B. Levita (D.A.A.G.), Captain P.O. Sandilands (A.S.C.), Major R. Kely (A.D.C.), Lt. I.V. Paton (A.D.C.), Major E. Williams (A.P.M.), Captain A.A. McHardy (Signalling Officer), and Lt. O. Schwikkard (Natal Scouts)." [3]

Watkin Williams writes: "But it would seem that Roberts sensed the need to give credit where credit was due, for in his covering despatch of March 28, he states: 'I trust that Her Majesty's Government will agree with me in thinking that credit is due to the General Officer in Chief Command, to the subordinate General (Warren) and other Officers, and last but not least, to the brave soldiers who marched and fought almost without cessation from 15th January to 28th February."

Upon this Warren comments: "Thus Lord Roberts acknowledges what General Buller ignores – i.e the position I held in this campaign and the credit due to me as the 'subordinate General', who, General Buller in his Despatches sought to show, oscillating between the 'insubordinate General' and the 'incompetent General'. "

Says Williams: "Among the many congratulatory telegrams which Warren received on the relief of Ladysmith was one from Abe Bailey [the gold mining magnate who at the start of the war had wanted to join Warren's division] saying 'Heartiest congratulations. I knew you would do it.'

" . . . Many years later when Lady White was discussing the Natal Campaign at a dinner table, she remarked to her neighbour, 'Of course, my husband knew all along that it was really Sir Charles Warren who relieved Ladysmith . . ." [4]

But the war was not over yet – although the immediate object of the Natal Field Force was.

From the February 28 on, the Colonial forces were given the chance to join with the Roberts juggernaut marching to Pretoria, or be disbanded.

Buller's troops in Natal would obviously join Roberts. But an even more important line of advance, writes Watkin Williams, was to be followed by a force marching up from the south, of which the troops under General Gatacre would form the nucleus.

Roberts proposed to place General White, for whom "there would no longer be any suitable occupation in Natal" in command of this force, the objective of whose advance would be to clear the enemy out of the south-east corner of the Free State – and to open up railway communication with Bloemfontein.

"For this purpose", says *The Times History*, "Gatacre's little force at Stormberg was quite inadequate, and the matter being one of paramount importance, Roberts telegraphed to Buller on February 24 to send Sir George White and Warren's Division to East London as soon as the relief had been accomplished.

"Such a reduction to meet the urgent needs of the main theatre of war would in no way have crippled the Natal Army, which, immediately after the relief, numbered 55,000 men."

But, says Williams, from the very first Buller was strongly opposed to any part of his force being taken away, and protested to Roberts to this effect.

In reply Roberts telegraphed back from Paardeberg telling him to stand on the strict defensive and send off the 5th Division at once to East London. But Sir George White was ill and his position was immediately solved by his being invalided home.

On March 4 – the day following the march into Ladysmith – Warren received orders to proceed with his division to Durban, *en route* for the Cape.

"There were very cheerful faces seen about," he writes, "in spite of the sick atmosphere which hung about this scene of four months investment." [5]

But there was to be a surprise, a nasty one for Warren and his division.

On March 6, Warren, says Williams, recorded that he "took leave of General Buller and in a very joyful frame of mind proceeded south".

Remember that the *Spioenkop Despatches* had not yet been debated, and thus Warren still had no idea of Buller's "not necessarily for publication" despatch, nor the fact that he was not among those top officers mentioned in despatches.

Williams says that after bivouacking that night a short distance north of Colenso, Warren rode out early the next morning with nearly all his staff to make a pilgrimage to Spioenkop, where the Roman Catholic chaplain wished to bless a grave.

Warren's account runs: "On such excurions as this we had to be careful against sniping, and with a large party we had vedettes on our front and flanks, but any sniping by the Boers was improbable.

"On arrival at the Tugela, north of Mount Alice, it was found that the grave to be blessed was on the south side and we were on the north side. Here was a dilemma.

"The Tugela was rather in flood and flowing from 5 to 6 knots. But Father Collins was not to be beaten by the Tugela. He was a strong swimmer, and his orderly said that he could swim well; so they both stripped naked and waded in carefully, as Father Collins was holding some sacred vessel on his head and the orderly had to carry Father Collins' vestments.

"They started a great distance above the place where they had to land, and were carried down stream and landed safely on the south bank.

"Then we saw a very strange and very impressive sight: Father Collins in his buff, covered only by very light canonicals and carrying some religious vessel, while his orderly marched behind, stark naked but with great dignity. Thus the ceremony was carried through – possibly one of the most impressive ceremonies I have ever witnessed – and we all from our side of the river took part in it.

"It was a blazing hot day and I thought that orderly's back would be one long blister, but he would not allow that he had felt any discomfort.

"Then we went up Spioenkop. It did not seem much of a hill to us, tackling it at our leisure. There was water enough for 50,000 men at the bottom, and a good pond at the top.

"General Coke was with me and we came to the conclusion that it ought not to have been abandoned. That is still an open question, but I felt that even so we ought to have retaken it the next morning." [6]

Warren's engineer, Colonel Sim, wrote in his diary: "We reached Spioenkop about 12.30 and had a picnic lunch by a spring at the top, and then discussed the view and position, and I made an eyesketch map of the hill.

"The view of the whole country, from Doorn Kop right round to Acton Homes, is splendid and one can now quite realise exactly how affairs took place . . . Spioenkop makes a distinct *salient* in the Boer line, and . . . being naturally a weak spot in their line was not strongly held by them, and was gained by us, but we failed owing to the attack not being assisted by any other attack on the neighbouring parts.

"The top of the hill was taken at night, but the attacking force entrenched on the actual top and not on the crest facing the Boers, the result being that in addition to shelling the top their marksmen were able to creep up to the crest, about 100 to 40 yards from our trenches, under cover of the steep hill (as at Majuba), and pick off our men.

"But if, after our men had so gallantly held the hill all day, instead of retiring at night a battalion or two had been sent forward from the reserve, they could have driven the Boers away from Spioenkop and, turning to the left, have driven them right along their position from the flank.

"The attack from Spearman's of two battalions on the hills east of the Kop [the capture of the Twin Peaks by the King's Royal Rifles, under Lyttleton's orders] was also well timed and valuable, but the retirement of these again at once, by order of Sir R. Buller, gave away the whole advantage.

"There cannot be the least doubt that with a little energy the Boers' position could have been pierced then, and they recognised this as they were actually on the trek when the hill was abandoned."

On the morning of Thursday, March 8, the division entrained at Colenso for Pietermaritzburg, where they arrived that evening and had two clear days to rest and enjoy the luxury of clean clothes and a short spell of relatively civilised existence.

Late on the Saturday night they left Pietermaritzburg by train for Durban, where they embarked in the liner *Hawardan Castle* on Sunday morning.

But then disaster struck.

"We were within three hours of sailing," Warren writes, "when our transit was counter-ordered and we were told to remain in Natal. It was a terrible blow to us all."

It was the second time this had happened. Warren, as has been stated elsewhere, was pulled off the train at De Aar at the beginning of the war, and told to return to the Cape, and move on to Natal.

What had happened?

Buller told the Commission: "I acknowledged Lord Roberts' telegram [asking that the 5th Division be sent to the Cape] saying: 'I note your wishes. I will send at once the Fifth Division and 14th Hussars, as both units have detachments at the Cape. I wish to keep the artillery and Royal Engineers of the division. Of the Ladysmith force the infantry will not be fit for some time; their cavalry and infantry will require, I think, six weeks – they say three months – before they can move . . .'

"Lord Roberts replied on the 6th directing me to send the Fifth Division and 14th Hussars to East London . . .

"By the 9th I began to feel the pressure of the returning enemy, and I telegraphed to Lord Roberts, whose troops had by this time occupied Burghersdorp that I thought the Fifth Division would be of more value to him if left with me than if sent to East London. I said: 'I fear that if I remain sedentary the Boers will commence raiding, and I think I ought to repair the line to Elandslaagte and strike at Dundee . . . this would turn enemy's position and probably save the railway line to Newcastle.

"On the 10th, Lord Roberts authorised me to delay the departure of the Fifth Division . . . I at once recalled the Fifth Division some of whom were already on board ship . . ." [7]

Says Williams: "Everyone from Warren downwards was completely in the dark as to their future movements or destination. On Wednesday, March 14, orders came for the Division to return to Pietermaritzburg, and encamp there.

"Before leaving Durban, Warren visited the hospital ship in Durban harbour, and talked to a number of wounded men from his Division.

"After six days in Pietermaritzburg without receiving further orders, Warren was at last instructed – on March 21 – to strike camp at once and return by train that day to Ladysmith – and thus he found himself back in exactly the same position as he had been in three weeks before, but with nothing accomplished.

" 'I got back from Ladysmith', he writes, 'on March 22, and visited General Buller on the 25th. He was most affectionate and proposed many things, but they were all knocked on the head by an order for Masterly Inactivity, from Lord Roberts.'

"The explanation of the Vth Division's fruitless journey to Durban, and of the inactivity which ensued on its return to the front, is to be found in the disagreement which took place between Roberts and Buller about the respective strength of the forces which each required . . .

"At an early stage in the telegraphic controversy which lasted throughout the whole of March and April, and in which between 40 and 50 telegrams passed, Roberts conceded to Buller's request for the return of the Vth Division; but even so Buller raised objections." [8]

"And so," says *The Times History*, "the discussion went on; the result was in each and every case the same, failure on the part of Roberts to get Buller to move. Finally despairing of getting any co-operation from Buller, Roberts, on April 8, took from him Hunter's Division and the Imperial Light Horse and told him to remain on the defensive. The two months that followed the relief of Ladysmith were, therefore, a time of complete inaction for the Natal army." [9]

Warren's narrative of the campaign describes a ludicrous situation which developed when he returned to Ladysmith: "I was ordered to move my Division on the 5th April across the Modder Spruit to Elandslaagte on the Sunday River, for the health of my troops.

"When I arrived there I found that about a mile and a half in front of me was the 2nd Division under General Clery; neither of us had received any orders as to how we were to co-operate in case of attack by the Boers, and we heard that they were in force not far from us.

"As General Clery and I had different views on many military subjects it seemed to me that in case of attack by the Boers we should not be well placed for efficiency.

"I went to see General Clery and had lunch with him, and enjoyed it immensely as he had a good cook [Warren lived in all respects the severest life of any General Officer in the army, he and his staff habitually fed on the normal diet of the troops – bully beef and commissariat biscuits] but neither at lunch nor afterwards could we come to any conclusion as to how we were to act.

"General Clery saw no difficulty in us having separate commands, and said he had been some days with Sir Archibald Hunter in these conditions without finding any difficulty.

"I told him that if General Lyttleton were in command of the 2nd Division I should not trouble myself with the question, because we usually thought alike, and no doubt he and General Hunter thought alike too.

"But quite apart from this I did not like the position held by General Clery, and as we each had to have our own outposts and look-out duties, the troops had a good deal of unecessary work . . .

"On the 11th April I received two memoranda from General Buller criticising General Clery's position and telling me how I should act to set matters right.

"I sent word that I knew how to act, but I was powerless to do so if half the force was outside my command. But General Buller failed to understand what I wanted, so the following morning I sent Major Kelly on a personal mission to General Buller to say that I did not care who was put in command – General Clery or someone else – but there must be someone in command, and that if he left matters as they were and there was a fiasco, I should decline all responsibility for its occurrence. Major Kelly had a most amusing interview, but eventually he came back with the following written order:

" '12 April. Lt.-General Sir Charles Warren. You will assume command of all the troops in the vicinity of Elandslaagte, viz: the 2nd Division and Naval Brigade, the Vth Division and the 3rd Mounted Brigade. By order. A.G. Miles, Col, C of S.'

"As soon as this order arrived General Clery could take my orders without loss of dignity, and we put matters through and were no longer troubled by Boer attacks.

"General Buller came to see me after I had got things straight, and said: 'I am much indebted to you for what you have done; you have relieved my mind of a great weight. I have been troubled for some time at having no mobile force at my disposal, and you have enabled me to possesss one in the force you now command, and I am greatly obliged to you.'

"But", writes Williams, "Warren was destined to remain in command of the troops at Elandslaagte for no more than one short week, before he was at last – and quite unexpectedly – transferred to the field of action for which he was best fitted by his previous experience and to which his disposition was, perhaps, particularly well suited.

"He describes the event as follows: 'On the 18th April General Buller sent me a telegram from Lord Roberts, stating that the High Commissioner (Sir Alfred Milner) had urged that a General officer should be made Military Governor of part of the Cape Colony north of the Orange River; it further stated that as Lord Roberts and the High Commissioner agreed that my local knowledge would be very valuable in this capacity, Lord Roberts desired that I may be sent if I could be spared.

" 'I wired to General Buller that I would not willingly be severed from my Division unless the change was recognised as a promotion.

" 'In his reply, he asked me to come over and see him: this I did and we had a most interesting conversation, of which I made notes at the time. At first he seemed unwilling to let me go, for he said I was a difficulty because I had the faculty of absorbing power wherever I went, and he did not like me to go from under his eyes.

" 'I was a difficulty, I knew; but knowing the type of country and having previously been in so many tight corners in similar circumstances, I could see short cuts out of them which he could not see till they were accomplished.

" . . . 'I told him he was quite wrong, and that I hoped he would some day realize how much he had misjudged me.

"The curious point is that though we both spoke in very strong terms, yet we remained in the best of humours, and when we came out to lunch everyone thought that we had been having a capital interview.

" 'It was one of those occasions when the question involved was too big to look upon as a personal one. I had saved his reputation; I had made it possible for him to relieve Ladysmith, and yet he had forgotten all of this.

" 'He said that if I could convince him that I was right, he would give in. I laughed and said I should not attempt to alter his wrong views which were too firmly ingrained to be changed.

" 'We parted that day on the best of terms, and when I later read his unkind reflections in the *Spioenkop Despatches* of the 30th January I always expected, even to the last, that he would one day say that he had retracted them.

" 'But when he brought the matter out all over again before the Royal Commission, and again later in the *Daily Mail* and other dailies, I could only say to him, telepathically, "Buller, there is one subject on which you will allow of no retirement, namely your finding fault with a subordinate."'

"The practical outcome . . . was that Warren was to be promoted to the post of Military Governor of Griqualand West, with a small field force under his command.

"Nothing now remained for him to do before embarking with his personal Staff for the Cape Colony, but to say good-bye . . .

"On the morning of April 23rd, Warren and his two A.D.Cs left Ladysmith with their orderlies, grooms and horses by train for Durban. Here they embarked on board the *Pavonia* for Cape Town." [10]

Warren's affairs in the Northern Cape – successful as they were – are out of the scope of this book, but at the beginning of August he was in Cape Town, having disbanded his Expeditionary Force, on his way home to England.

In Cape Town he saw for the first time, in the public newspapers, copies of two of Buller's despatches of January 30 (of the "secret" despatch he remained unaware of until its publication in 1902), commenting unfavourably on his action when in command on Spioenkop.

He at once wrote, on August 8, says Williams, a despatch to Lord Roberts to supplement his own previous report "with such additional information and explanations as will show several points under a very different aspect".

This despatch, however, was never published, and to Warren's later letters on the subject he received nothing but a curt reply requesting him *not* to discuss the matter further or to *attempt any defence of his cause.*

Like Coke. Like Long.

Warren regarded the whole matter as too big to be a personal one. Had it been otherwise, writes Williams, there would have been no lack of opportunity for him to show a personal bias, for at the time when he arrived in Cape Town – and for that matter when he got back to England – society gossip was full of absurdly malignant statements which sought to damage Buller's reputation.

All these statements Warren, from a personal knowledge, vigorously denied.

The then *Cape Argus* in fact carried this paragraph: "Sir Charles Warren arrived at Cape Town to find the air thick with rumours as to the conduct and personal habits of General Buller.

"Sir Charles Warren, whatever his faults as a soldier, is a man of the highest honour, and although he had no reason to love his old chief, he was practically the only man in Cape Town who championed the cause of Buller.

"To dozens of persons when in Cape Town on that occasion Sir Charles Warren vigorously denied the truth of the libels to which reference has been made above."

At the end of August he returned to his home at Ramsgate, and absorbed himself in completing literary work which had been begun in earlier and busier years.

In 1902 he published *On the Veld in the Seventies*, and in 1903 *The Ancient Cubit and our Weights and Measures.*

He also had a long and detailed statement to prepare for the Commission, and finally he provided Leo Amery with much information on the Natal Campaign.

In November 1902, Warren was one of the General Officers chosen to act as pall-bearers at the funeral of Prince Edward of Saxe-Weimar at Chichester Cathedral. He was at this time frequently speaking on behalf of the Palestine Exploration Fund, the London Missionary Society and the Church of England Temperance Society, as well as for the St John Ambulance Brigade, of which he was Life President.

Why did Warren, the thorough gentleman, remain silent on his atrocious treatment by Sir Redvers Buller?

Watkin Williams provides the answer, and says the story is told in a letter

267

Last resting place of a hero. The grave of Sir Charles Warren, and his wife, in the ancient graveyard at Westbere, three miles from Canterbury. The grave is in the open, with flowers all around. (Picture: the Author.)

Warren wrote to Sir Bartle Frere in October 1924: "I am just completing an episode in my life which has lasted 23 years. When I arrived in England in 1901, I consulted General Sir Alexander Montgomery-Moore, then commanding at Aldershot, as to what I should do about Sir R. Buller's strictures on my action in Natal.

"He had very strict views on such subjects, and he said that according to military etiquette no subordinate officer, right or wrong, could controvert hostile remarks of his C. in Chief during war, and that I must grin and bear it, right or wrong.

"Since then we have had plenty of cases where subordinates have brought their cases before the public, but I do not know whether they have been justified.

"Anyhow, as matters then stood I felt his advice was right, but I wanted to do *something,* and asked him what I could do. He said, 'Wait 20 years, and then do what you like.' I said, 'I shall not probably live so long; what can I do now? He said: 'There is only one thing you can do. Begin all over again in some other line, and show the world you are not the idiot Buller makes you out to be. Show you can lead men, and you have superior ability.'

"So I turned away and made up my mind . . . I determined to go in for education of boys; and, to show my ability, I determined to make order out of the confused chaos of weights and measures, and also to find out what's the matter with the earth's position – as no astronomers, as yet, have been able to find any law for the position of the planets."

General Sir Charles Warren, CCMG, KCB, FRS, died on the evening of Friday, January 21, 1927 in Weston Super Mare. A memorial service was held in the Weston Parish Church on Tuesday the 25th. The coffin was draped with the Union Jack and on it was placed the Stellaland Republic banner which had been presented to Warren by Queen Victoria.

Also there was placed his General's cocked hat, his decorations and his police sword.

Afterwards the coffin was taken by road to Canterbury cathedral, where it was lain in state in the chapel at the east end of the cryst.

King George V was represented by General Sir Alexander Godley, GOC of the Southern Command; the War Office by Major-General P.G. Grant, Commandant of the School of Military Engineering at Chatham; Colonel H.L. Pritchard represented the Royal Engineers and Mrs G.H. Edwards represented the Chief Commissioner of Metropolitan Police.

Says Williams: "The coffin was then taken out through the West door to the waiting gun-carriage, and the long procession – it was over a half mile long, with its escort of 400 troops – began to wind its way through the narrow streets of Canterbury, out into the country and across the marshes, through the village of Sturry and up the hill to the little churchyard at Westbere.

"The whole of Canterbury had come out to pay its last tribute . . . one saw here and there some grey-haired old soldier wearing the medals of his African campaigns . . . press his way through to the front and raise his hat in token of respect.

"The January wind blew cold across the marshes and the feathers of the cocked hat on the coffin fluttered in the breeze.

"The three mile march was long, but outside the city the procession had broken into quick time, and the measured tread of the soldiers' feet was like a solemn rhythm of applause as the warrior neared his final resting place. Half way up Westbere hill the slow time began again as the band burst forth with Beethoven's Funeral March and the cortege turned down the narrow lane to the churchyard gates.

"The grave had been dug next to my grandmother's, a few feet away from the old garden fence . . . then the firing party fired their last salute. Buglers played the Last Post and Reveille echoed as the sound of trumpets on the other side . . ." [11]

And so passed a true hero of the Boer War.

I sat in the tiny graveyard at Westbere for some time with the spirit of Sir Charles Warren, on a trip to Britain in 1992.

The Oaks – his huge house that overlooks the graveyard – is very much still there, and Sir Charles and Lady Warren are buried among buttercups and trees, for the cemetery is not cluttered.

There are birds, and nearby a tiny church.

All is peace . . .

SOURCES

1. *The Times History*, Vol. 4, pp 165,166.
2. *South African Despatches*, Vol. 2, Natal Field Army.
3. *Life of General Sir Charles Warren*, by Watkin Williams.
4. Ibid.
5. Ibid.
6. Ibid.
7. *Commission on the War in South Africa*.
8. *Life of General Sir Charles Warren*, by Watkin Williams.
9. *Times History*, Vol. 4, p. 168.
10. *Life of General Sir Charles Warren*, by Watkin Williams.
11. Ibid.

CHAPTER THIRTY

The End for Buller

Sacked out of hand over the "Surrender Telegram"

Lieutenant-General Sir Ian Hamilton arrived in Natal as Assistant Adjutant General – in fact Chief Staff Officer to Sir George White in Ladysmith. But one day after landing at Durban he was superseded by Sir Archibald Hunter, who had come out in advance to become Sir Redvers Buller's Chief Staff Officer. But as Buller had not yet arrived, he took the position with Sir George White.

Hamilton, instead, was given an infantry brigade. He had also been recommended for the Victoria Cross for action at Elandslaagte, but it was disallowed by Buller – because a General officer was not meant to expose himself to enemy fire to such an extent. And in any case an officer was expected to show extraordinary courage.

Hamilton had fought at Majuba, and of his bravery there was no question.

In Sir George White's despatches of December 2, 1899 he says of Hamilton: "Colonel I. Hamilton, C.B., D.S.O., has acted as brigadier-general in command of a brigade since my headquarters have been established at Ladysmith; I have made a special recommendation in favour of this officer for the manner in which he led the infantry at Elandslaagte on October 21 and consider him an officer of special ability who is well fitted for higher rank and command."

And again, on March 23: "Colonel I.S.M. Hamilton, C.B., D.S.O., Commanding 7th Brigade and in charge of section C of the defences, has, during the whole of the operations of the defence, been in charge of the most exposed and most extended front, including the immense position of Caesar's Camp and Wagon Hill over 4 miles in perimeter. I cannot speak too highly of his indefatigable zeal in organising the defence of his front, and in keeping up the hearts of all under him by his constant and personal supervision. His leadership on 6th January [the Boer attack on Wagon Hill and Caesar's Camp] was the most marked factor in the success of the defence." [1]

It was in Ladysmith, says Julian Symons, that Buller's Generals and staff learned for the first time of the "surrender telegram" Buller had sent after the battle of Colenso.

And it was Hamilton who wrote to journalist-historian Spencer Wilkinson in London that a hundred of Buller's officers had talked to him, and that from General to subaltern they had all lost confidence in "Sir Reverse, as they call him".

What angered Hamilton and the others in Ladysmith was Buller's conviction now that everything he had done was for the best.

Hamilton, says Symons, wrote Roberts a letter on March 14, 1900: "Buller was very rude to Sir George and spoke to him in the vilest way of you and Kitchener, whom he appears to dislike and to attribute dishonest motives to, almost as much as he does you. I never gave him the chance to be nasty to me, but contented myself with a very distant salute," and to Spencer

Wilkinson: "After the battle he wired us that we had better fire off our ammo and make the best terms we could. We thought at first our cypher and helio must have fallen into the hands of the Boers, it seemed so incredible that the great Buller of all men could be giving such unworthy counsel. He recovered himself in about three days and then became as boastful as ever."

And Hamilton followed it up by saying: "Buller is no use . . . It is a question of life or death of our selves here as well as of the empire in general, and I write to beg you to use all your influence to get the man recalled before he does more mischief." [2]

But, says Symons, Buller was not recalled.

He stayed in South Africa, as Roberts's second in command until October. Lansdowne, in fact, suggested after reading some of the telegrams sent by Buller to Roberts, that Buller's mind was unhinged!

But because of his immense popularity with his men – without doubt he was a soldiers' man and made sure they came first – no-one cared to consider the idea of removing him.

Dundonald, like Warren, found Buller to be irritable one day, pleasant the next. Dundonald said to him: "You are a changed Buller, you are not the Buller I knew in the Sudan."

Buller is reported to have said: "It is true, my dear Dundonald, I am changed, and what changed me was the indoor life at that cursed War Office, those long hours, day after day, without exercise, for I used to work there long after others had gone."

Towards the end of 1900, Roberts was recalled to Britain to take over from Lord Wolseley as Commander-in-Chief of the British Army, and Buller went about the same time. As far as they were concerned Pretoria had been captured, there were a few commandos still loose in the Northern Transvaal, and the war was over.

Of course it was not. But that is out of the scope of this work.

Buller and Roberts left South Africa in clouds of military glory.

As he made his way down through Natal by train, Buller was feted at every stop. At Pietermaritzburg, for instance, he was presented with an address at an open air meeting on the market square by the Deputy-Mayor, Mr P. F. Payn, chairman of the Buller testimonial committee. It read, in part: "When our land was threatened with ruin, you chose to sacrifice your original plan, which promised speedy and assured success, and decided to stem the tide of invasion in Natal . . . Your self sacrificing action was justified by subsequent events, and Natal was saved from a catastrophe which would have crippled her for many years . . . Your qualities as a soldier have won for you the admiration of the Empire . . . the confidence of the men whom you so often led to victory and the heartfelt gratitude of the Colonists of Natal.

"We recognise in you a worthy example of the great soldiers who, from generation to generation, have formed and perpetuated the unparalleled traditions of the British Empire, men in whom military sagacity of the highest order has been displayed . . ." [3]

Buller was received with a "storm of cheers".

But it was what he had to say that was important. Nay, vital.

He admitted, perhaps for the first time at an open meeting, his failures had lost him the command in South Africa.

He said: "I have been found fault with by all the so-called military critics of the English Press. I have been pelted with criticism from German, French and Italian critics. I have been told I allowed the enemy to dictate my strategy. I was told I was incapable of fulfiling the plans I left England with.

"But I was not told the truth, that the conditions under which these plans were made had been altered when I arrived in South Africa . . . Well I did what I thought right . . .

"At the moment I had to decide to come to Natal, I received a telegram from Sir Evelyn Wood [Buller's commanding officer in the Zulu War of 1879]. His military knowledge and soldierly spirit enabled him to see by intuition the difficulties to be faced, and the telegram was, 'If you have any trouble in Natal, allow me to come out and serve under you.' I was never so tempted in my life to take a man at his word, but wired back to him and said I looked on the journey to Natal as a forlorn hope.

"I was aware that if I failed at Ladysmith the first shot, I should run the risk of losing the command in South Africa.

"I think I would have been a coward if I had asked Sir Evelyn Wood, who was senior to me, and a better man, to come out here, and take the risk I was in great anxiety about myself.

"I came here, and failed at my first attempt to to relieve Ladysmith, and I lost the command in South Africa, and I think rightly. I had taken on a task, and I was bound to see it through. . ." [4]

Buller landed at Southampton on November 9, 1900. Lord Wolseley, his friend, was there to meet him, and large crowds gathered wherever he went.

Nothing was yet known publicly of the "surrender" telegram, little of the true story of Spioenkop. And for Buller there was no sign of the wrath to come . . .

And no sign of the already deteriorated relationship between Roberts and Buller.

There are anonymous sources which say Roberts had never forgiven Buller for allowing the Honourable Freddy to ride out in his fatal attempt to bring back the Colenso guns.

Freddy's death was Buller's fault – and once given the chance, Roberts would exact his revenge.

One source even attributes the maelstom of farm burning – the nauseous policy of scorched earth begun by Roberts, but honed finely by Kitchener – to the death of Freddy. The Boers, apart from Buller, had taken Roberts's only son from him – and they would pay.

That Roberts was exasperated by Buller is evident in the telegrams they exchanged. That Roberts kept his temper in the face of Buller's pleas for more men, more equipment and his apparent fear of attacking the enemy, is a measure of Roberts's gentlemanly self-control.

It is entirely possible he hated Buller.

Like Warren, Buller's temper was famous. The government awaited Buller's arrival back home with trepidation: What would he say? What would he do?

Says Symons: "Almost everybody was afraid of his temper, which Buller spoke of as malady from which he had suffered all his life. ~'Since Old Eton days', he once told Lord Esher, 'I have had a formula for myself, 'Remember Dunmore.'

"This referred to an occasion at Eton when he had been playing football and had had a chance of taking a kick at goal. He had not taken it because he was too busy kicking Dunmore.'

". . . In November, Lansdowne wrote to Roberts . . . 'Buller has been tremendously feted and, so far, has bridled his tongue in public.'

". . . The 'surrender' telegram had never been made public, but its general nature was known to all of White's staff officers, and rumours about the telegram appeared frequently in the press.

" . . . But the press attacks and innuendoes made him steadily angrier. His anger was increased by the fact that he had been more or less passed over in the distribution of honours, being awarded only the G.C.M.G. (Grand Cross of St Michael and St George)." [5]

Buller blamed Roberts. But Roberts had nothing to do with it – in fact he had suggested Buller should be given a peerage, an idea rejected by the government.

"But," says Symons, "Buller had reached a point where he attributed almost all of his misfortunes to Roberts. In July he had been formally rebuked because he had appeared at a bazaar for war charity in plain clothes, although troops were present in uniform.

"The King was displeased, and Roberts communicated this displeasure. Buller's apology was grudging: 'I confess your letter surprised me. But of course if the King thinks I ought to have been in uniform there is no more to be said, and I am very sorry I was not.'"

Buller's end came suddenly in October.

"The occasion," writes Symons, "was a luncheon given by the Queen's Westminister Volunteers. Sir Howard Vincent was in the chair and he coupled the toast of the regiment with the name of Buller. The reply to the toast was made in terms which suggest that Buller had, as Wolseley put it, too much champagne on board.

"He (Buller) told how he had been visited at Aldershot by an international spy, who had first talked mysteriously about the Transvaal Secret Service, and then suggested that Buller should give up the Aldershot command. The conversation between them continued:

"BULLER: 'Thank you very much. I do not know that I need to do so. Why should I do so?'

"SPY: 'I will tell you. You have got enemies, men who mean to get you out of the way and they will get you out of the way, and you had better get out of it quietly.'

"BULLER: 'I am a fighting man, and if what you say were really so, I am much more likely to stop here than to leave. If it is necessary for me to use that information, I shall.'

"SPY: 'You can.'

"Buller went on to say that *The Times* had said he was not fit to be in command of the First Army Corps. 'I assert that there is no one in England junior to me who is as fit as I am. *(Cheers)*. I say so. I challenge *The Times* to say who is the man they have in their eye more fit than I am?

"He told in detail his version of the 'surrender' telegram, which had been mentioned in *The Times* by Amery [Leo, editor of *The Times History of the War*)] 'writing pseudonymously. 'I challenge *The Times* to bring their scribe, *Reformer,* into the ring. Let us know who he is, by what right he writes, what his name is, what his authority is. Let him publish his telegram. Then I will publish a certified copy of the telegram I sent and the public shall judge me. I am perfectly ready to be judged.' " [6]

It may be well here to look again at the "surrender" telegram and then examine Buller's muddled, confused explanation to the Commission over it.

The telegram sent to White from Buller read: "*Clear line. No 88, 16th December.* I tried Colenso yesterday, but failed; the enemy is too strong for my force, except with siege operations, and those will take one full month to prepare. Can you last so long? If not, how many days can you give me in which to take up defensive position? After which I suggest you firing away as much ammunition as you can, and making best terms you can. I can remain here if you have alternative suggestion, but unaided I cannot break in. I find my infantry cannot fight more than 10 miles from camp, and then only if water can be got, and it is scarce here."

(There is a correction note in the Commission's report, presumably added by the War Office. It reads: "In his No. 92 of 17th, Buller said above message had been signalled correctly, but asked us to make the following corrections: Strike out from 'if not, how many' down to 'after which' inclusive, and substitute 'how many days can you hold out?' Add to end of message 'whatever happens recollect to burn your cipher, decipher, and code books, and all deciphered messages'.")

The contents of telegram No. 92 appear in the paragraphs that follow.

The Commissions proceedings went as follows:

CHAIRMAN: "I mentioned that we have the telegrams before us because it might save you going through them in detail. We have all these telegrams."

BULLER: "The only point with regard to those telegrams to which I attach the slightest importance really is the fact one telegram which I was ordered to publish is not in the shape in which I sent it, and that the following telegram which conveyed a very different impression from what was sought to be conveyed by the publication that was made, was not published.

"My No 92 was followed by my 93, and my 92, of which rather a strong point was made, was not published as I sent it, but published as it was said to have been deciphered. I have given it in the narrative as I sent it."

SIR JOHN EDGE: "What is the date of that?"

BULLER: "The 16th December."

SIR GEORGE TAUBMAN-GOLDIE: "It is quoted in a series before us?"

BULLER: "Exactly, but those are wrong. That is the point. In all the telegrams I was ordered to publish (and I protested against publishing them wrongly) I was told to publish them textually as they were given to me, and to some of mine were given the dates on which I sent them and to others were given the dates on which Sir George White received them.

"As regards that particular telegram, No. 92, the date of the receipt by Sir George White, the 17th, is given, but I sent it on the 16th. My original telegram gave its own date as I think all my telegrams did, but the War Office left the date out. I have given the reference to it at the bottom of my statement."

CHAIRMAN: "We do not seem to have that."

BULLER: "That is what I am afraid of."

CHAIRMAN: "Would you like to look at this document again?" [handing the paper to the witness].

BULLER: "That is it, you see; that is what was done, No. 88 was published and hung on to No. 92, but as a matter of fact No. 88 was answered by Sir George White long before he received No. 92. This was not fair – that is all."

CHAIRMAN: "Will you read your No. 92?"

BULLER: "Yes."

TAUBMAN-GOLDIE: "Are you confident of the date being the 16th because in their correction note they say it was the 17th again."

BULLER: "I am absolutely confident. A clerk brought me No. 88 which I thought was an important telegram. I had had it repeated by the signaller and sent back to me, and he brought me the signaller's returned telegram. I wanted to alter it. You will see in that series of telegrams that in no two telegrams did Sir George White ever give me the same period for which his supplies could last. I said in the original telegram 'How long'; I wanted to alter it to 'how many days.' I was on my horse at the time, and I gave the clerk instructions to strike out the words 'how long' and put in 'how many days.' By mistake too many groups seem to have been struck out. I may say I never saw that telegram until after I got to England."

CHAIRMAN: "Which? No. 92?"

BULLER: "Yes, my No. 92. I did not pay any attention to it. It was meant to be a verbal correction. I put into the end of it the remark about the ciphers because at that very moment I had received a letter from the person who sent me my best information telling me that they were satisfied that the Boers had got a certain number of cipher or code telegrams over which the deciphering had been written, and therefore those groups they would have been able to read in future."

CHAIRMAN: "I think it would be better that you should give us the actual text of No. 92."

BULLER: ". . . My message, No. 88 cipher. Groups 31 to 43 were correctly sent, but in place of them and of first number of 44 Group, read as follows: 'How many days can you hold out?' Also add to end of message, 'Whatever happens recollect to burn your cipher and decipher and code books and deciphered messages.'

"It is a stupid telegram; it is not a telegram I ought to have sent, but it was sent in the hurry, and I never knew anything about it until I got to England, as no acknowledgement of it was ever received. Sir George White never acknowledged it. He acknowledged No. 88, but when I was given the chance of publishing his acknowledgment, and did so, I was not allowed to complete it by showing that he acknowledged No. 88 only. He said: 'Your No. 88 of today received.'

"He did not refer to No. 92."

CHAIRMAN: "I think that appears in the telegrams.

BULLER: "Yes, but it did not appear in what the War Office gave me to publish."

CHAIRMAN: "But it appears now?"

BULLER: "Yes, confidentially to you, but it has not appeared in public."

VISCOUNT ESHER: "It is No. 92 which you speak of when you say it is a stupid telegram?"

BULLER: "Yes, I followed it with No. 93 . . . No. 92 in the way in which it was published was published rather to give colour to the fact that in No. 88 I had suggested to Sir George White he ought to surrender, and it was published, no doubt, for that reason, but if they had also published No. 93 I do not think it would have been possible for anyone to have given it that meaning."

TAUBMAN-GOLDIE: "Would you explain that?"

BULLER: "My No. 93 was: 'I find I cannot take Colenso, and I cannot stay in force near there as there is no water, but I am leaving there as large a force as I can to help you; but recollect that in this weather my infantry cannot be depended on to march more than ten miles a day. Can you suggest anything for me to do? I think in about three weeks from now I could take Colenso, but I can never get to Onderbroek.'

"No man would have sent that who had the moment before ordered the man to consider the possibilities of surrender. I ask too is it common sense to suppose that a General ordering an officer to surrender would do so covertly by elimination of words from a previous order? No officer would think of obeying without question such an order so conveyed.

"That telegram, No. 93, as you have it, is not my original telegram; it is one of those which have been altered."

TAUBMAN-GOLDIE: "Do you mean that if your second telegram had been published as you sent it it would have explained No. 88?"

BULLER: "Yes, if No. 93 had been published."

TAUBMAN-GOLDIE: "And that it would have explained it in such a way that it would have been clear that you did not mean Sir George White to surrender?"

BULLER: "What I mean is that by putting my No.92 in this paper as a note to No.88, it is fairer than it was; but what was published before by the War Office was my No. 92 given in extenso, as it was assumed to have altered No.88 the original telegram in the words in which I sent it not being given."

TAUBMAN-GOLDIE: "Of course we only want to give you an opportunity of making any explanation which you wish, but the question which will always arise is this: what is the meaning of those words 'After which I suggest your firing away as much ammunition as you can and making best terms you can'?

BULLER: "The meaning of those words was this: I was face to face with a man who had a better force theoretically, a more experienced force, and a larger available force to help himself than I had to help him. [Buller is talking about White – author.]

"In his telegrams he has thrown the whole onus of his relief upon me; he could not come out, he could not go large and could only help me in a particular hole, the most difficult place to get to.

"As I say, the onus of his relief was thrown upon me, and practically he had got into Ladysmith, and was directing me, as he did then and afterwards, to bring the whole forces of the Empire to get him out.

"I am satisfied in my own mind that if I had been in Ladysmith with that force I could have come out any morning or evening that I wished to from Wagon Hill and along the line of the watershed; there is a very interesting watershed there.

"I happen to know Ladysmith very well myself. In 1881 I selected Ladysmith as a defensible position against the Boers, who had at that time no guns; and therefore I knew the country. From Wagon Hill it comes round, you turn at the end of Bester's spruit and come on to the next high hill and then you go down a little at the top of Onderbroek and come out at Groblers on the top of the hill, so that the whole way out of Ladysmith he would have had a strong artillery positions to take up and help his attack as he came along.

"There could have been no difficulty whatever in getting out of Ladysmith provided he could be received at the bottom of the hill, where I hoped to be able to receive him.

"And that is what I expected to be able to do for him.

"I did consider that Sir George White was a man who could never give up Ladysmith if he could possibly keep it, but I did not consider that he had much initiative for active fighting, and I thought that the most effective lever I could employ to move him would be the warning that unless he could offer me active assistance he might possibly have to surrender.

"At any rate I think I may claim that he felt it so because in his reply to my No.88 you noticed he introduced a subject that I never mentioned. He says, 'I cannot cut my way out to you.'

"It is put in the paper you have given me 'I fear I could not cut my way to you.'

"He brings that in. I do not wish to say anything against Sir Geroge White, but if I have to defend myself I have to tell the truth. It will be found later on that Sir George White came to the conclusion that I should not be able to help he did then offer to try and cut his way out, but not till then (that was about 28th January. . .) although at that time he had only 7,000 men whom he could put in the field. At the time when I asked him to suggest how he could do something to help me he had over 12,000 men and he suggested nothing."

CHAIRMAN: " . . . He could have made a movement out with his troops to meet you, but could not have taken either his non-combatants or his stores out."

BULLER: "But his non-combatants would have been perfectly safe; the Boers did not kill non-combatants, and if he had joined me we should have defeated the Boers the next day . . .

"I wanted him to retire from Ladysmith. I would not have cared what happened to Ladysmith if I got him out. He might have left all his guns behind and it would not have mattered. I did suggest to him the point that he might fire away all his ammunition; that was part of the original idea . . ."

CHAIRMAN: "Please understand that I am not arguing the point; I am only trying to make clear what you meant."

BULLER: "I also do not want to argue it. I only want to make it quite clear; that was my point, that short of positively ordering him I did everything I could to induce him to do something."

CHAIRMAN: "But the movement which you suggested was a movement for his troops which were fit to take the field to join you, but to abandon for a time at any rate the position of Ladysmith, to be occupied by the Boers if they chose to walk into it."

BULLER: "Nothing would have pleased me more than to have got the Boers into Ladysmith. The possession of Ladysmith was of no use to anybody. It was of use to Sir George White to protect himself, but it was of no strategic value as long as there were no troops to bar us. It did not close the passage of the Tugela in any way; it was 16 miles from the Tugela."

CHAIRMAN: "I am not going into the question of strategy, but the Boers would then have walked in and taken possession of the place and you would have had to make operations which might not have taken place in Ladysmith itself but you would have had to make operations afterwards to drive them back?"

BULLER: "I had to make those operations in any case in order to get to Sir George White."

CHAIRMAN: " . . . But still if one of the forces is in a town, and that town is occupied by the enemy, you speak of it as an abandonment of that place to the enemy?"

BULLER: "A few tin houses – a village; but I deny that if we had met, Ladysmith would have been occupied by the Boers. We should then have been on the hills and they could not have got in."

VISCOUNT ESHER: " . . . You did not ask Sir George White directly, in so many words, Can you or can you not come out of Ladysmith? There is no telegram which shows that; there is only your obscure telegram, if I may say so, which has been so misinterpreted according to you?"

BULLER: "I admit the criticism, but I can only say that I should do it again with the same man. . ."

SIR JOHN EDGE: " . . . Read in any way that it is possible to read your heliogram No. 88 of the 16th December, could it be read to mean that Sir George White should surrender before the very last moment?"

BULLER: "I do not think it could."

SIR JOHN EDGE: "I do not think so either."

BULLER: "I do not honestly think it could; I know I wrote it with extreme care; it was not a very easy telegram to write. I did feel at the time that if was of enormous importance to me to get rid of the incubus of Ladysmith, and that if I could have got Sir George White out at any price, at any sacrifice, I should have done so.

"I did think I was using words that would spur him on to give me some idea of what he could do."

SIR JOHN EDGE: "But even without your explanation, which I think fully explains why you worded the heliogram in that way, I cannot see how it could be read as a suggestion that he should make any surrender before the very last moment – until the very last moment."

BULLER: "I am very much obliged to you for saying that. I can truly say that is my impression also."

There is a postscript. Buller says: "I may also mention that although, for some reason of which I am quite unaware, the War Office asked Sir George White for all his correspondence with me, they did not do me the honour of asking me for my correspondence with Sir George White, so that that print is only a one-sided document. I have never had a single question or Inquiry of any sort, kind or description addressed to me by the War Office with regard to my operations in Natal or anything connected with them. [7]

St John Broderick had become Secretary of State for War at the same time as Roberts had been appointed chief of the army.

After Buller's speech to the Queen's Westminister Volunteers, Broderick sent a telegram to Roberts: Now Buller had to go, was its gist.

Buller must first be asked to admit that he had made the speech; next, the substance of it must be telegraphed to the King at Balmoral; and third he must be replaced in his command.

King Edward agreed. But Buller, after a loud scene with Broderick, in which he complained of Roberts, of White and the way in which he had been treated, refused to quit, and appealed to the King, saying he regretted making the speech, but that he thought his speech alone should not be made the grounds of depriving him of his position and driving him from a service of 43 years.

The King, says Symons, was unmoved.

On October 23, 1901 it was announced that Buller had been relieved of his command and retired on half pay.

He was replaced at Aldershot by Hildyard. [8]

"And so", says his official biographer, Colonel C.H. Melville, "nothing was said of the good work he had done during the first weeks of his command in South Africa, nothing of his splendid administrative work, nothing of his skilful manoeuvres in the summer and autumn of 1900." [9]

Later he laments: "It is worth remembering that Sir Redvers had every right to feel a deeply injured man. Not for any dereliction of duty, but for one error of judgement he had been publicly degraded, and all his good work in the previous 40 years ignored . . ." [10]

On September 9, 1905, Buller attended, what is rare for any man to attend, the unveiling of an equestrian statue of himself in Exeter, to be unveiled by Lord Wolseley, the friend whom he loved and the leader whom he honoured above all men. Unfortunately, Lord Wolseley was not in a fit state of health to face the journey.

The statue, which represents the General in full uniform, wearing a greatcoat, stands at the end of Queen's Street.

Buller's health remained good after his retirement, in spite of the hardworking life he had lived, and it was not until 1907 that signs of serious illness showed themselves. As long as he could, however, he still held on to the various duties that he had imposed upon himself.

Through the trees and dank undergrowth the plinth marking the last resting place of Sir Redvers Buller can just be seen. It lies in the churchyard at Crediton, in Devon. The man in charge thought Sir Redvers was buried in Westminster Abbey. He is not. (Picture: the author.).

Even in the final three months of his life, when he had at last to lead the life of an invalid, and often suffered much pain, he did as much work as could be carried out by letter, and drove about his estate supervising any work that was going on.

Long before the end, he knew that recovery was hopeless, but he never uttered a word of complaint or gave a sign of impatience. As increasing weakness and pain cut down the range of his activities, he adapted himself to each inevitable new limitation, and managed to provide himself with some new interest of occupation suited to his powers.

The prospect of death he faced with absolute equanimity, his only anxiety being how he might make his illness as little distressing to others as possible.

Towards the last day of May 1908, he had to take to his bed.

"In the earliest hours of the 2nd of June the end came. I am dying, he quietly remarked . . .'I think it is time to go to bed now.'

"Three days later he was buried in Crediton churchyard. A battalion of the Devons and one of his own riflemen formed his last escort. The two miles of road that lead from Downes to Crediton were lined on either side with people who had come, many of them from long distances, to show their respect to the great soldier, the kindly squire, the good neighbour, the friend of all that were needy or wanted a helper, the man without fear and without reproach . . .

"There was but little of the splendour that has marked the passage to the tomb of other great commanders, but the quiet country funeral, and the grave in a quiet country churchyard, suited better with the humble, unpretentious character of Redvers Buller than a procession through the London streets and a grave in the Abbey or St Paul's . . ." [11]

Buller's grave is in a corner of the tiny Crediton church. It is hard to find. When I visited there a few years ago, the verger told me: "Sir Redvers Buller? Good heaven no, he's not buried here – he's buried in Westminster Abbey!"

But he is not.

Beneath a replica Victoria Cross, his monument states simply: Redvers Henry Buller, of Downes, General. Born December 7 1839, died 2 June 1908.

There is an ornamental archway in the medieval church and a memorial placed there by his only child, Georgiana, who is also buried in the Buller family grave.

SOURCES

1. *South Africa Despatches*, Vol. 2: Natal Field Army.
2. *Buller's Campaigns*, by Julian Symons.
3. *Natal Volunteer Record*, Robinson & Co, Durban.
4. Ibid.
5. *Buller's Campaigns*, by Julian Symons.
6. *Commission on the War in South Africa.*
7. Ibid.
8. *Buller's Campaigns.*
9. *Sir Redvers Buller,* Colonel C.H. Melville Vol. 2.
10. Ibid.
11. Ibid.

EPILOGUE

War of another kind

Tussles with the authority

In July 1984, I visited the Back Route for the first time in some five years. Cape Town, where I was living, is a long way from Natal, and while visits to Durban came around often enough, it was awkward getting up to Ladysmith.

But that year I determined to spend at least four days there, visiting the places I needed to see. It was a bitter and angry experience, and I went home and wrote a piece I headlined "Vandalism with a Sinister Twist: The Big Business War".

It was published in Cape Town's *Weekend Argus* of August 18, and the *Daily News*, Durban, on August 23. It was also picked up by the Johannesburg *Sunday Times* of August 23.

I wrote: "A wave of vandalism with a sinister twist has shocked people in and around Ladysmith. Targets are South African War graves and monuments, some of them ripped apart with sledgehammers and pickaxes. Also hit is the grave of Voortrekker leader Gert Maritz who is buried at Blaauwkrantz, near Colenso.

"The site of the Armoured Train Incident, where Winston Churchill was captured near Frere – it also marks the graves of soldiers – was also desecrated. A bag of coins was found at the grave site.

"Almost nothing is left of the Pieters monument marking the last battle between British troops and burghers before the siege of Ladysmith was lifted.

"The monument is on a hill along the 'Back Route'. But a climb to the top reveals amazing destruction. The plaque has been hammered out. Sledgehammers have been used to rip huge, cemented stones apart. They lie strewn around the summit, exposing the empty hollow interior of the monument.

"The cairn marking the place where Colonel William Dick-Cunyngham VC (Afghan War, 1878–80) was mortally wounded by a stray bullet was also desecrated.

[What was worse: the area around this monument had been used as a dump, and a carcase of a dead dog had been left to rot close by.]

"Two monuments at Nicholson's Nek, on the farm Hydewood were also severely damaged. 'To get to the monuments one has to go through the entrance to my farm,' says George Tatham, a Ladysmith businessman and noted historian.

" 'We saw nobody. I visit the monuments regularly. Whoever damaged them used sledgehammers.

" 'It was the same story as all the others around here. The vandals attempted to get into the heart of the monument by removing the name plaque. Whoever they are, they don't seem to realise that people are not buried there. The monuments mark the battle sites only . . . ' "

One person I spoke to told of her horror visiting a long trench-grave between Inniskilling (Hart's) Hill and Railway Hill and finding bones protruding from the ground. The grave had been exhumed some years before – the Brave Burghers reburied on top of Ladysmith's Platrand, also causing the comment: "What the Boers never achieved in life (the capture of Wagon Hill, or Platrand as it is now known) they achieved in death!"

Whose bones were they? The answer came much later, and is reflected further on.

I wrote: "Mrs Paddy Odendaal, who voluntarily looks after the Chieveley graveyard where the Hon. Freddy Roberts, VC, only son of Lord Roberts, lies buried, told me how her husband had come upon the desecration of Gert Maritz's grave.

" 'We owned Blaauwkrantz farm on which the grave and memorial stand. We sold it recently and my husband went down there to see to something and almost surprised the vandals. They had dug beneath the memorial plinth.' "

The story went on in that vein, with pictures.

The point was that the Boer War was, and still is, big business. Artefacts – ghoulish possessions of the dead – can bring in big money. But the desecration by sledgehammers was something new. A South African Police spokesman in Ladysmith told me at the time: "There is a story going around among young Africans that a fortune is buried behind the plaques. The money left behind is a sort of peace offering for disturbing the dead."

I wrote: "Hundreds of people, many from overseas, now visit major battle-fields at Ladysmith and Kimberley every day. Both towns were besieged and thus indelibly written into history books forever. Tourists, whose forefathers fought on the dry, dusty plains of the South African veld, now specifically go looking for those very same battlefields.

"Many of them go away disappointed. The graves are either in a shocking condition, or cannot be found at all . . . The conclusion is a serious one – not only are British war graves a cause for serious concern, but also the graves of brave burghers . . ."

Then, Dr Fred Clarke, who was the Natal Provincial Council's MEC for Museums and National Monuments, wrote to Mr Michael Green, the then Editor of the *Daily News*: "There have been several press articles recently on the vandalism of South African War graves. The occasions were 9 September 1984, *Sunday Times*, 23 August 1984 *Daily News*, 18th August 1984 *Argus*.

"There is an obvious similarity in these articles and even phrases have been repeated, so I am sending you a copy of the report sent to me by my department which details the queries with the earnest request that before any further publicity is given, the attached report is read."

The similarity between the reports in The *Daily News* and the *Argus* is obvious – they were both written by me. *The Sunday Times* report is just as obvious – the late Flash Seaton, the reporter concerned, took his quotes from my August 18 report in *Weekend Argus*, unknown to me.

Dr Clarke's report was a grim litany of destruction. But every site I had mentioned, he confirmed had been damaged. Repairs had, or were about to, be done.

And in fact the South African War Graves Board had moved pretty swiftly by removing plaques and monuments into safekeeping of the Public Works Department in Ladysmith, until the sites could be redone.

One of the biggest eyesores was, until recently, a quarry used by the national rail carrier then called South African Railways, and begun in the 1930s on the western side of Inniskilling (Hart's) Hill. The National Monuments Council (NMC), Dr Clarke wrote, had attempted to arrange its closure in 1968 but the best the SAR would do was to restrict operations to save the monument on its south side (Connaught Rangers) and the Boer trenches on the north side.

But the quarry had already cut the hill – part of Churchill's "Hill of Whispering Death" – in half. Dr Clarke wrote that two attempts had been made to persuade the minister concerned to close the quarry, without result.

However, he wrote, when the area was visited on August 20, 1984 – some weeks after my stories had been published – it appeared that the contractor was working outside the limits agreed to, and the fact had been reported to the NMC.

In all my visits to Ladysmith one name kept on coming up – Llewellyn Hyde: "Speak to Wally Hyde," they said, "he knows." However, Hyde was always "out".

I discovered why. With some Zulu helpers, a truck, and his dog, Nonsense, it was his job to repair all war graves in Natal and KwaZulu. Bearing in mind that Natal was the battleground of South African history, that was indeed a formidable task.

Hyde went everywhere. For weeks, he was away. He had an office in the Public Works Department's Ladysmith headquarters, but it was always closed. Someone once directed me to his house, on the Windsor Dam road, some five kilometres outside of Ladysmith.

I found it – including the Jaguar he had up on blocks – and his hundred or so cats. Under shelter were headstones and monument plaques he was fixing up. Of him, however, there was no sign.

I wrote to Dr Clarke, asking more questions about the state of the monuments and graves and in December 1984 he replied confirming action had indeed been taken.

The Monument to Colonel Dick-Cunyngham, he wrote, had been restored. "The health service of the Ladysmith Municipality is responsible for clearing away any litter in the vicinity, and the South African Police have been requested to patrol the area regularily, especially at weekends. When inspected two weeks ago, the area was in good order.

"The Boer Grave between Hart's Hill and Railway Hill: The report which was drawn up after the newspaper article appeared, was sent to the National Monuments Council, thus Dr (Chris) Loedolf (the then head of the NMC in Cape Town) must have had knowledge of it.

"The Burghergraftekomitee of the National Monument's Council considered the newspaper article [quoting the person who found bones in the Inniskilling-Hart's Hill trench-grave] but were of the opinion that any bones found must have been those of animals, as a very thorough search was made when the exhumations were undertaken. A search made subsequently to the newspaper article has revealed no human remains . . ."

[They were right as I subsequently found out: Game was plentiful, even in the worst of the fighting.]

"Quarry at Inniskilling-Hart's Hill: The National Monuments Council is continuing its representations regarding Hart's Hill, including the matter of the probability that the contractor may be working outside the prescribed limits."

He also wrote: "Any help from the public will be very welcome because we believe that involving people in preservation work is one of the best ways of making them appreciate their cultural heritage . . .

"It might be mentioned that Maritzburg College have assisted us in renovating several military cemeteries, while the students of the Durbanse Onderwyskollege have, since 1968, given up one vacation per year to work on an historical site. Many other groups, societies and private persons have assisted us on a more irregular basis . . ."

In September of 1985, I finally tracked "Wally" Hyde down. He was redoing the Somerset Light Infantry monument on the "Back Route", changing the approach to what had been a pitted plinth surrounded by barbed wire – to keep cattle away.

Gaunt and aristocratic, Hyde turned out to be a sensitive historian, whose mother was related to the Louis Napoleons of France. Later we met again at his Ladysmith office. It was a revelation: the office was a small museum, filled with books and artefacts, badges – and people. Hyde's reputation as an historian, restorer and friend, was known and respected. There were people from Britain, Australia and Canada who had specially come to Ladysmith to see "Wally" Hyde.

There was, too, an American anthropological student who had spent some days with Wally out in the wilds of Zululand – Wally had to, then, do Zulu War graves as well.

Most of the people were in search of ancestors who had fought in The War, substantiating my original story in 1984 that the Boer War is big business. Hyde, the grave-digger, knew, mostly, what had happened to the soldiers of the Queen the visitors were seeking.

Hyde talked easily of his family history and priceless possessions; of a hunting relative who was taken by a lion outside Ladysmith; of the grief when the Prince Imperial fell in the Zulu War; of the visit by Prince Louis Naopleon's mother to the Hyde family; of the ancient family silver that was destroyed in a fire.

And of the family connection to Britain's royals? It is a story he was loath to discuss, but proved it beyond doubt with a reference in *Burke's Peerage*.

Hyde always said he, one day, was going to write a book "straightening out the facts" of the actions in which the heroes of both sides perished. If anyone knew the real story of what went on in the maelstrom of death on the hillsides outside Ladysmith, it was Hyde.

But he never got a chance: he died in 1992.

The last letter I received from Dr Clarke was in September 1985. He wrote: "I read your . . . article on Mr Lewellyn Hyde with great interest. He was known to me as a very enthusiastic historian who did a good restoration job . . .

"There is a surge of enthusiasm in Natal in the conservation of history . . . We are about to conclude (the documents are in front of me now) an agreement with the Swedish Evangelistic Church for a 99 year lease on Rorke's Drift, and a 25 year lease on Spioenkop is imminent . . ."

It was my last communication with a man I had come to respect, although never met. A wartime hero, he went into hospital for what was to be a minor operation. While under anaesthetic, something went amiss. Dr Clarke never regained consciousness, and two years ago his wife applied for permission to have him taken off his life-support system.

His funeral, in Durban, was attended by dignitaries from far and wide.

It is significant that after each story on the "Back Route" things improved. Cemeteries that had been hidden for years in shoulder-high elephant grass suddenly re-emerged.

What came to light, too, were single graves between the Tugela River and Railway Hill – graves that had, indeed, been "lost" for years.

During one visit I was surprised by the extent of the clean-up.

But in 1987, I was tipped off that the unthinkable was about to happen – a new road linking a new industrial area outside Ladysmith – Ezakheni – with Colenso was going to be built, using and extending the existing "Back Route" road.

This would mean, said my informant, that all the graves would have to go.

Despite the cost and the time, I made a lightning trip to Durban and Ladysmith. All the signs were there – heavy bulldozers were in action at the Colenso end, and at Pieters station. Indeed a new highway was already being constructed from Ladysmith to Ezakheni at Pieters. Factories were under construction.

What was worse, a new quarry had suddenly made its appearance above the Langverwacht spruit, near the historic Pom-Pom bridge, and one monument, erected by soldiers of the Royal Dublin Fusiliers – Queen Victoria's "Poor Irishmen" – had vanished completely.

Not only that, the old quarry was still eating away the western side of Inniskilling–Hart's Hill but piles of stones were coming perilously close to engulfing a monument at the foot of the hill to the Connaught Rangers.

I spent much time on the telephone to various officials in Pietermaritzburg and Ladysmith. No-one would talk. Not to a journalist.

Back in Cape Town, and before launching into print, I wrote to the then Director of the NMC, Dr Chris Loedolf, lamenting the fact of the road, and attaching many questions.

In July, he wrote back to me saying: "Thank you again for your letter of the 14th July and being given the opportunity of replying to your many questions . . . before going into print.

"The use of the road through the 'Back Route' is unavoidable," wrote Dr Loedolf, "and will undoubtedly increase as the industrial and residential complex of the city of Ezakheni expands, which is the main reason for the construction of the new tarred road."

But what was immediately obvious was that the road had been rerouted to pass to the west of the "Back Route" itself. The graves, the monuments, indeed the original road itself would remain intact.

Dr Loedolf wrote: "The new quarry above Langverwachtspruit has been mined for the sole purpose of providing metal for hardening of the new road . . .

"This quarry will continue to be mined until the metal is no longer required. The reason for the quarry being mined in the area is purely a contractual arrangement between the Natal Roads Department and the owner of the farm.

"The contractor will be required to restore the slope and cover the open-cast mine on completion of its use."

Dr Loedolf kindly enclosed a map of the route the new road would take, and said: "The Onderbroekspruit military cemetery and the monument to the 2nd Battalion Somerset Light Infantry (13th Regiment of Foot) has by design been included within the new road reserve.

"Following negotiations with the contractors and the NRD a lay-by has been provided for visitors at each site.

"Hart's–Inniskilling Hill is not affected by the new road as it proceeds behind to the north-west of this hill."

On the quarry eating away Inniskilling–Hart's Hill, Dr Loedolf wrote: "The quarry commenced operations in the 1930s – strangely enough no one protested at the desecration of the countryside nor the historical implications until the National Monuments Council commenced negotiations with the South African Transport Services in the 1960s when agreement was reached to limit the extent of the operations. Since then the National Monuments Council has hoped to close down these operations.

"This has included a deputation to interview the Minister of Transport Services. Since then the Council has with very little success repeatedly endeavoured to have the quarry shut down."

On the Connaught Rangers monument at the foot of the hill: "It is admitted that there is a large accumulation of chipping material on the other side of the road to that on which this monument stands but as a result it does not constitute any danger to the monument at all.

"There does not seem to be any chance of the quarry ceasing mining operations at present. We are aware that the overburden from the quarry area has been piled as an accumulation on the area which the SA Transport Services have agreed not to mine. This, however, is a temporary measure and will be removed in due course.

"The SA Transport Services have now concurred that the mining of the quarry should be accomplished downwards in the next few years so the present quarry face will not be extended in the short term . . .

"The British War Graves Committee is aware of the damage incurred to the 1st Battalion Royal Inniskilling Fusiliers monument on the summit of the Hill which will be attended to as soon as blasting operations cease. At the moment the public is prohibited from access to the area but as soon as the danger has passed the fencing will be replaced around the quarry, signposts erected and the public allowed into the area in accordance with the negotiated agreement . . .

"It should be pointed out that the National Monuments Council was the first organisation to take action and have never deviated from the idea that the area should be preserved.

"The Wynne Hill area is private property. Through representation by the National Monuments Council the owner has agreed under certain conditions to allow public access to the many graves on the hill which will be implemented when the new road is completed.

"Access to the Connaught Rangers monument and the adjacent cemetery at the foot of Inniskilling–Hart's Hill will not be affected by the new tarred road, but it should be remembered that the road between the Somerset Light Infantry monument and the quarry will no longer be an official road and access to the monument will be from the Pieter's station side.

"The Boer trench in the valley between Hart's (Inniskilling) Hill and Railway Hill has been fenced and declared a National Monument. The British headstones nearby were moved for the purposes of safety and will be re-erected at the relevant monument and cemeteries in the area when these have been restored and repaired.

[And that is what happened to the monument I had thought had vanished completely!]

"It is very much the intention in due course to erect cairns with suitable descriptions and explanatory diagrams and maps as soon as the new tarred road is completed. It is envisaged for instance that two will be erected at the monument to the Somerset Light Infantry, one at the viewsite on the crest of Wyne Hill on the verge of the road. This site was kindly brought to our attention by the contractors. There is also one cairn planned for Pieters Hill.

"Long before the planning of the road was finally decided the road planners in company with National Monuments Council representative in Natal, spent several days studying the various possible routes through the Pieter's Hill area paying particular attention to the impact on the historical and general environment aspects and implications of the route. The tarred road at present under construction was considered the one which would do the least damage to the environment . . ."

Dr Loedolf's letter answered my questions and, with the pictures I had taken on my recent visit, I went into print. However, the bugbear was still that Inniskilling quarry, spewing dust and eating away at the hill.

In 1989, I moved back to the *Daily News* in Durban to research *The Road to Infamy*. Of course, the "Back Route" was now right on my doorstep. A few weeks after being back in Durban, I headed for Ladysmith.

The transformation of the "Back Route" was amazing.

Using pictures I had just taken, as well as pictures taken over a period of nine years, I went into print under the headline "*Clean-up at the Graves of Wrath*", which appeared on Saturday May 5, 1990.

I wrote: "They've done it! Not completely of course. But the once-vandalised monuments and graves along the 12-kilometre dirt road that marks one of the bloodiest battles of the South African War – the final push to relieve besieged Ladysmith – have been re-done. And what is more even improved.

"It has taken more than five years – and a lot of acrimonious debate. But finally the pitiful graves are looking smart – fitting memorials to war heroes.

"New railings, stone and cement walls and chips of white marble have replaced broken barbed wire fences, vandalised headstones, high untamed grass – and mud . . .

"Only one blot still remains on the landscape – a quarry that has already 'eaten' away much of Inniskilling Hill and the graves that were once on top of it . . ."

Everything the NMC had said they would do, appeared to have been done.

Finally came even better news. On July 5, 1990 the Administrator of Natal, Mr C.J. van R. Botha, issued a statement on behalf of the Minister of Transport, Public Works and Land Afffairs announcing the closure, by September of 1992, of the Inniskilling Hill quarry.

The statement read: "The mining of railway ballast from a quarry on Hart's Hill, which commenced in the 1930s, has begun to pose an increasing threat to the famous South African War battlefield site, not only because the quarry has become very large and unsightly in recent years, but because it has started encroaching towards the area where the main Boer forces were deployed in February 1900 on the northern slopes of the hill.

"In view of the serious threat posed to one of the country's most historically important tourist sites" . . . alternative sites were to be looked at.

One, said the statement, had been located, and that mining would cease on September 30, 1992.

"In the interim period Transnet (the old SAR) has given the assurance that it will continue to strictly observe a long-standing agreement with the National Monuments Council not to expand the quarry operations into the area demarcated for preservation. Transnet also confirmed that restoration work has recently been carried out on the northern slopes, while arrangements have also been made for the removal of dumped overburden on the hill slopes . . ."

In 1992, the quarry was closed.

A question mark hangs over the future, however. Ezakheni township, under the control of the KwaZulu government, has featured in scenes of ANC–Inkatha violence as plans for a new democratic South Africa evolved.

The industrial complex is vital to the needs of the population – but it is too close to the "Back Route" for comfort.

How the National Monuments Council and the aspirations of the locals will deal with this historic area will be interesting. But the locals, who could identify the Boer sites as those belonging to the "oppressor", need to remember one thing: the graves are not those of the Boer fighters for freedom, who have been moved to Ladysmith, but soldiers of Queen Victoria.

Finally, I like to think that the continued exposure of conditions along the "Back Route" and the quarry, resulted in the clean-up. If so, the basis of a soft form of investigative journalism is alive and well . . .

In 1977 I received a postscript to the whole Spioenkop saga. It came from Westville, Natal, and read: "Spioenkop and Potgieter's Drift belonged to my father Mathrinus Jacobus Potgieter at the time of the Boer War.

"As the graves and monuments were on his farm he cared for them and received a letter . . . thanking him for doing so . . .

"Potgieter's Drift's correct and legal name is Labuschagne's Kraal and was a grant farm for my great-grandfather.

"The name was changed with the war to Potgieter's Drift. My grandfather Gerhardus Cornelius Potgieter married Petronella Labuschagne and had a farm in the Orange Free State, and after his death his family moved to Labuschagne's Kraal.

"When my maternal Grandfather, Paul Michiel Bester, founder of Harrismith, and its first Landrost died, he left my mother 1,800 Pounds (Sterling) and it was this money that bought Spioenkop. I have a copy of the title deeds.

" . . . I celebrated my 84th birthday last week. I was six years old when the Boer War started.

"Sincerely,

"Eugenie Reid (born Potgieter)".

The shocking state of the Hart's Hollow graves when the author came across them some 15 years ago. They were almost hidden in thick undergrowth, the iron railings around them were broken, as were the gravestones. It led to the publication of the first report in Weekend Argus, *in Cape Town, and the* Daily News *in Durban, and acrimonious correspondence between the Province of Natal and the author. However, the campaign to clean up the graves was begun with regular hard-hitting reports. (Picture: the author.)*

Index

was ambushed, page 68. See also Dundonald; Watkins-Pitchford; Haldane; Frere. Churchill's comments on Buller's vast army on the march between Frere and Springfield, "utterly precludes all possibility of surprise", page 121. Describes Battle of Monte Cristo and Hlangwane, see chapters on Battle of Pieters.

Colenso: Village on the banks of the Tugela. First of Buller's reverses, on December 15, 1899. White sends single battalion from besieged Ladysmith to guard Colenso railway bridge "for the Colony", page 39. Buller – "I never attacked", page 73. Descriptions of, before the battle – Davitt, Bennett Burleigh and JB Atkins, pages 73, 74, 75. Conspiracy of silence, page 73. Attack on, page 79.

Colenso VCs: The Hon. Frederick Hugh Sherston Roberts; Walter Norris Congreve; William Babtie; Hamilton Lyster Reed; George Edward Nurse, and Captain Henry Norton Schofield, pages 96-100.

Commission: (on the War in South Africa) sat at St Stephen's House, London Embankment, 1902-1903. Details of; warrant for; Commissioners, page 6.

Congreve: Walter Norris, went to help bring in Long's guns, under withering hail of Boer fire, but landed in a donga with Long. Dragged Hon. Frederick Sherston Roberts, Lord Roberts's only son, who rode with Congreve in an heroic bid to retrieve Buller's guns, to safety. Awarded VC, page 93. How he brought mortally wounded Roberts to safety, page 96. See Roberts, Frederick Sherston.

Correspondents: Bitterness at being restricted. No mention to be made of Buller's arrival in Natal, page 41. Also not permitted on the battlefield at Colenso, Spioenkop, Vaalkrantz and Pieters, page 41.

Crofton: Colonel Malby, confirms that the wrong "All is lost" message was sent to Sir Charles Warren from the top of Spioenkop, page 150.

Davitt: Michael; Irish MP and author of *The Boer Fight for Freedom*, banned in Britain. Gave up his seat in the House of Commons to join Kruger. Called the war "the most dishonourable and unchristian war which has ever disgraced a civilised age," page 40. Predicts a defeat at Colenso, December 15, 1899, page 74. Writes on Spioenkop.

Dum Dum Bullets: (See also Brackenbury, Sir Henry; and Knox, Sir Ralph Henry). Mark IV expanding bullet was to be official bullet for the British Army all over the world; 66 million Mark IV bullets delivered throughout the Empire, including South Africa, by March 1899; Recalled after they had "stripped" in conditions of heat and dust. (See Hague Convention), page 23. Confirmation that "Dum Dums were to be used, page 24. Withdrawal of, page 24. See Knox. See Brackenbury. Found among Boer ammunition after the Battle of Pieters, page 253. See Blake-Knox.

Dundonald: General Lord Douglas; Maintained he had reached Ladysmith first. Disputed by Major Hubert Gough and Herbert Watkins-Pitchford, page 36. See also Churchill, Watkins-Pitchford.

Durban: Busy wharves in October 1899. Boers – "We'll be eating fish there and drive the British back to Britain", page 26. Critical to protect, page 27. Also see Scott, Captain Percy. "Vierkleur" would have flown over Durban, Botha, if not for Captain Scott, page 30. Defence of Durban-Scott divided surroundings into three separate commands, page 31. Defence of, completed, page 31. Life under martial law, night passes, page 31. See also: Fort Denison, Fort Hartley. *HMS Terrible.*

Emmet: Cherrie, Field Cornet. Brother-in-Law of Louis Botha, organised Long's "lost" guns to be taken across the Tugela and, later, used by the Boers, page 92.

"Flasher": Unit to communicate with Ladysmith. Searchlight on converted railway carriage made in Durban, sent to Frere, page 32. See Scott, Captain Percy.

Food: Poor quality of for troops. Tinned meat – troops had to carry 1lbn tin with them. Much of the meat thrown away, page 19. Tea came in a compressed cake, much thrown away, page 20. Preserved milk did not keep in the warm climate, page 21. See Richardson.

Fort Denison: Windermere Road. One of Captain Percy Scott's "forts" for the protection of Durban, page 31.

Fort Hartley: Umgeni Road. One of Captain Percy Scott's "forts" for the protection of Durban, page 31.

French: General John Denton Pinkstone. On the last train out of Ladysmith before it was besieged. Later relieved the Siege of Kimberley, and pulled Boers away from Ladysmith laagers to help General Piet Cronje who surrendered at Paardeberg, page 37.

Frere: Village between Estcourt and Colenso. Flies, mud and the troops, page 62. Staging post and headquarters, page 63. On wreckage of the armoured train from which Winston Churchill was captured from, page 65.

Gough: Major Hubert; The first man into Ladysmith, with Colonial Irregulars, Natal Carbineers, Natal Mounted Rifles, Border Mounted Rifles, Natal Police and Imperial Light Horse, at 4pm on February 28, 1900, page 35. Disputed by Dundonald and Churchill; confirmed by Watkins-Pitchford.

"Gun Run": Naval competition, first carried out in Portsmouth in 1900. Now part of every military "tattoo", page 30.

Hague Convention: Britain not party to convention which banned all use of Dum Dum bullets. Britain declined to be bound by it, page 23.

Haldane: Aylward. Officer in charge of the Armoured Train when Churchill was captured.

Hely-Hutchinson: Sir Walter, Governor of Natal; Against withdrawal of British troops from Glencoe, page 46. Terrified the Boers would reach Pietermaritzburg and then Durban, page 47.

Hlangwane: "The Key to Ladysmith." A hillock to the right of Colenso, from the slopes and top of which, British guns could have pounded a way through to Colenso in December 1899, but was not attacked until the fourth and final push, page 94. Louis Botha blamed French press for disclosing the "secret of Hlangwane" to the world in December 1899, page 95. Warren, after the defeat at Spioenkop and withdrawal from Vaalkrantz, again suggests an attack on Hlangwane. Buller accepts, page 210. See The Beginning of the End, page 214, etc.; Attack on, page 225.

Hunter: Sir Archibald. Chief of Staff to Sir George White in Ladysmith. On Ladysmith: Why White had to hold the town against all odds, page 55. Clarifies Defence Plan – Sir George White wanted the troops concentrated under him, page 56. Fall of Ladysmith accepted as a "sign to the Zulu nation. If it had fallen the Zulus would have risen up in revolt, page 59. On Ladysmith – The use of telephones to direct the Battle of Wagon Hill on January 6, 1900, page 59. On the motor car – It would serve the army well, page 59. See also Telephones.

"Jerusalem" Warren: Sir Charles Warren's work for the Palestine Exploration Fund, page 109; Underground survey of Jerusalem, 110; Notes still being used today by Israeli archaeologists in Jerusalem, mainly Dan Bahat, page 110.

Kitchener: Horatio Lord; at the Commission, page 6.

Knox: Sir Ralph Henry, Permanent Under Secretary for War. Confirmation that "Dum Dum" bullets were to be Britain's official bullet. Withdrawn because of "stripping", page 24.

Ladysmith Siege Band: Played daily for physical drill and concerts with instruments made from tubs, covered by sheepskin and tin whistles, page 38.

Ladysmith: Besieged for 118 days from November 2, 1899 to February 28, 1900. First man in to lift the siege was Major Hubert Gough, with Colonial Irregular Troops, at 4pm on February 28, 1900. Disputed by Churchill, confirmed by Watkins-Pitchford, a Ladysmith resident, page 35. Said to be surrounded by 25 000 Boers, page 41. Locomotive centre, with coal. Also stocked up with food, ammunition, medical stores, page 58. Regiments there, in November 1899, page 63. Abandonment of White's force is regarded by the government as national disaster – telegram to Buller from Lord Lansdowne, after Colenso, page 81. Buller enters, page 257.

Lambton: Rear Admiral the Honourable Headworth. In charge of Naval guns during the siege in Ladysmith. On the "bad" shooting by the Navy, page 60. On the "bad" shooting of the Army "numbskulls", page 60.

Lambton: The Hon. D'Arcy. Author of a long time anonymous work: Sir Charles Warren and Spioenkop – A Vindication, by "Defender", page 11.

Lanterns: Fitting for candles too small; leaked because of poor fit, page 21.

Long: Colonel Charles. In charge of the "lost" guns, and the man Buller blamed for the defeat at Colenso, page 89. "The idea of abandoning the guns never entered my head", says Long, page 89.

Long Tom: Visited by hundreds of Boer "thrillseekers" from Johannesburg and Pretoria in November 1899, page 41.

Lansdowne: Marquess of, Secretary of War, Telegram to Buller. "Abandonment of White's force regarded by the government as national disaster", December 16, page 81. Refutes Buller's statement that he, Buller, had had no orders before going to South Africa, page 105.

Lyddite: Effects of, during the Battle of Pieters, page 230. Effectiveness of, page 230.

Lyttleton: General Neville; On Buller's refusal to attack retreating Boers at Modder Spruit. "Few commanders have so wantonly thrown away an opportunity. They were at our mercy," page 42. Attacked Twin Peaks during Battle of Spioenkop sucessfully, but withdrawn by Buller. See Spioenkop chapters.

Maps: Carried by pigeons from Ladysmith. See Pigeons.

Motor Cars: Would come in useful to move troops about – Sir Archibald Hunter, page 59.

Mud: An army on the march, page 121.

Natal Field Force: Commanded by Sir Redvers Buller and Sir Charles Warren. Disbanded on October 19, 1900. Comprised some 75,000 troops, 30,000 horses, 120 guns. 300,000 tons of supplies were received in Durban and forwarded to the fronts, and 25,000 men, Natalian, Uitlander, Zulu and Hindu had served in one way or another, page 42.

Natal Scheme of Defence: Formulated before the war by Generals Goodenough and Butler as a measure to protect Natal and Ladysmith from attack, page 54.

"Natives" and the War: British were worried how some 750,000 Zulus would react if the British retreated, page 46. See White. See Hunter.

Penn-Symons: Sir William, at Talana. Buried in the English churchyard, page 15. Arrived in May, 1899, page 45. Confident that troops could hold Glencoe, page 46.

Pietermaritzburg: Critical to protect, page 27.

Pieters: Battle for: The juggernaut begins to roll, page 217; The hill of hideous whispering death, page 226; Inniskilling Hill, Hart's Hollow, page 240; Victory on Majuba Day, page 243.

Pigeons: (See White, Sir George.) Used by White to carry messages to and from Ladysmith. Also, greetings to the Prince of Wales on his birthday, page 32. Also used to carry map, cut into four portions, showing Ladysmith situation, page 32.

Reitz: Denys. With the Boers; Son of President Reitz of the Orange Free State. On the retreat by the Boers to Modder Spruit during the Battle of Pieters. "If the British had fired one single gun, everything would have fallen into their hands," page 37. See also Spioenkop chapters.

Richardson: Sir W.O. Deputy Adjutant General for Supplies, page 13. On the dearth of material available. Dearth of equipment for Horse Artillery, Field Artillery, gun ammunition, page 17. Lack of equipment for Horse harnesses; machine guns; Cavalry saddlery; Infantry accoutrements; mule harnesses; cavalry swords; tents, camp equipment, small arms ammunition; general stores, page 18. Tinned meat, large portion sent to South Africa found to be unfit for consumption, page 20. Tobacco; came in wooden cases which could not reach battlefield, page 20.

Rifle Sights: Faulty. Lee Enfield sights shot 18 inches to the right over 500 yards. Defect noticed only after shipped to South Africa, page 24.

Road to Infamy: It exists on the back road between Colenso and Ladysmith, page 9.

Roberts: Field Marshal, Sir Frederick Sleigh. Commander-in-Chief of British Forces in South Africa until the surrender of Pretoria in 1900. Ladysmith a bad selection for a base. But there was no other choice, page 54. Appointed to commander-in-chief of the Army in South Africa after the loss at Colenso, December 1899, page 82. Roberts sends Spioenkop Despatches to London, after the battle, blaming Thorneycroft and hinting at Warren's "ineptidude", page 136 etc. Roberts to Buller: "Ladysmith must be relieved at any cost", page 203; Roberts turns on Buller, finally condemning and castigating his defeatist attitude, page 210.

Roberts: The Hon. Frederick Hugh Sherston, only son of Lord Roberts. Shot in the abdomen during the heroic but vain attempt to bring in Long's guns at Colenso, December 15, 1899. Died two days later. Awarded the posthumous VC, page 96. See Congreve. Could his life have been saved? Page 100.

Scott: Captain Percy of *HMS Terrible*. Converted 12lb. 12cwt deck guns to field guns. Appointed Military Governor of Durban, page 27. Scott converted *HMS Terrible*'s 4.7in guns to field guns, page 29. Refuses passage to Boer sympathisers' Ambulance, page 31.

Searchlight: Ladysmith "Flasher". See "Flasher", page 32.

Soap: The supply of, non-existent, page 14.

Spioenkop: Warren proposes, for the first time, an attack on Spioenkop, to which Buller agrees, page 127. Warren asks for long-range guns to counter ones near the top, Buller refuses, page 127; the battle begins, page 135-205. What really took place on top, page 143, etc; Wrong message signalled to Warren from top of Spioenkop, accusations and refutation, page 149, etc. Aftermath, page 197.

Spioenkop Despatches: To be read in conjunction with the chapters on Spioenkop. Not all of them were published which gave a false impression of the actions of Sir Charles Warren, who ultimately has gone down in history as the man who "lost" Spioenkop. Published in the Easter recess of 1900, page 137 etc. The Spioenkop Debates, the silence that shocked a nation, and why the Despatches were withheld by the government, Page 182, etc. House of Commons Debate, page 193, etc.

Spearman's farm: Hospital point, behind Buller's headquarters on Mount Alice, page 121.

Springfield: Village in Natal midlands, today Winterton, page 121.

Stainbank, Trooper H.M. On the poor condition of the Ladysmith garrison, page 38.

"Starvation City": Ladysmith. A description by Surgeon Sir Frederick Treves, page 38.

Supplies: Dearth of, page 14. Biscuits came in 1lb tin, page 19. Clothing, lack of, page 19. Meat came in 1lb tim, contents often discarded, page 19. Tea, came in a compressed cake, page 20. Ambulances, of little use, page 21. Baggage wagons of little use, page 21. Milk, preserved. Many brands won't keep in the climate, page 21. See Brackenbury.

Surrenders: 225 listed between October 1899, and the occupation of Pretoria in May 1900, page 8. Nicholson's Nek, surrender of 954 officers and men, page 15. Colonel G.M. Bullock, in donga at Colenso, page 93.

Surrender Telegram: "Can you last so long? If not how many days can you give me in which to take up a defensive position. After which I suggest you firing away as much ammunition as you can and making the best terms (with the Boers) as you can", page 79. Questioned on it by the Commission, page 273 etc. Finally Buller is sacked over it, Page 278.

Talana: Page 15. See Penn-Symons.

Telegrams: The major source of communication. Here are a selected few. Buller to Captain Percy Scott on Durban: "Make yourself as snug as possible, page 32. Buller to White: "Stay in Ladysmith", page 39. White to Buller: "I cannot leave Ladysmith," page 39. Ladysmith the most advanced post I could

retires to Weston-Super-Mare, and dies on the evening of Friday, January 21, 1927. He is buried at Westbere cemetery, in front of his old house The Oaks, near Canterbury, page 268, etc.

Watkins-Pitchford, Herbert: Besieged in Ladysmith. Wrote in his diary: "Dundonald had no more hand in the Relief of Ladysmith than I had," page 36.

White, Sir George: Commander of the forces besieged in Ladysmith. Sailed from Southampton, September 16, 1899. Without orders. Arrived in Durban on October 7, 1899. Davitt calls the siege a triumph for the British in sheer endurance, page 41. White - why I am confident of holding out at Ladysmith, page 41. Deceived into believing there were 25,000 Boers surrounding him at Ladysmith, page 41. Why I stayed in Ladysmith, page 44. Ladysmith the most advanced post I could hold on to, page 46. However not confident that Penn-Symons would be able to hold out at Glencoe, page 46. My task, the protection of the Colony, page 47. The reasons for holding on to Ladysmith, page 47. My holding it resulted in the complete overthrow of the Boer battle plan, page 52. On Ladysmith: Why it was right to hold it, page 57. White - ready to help Buller, on the wrong day, thanks to Buller's change of plan, page 78. Invalided home.

Wolseley, Viscount (Sir Garnet Joseph): Commander-in-Chief of the British Army between 1895-1901. On Glencoe, Ladysmith and the Schemes of Defence - No-one ever thought troops would occupy Ladysmith. And no-one would dream of holding it, page 49. Ladysmith in a very bad geographic position, page 49. No-one told White to hold it, page 49. On Buller's defeat at Colenso: "Were I in his place, I should resign at once . . .", page 82.